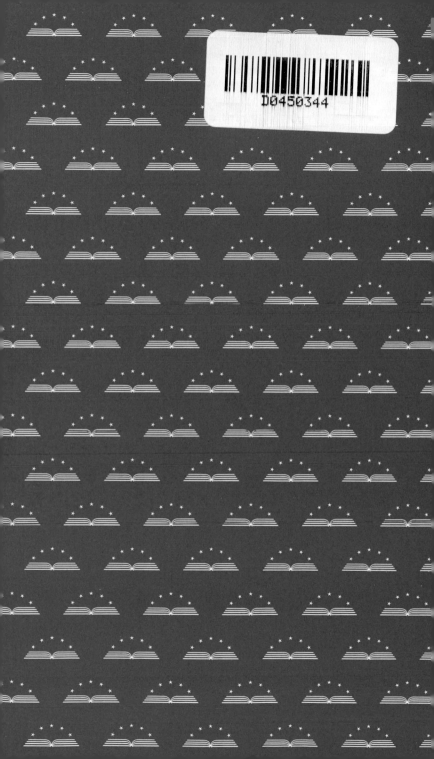

Library of America, a nonprofit organization,
champions our nation's cultural heritage
by publishing America's greatest writing in
authoritative new editions and providing resources
for readers to explore this rich, living legacy.

PHILIP ROTH

PHILIP ROTH

WHY WRITE?

COLLECTED NONFICTION
1960–2013

THE LIBRARY OF AMERICA

Contents

THREE

Explanations

Preface

THE FIRST pieces printed here belong to an early and embattled period of my writing career. They are included for the sake of the record—in May 2014, fifty-five years after my story "Defender of the Faith" was published in *The New Yorker* and promptly deemed an affront to Jews by any number of the magazine's Jewish readers, I received an honorary degree from the Jewish Theological Seminary that I trust signaled an end to the antagonism from the institutional and establishment Jewish sources that had commenced with my beginnings as a published writer in my mid-twenties. The publication of *Portnoy's Complaint* (1969)—which found an audience greater by far than any book of mine would garner again—certainly did little to ameliorate this conflict and accounts for why there are several pieces reprinted here examining the origins of that inflammatory book, its astonishing reception, and its continuing impact on my reputation in some circles, if not any longer as an anti-Semite then, hardly any less offensively, as a misogynist. (See the interview with *Svenska Dagbladet.*)

Of my thirty-one published books, twenty-seven have been works of fiction. Aside from *Patrimony* (1991), which recounted my father's final illness and death, and *The Facts* (1988), a brief autobiography about my development as a writer, what nonfiction I have written has arisen mainly from a provocation —responding to the charges of anti-Semitism and Jewish self-hatred—or to answer a request for an interview by a serious periodical or to acknowledge my acceptance of an award or to mark a milestone birthday or to mourn the death of a friend.

The Kafka piece with which the volume begins came to be written after I had spent a happy semester at the University of Pennsylvania teaching all of Kafka's major fiction along with his anguished "Letter to His Father" and Max Brod's biography. This hybrid essay-story was a first attempt at an approach that I would take up again more extensively in *The Ghost Writer* (1979) and *The Plot Against America* (2004): imagining history as it had not actually occurred, first as in "I Always Wanted You to Admire My Fasting" by my conjuring up Kafka's years in America as a—my—Hebrew school teacher, and years later by my inventing alternative biographies for Anne Frank and then for Charles Lindbergh as well as for my own immediate family. In the essay "My Uchronia," written for the *New York Times Book Review* to accompany its review of *The Plot Against America*, I explain the strategies I came up with to make credible reality of an imaginary 1940s America allied with Nazi Germany under President Lindbergh.

I lived in London for half of each year from 1977 to 1988 and out of that residency came key interviews in *Shop Talk* (2001), which is reprinted here in its entirety. Ivan Klíma in Prague, Milan Kundera in Prague and Paris (and London and Connecticut), Primo Levi in Turin, Aharon Appelfeld in Jerusalem, Edna O'Brien in London—all these important writers were at most a few hours away by plane from my London home and so I was able easily to travel to and fro during those years cultivating and enjoying the friendships from which these conversations emerged. Ivan and Milan I had been introduced to in 1973, five years after the collapse of the Prague Spring, in totalitarian Communist Prague, and in the speech "A Czech Education," delivered to American PEN in 2013, I present a picture of the fraught circumstances of our subsequent meetings.

When I traveled to Italy to see Primo Levi at his home in the fall of 1986, we had already met the previous spring in London, where he had come to deliver some lectures and where we were brought together by a mutual friend. How very *sound* he'd seemed to me during the four days we spent talking away in his study in Turin. How vivacious a man! Enviably rooted was how I described him in the introduction to our conversation, "thoroughly adapted to the totality of the life around him." In the months that followed my visit, we communicated by mail and I invited him to come to America for a visit when I got home the following year—I believed I had made a new and wonderful friend. But the friendship was never to evolve. In the spring he committed suicide, this great writer who only months before I had taken from his alert, lively demeanor to be so sound and vivacious and rooted.

The volume closes with an address I gave on March 19, 2013, at my eightieth birthday celebration in my hometown of

Newark, at the Newark Museum's Billy Johnson Auditorium,
to an audience of several hundred guests and friends. I have
never enjoyed a birthday more. In attendance were some of
my oldest, lifelong friends, boys I'd grown up with in the
Jewish Weequahic section of Newark, and many of the numerous other friends I have made all over throughout a lifetime.
The evening was organized by the Philip Roth Society and the
Newark Preservation and Landmarks Committee and my talk
was preceded by remarks about my work from Jonathan Lethem,
Hermione Lee, Alain Finkielkraut, and Claudia Roth Pierpont.
I was introduced by a friend of many decades, the great Irish
novelist Edna O'Brien, who may have surprised some in the
audience but didn't surprise me when she said, "The defining
influences on him are his parents, his father Herman, the hard-
working Jew in a Gentile insurance colossus, and the mother's
faithful husbandry."

I ended my address that evening ("The Ruthless Intimacy of
Fiction") with a brief reading from *Sabbath's Theater*, a scene
taken from near the end of the book in which Mickey Sabbath,
as isolated and bereft as he has ever been, visits the seashore
graveyard where all of his beloved family members are buried.
Among them is Morty, the older brother he adored, whose
bomber had been shot down over the Japanese-occupied Philippines only months before the conclusion of World War II,
when Sabbath was still a vulnerable boy—indeed, it is this unthinkable childhood blow that, for Sabbath, will determine
everything thereafter. This cemetery scene winds up with Sabbath placing a pebble atop each of their gravestones and, after
having been flooded with the tenderest memories of them all,
saying to his dead, quite simply, "Here I am."

I say the same now. Here I am, out from behind the disguises and inventions and artifices of the novel. Here I am,
stripped of the sleight of hand and denuded of all those masks
that have conferred such imaginative freedom as I have been
able to muster as a writer of fiction.

ONE

READING MYSELF
AND OTHERS

"I Always Wanted You to Admire My Fasting"; or, Looking at Kafka

"I always wanted you to admire my fasting," said the hunger artist. "We do admire it," said the overseer, affably. "But you shouldn't admire it," said the hunger artist. "Well then we don't admire it," said the overseer, "but why shouldn't we admire it?" "Because I have to fast, I can't help it," said the hunger artist. "What a fellow you are," said the overseer, "and why can't you help it?" "Because," said the hunger artist, lifting his head a little and speaking, with his lips pursed, as if for a kiss, right into the overseer's ear, so that no syllable might be lost, "because I couldn't find the food I liked. If I had found it, believe me, I should have made no fuss and stuffed myself like you or anyone else." These were his last words, but in his dimming eyes remained the firm though no longer proud persuasion that he was still continuing to fast.

—Franz Kafka, "A Hunger Artist"

I

I AM looking, as I write of Kafka, at the photograph taken of him at the age of forty (my age)—it is 1924, as sweet and hopeful a year as he may ever have known as a man, and the year of his death. His face is sharp and skeletal, a burrower's face: pronounced cheekbones made even more conspicuous by the absence of sideburns; the ears shaped and angled on his head like angel wings; an intense, creaturely gaze of startled composure—enormous fears, enormous control; a black towel of Levantine hair pulled close around the skull the only sensuous feature; there is a familiar Jewish flare in the bridge of the nose, the nose itself is long and weighted slightly at the tip—the nose of half the Jewish boys who were my friends in high school. Skulls chiseled like this one were shoveled by the thousands from the ovens; had he lived, his would have been among them, along with the skulls of his three younger sisters.

Of course it is no more horrifying to think of Franz Kafka in Auschwitz than to think of anyone in Auschwitz—it is just horrifying in its own way. But he died too soon for the Holocaust.

Written in 1973.

Had he lived, perhaps he would have escaped with his good friend Max Brod, who found refuge in Palestine, a citizen of Israel until his death there in 1968. But *Kafka* escaping? It seems somehow implausible for one so fascinated by entrapment and careers that culminate in anguished death. Still, there is Karl Rossmann, his American greenhorn. Having imagined Karl's escape to America and his mixed luck here, could not Kafka have found a way to execute such an escape for himself? The New School for Social Research in New York becoming *his* Great Nature Theatre of Oklahoma? Or perhaps, through the influence of Thomas Mann, a position in the German department at Princeton . . . But then, had Kafka lived, it is not at all certain that the books of his which Mann celebrated from *his* refuge in New Jersey would ever have been published; eventually Kafka might either have destroyed those manuscripts that he had once bid Max Brod to dispose of at his death or, at the least, continued to keep them his secret. The Jewish refugee arriving in America in 1938 would not then have been Mann's unmatched "religious humorist" but a frail and bookish fifty-five-year-old bachelor, formerly a lawyer for a government insurance firm in Prague, retired on a pension in Berlin at the time of Hitler's rise to power—an author, yes, but of a few eccentric stories, mostly about animals, stories no one in America had ever heard of and only a handful in Europe had read; a homeless K., but without K.'s willfulness and purpose, a displaced Karl, but without Karl's youthful spirit and resilience; just a Jew lucky enough to have escaped with his life, in his possession a suitcase containing some clothes, family photos, Prague mementos, and the manuscripts, still unpublished and in pieces, of *Amerika*, *The Trial*, *The Castle*, and (stranger things happen) three more fragmented novels, no less remarkable than the bizarre masterworks that he keeps to himself out of oedipal timidity, perfectionist madness, and insatiable longings for solitude and spiritual purity.

July 1923: Eleven months before he will die in a Vienna sanatorium, Kafka somehow finds the resolve to leave Prague and his father's home for good. Never before has he even remotely succeeded in living apart, independent of his mother, his sisters, and his daunting father, nor has he been a writer other

than in those few evening hours when he is not working in the
legal department of the Workers' Accident Insurance Office in
Prague; since taking his law degree at the university, he has
been by all reports the most dutiful and scrupulous of employees, though he finds the work tedious and enervating. But in
June of 1923—having some months earlier been pensioned
from his job because of his illness—he meets a young Jewish
girl of nineteen at a seaside resort in Germany, Dora Dymant,
an employee at the vacation camp of the Jewish People's Home
of Berlin. Dora has left her Orthodox Polish family to make a
life of her own (at half Kafka's age); she and Kafka—who has
just turned forty—fall in love. Kafka has by now been engaged
to two rather more conventional Jewish girls—twice to one of
them—hectic, anguished engagements wrecked largely by his
fears. "I am mentally incapable of marrying," he writes his father in the forty-five-page letter he gave to his mother to deliver. ". . . the moment I make up my mind to marry I can no
longer sleep, my head burns day and night, life can no longer
be called life." He explains why. "Marrying is barred to me,"
he tells his father, "because it is your domain. Sometimes I
imagine the map of the world spread out and you stretched di-
agonally across it. And I feel as if I could consider living in only
those regions that are not covered by you or are not within your
reach. And in keeping with the conception I have of your magnitude, these are not many and not very comforting regions—
and marriage is not among them." The letter explaining what is
wrong between this father and this son is dated November 1919;
the mother thought it best not even to deliver it, perhaps for
lack of courage, probably, like the son, for want of hope.

During the following two years, Kafka attempts to wage an
affair with Milena Jesenká-Pollak, an intense young woman of
twenty-four who has translated a few of his stories into Czech
and is most unhappily married in Vienna; his affair with Milena,
conducted feverishly, but by and large through the mails, is
even more demoralizing to Kafka than the fearsome engagements to the nice Jewish girls. Those fiascos aroused only the
paterfamilias pining that he dared not indulge, a hunger inhibited by his exaggerated awe of his father—"spellbound," says
Brod, "in the family circle"—and the hypnotic spell of his own
seclusion; but the Czech Milena, impetuous, frenetic, indifferent

to conventional restraints, a woman of appetite and anger, arouses more elemental yearnings and more elemental fears. According to a Prague critic, Rio Preidner, Milena was "psychopathic"; according to Margaret Buber-Neumann, who lived two years beside her in the German concentration camp where Milena died following a kidney operation in 1944, she was powerfully sane, extraordinarily humane and courageous. Milena's obituary for Kafka was the only one of consequence to appear in the Prague press; the prose is strong, so are the claims she makes for Kafka's accomplishment. She is still only in her twenties, the dead man is hardly known as a writer beyond his small circle of friends—yet Milena writes: "His knowledge of the world was exceptional and deep, and he was a deep and exceptional world in himself. . . . [He had] a delicacy of feeling bordering on the miraculous and a mental clarity that was terrifyingly uncompromising, and in turn he loaded on to his illness the whole burden of his mental fear of life. . . . He wrote the most important books in recent German literature." One can imagine this vibrant young woman stretched across the bed, as awesome to Kafka as his own father spread out across the map of the world. His letters to her are disjointed, unlike anything else of his in print; the word "fear" appears on page after page. "We are both married, you in Vienna, I to my Fear in Prague." He yearns to lay his head upon her breast; he calls her "Mother Milena"; during at least one of their two brief rendezvous, he is hopelessly impotent. At last he has to tell her to leave him be, an edict that Milena honors, though it leaves her hollow with grief. "Do not write," Kafka tells her, "and let us not see each other; I ask you only to quietly fulfill this request of mine; only on those conditions is survival possible for me; everything else continues the process of destruction."

Then, in the early summer of 1923, during a visit to his sister, who is vacationing with her children by the Baltic Sea, he finds young Dora Dymant, and within a month Franz Kafka has gone off to live with her in two rooms in a suburb of Berlin, out of reach at last of the "claws" of Prague and home. How can it be? How can Kafka, in his illness, have accomplished so swiftly and decisively the leave-taking that was beyond him in his healthiest days? The impassioned letter writer who could equivocate interminably about which train to catch to Vienna to meet with Milena (if he should meet with her for the weekend at all); the bourgeois suitor in the high collar, who, during his drawn-out agony of an engagement with the proper Fräulein Bauer, secretly draws up a memorandum for himself, countering the arguments "for" marriage with the arguments "against"; the poet of the ungraspable and the unresolved, whose belief in an immovable barrier separating the wish from its realization is at the heart of his excruciating visions of defeat; the Kafka whose fiction refutes every easy, touching, humanish daydream of salvation and justice and fulfillment with densely imagined counterdreams that mock all solutions and escapes—this Kafka *escapes*. Overnight! K. penetrates the Castle walls—Joseph K. evades his indictment—"a breaking away from it altogether, a mode of living completely outside the jurisdiction of the Court." Yes, the possibility of which Joseph K. has just a glimmering in the Cathedral, but can neither fathom nor effectuate—"not . . . some influential manipulation of the case, but . . . a circumvention of it"—Kafka realizes in the last year of his life.

Was it Dora Dymant or was it death that pointed the new way? Perhaps it could not have been one without the other. We know that the "illusory emptiness" at which K. gazed, upon first entering the village and looking up through the mist and the darkness to the Castle, was no more vast and incomprehensible than the idea of himself as husband and father was to the young Kafka; but now, it seems, the prospect of a Dora forever, of a wife, home, and children everlasting, is no longer the terrifying, bewildering prospect it would once have been, for now "everlasting" is undoubtedly not much more than a matter of months. Yes, the dying Kafka is determined to marry, and writes to Dora's Orthodox father for his daughter's hand. But the imminent death that has resolved all contradictions and uncertainties in Kafka is the very obstacle placed in his path by the young girl's father. The request of the dying man Franz Kafka to bind to him in his invalidism the healthy young girl Dora Dymant is—denied!

If there is not one father standing in Kafka's way, there is another—and another behind him. Dora's father, writes Max Brod in his biography of Kafka, "set off with [Kafka's] letter to

consult the man he honored most, whose authority counted
more than anything else for him, the 'Gerer Rebbe.' The rabbi
read the letter, put it to one side, and said nothing more to
Dora's father than the single syllable, 'No.'" *No.* Klamm himself could have been no more abrupt—or any more removed
from the petitioner. *No.* In its harsh finality, as telling and inescapable as the curselike threat delivered by his father to "The
Judgment"'s Georg Bendemann, that thwarted fiancé: "Just
take your bride on your arm and try getting in my way. I'll
sweep her from your very side, you don't know how!" *No.*
Thou shalt not have, say the fathers, and Kafka concedes that
he shan't. The habit of obedience and renunciation; also, his
own distaste for the infirm and reverence for strength, appetite, and health. "'Well, clear this out now!' said the overseer,
and they buried the hunger artist, straw and all. Into the cage
they put a young panther. Even the most insensitive felt it refreshing to see this wild creature leaping around the cage that
had so long been dreary. The panther was all right. The food
he liked was brought him without hesitation by the attendants;
he seemed not even to miss his freedom; his noble body, furnished almost to the bursting point with all that it needed,
seemed to carry freedom around with it too; somewhere in his
jaws it seemed to lurk; and the joy of life streamed with such
ardent passion from his throat that for the onlookers it was not
easy to stand the shock of it. But they braced themselves,
crowded round the cage, and did not want ever to move away."
So no is no is no is no—he already knew as much himself. A
healthy young girl of nineteen cannot, *should* not, be given in
matrimony to a sickly man twice her age, who spits up blood
("I sentence you," cries Georg Bendemann's father, "to death
by drowning!") and who shakes in his bed with fevers and chills.
What sort of un-Kafka-like dream had Kafka been dreaming?

And those nine months spent with Dora have still other
"Kafkaesque" elements: a fierce winter in quarters inadequately
heated; the inflation that makes a pittance of his own meager
pension, and sends into the streets of Berlin the hungry and
needy whose suffering, says Dora, turns Kafka "ash-gray"; and
his tubercular lungs, flesh transformed and punished. Dora
cares for the diseased writer as devotedly and tenderly as
Gregor Samsa's sister in "The Metamorphosis" does for her

brother, the repellent bug. Gregor's sister plays the violin so beautifully that Gregor "felt as if the way were opening before him to the unknown nourishment he craved"; he dreams, in his condition, of sending his gifted sister to the Conservatory! Dora's music is Hebrew, which she reads aloud to Kafka, and with such skill that, according to Brod, "Franz recognized her dramatic talent; on his advice and under his direction she later educated herself in the art . . ."

Only Kafka is hardly vermin to Dora Dymant, *or to himself.* Away from Prague and his father's home, Kafka, at forty, seems at last to have been delivered from the self-loathing, the self-doubt, and the guilt-ridden impulses to dependence and self-effacement that had nearly driven him mad throughout his twenties and thirties; all at once he seems to shed the pervasive sense of hopeless despair that informs the great punitive fantasies of *The Trial,* "In the Penal Colony," and "The Metamorphosis." Years earlier, in Prague, he had directed Max Brod to destroy all his papers, including the three unpublished novels, upon his death; now, in Berlin, when Brod introduces him to a German publisher interested in his work, Kafka consents to the publication of a volume of four stories, and does so, says Brod, "without much need of long arguments to persuade him." With Dora to help, he diligently resumes the study of Hebrew; despite his illness and the harsh winter, he travels to the Berlin Academy for Jewish Studies to attend a series of lectures on the Talmud—a Kafka quite transfigured from the estranged melancholic who once wrote in his diary, "What have I in common with the Jews? I have hardly anything in common with myself and should stand very quietly in a corner, content that I can breathe." And to further mark the alteration, there is ease and happiness with a woman: with this young and adoring companion, he is playful, he is pedagogical, and, one would guess, in light of his illness (*and* his happiness), he is chaste. If not a husband (such as he had striven to be to the conventional Fräulein Bauer), if not a lover (as he struggled in vain to be with the vivacious Milena), he would seem to have become something no less miraculous in his scheme of things: a father, a kind of father to this sisterly, mothering daughter. *As Franz Kafka awoke one morning from uneasy dreams he found himself transformed in his bed into a father, a writer, and a Jew.*

"I have completed the construction of my burrow," begins the long, exquisitely tedious story that he wrote that winter in Berlin, "and it seems to be successful. . . . Just the place where, according to my calculations, the Castle Keep should be, the soil was very loose and sandy and had literally to be hammered and pounded into a firm state to serve as a wall for the beautifully vaulted chamber. But for such tasks the only tool I possess is my forehead. So I had to run with my forehead thousands and thousands of times, for whole days and nights, against the ground, and I was glad when the blood came, for that was proof that the walls were beginning to harden; in that way, as everybody must admit, I richly paid for my Castle Keep."

"The Burrow" is the story of an animal with an acute sensitivity to peril whose entire life is organized around the principle of defense, and whose deepest longings are for security and serenity. With teeth and claws—*and* forehead—the burrower constructs an elaborate and ingeniously intricate system of underground chambers and corridors that are designed to afford it some peace of mind; however, while this burrow does succeed in reducing the sense of danger from without, its maintenance and protection are equally fraught with anxiety: "these anxieties are different from ordinary ones, prouder, richer in content, often long repressed, but in their destructive effects they are perhaps much the same as the anxieties that existence in the outer world gives rise to." The story (whose ending is lost) terminates with the burrower morbidly preoccupied with distant subterranean noises that cause it "to assume the existence of a great beast," itself burrowing in the direction of the Castle Keep.

Another grim tale of entrapment, and of obsession so absolute that no distinction is demonstrable between character and predicament. Yet this fiction imagined in the last "happy" months of Kafka's life is touched by a spirit of personal reconciliation and sardonic self-acceptance, by a tolerance of one's own brand of madness, that is nowhere apparent in "The Metamorphosis." The piercing masochistic irony of the earlier animal story—as of "The Judgment" and *The Trial*—has given way here to a critique of the self and its profoundest fixations that, though bordering on mockery, no longer seeks to resolve

itself in images of the uttermost humiliation and defeat. Yet
there is more here than a metaphor for the insanely defended
ego, whose striving for invulnerability produces an elaborate
stronghold of protection that must in its turn become the object of perpetual concern—there is also an unromantic and
hardheaded fable about how and why art is made, a portrait of
the artist in all his ingenuity, anxiety, isolation, dissatisfaction,
relentlessness, secretiveness, paranoia, and self-addiction, a
portrait of the magical thinker at the end of his tether, Kafka's
Prospero. It is an endlessly suggestive story, this story of life in
a hole. For, finally, remember the proximity of Dora Dymant
during the months that Kafka was at work on "The Burrow"
in the two underheated rooms that were their unsanctioned
home. Certainly a dreamer like Kafka need never have entered
the young girl's body for her tender presence to kindle in him
a fantasy of a hidden orifice that promises "satisfied desire,"
"achieved ambition," and "profound slumber," but that, once
penetrated and in one's possession, arouses the most terrifying
and heartbreaking fears of retribution and loss. "For the rest I
try to unriddle the beast's plans. Is it on its wanderings, or is it
working on its own burrow? If it is on its wanderings then
perhaps an understanding with it might be possible. If it should
really break through to the burrow I shall give it some of my
stores and it will go on its way again. It will go on its way
again, a fine story! Lying in my heap of earth I can naturally
dream of all sorts of things, even of an understanding with the
beast, though I know well enough that no such thing can
happen, and that at the instant when we see each other, more,
at the moment when we merely guess at each other's presence,
we shall blindly bare our claws and teeth . . ."

He died of tuberculosis of the lungs and larynx on June 3,
1924, a month before his forty-first birthday. Dora, inconsolable, whispers for days afterward, "My love, my love, my good
one . . ."

2

1942. I am nine; my Hebrew-school teacher, Dr. Kafka, is
fifty-nine. To the little boys who must attend his "four-to-five"
class each afternoon, he is known—in part because of his

remote and melancholy foreignness, but largely because we vent on him our resentment at having to learn an ancient calligraphy at the very hour we should be out screaming our heads off on the ball field—he is known as Dr. Kishka. Named, I confess, by me. His sour breath, sharply spiced with intestinal juices by five in the afternoon, makes the Yiddish word for "insides" particularly telling, I think. Cruel, yes, but in truth I would have cut out my tongue had I ever imagined the name would become legend. A coddled child, I do not yet think of myself as persuasive, or, quite yet, as a literary force in the world. My jokes don't hurt, how could they, I'm so adorable. And if you don't believe me, just ask my family and the teachers in my school. Already at nine, one foot in college, the other in the Catskills. Little borscht-belt comic that I am outside the classroom, I amuse my friends Schlossman and Ratner on the dark walk home from after-hours Hebrew school with an imitation of Kishka, his precise and finicky professional manner, his German accent, his cough, his gloom. "Doctor *Kishka*!" cries Schlossman, and hurls himself savagely against the newsstand that belongs to the candy-store owner whom Schlossman drives just a little crazier each night. "Doctor Franz—Doctor Franz—Doctor Franz—*Kishka*!" screams Ratner, and my chubby little friend who lives upstairs from me on nothing but chocolate milk and Mallomars does not stop laughing until, as is his wont (his mother has asked me "to keep an eye on him" for just this reason), he helplessly wets his pants. Schlossman takes the occasion of Ratner's humiliation to pull the sodden little boy's paper out of his notebook and wave it in the air—it is the assignment Dr. Kafka has just returned to us, graded; we were told to make up an alphabet of our own, out of straight lines and curved lines and dots. "That is all an alphabet is," he had explained. "That is all Hebrew is. That is all English is. Straight lines and curved lines and dots." Ratner's alphabet, for which he received a C, looks like twenty-six skulls strung in a row. I received my A for a curlicued alphabet, inspired largely (as Dr. Kafka seems to have surmised, given his comment at the top of the page) by the number eight. Schlossman received an F for forgetting even to do it—and a lot he seems to care. He is content—he is *overjoyed*—with things as they are. Just waving a piece of paper in the air and screaming, "Kishka! Kishka!" makes him deliriously happy. We should all be so lucky.

At home, alone in the glow of my goose-necked "desk" lamp (plugged after dinner into an outlet in the kitchen, my study), the vision of our refugee teacher, sticklike in a fraying three-piece navy-blue suit, is no longer very funny—particularly after the entire beginners' Hebrew class, of which I am the most studious member, takes the name Kishka to its heart. My guilt awakens redemptive fantasies of heroism, I have them often about the "Jews in Europe." I must save him. If not me, who? The demonic Schlossman? The babyish Ratner? And if not now, when? For I have learned in the ensuing weeks that Dr. Kafka rents a room in the house of an elderly Jewish lady on the shabby lower stretch of Avon Avenue, where the trolley still runs and the poorest of Newark's Negroes live. A *room*. And *there*! My family's apartment is no palace, but it is ours at least, so long as we pay the $38.50 a month in rent for the five rooms; and though our neighbors are not rich, they refuse to appear poor or to be meek and beaten down. Tears of shame and sorrow in my eyes, I rush into the living room to tell my parents what I have heard (though not that I heard it during a quick game of "aces up" played a minute before class against the synagogue's rear wall—worse, played directly beneath a stained-glass window embellished with the names of the dead): "My Hebrew teacher lives in a *room*."

Invite him to dinner, my mother says. *Here?* Of course here —Friday night; I'm sure he can stand a home-cooked meal, she says, and a little pleasant company. Meanwhile, my father gets on the phone to call my Aunt Rhoda, who lives with my grandmother and tends her and her potted plants in the apartment house at the corner of our street. For nearly two decades my father has been introducing my mother's "baby" sister to the Jewish bachelors and widowers of north Jersey. No luck so far. Aunt Rhoda, an "interior decorator" in the dry-goods department of the Big Bear, a mammoth merchandise and produce market in industrial Elizabeth, wears falsies (this information by way of my older brother) and sheer frilly blouses, and family lore has it that she spends hours in the bathroom every day applying powder and sweeping her stiffish

hair up into a decorative display atop her head; but despite all
the dash and drama, she is, in my father's words, "still afraid of
the facts of life." He, however, is undaunted, and administers
therapy regularly and gratis: "Let 'em squeeze ya, Rhoda—it
feels good!" I am his flesh and blood, I can reconcile myself to
such scandalous talk in our kitchen—*but what will Dr. Kafka
think?* Oh, but it's too late to do anything now. The well-meant
machinery of matchmaking has been set in motion by my undiscourageable father, and the smooth engines of my proud
homemaking mother's celebrated hospitality are already purr-
ing away. To throw my body into the works in an attempt to
bring it all to a halt—well, I might as well try to bring down
the New Jersey Bell Telephone Company by leaving our re-
ceiver off the hook. Only Dr. Kafka can save me now. But to
my muttered invitation, he replies, with a formal bow that
turns me scarlet—who has ever seen a person do such a thing
outside of a movie house?—he replies that he would be *honored* to be my family's dinner guest. "My aunt," I rush to tell
him, "will be there too." It appears that I have just said something mildly humorous; odd to see Dr. Kafka smile. Sighing,
he says, "I will be delighted to meet her." Meet her? He's
supposed to *marry* her. How do I warn him? And how do I
warn Aunt Rhoda (a very great admirer of me and my grades)
about his smelly breath, his roomer's pallor, his Old World
ways, so at odds with her up-to-dateness? My face feels as if it
will ignite of its own—and spark the fire that will engulf the
synagogue, Torah and all—when I see Dr. Kafka scrawl our
address in his notebook, and beneath it, some words *in German*. "Good night, Dr. Kafka!" "Good night, and thank you,
thank you." I turn to run, I go, but not fast enough: out on
the street I hear Schlossman—that fiend!—announcing to my
classmates, who are punching one another under the lamplight
down from the synagogue steps (where a card game is also in
progress, organized by the bar mitzvah boys): "Roth invited
Kishka to his *house*! To *eat*!"

Does my father do a job on Kafka! Does he make a sales
pitch for familial bliss! What it means to a man to have two fine
boys and a wonderful wife! Can Dr. Kafka imagine what it's
like? The thrill? The satisfaction? The pride? He tells our visitor
of the network of relatives on his mother's side that are joined

in a "family association" of over two hundred people located in seven states, including the state of Washington! Yes, relatives even in the far Far West: here are their photographs, Dr. Kafka; this is a beautiful book we published entirely on our own for five dollars a copy, pictures of every member of the family, including infants, and a family history by "Uncle" Lichtblau, the eighty-five-year-old patriarch of the clan. This is our family newsletter, which is published twice a year and distributed nationwide to all the relatives. This, in the frame, is the menu from the banquet of the family association, held last year in a ballroom of the "Y" in Newark, in honor of my father's mother on her seventy-fifth birthday. My mother, Dr. Kafka learns, has served *six consecutive years* as the secretary-treasurer of the family association. My father has served a two-year term as president, as has each of his three brothers. We now have fourteen boys in the family in uniform. Philip writes a letter on V-mail stationery to five of his cousins in the army every single month. "Religiously," my mother puts in, smoothing my hair. "I firmly believe," says my father, "that the family is the cornerstone of everything."

Dr. Kafka, who has listened with close attention to my father's spiel, handling the various documents that have been passed to him with great delicacy and poring over them with a kind of rapt absorption that reminds me of myself over the watermarks of my stamps, now for the first time expresses himself on the subject of family; softly he says, "I agree," and inspects again the pages of the family association book. "Alone," says my father, in conclusion, "alone, Dr. Kafka, is a stone." Dr. Kafka, setting the book gently down upon my mother's gleaming coffee table, allows with a nod that that is certainly so. My mother's fingers are now turning in the curls behind my ears; not that I even know it at the time, or that she does. Being stroked is my life; stroking me, my father, and my brother is hers.

My brother goes off to a Boy Scout meeting, but only after my father has him stand in his neckerchief before Dr. Kafka and describe to him the skills he has mastered to earn each of his badges. I am invited to bring my stamp album into the living room and show Dr. Kafka my set of triangular stamps from Zanzibar. "Zanzibar!" says my father rapturously, as though I, not even ten, have already been there and back. My father accompanies Dr. Kafka and me into the "sun parlor," where my tropical fish swim in the aerated, heated, and hygienic paradise I have made for them with my weekly allowance and Hanukkah *gelt*. I am encouraged to tell Dr. Kafka what I know about the temperament of the angelfish, the function of the catfish, and the family life of the black mollie. I know quite a bit. "All on his own he does that," my father says to Kafka. "He gives me a lecture on one of those fish, it's seventh heaven, Dr. Kafka." "I can imagine," Kafka replies.

Back in the living room my Aunt Rhoda suddenly launches into a rather recondite monologue on "Scotch plaids," intended, it would appear, for the edification of my mother alone. At least she looks fixedly at my mother while she delivers it. I have not yet seen her look directly at Dr. Kafka; she did not even turn his way at dinner when he asked how many employees there were at the Big Bear. "How would I know?" she had replied, and then continued right on conversing with my mother, about a butcher who would take care of her "under the counter" if she could find him nylons for his wife. It never occurs to me that she will not look at Dr. Kafka because she is shy—nobody that dolled up could, in my estimation, be shy. I can only think that she is outraged. *It's his breath. It's his accent. It's his age.*

I'm wrong—it turns out to be what Aunt Rhoda calls his "superiority complex." "Sitting there, sneering at us like that," says my aunt, undisguisedly superior now herself. "Sneering?" repeats my father, incredulous. "Sneering and laughing, yes!" says Aunt Rhoda. My mother shrugs. "*I* didn't think he was laughing." "Oh, don't worry, by himself there he was having a very good time—*at our expense*. I know the European-type man. Underneath they think they're all lords of the manor," Rhoda says. "You know something, Rhoda?" says my father, tilting his head and pointing a finger, "I think you fell in love." "With *him*? Are you *crazy*?" "He's too quiet for Rhoda," my mother says. "I think maybe he's a little bit of a wallflower. Rhoda is a very lively person, she needs lively people around her." "Wallflower? Franz? He's not a wallflower! He's a gentleman, that's all. And he's lonely," my father says assertively, glaring at my mother for going over his head like this *against*

Kafka. My Aunt Rhoda is nearing forty—it is not exactly a shipment of brand-new goods that he is trying to move. "He's a gentleman, he's an educated man, and I'll tell you something, he'd give his eyeteeth to have a nice home and a wife." "Well," says my Aunt Rhoda, "let him find one then, if he's so educated. Somebody who's his equal, who he doesn't have to look down his nose at with his big sad refugee eyes!" "Yep, she's in love," my father announces, squeezing Rhoda's knee in triumph. "With him?" she cries, jumping to her feet, taffeta crackling around her like a bonfire. "With *Kafka?*" she snorts. "I wouldn't give an old man like that the time of day!"

Dr. Kafka calls and takes my Aunt Rhoda to a movie. I am astonished, both that he calls and that she goes; it seems there is more desperation in life than I have come across yet in my fish tank. Dr. Kafka takes my Aunt Rhoda to a play performed at the "Y." Dr. Kafka eats Sunday dinner with my grandmother and my Aunt Rhoda and, at the end of the afternoon, accepts with that formal bow of his the mason jar of mushroom and barley soup that my grandmother presses him to carry back to his room with him on the No. 8 bus. Apparently he was very taken with my grandmother's jungle of potted plants—and she, as a result, with him. Together they spoke in Yiddish about gardening. One Wednesday morning, only an hour after the store has opened for the day, Dr. Kafka shows up at the dry-goods department of the Big Bear; he tells Aunt Rhoda that he just wants to see where she works. That night he writes in his diary: "With the customers she is forthright and cheery, and so managerial about 'taste' that when I hear her explain to a chubby young bride why green and blue do not 'go,' I am myself ready to believe that Nature is in error and R. is correct."

One night, at ten, Dr. Kafka and Aunt Rhoda come by unexpectedly, and a small impromptu party is held in the kitchen—coffee and my mother's marble cake, even a thimbleful of whiskey all around, to celebrate the resumption of Aunt Rhoda's career on the stage. I have only heard tell of my aunt's theatrical ambitions. My brother says that when I was small she used to come to entertain the two of us on Sundays with her puppets—she was at that time employed by the W.P.A. to travel around New Jersey and put on marionette shows in

schools and even in churches; Aunt Rhoda did all the voices
and, with the help of a female assistant, manipulated the man-
ikins on their strings. Simultaneously she had been a member
of the Newark Collective Theater, a troupe organized primarily
to go around to strike groups to perform *Waiting for Lefty*.
Everybody in Newark (as I understood it) had had high hopes
that Rhoda Pilchik would go on to Broadway—everybody except my grandmother. To me this period of history is as difficult to believe in as the era of the lake dwellers, which I am
studying in school; people say it was once so, so I believe them,
but nonetheless it is hard to grant such stories the status of the
real, given the life I see around me.

Yet my father, a very avid realist, is in the kitchen, schnapps
glass in hand, toasting Aunt Rhoda's success. She has been
awarded one of the starring roles in the Russian masterpiece
The Three Sisters, to be performed six weeks hence by the amateur group at the Newark Jewish "Y." Everything, announces
Aunt Rhoda, everything she owes to Franz and his encouragement. One conversation—"One!" she cries gaily—and Dr.
Kafka had apparently talked my grandmother out of her lifelong belief that actors are not serious human beings. And what
an actor *he* is, in his own right, says Aunt Rhoda. How he had
opened her eyes to the meaning of things, by reading her the
famous Chekhov play—yes, read it to her from the opening
line to the final curtain, all the parts, and actually left her in
tears. Here Aunt Rhoda says, "Listen, listen—this is the first
line of the play—it's the key to everything. Listen—I just think
about what it was like the night Pop passed away, how I wondered what would become of us, what would we do—and,
and, *listen*—"

"We're listening," laughs my father. So am *I* listening, from
my bed.

Pause; she must have walked to the center of the kitchen li-
noleum. She says, sounding a little surprised, "'It's just a year
ago today that father died.'"

"Shhh," warns my mother, "you'll give the little one nightmares."

I am not alone in finding my aunt a "changed person"
during the weeks of rehearsal. My mother says this is just what
she was like as a little girl. "Red cheeks, always those hot, red

cheeks—and everything exciting, even taking a bath." "She'll calm down, don't worry," says my father, "and then he'll pop the question." "Knock on wood," says my mother. "Come on," says my father, "he knows what side his bread is buttered on—he sets foot in this house, he sees what a family is all about, and believe me, he's licking his chops. Just look at him when he sits in that club chair. This is Franz Kafka's dream come true." "Rhoda says that in Berlin, before Hitler, he had a young girl friend, years and years it went on, and then she left him. For somebody else. She got tired of waiting." "Don't worry," says my father, "when the time comes I'll give him a little nudge. He ain't going to live forever, either, and don't think he don't know it."

Then one weekend, as a respite from the "strain" of nightly rehearsals—which Dr. Kafka regularly visits, watching in his hat and coat at the back of the auditorium until it is time to accompany Aunt Rhoda home—the two take a trip to Atlantic City. Ever since he arrived on these shores Dr. Kafka has wanted to see the famous boardwalk and the horse that dives from the high board. But in Atlantic City something happens that I am not allowed to know about; any discussion of the subject conducted in my presence is in Yiddish. Dr. Kafka sends Aunt Rhoda four letters in three days. She comes to us for dinner and sits till midnight crying in our kitchen. She calls the "Y" on our phone to tell them (weeping) that her mother is still ill and she cannot come to rehearsal again—she may even have to drop out of the play. No, she can't come, she can't, her mother is too ill, she herself is too upset! goodbye! Then back to the kitchen table to cry. She wears no pink powder and no red lipstick, and her stiff brown hair, down, is thick and spiky as a new broom.

My brother and I listen from our bedroom, through the door that he has pushed ajar.

"Have you ever?" says Aunt Rhoda, weeping. "Have you *ever*?"

"Poor soul," says my mother.

"*Who?*" I whisper to my brother. "Aunt Rhoda or—"

"Shhhh!" he says. "Shut *up!*"

In the kitchen my father grunts. "Hmm. Hmm." I hear him getting up and walking around and sitting down again—and then grunting. I am listening so hard that I can hear the letters being folded and unfolded, stuck back into their envelopes, then removed to be puzzled over yet one more time.

"Well?" demands Aunt Rhoda. "*Well?*"

"Well what?" answers my father.

"Well, what do you want to say *now*?"

"He's *meshugeh*," admits my father. "Something is wrong with him all right."

"But," sobs Aunt Rhoda, "no one would believe me when *I* said it!"

"Rhody, Rhody," croons my mother in that voice I know from those two times that I have had to have stitches taken, or when I have awakened in tears, somehow on the floor beside my bed. "Rhody, don't be hysterical, darling. It's over, kitten, it's all over now."

I reach across to my brother's twin bed and tug on the blanket. I don't think I've ever been so confused in my life, not even by death. The speed of things! Everything good undone in a moment! By what? "*What?*" I whisper. "*What is it?*"

My brother, the Boy Scout, smiles leeringly and, with a fierce hiss that is no answer and enough answer, addresses my bewilderment: "Sex!"

Eleven years later, a junior at college, I receive an envelope from home containing Dr. Kafka's obituary, clipped from *The Jewish News*, the tabloid of Jewish affairs that is mailed each week to the homes of the Jews of Essex County. It is summer, the semester is over, but I have stayed on at school, alone in my room in the town, trying to write short stories. I am fed by a young English professor and his wife in exchange for babysitting; I tell the sympathetic couple, who are also loaning me the money for my rent, why it is I can't go home. My fights with my father are all I can talk about at their dinner table. "Keep him away from me!" I scream at my mother. "But, darling," she asks me, "what is going on? What is this all about?"—the very same question with which I used to plague my older brother, asked now of me and out of the same bewilderment and innocence. "He *loves* you," she explains.

But that, of all things, seems to me precisely what is blocking my way. Others are crushed by paternal criticism—I find myself oppressed by his high opinion of me! Can it possibly be

true (and can I possibly admit) that I am coming to hate him
for loving me so? praising me so? Everything he says drives me
nuts. But that makes no sense—the ingratitude! the stupidity!
the perversity! Being loved is so obviously a blessing, *the* blessing,
praise such a rare bequest. Only listen late at night to my closest friends on the literary magazine and in the drama society
—they tell horror stories of family conflict and misery to rival
The Way of All Flesh, they return shell-shocked from vacations,
drift back to school as though from the wars. "What's going
on?" my mother begs me to tell her; but how can I, when I
myself don't fully believe that this is happening to us, or that I
am the one who is making it happen. That they, who together
cleared all obstructions from my path, should seem now to be
my final obstruction! All that we have constructed together
over the course of two century-long decades, and look how I
must bring it down—in the name of this tyrannical need that I
call my "independence"! My mother, keeping the lines of
communication open, sends a note to me at school: "We miss
you"—and encloses the brief obituary notice. Across the margin at the bottom of the clipping, she has written (in the same
hand with which she wrote notes to my teachers and signed
my report cards, in that very same handwriting that once eased
my way in the world), "Remember poor Kafka, Aunt Rhoda's
beau?"

"Dr. Franz Kafka," the notice reads, "a Hebrew teacher at
the Talmud Torah of the Schley Street Synagogue from 1939
to 1948, died on June 3 in the Deborah Heart and Lung Center
in Brown Mills, New Jersey. Dr. Kafka had been a patient there
since 1950. He was 70 years old. Dr. Kafka was born in Prague,
Czechoslovakia, and was a refugee from the Nazis. He leaves
no survivors."

He also leaves no books: no *Trial*, no *Castle*, no Diaries.
The dead man's papers are claimed by no one, and disappear—
all except those four "*meshugeneh*" letters that are, to this day,
as far as I know, still somewhere in among the memorabilia
accumulated by my spinster aunt, along with a collection of
Broadway Playbills, sales citations from the Big Bear, and
transatlantic steamship stickers.

Thus all trace of Dr. Kafka disappears. Destiny being destiny,
how could it be otherwise? Does the Land Surveyor reach the

Castle? Does K. escape the jurisdiction of the Court, or Georg Bendemann the judgment of his father? "'Well, clear this out now!' said the overseer, and they buried the hunger artist, straw and all." No, it simply is not in the cards for our Kafka ever to become *the* Kafka—why, that would be stranger even than a man turning into an abominable insect. No one would believe it, Kafka least of all.

Writing American Fiction

S EVERAL WINTERS back, while I was living in Chicago, the city was shocked and mystified by the death of two teenage girls. So far as I know, the populace is mystified still; as for the shock, Chicago is Chicago, and one week's dismemberment fades into the next's. The victims this particular year were sisters. They went off one December night to see an Elvis Presley movie, for the sixth or seventh time we are told, and never came home. Ten days passed, and fifteen and twenty, and then the whole bleak city, every street and alley, was being searched for the missing Grimes girls, Pattie and Babs. A girl friend had seen them at the movie, a group of boys had caught a glimpse of them afterward getting into a black Buick, another group said a green Chevy, and so on and so forth, until one day the snow melted and the unclothed bodies of the two girls were discovered in a roadside ditch in a forest preserve west of Chicago. The coroner said he didn't know the cause of death, and then the newspapers took over. One paper ran a drawing of the girls on the back page, in bobby socks and Levi's and babushkas: Pattie and Babs a foot tall, and in four colors, like Dixie Dugan on Sundays. The mother of the two girls wept herself right into the arms of a local newspaper lady, who apparently set up her typewriter on the Grimeses' front porch and turned out a column a day, telling us that these had been good girls, hard-working girls, average girls, churchgoing girls, et cetera. Late in the evening one could watch television interviews featuring schoolmates and friends of the Grimes sisters: the teenage girls look around, dying to giggle; the boys stiffen in their leather jackets. "Yeah, I knew Babs, yeah, she was all right, yeah, she was popular . . ." On and on, until at last comes a confession. A skid-row bum of thirty-five or so, a dishwasher, a prowler, a no-good named Benny Bedwell, admits to killing both girls, after he and a pal cohabited with them for several weeks in various flea-bitten hotels. Hearing the news, the

Originally a speech delivered at Stanford University, which co-sponsored with *Esquire* magazine a symposium on "Writing in America Today" (1960).

weeping mother tells the newspaper lady that the man is a liar—her girls, she insists now, were murdered the night they went off to the movie. The coroner continues to maintain (with rumblings from the press) that the girls show no signs of having had sexual intercourse. Meanwhile, everybody in Chicago is buying four papers a day, and Benny Bedwell, having supplied the police with an hour-by-hour chronicle of his adventures, is tossed in jail. Two nuns, teachers of the girls at the school they attended, are sought out by the newspapermen. They are surrounded and questioned, and finally one of the sisters explains all. "They were not exceptional girls," the sister says, "they had no hobbies." About this time, some good-natured soul digs up Mrs. Bedwell, Benny's mother, and a meeting is arranged between this old woman and the mother of the slain teenagers. Their picture is taken together, two overweight, overworked American ladies, quite befuddled but sitting up straight for the photographers. Mrs. Bedwell apologizes for her Benny. She says, "I never thought any boy of mine would do a thing like that." Two weeks later, maybe three, her boy is out on bail, sporting several lawyers and a new one-button-roll suit. He is driven in a pink Cadillac to an out-of-town motel where he holds a press conference. Yes, he is the victim of police brutality. No, he is not a murderer; a degenerate maybe, but even that is changing. He is going to become a carpenter (a carpenter!) for the Salvation Army, his lawyers say. Immediately, Benny is asked to sing (he plays the guitar) in a Chicago night spot for two thousand dollars a week, or is it ten thousand? I forget. What I remember is that suddenly, into the mind of the onlooker, or newspaper reader, comes The Question: is this all public relations? But of course not—two girls are dead. Still, a song begins to catch on in Chicago, "The Benny Bedwell Blues." Another newspaper launches a weekly contest: "How Do You Think the Grimes Girls Were Murdered?" and a prize is given for the best answer (in the opinion of the judges). And now the money begins to flow; donations, hundreds of them, start pouring in to Mrs. Grimes from all over the city and the state. For what? From whom? Most contributions are anonymous. Just the dollars, thousands and thousands—the *Sun-Times* keeps us informed of the grand total. Ten thousand, twelve thousand, fifteen thousand. Mrs.

Grimes sets about refinishing and redecorating her house. A stranger steps forward, by the name of Shultz or Schwartz—I don't really remember—but he is in the appliance business and he presents Mrs. Grimes with a whole new kitchen. Mrs. Grimes, beside herself with appreciation and joy, turns to her surviving daughter and says, "Imagine me in that kitchen!" Finally, the poor woman goes out and buys two parakeets (or maybe another Mr. Shultz presents them as a gift); one parakeet she calls Babs, the other Pattie. At just about this point, Benny Bedwell, doubtless having barely learned to hammer a nail in straight, is extradited to Florida on the charge of having raped a twelve-year-old girl there. Shortly thereafter I left Chicago myself, and so far as I know, though Mrs. Grimes hasn't her two girls, she has a brand-new dishwasher and two small birds.

And what is the moral of the story? Simply this: that the American writer in the middle of the twentieth century has his hands full in trying to understand, describe, and then make *credible* much of American reality. It stupefies, it sickens, it infuriates, and finally it is even a kind of embarrassment to one's own meager imagination. The actuality is continually outdoing our talents, and the culture tosses up figures almost daily that are the envy of any novelist. Who, for example, could have invented Charles Van Doren? Roy Cohn and David Schine? Sherman Adams and Bernard Goldfine? Dwight David Eisenhower?

Several months back, most of the country heard one of the candidates for the Presidency of the United States say something like, "Now if you feel that Senator Kennedy is right, then I sincerely believe you should vote for Senator Kennedy, and if you feel that I am right, I humbly submit that you vote for me. Now I feel, and this is certainly a personal opinion, that I am right . . ." and so on. Though it did not appear this way to some thirty-four million voters, it still seems to me a little easy to ridicule Mr. Nixon, and it is not for that reason that I have bothered to paraphrase his words here. If one was at first amused by him, one was ultimately astonished. Perhaps as a satiric literary creation, he might have seemed "believable," but I myself found that on the TV screen, as a real public figure, a political fact, my mind balked at taking him in. Whatever else the television debates produced in me, I should point out, as a literary curiosity, they also produced professional envy. All the machinations over make-up and rebuttal time, all the business over whether Mr. Nixon should look at Mr. Kennedy when he replied, or should look away—all of it was so beside the point, so fantastic, so weird and astonishing, that I found myself beginning to wish I had invented it. But then, of course, one need not have been a fiction writer to wish that *someone* had invented it, and that it was not real and with us.

The daily newspapers, then, fill us with wonder and awe (is it possible? is it happening?), also with sickness and despair. The fixes, the scandals, the insanity, the idiocy, the piety, the lies, the noise . . . Recently, in *Commentary*, Benjamin De-Mott wrote that the "deeply lodged suspicion of the times [is] namely, that events and individuals are unreal, and that power to alter the course of the age, of my life and your life, is actually vested nowhere." There seems to be, said DeMott, a kind of "universal descent into unreality." The other night—to give a benign example of the descent—my wife turned on the radio and heard the announcer offering a series of cash prizes for the three best television plays of five minutes' duration written by children. It is difficult at such moments to find one's way around the kitchen. Certainly few days go by when incidents far less benign fail to remind us of what DeMott is talking about. When Edmund Wilson says that after reading *Life* magazine he feels he does not belong to the country depicted there, that he does not live in this country, I understand what he means.

However, for a writer of fiction to feel that he does not really live in his own country—as represented by *Life* or by what he experiences when he steps out the front door—must seem a serious occupational impediment. For what will his subject be? His landscape? One would think that we might get a high proportion of historical novels or contemporary satire—or perhaps just nothing. No books. Yet almost weekly one finds on the best-seller list another novel which is set in Mamaroneck or New York City or Washington, with characters moving through a world of dishwashers and TV sets and advertising agencies and senatorial investigations. It all *looks* as though the writers are turning out books about our world. There is *Cash McCall* and *The Man in the Gray Flannel Suit* and *Marjorie*

Morningstar and *The Enemy Camp* and *Advise and Consent*, and so on. But what is noteworthy is that these books aren't very good. Not that the writers aren't sufficiently horrified with the landscape to suit me—quite the contrary. They are generally full of concern for the world about them; finally, however, they just don't imagine the corruption and vulgarity and treachery of American public life any more profoundly than they imagine character—that is, the country's private life. All issues are generally solvable, suggesting that they are not so much awe-struck or horror-struck as they are provoked by some topical controversy. "Controversial" is a common word in the critical language of this literature, as it is, say, in the language of the TV producer.

It is hardly news that in best-sellerdom we frequently find the hero coming to terms and settling down in Scarsdale, or wherever, knowing himself. And on Broadway, in the third act, someone says, "Look, why don't you just love each other?" and the protagonist, throwing his hand to his forehead, cries, "God, why didn't *I* think of that!" and before the bulldozing action of love, all else collapses—verisimilitude, truth, and interest. It is like "Dover Beach" ending happily for Matthew Arnold, and for us, because the poet is standing at the window with a woman who understands him. If the literary investigation of our era were to become solely the property of Wouk, Weidman, Sloan Wilson, Cameron Hawley, and Broadway's *amor-vincit-omnia* boys it would be unfortunate indeed—like leaving sex to the pornographers, where again there is more to what is happening than first meets the eye.

But the times have not yet been given over completely to lesser minds and talents. There is Norman Mailer. And he is an interesting example of a writer in whom our era has provoked such a magnificent disgust that dealing with it in fiction has almost come to seem, for him, beside the point. He has become an actor in the cultural drama, the difficulty of which is that it leaves one with less time to be a writer. For instance, to defy the civil-defense authorities and their H-bomb drills, you have to take off a morning from the typewriter and go down and stand outside of City Hall; then, if you're lucky and they toss you in jail, you have to give up an evening at home and your next morning's work as well. To defy Mike Wallace, or challenge his principle-less aggression, or simply use him or straighten him out, you must first be a guest on his program* —there's one night shot. Then you may well spend the next two weeks (I am speaking from memory) disliking yourself for having gone, and then two more writing an article attempting to explain why you did it and what it was like. "It's the age of the slob," says a character in William Styron's new novel. "If we don't watch out they're going to drag us under. . . ." And the dragging under can take many forms. We get, from Mailer, for instance, a book like *Advertisements for Myself*, a chronicle for the most part of why I did it and what it was like—and who I have it in for: his life as a substitute for his fiction. An infuriating, self-indulgent, boisterous, mean book, not much worse than most advertising we have to put up with—but, taken as a whole, curiously moving in its revelation of despair so great that the man who bears it, or is borne by it, seems for the time being to have given up on making an imaginative assault upon the American experience, and has become instead the champion of a kind of public revenge. However, what one champions one day may make one its victim the next; once having written *Advertisements for Myself*, I don't see that you can write it again. Mailer probably now finds himself in the unenviable position of having to put up or shut up. Who knows—maybe it's where he wanted to be. My own feeling is that times are tough for a fiction writer when he takes to writing letters to his newspaper rather than those complicated, disguised letters to himself, which are stories.

The last is not intended to be a sententious, or a condescending remark, or even a generous one. However one suspects Mailer's style or his motives, one sympathizes with the impulse that leads him to want to be a critic, a reporter, a sociologist, a journalist, or even the Mayor of New York. For what is particularly tough about the times is writing about them, as a serious novelist or storyteller. Much has been made, much of it by the writers themselves, of the fact that the American writer has no status, no respect, and no audience. I

*In the late fifties and early sixties, Mike Wallace, now a seasoned CBS correspondent, ran an exceedingly abrasive TV interview show; I appeared there to be cross-examined by him after *Goodbye, Columbus* won a National Book Award.

am pointing here to a loss more central to the task itself, the loss of a subject; or, to put it another way, a voluntary withdrawal of interest by the fiction writer from some of the grander social and political phenomena of our times.

Of course there have been writers who have tried to meet these phenomena head-on. It seems to me I have read several books or stories in the past few years in which one character or another starts to talk about "The Bomb," and the conversation usually leaves me feeling less than convinced, and in some extreme instances, with a certain amount of sympathy for fallout; it is like people in college novels having long talks about what kind of generation they are. But what then? What can the writer do with so much of the American reality as it is? Is the only other possibility to be Gregory Corso and thumb your nose at the whole thing? The attitude of the Beats (if such a phrase has meaning) is not entirely without appeal. The whole thing is a joke. America, ha-ha. But that doesn't put very much distance between Beatdom and its sworn enemy, best-sellerdom—for is America, ha-ha, really any more than America, hoo-ray, stood upon its head?

Now it is possible that I am exaggerating the serious writer's response to our cultural predicament and his inability or unwillingness to deal with it imaginatively. There seems to me little, in the end, to prove an assertion about the psychology of a nation's writers, outside, that is, of their books themselves. In this case, unfortunately, the bulk of the evidence is not books that *have* been written but the ones that have been left unfinished, and those that have not even been considered worth the attempt. Which is not to say that there have not been certain literary signs, however, certain obsessions and innovations, to be found in the novels of our best writers, supporting the notion that the social world has ceased to be as suitable or as manageable a subject as it once may have been.

Let me begin with some words about the man who, by reputation at least, is *the* writer of the age. The response of college students to the work of J. D. Salinger indicates that perhaps he, more than anyone, has not turned his back on the times but, instead, has managed to put his finger on whatever struggle of significance is going on today between self and culture. *The Catcher in the Rye* and the recent stories in *The New Yorker* having to do with the Glass family surely take place in the immediate here and now. But what about the self, what about the hero? The question is of particular interest here, for in Salinger, more than in most of his contemporaries, the figure of the writer has lately come to be placed directly in the reader's line of vision, so that there is a connection, finally, between the attitudes of the narrator as, say, brother to Seymour Glass, and as a man who writes by profession.

And what of Salinger's heroes? Well, Holden Caulfield, we discover, winds up in an expensive sanitarium. And Seymour Glass commits suicide finally, but prior to that he is the apple of his brother's eye—and why not? He has learned to live in this world—but how? By not living in it. By kissing the soles of little girls' feet and throwing rocks at the head of his sweetheart. He is a saint, clearly. But since madness is undesirable and sainthood, for most of us, out of the question, the problem of how to live *in* this world is by no means answered; unless the answer is that one cannot. The only advice we seem to get from Salinger is to be charming on the way to the loony bin. Of course, Salinger is under no obligation to supply advice of any sort to writers or readers—still, I happen to find myself growing more and more curious about this professional writer, Buddy Glass, and how *he* manages to coast through life in the arms of sanity.

There is in Salinger the suggestion that mysticism is a possible road to salvation; at least some of his characters respond well to an intensified, emotional religious belief. Now my own reading in Zen is minuscule, but as I understand it from Salinger, the deeper we go into this world, the further we can get away from it. If you contemplate a potato long enough, it stops being a potato in the usual sense; unfortunately, however, it is the usual potato that we have to deal with from day to day. For all his loving handling of the world's objects there seems to me, in Salinger's Glass family stories as in *The Catcher*, a spurning of life as it is lived in the immediate world—this place and time is viewed as unworthy of those few precious people who have been set down in it only to be maddened and destroyed.

A spurning of our world—though of a different order—occurs in the work of another of our most gifted writers,

Bernard Malamud. Even when Malamud writes a book about baseball, *The Natural*, it is not baseball as it is played in Yankee Stadium but a wild, wacky game, where a player who is instructed to knock the cover off the ball promptly steps up to the plate and does just that: the batter swings and the inner core of the ball goes looping out to center field, where the confused fielder commences to tangle himself in the unwinding sphere; then the shortstop runs out and, with his teeth, bites the center fielder and the ball free from one another. Though *The Natural* is not Malamud's most successful book, it is at any rate our introduction to his world, which is by no means a replica of our own. There are really things called baseball players, of course, and really things called Jews, but there much of the similarity ends. The Jews of *The Magic Barrel* and the Jews of *The Assistant* are not the Jews of New York City or Chicago. They are Malamud's invention, a metaphor of sorts to stand for certain possibilities and promises, and I am further inclined to believe this when I read the statement attributed to Malamud which goes, "All men are Jews." In fact, we know this is not so; even the men who are Jews aren't sure they're Jews. But Malamud, as a writer of fiction, has not shown specific interest in the anxieties and dilemmas of the contemporary American Jew, the Jew we think of as characteristic of our times. Rather, his people live in a timeless depression and a placeless Lower East Side; their society is not affluent, their predicament is not cultural. I am not saying—one cannot, of Malamud—that he has spurned life or an examination of its difficulties. What it is to be human, and to be humane, is his deepest concern. I do mean to point out that he does not—or has not yet—found the *contemporary* scene a proper or sufficient backdrop for his tales of heartlessness and heartache, of suffering and regeneration.

Now, Malamud and Salinger cannot, of course, be considered to speak for all American writers, and yet their fictional response to the world about them—what they choose to emphasize or ignore—is of interest to me simply because they are two of the best. Of course there are plenty of other writers around, capable ones too, who do not travel the same road; however, even among these others, I wonder if we may not be witnessing a response to the times, less apparently dramatized perhaps than the social detachment in Salinger and Malamud, but there in the body of the work nonetheless.

Let us take up the matter of prose style. Why is everybody so bouncy all of a sudden? Those who have been reading Saul Bellow, Herbert Gold, Arthur Granit, Thomas Berger, and Grace Paley will know to what I am referring. Writing recently in *The Hudson Review*, Harvey Swados said that he saw developing "a nervous muscular prose perfectly suited to the exigencies of an age which seems at once appalling and ridiculous. These are metropolitan writers, most of them are Jewish, and they are specialists in a kind of prose-poetry that often depends for its effectiveness as much on how it is ordered, or how it looks on the printed page, as it does on what it is expressing. This is risky writing . . ." Swados added, and perhaps it is in its very riskiness that we can discover some kind of explanation for it. I'd like to compare two short descriptive passages, one from Bellow's *The Adventures of Augie March*, the other from Gold's new novel, *Therefore Be Bold*, in the hope that the differences revealed will be educational.

As numerous readers have already pointed out, the language of *Augie March* combines literary complexity with conversational ease, joins the idiom of the academy with the idiom of the streets (not all streets—certain streets); the style is special, private, energetic, and though at times unwieldy, it generally serves Bellow brilliantly. Here, for instance, is a description of Grandma Lausch:

> With the [cigarette] holder in her dark little gums between which all her guile, malice, and command issued, she had her best inspirations of strategy. She was as wrinkled as an old paper bag, an autocrat, hard-shelled and jesuitical, a pouncy old hawk of a Bolshevik, her small ribboned gray feet immobile on the shoekit and stool Simon had made in the manual-training class, dingy old wool Winnie [the dog] whose bad smell filled the flat on the cushion beside her. If wit and discontent don't necessarily go together, it wasn't from the old woman that I learned it.

Herbert Gold's language has also been distinctly special, private, energetic. One notices in the following passage from *Therefore Be Bold* that here too the writer begins by recognizing a physical similarity between the character to be described and some unlikely object, and from there, as in Bellow's Grandma Lausch passage, attempts to wind up, via the body, making a discovery about the soul. The character described is named Chuck Hastings.

> In some respects he resembled a mummy—the shriveled yellow skin, the hands and head too large for a wasted body, the bottomless eye sockets of thought beyond the Nile. But his agile Adam's apple and point-making finger made him less the Styx-swimmer dog-paddling toward Coptic limbos than a high school intellectual intimidating the navel-eyed little girls.

First, the grammar: ". . . bottomless eye sockets of thought beyond the Nile." Is the thought beyond the Nile, or the eye sockets? What does it mean to be beyond the Nile anyway? These grammatical difficulties have little in common with the ironic inversion with which Bellow's description begins: "With the holder in her dark little gums between which all her guile, malice, and command issued . . ." Bellow goes on to describe Grandma Lausch as an "autocrat," "hard-shelled," "jesuitical," "a pouncy old hawk of a Bolshevik"—imaginative certainly, but tough-minded, *exact*. Of Gold's Chuck Hastings, however, we learn, "His agile Adam's apple and point-making finger made him less the Styx-swimmer dog-paddling toward Coptic limbos," etc. . . . Language in the service of the narrative, or literary regression in the service of the ego? In a recent review of *Therefore Be Bold*, Granville Hicks quoted this very paragraph in praise of Gold's style. "This is high-pitched," Mr. Hicks admitted, "but the point is that Gold keeps it up and keeps it up." I take it the sexual pun is not deliberate; nevertheless, it might serve as a reminder that exhibitionism and passion are not one and the same. What we have here is not stamina or vitality but reality taking a back seat to personality—and not the personality of the imagined character, but of the writer who is doing the imagining. Bellow's description seems to arise out of a writer's firm grasp of his character: Grandma Lausch *is*. Behind the description of Chuck Hastings there seems to me something else that is being said: Herbert Gold is.

Now, I am not trying to sell selflessness here. Rather, I am suggesting that this nervous muscular prose that Swados talks about may perhaps have something to do with the unfriendly relations that exist between the writer and the culture. The prose suits the age, Swados suggests, and I wonder if it does not suit it, in part, because it rejects it. The writer thrusts before our eyes—it is in the very ordering of his sentences—*personality*, in all its separateness and specialness. Of course, the mystery of personality may be nothing less than a writer's ultimate concern; and certainly when the muscular prose is revealing of character and evocative of an environment—as in *Augie March*—it can be wonderfully effective; at its worst, however, as a form of literary onanism, it seriously curtails the fictional possibilities, and may perhaps be thought of as a symptom of the writer's loss of the community—of what is *outside* himself —as subject.

True, the bouncy style can be understood in still other ways as well. It is not surprising that most of the practitioners Swados points to are Jewish. When writers who do not feel much of a connection to Lord Chesterfield begin to realize that they are under no real obligation to try and write like that distinguished old stylist, they are likely enough to go out and be bouncy. Also, there is the matter of the spoken language which these writers have heard, as our statesmen might put it, in the schools, the homes, the churches and the synagogues of the nation. I would even say that when the bouncy style is not an attempt to dazzle the reader, or one's self, but to incorporate into American literary prose the rhythms, nuances, and emphases of urban and immigrant speech, the result can sometimes be a language of new and rich emotional subtleties, with a kind of backhanded charm and irony all its own, as in Grace Paley's book of stories *The Little Disturbances of Man*.

But whether the practitioner is Gold, Bellow, or Paley, there is a further point to make about the bounciness: it is an expression of pleasure. However, a question: If the world is as crooked and unreal as it feels to me it is becoming, day by day; if one feels less and less power in the face of this unreality; if the inevitable end is destruction, if not of all life, then of much that is valuable and civilized in life—then why in God's name is the writer pleased? Why don't all our fictional heroes wind up in institutions, like Holden Caulfield, or suicides, like Seymour Glass? Why is it that so many of them—not just in books by Wouk and Weidman but in Bellow, Gold, Styron, and others—wind up affirming life? For surely the air is thick these days with affirmation, and though we shall doubtless get our annual editorial this year from *Life* calling for affirmative novels, the fact is that more and more books by serious writers seem to end on a note of celebration. Not just the tone is bouncy, the moral is bouncy too. In *The Optimist*, another of Gold's novels, the hero, having taken his lumps, cries out in the book's last line, "More. More. More! More! More!" Curtis Harnack's novel, *The Work of an Ancient Hand*, ends with the hero filled with "rapture and hope" and saying aloud, "I believe in God." And Saul Bellow's *Henderson the Rain King* is a book given over to celebrating the regeneration of the heart, blood, and general health of its hero. Yet it is of some importance, I think, that the regeneration of Henderson takes place in a world that is thoroughly and wholly imagined, *but that does not really exist*. It is not the tumultuous Africa of the newspapers and the United Nations discussions that Eugene Henderson visits. There is nothing here of nationalism or riots or apartheid. But why should there be? There is the world, and there is also the self. And the self, when the writer turns upon it all his attention and talent, is revealed to be a most remarkable thing. First off, it exists, it's real. *I am*, the self cries out, and then, taking a nice long look, it adds, *and I am beautiful*.

At the conclusion to Bellow's book, his hero, Eugene Henderson, a big, sloppy millionaire, is returning to America, coming home from a trip to Africa, where he has been plague fighter, lion tamer, and rainmaker; he is bringing back with him a real lion. Aboard the plane he befriends a small Persian boy, whose language he cannot understand. Still, when the plane lands at Newfoundland, Henderson takes the child in his arms and goes out onto the field. And then:

> Laps and laps I galloped around the shining and riveted body of the plane, behind the fuel trucks. Dark faces were looking from within. The great, beautiful propellers were still, all four of them. I guess I felt it was my turn now to move, and so went running—leaping, leaping, pounding, and tingling over the pure white lining of the gray Arctic silence.

And so we leave Henderson, a very happy man. Where? In the Arctic. This picture has stayed with me since I read the book a year ago: of a man who finds energy and joy in an imaginary Africa, and celebrates it on an unpeopled, ice-bound vastness.

Earlier I quoted from Styron's new novel, *Set This House on Fire*. Now Styron's book, like Bellow's, also tells of the regeneration of an American who leaves his own country and goes abroad for a while to live. But where Henderson's world is wildly removed from our own, Kinsolving, Styron's hero, inhabits a place we immediately recognize. The book is thick with detail that twenty years from now will probably require extensive footnotes to be thoroughly understood. The hero is an American painter who has taken his family to live in a small town on the Amalfi coast. Cass Kinsolving detests America, and himself. Throughout most of the book he is taunted, tempted, and disgraced by Mason Flagg, a fellow countryman, who is rich, boyish, naïve, licentious, indecent, cruel, and stupid. Kinsolving, by way of his attachment to Flagg, spends most of the book choosing between living and dying, and at one point, in a tone that is characteristic, says this about his expatriation:

> . . . the man I had come to Europe to escape [why he's] the man in all the car advertisements, you know, the young guy waving there—he looks so beautiful and educated and everything, and he's got it *made*, Penn State and a blonde there, and a smile as big as a billboard. And he's going places. I mean electronics. Politics. What they call communication. Advertising. Saleshood. Outer space. God only knows. And he's as ignorant as an Albanian peasant.

However, despite all his disgust with what American public life can do to a man's private life, Kinsolving, like Henderson, comes back to America at the end, having opted for existence. But the America that we find him in seems to me to be the America of his childhood, and (if only in a metaphoric way) of everyone's childhood: he tells his story while he fishes from a boat in a Carolina stream. The affirmation at the conclusion is not as go-getting as Gold's "More! More!" or as sublime as

Harnack's "I believe in God," or as joyous as Henderson's romp on the Newfoundland airfield. "I wish I could tell you that I had found some belief, some rock . . ." Kinsolving says, "but to be truthful, you see, I can only tell you this: that as for being and nothingness, the only thing I did know was that to choose between them was simply to choose being . . ." Being. Living. Not where one lives or with whom one lives—but *that* one lives.

And what does all of this add up to? It would, of course, drastically oversimplify the making of fiction to suggest that Saul Bellow's book or Herbert Gold's prose style arise ineluctably out of our distressing cultural and political predicament. Nonetheless, that the communal predicament *is* distressing weighs upon the writer no less, and perhaps even more, than upon his neighbor—for to the writer the community is, properly, both subject and audience. And it may be that when this situation produces not only feelings of disgust, rage, and melancholy but impotence too, the writer is apt to lose heart and turn finally to other matters, to the construction of wholly imaginary worlds, and to a celebration of the self, which may, in a variety of ways, become his subject, as well as the impetus that establishes the perimeters of his technique. What I have tried to point out is that the vision of self as inviolable, powerful, and nervy, self imagined as the only seemingly real thing in an unreal-seeming environment, has given some of our writers joy, solace, and muscle. Certainly to have come through a serious personal struggle intact, simply to have survived, is nothing to be made light of, and it is for just this reason that Styron's hero manages to engage our sympathies right down to the end. Still, when the survivor cannot choose but be ascetic, when the self can only be celebrated as it is excluded from society, or as it is exercised and admired in a fantastic one, we then do not have much reason to be cheery. Finally, for me there is something unconvincing about a regenerated Henderson up on the pure white lining of the world dancing around that shining airplane. Consequently, it is not with this scene that I should like to conclude, but instead with the image of his hero that Ralph Ellison presents at the end of *Invisible Man*. For here too the hero is left with the simple stark fact of himself. He is as alone as a man can be. Not that he hasn't gone out into the world; he has gone out into it, and out into it, and out into it—but at the end he chooses to go underground, to live there and to wait. And it does not seem to him a cause for celebration either.

New Jewish Stereotypes

I FIND that I am suddenly living in a country in which the Jew has come to be—or is allowed for now to think he is—a cultural hero. Only recently on the radio I heard a disc jockey introducing the theme song from the new movie *Exodus*. The words were to be sung by Pat Boone. The disc jockey made it clear that this was the "only authorized version of the song." Authorized by what? For whom? Why? No further word from the d.j. Only a silence crackling with piety, and then Mr. Boone, singing out of something less than a whirlwind—

> This land is mine,
> God gave this land to me!

I do not know whether I am moving up or down the cultural ladder, or simply sideways, when I recall that there has been the song "Exodus," preceded by the movie *Exodus*, preceded by the novel *Exodus*. However you slice it, there does not seem to be any doubt that the image of the Jew as patriot, warrior, and battle-scarred belligerent is rather satisfying to a large segment of the American public.

In an interview in the *New York Post*, Leon Uris, the author of the novel, claims that his image of the Jewish fighter is a good deal closer to the truth than images of Jews presented by other Jewish writers. I take it I am one of the others to whom Mr. Uris is referring—the *Post* clipping was mailed to me by a woman demanding some explanation for the "anti-Semitism and self-hatred" that she found in a collection of my short fiction that had just been published. What Uris told his interviewer, Joseph Wershba, was this:

> There is a whole school of Jewish American writers, who spend their time damning their fathers, hating their mothers, wringing their hands and wondering why they were born. This isn't art or literature. It's psychiatry. These writers are professional

Originally a speech delivered at Loyola University (Chicago) for a symposium on "The Needs and Images of Man," sponsored jointly by the Anti-Defamation League of B'nai B'rith and Loyola (1961).

apologists. Every year you find one of their works on the best seller lists. Their work is obnoxious and makes me sick to my stomach.

I wrote *Exodus* because I was just sick of apologizing—or feeling that it was necessary to apologize. The Jewish community of this country has contributed far more greatly than its numbers—in art, medicine, and especially literature.

I set out to tell a story of Israel. I am definitely biased. I am definitely pro-Jewish.

An author goes through everything his readers do. It was a revelation to me, too, when I was researching *Exodus* in Europe and in Israel. And the revelation was this: that we Jews are not what we have been portrayed to be. In truth, we have been fighters.

"In truth, we have been fighters." So bald, stupid, and uninformed is the statement that it is not even worth disputing. One has the feeling that, single-handedly, Uris has set out to counter with his new image of the Jew, the older one that comes down to us in those several stories, the punch line of which is, "Play nice, Jakie—don't fight." However, there is not much value in swapping one simplification for the other. What Uris might do, when he is not having revelations by way of "researching" novels, is to read a new book called *Dawn*, by Elie Wiesel. Wiesel is a Hungarian Jew now living in New York, and his first book, *Night*, was an autobiographical account of his experiences as a fifteen-year-old boy in Auschwitz and Buchenwald, those concentration camps, he writes, which "consumed my faith forever . . . murdered my God and my soul and turned my dreams to dust." *Dawn*, the second book, has for its background Jewish terrorist activities in Palestine that preceded the establishment of the State of Israel. The hero is assigned the task of executing a British major who has been taken hostage by the Jewish terrorists; the novel deals with the terrible hours the hero spends prior to the execution. I should like to tell Uris that Wiesel's Jew is not so proud to discover himself in the role of a fighter, nor is he able to find justification for himself in some traditional Jewish association with pugnacity or bloodletting. But actually it turns out that there is really no need to tell Uris anything of the sort; if we can believe a news item that we find in *Time* magazine, he already knows more than he lets on in the *New York Post*.

In Manhattan, *Time* reports,

> Captain Yehiel Aranowicz, 37 . . . one-time master of the blockade-running Israeli refugee ship "Exodus," reported some reservations back home about the best selling (4,000,000 copies to date) novel inspired by his 1947 heroics. "Israelis," he said, "were pretty disappointed in the book, to put it lightly. The types that are described in it never existed in Israel. The novel is neither history nor literature." . . . In Encino, California, *Exodus'* author Leon Uris rebutted: "You may quote me as saying, 'Captain who?' and that's all I have to say. I'm not going to pick on a lightweight. Just look at my sales figures."

Admittedly, it is not safe to indict a man solely on the basis of what *Time* quotes him as having said; it may even be *Time*'s pleasure to titillate its readers with another classic stereotype—the Jewish hustler who will sell anything for a price. There was a time when this image was helpful to certain Gentiles in describing the Jew. Now there is another way of describing him—there is the image that Mr. Uris has sold, the image millions have read about in his book and other millions will see flickering on the screen.

There is Leon Uris to make the Jew and Jewishness acceptable, appealing, and attractive, and there is that famous optimist and cracker-barrel philosopher, Harry Golden. The image of the Jew that Harry Golden presents has been analyzed to a turn in Theodore Solotaroff's recent essay in *Commentary*, "Harry Golden and the American Audience." Mr. Solotaroff points out that in Golden's three books, *For 2¢ Plain*, *Only in America*, and *Enjoy, Enjoy!* he "satisfied both Jewish nostalgia and Gentile curiosity" that "he presents with depressing clarity certain very real problems and conditions of our society in the past decade—a society characterized by its well-intentioned but soft, sloppy, equivocal thinking about itself. . . . Garnished with a little Manischewitz horseradish the perplexed banalities of the middle class come back to [the reader] as the wisdom of the ages."

Solotaroff thinks of horseradish; in matters Goldenian, I am a schmaltz man myself. It is interesting to observe that Golden, in replying to Solotaroff's comments, manages to lay the schmaltz on with one hand while trying to wipe it away with the other. In his newspaper, *The Carolina Israelite*, Golden writes that Solotaroff is dead wrong in accusing him of glamorizing life in the New York ghetto. With characteristic restraint and logic, Golden explains: "We Jews . . . not only had a society, but, quite frankly, a Jewish city, and this sense of community is what lends memories of the old East Side its glamour, and it is for this reason that the bulk of American Jewry up in the middle class lick their fingers over everything I write about the Lower East Side of New York. Sentiment alone could never sustain such amazingly wide-spread interest." The word is spelled sentimentality, and if *it* can't produce wide-spread interest, what can?

Popular Jewish interest in Golden and in Uris isn't hard to understand. For one thing, there is the pleasure of recognition, the kick that comes of seeing the words "kugel" and "latkes" in print. Then there is the romance of oneself: The Manly Hebrew Hero on the one hand, the Immigrant Success on the other. Harry Golden, a self-confessed Horatio Alger, furnishes us with the names of the judges, movie stars, scientists, and comedians who have risen from the Jewish Lower East Side to fame and fortune. But what of the Gentile interest? Four million people have bought copies of *Exodus*; two million, copies of *Only in America*; they can't all have been Jews. Why this Gentile interest in Jewish characters, history, manners, and morals? How does Pat Boone come to be singing the "only authorized version" anyway? Why not Moishe Oysher or Eddie Fisher?

One explanation Solotaroff offers for Golden's appeal is that Golden presents to his readers a world characterized by "vividness, energy, aspiration, discipline, and finally the warmth of life—that is, precisely those qualities which are said to be declining in the modern middle-class family and suburb." And there does seem to be fascination these days with the idea of Jewish emotionalism. People who have more sense than to go up to Negroes and engage them in conversation about "rhythm" have engaged me in conversation about Jewish "warmth." They think it is flattering—and they think it is true.

I do not believe that they think it is complicated; that warmth, when it does appear, does not just radiate itself—at the center there is usually a fire.

There are several Jewish graduate students in a class I teach at the Writing Workshop of the State University of Iowa, and during this last semester three of them wrote stories about a Jewish childhood; and in all three the emotional pitch of the drama ran very high. Curiously, or perhaps not so curiously, in each story the hero is a Jewish boy, somewhere between ten and fifteen, who gets excellent grades in school and is always combed and courteous. The stories, all told in the first person, have to do with a friendship that grows up between the hero and a Gentile neighbor or schoolmate. The Gentile is from a slightly lower class—Italian-American, in one instance, Tom Sawyer–American in another—and he leads the Jewish boy, who is of the middle class, into the world of the flesh. The Gentile boy has already had some kind of sexual experience. Not that he is much older than his Jewish sidekick—he has had a chance to find his way to adventure because his parents pay hardly any attention to him at all: they are divorced, or they drink, or they are uneducated and say "goddamn" all the time, or they just don't seem to be around that much to care. This leaves their offspring with plenty of time to hunt for girls. The Jewish boy, on the other hand, is watched—he is watched at bedtime, at study time, and especially at mealtime. Who he is watched by is his mother. The father we rarely see, and be- tween him and the boy there seems to be little more than a nodding acquaintance. The old man is either working or sleeping or across the table, silently stowing it away. Still, there is a great deal of warmth in these families—especially when compared to the Gentile friend's family—and almost all of it is generated by the mother. And it does not strike the young hero the way it strikes Harry Golden and his audience. The fire that warms can also burn and asphyxiate: what the hero envies the Gentile boy is his parents' *indifference*, and largely, it would seem, because of the opportunities it affords him for sexual adventure. Religion here is understood, not as the key to the mysteries of the divine and the beyond, but to the mystery of the sensual and the erotic, the awesome wonder of laying a hand on the girl down the street. The warmth these Jewish storytellers want then is the warmth to which the Gentiles seem (to them) to have such easy access, just as the warmth that Harry Golden's Gentiles envy him for is the warmth he tells them that Jews come by as a matter of course.

I hasten to point out that in these short stories the girls to whom the Gentile friend leads the young narrator are never Jewish. The Jewish women are mothers and sisters. The sexual yearning is for the Other. The dream of the shiksa—counterpart to the Gentile dream of the Jewess, often adjectivally portrayed as "melon-breasted." (See Thomas Wolfe.) I do not mean, by the way, to disparage the talent of these writing students by comparing their interest in a Jewish boy's dreams with the dreaminess you find in Golden: what the heroes of these stories invariably learn—as the Gentile comrades disappear into other neighborhoods or jail—are the burdensome contradictions of their own predicament.

Golden and Uris burden no one with anything. Indeed, much of their appeal is that they dissipate guilt, real and imagined. It turns out that the Jews are not poor innocent victims after all—all the time they were supposed to be being persecuted, they were having a good time being warm to one another and having their wonderful family lives. What they were developing—as one reviewer quoted by Solotaroff says of Harry Golden—was their "lovely Jewish slant on the world."

Ah, that lovely Jewish slant—its existence surely can soothe the conscience: for if the victim is not a victim, then the victimizer is probably no victimizer either. Along with the other comforts Golden offers, there is a kind of escape hatch for Gentiles who, if they have not been practicing anti-Semites, have at any rate been visited with distrustful, suspicious feelings about Jews, feelings which they are told they ought not to have. Golden assures them (as he assures the Jews) that we are a happy, optimistic, endearing people, and also that we live in a top-notch country—is not his career proof that bigotry does not corrode the American soul? There he is, a Jew—and one who speaks up, mind you—a respected citizen in a Southern city no less. Wonderful! And not in Sweden, or in Italy, or in the Philippines. Only—Golden tells them—in America!

This may be pleasant therapy for certain anxious, well-meaning Gentiles, in that they do not have to continue to feel guilty for crimes for which they do not in fact bear any responsibility; it may even unburden some halfhearted anti-Semites who don't like Jews because they don't like themselves for not liking Jews. But I do not see that it is very respectful to the Jews and the hard facts of their history. Or even to the validity of Gentile suspiciousness. For why shouldn't the Gentiles have suspicions? The fact is that, if one is committed to being a Jew, then he believes that on the most serious questions pertaining to man's survival—understanding the past, imagining the future, discovering the relation between God and humanity—he is right and the Christians are wrong. As a believing Jew, he must certainly view the breakdown in this century of moral order and the erosion of spiritual values in terms of the inadequacy of Christianity as a sustaining force for the good. However, who would care to say such things to his neighbor? Rather, what we witness daily in American life is the "socialization of the anti-social . . . the acculturation of the anti-cultural . . . the legitimization of the subversive." These phrases are Lionel Trilling's; he has used them to describe the responses many of his students have to the more extreme elements in modern literature. His words have for me an even broader cultural relevance: I refer to the swallowing up of difference that goes on around us continuously, that deadening "tolerance" that robs—is designed to rob—those who differ, diverge, or rebel of their powers. Instead of being taken seriously as a threat, a man is effectively silenced by being made popular. They are presently holding beatnik parties in the suburbs—which does not convince me that all men are brothers. On the contrary, they are strangers; that comes home to me every day when I read the newspaper. They are strangers, and they are enemies, and it is because that is how things are that it behooves us, not "to love one another" (which from all evidence appears to be asking for the moon), but to practice no violence and treachery upon one another, which, it would seem, is difficult enough.

But of course the Jews *have* done violence. It is the story of their violence that Leon Uris is so proud to tell to America. Its compensatory appeal to American Jews is not hard to understand, but again, what of the Gentiles? Why all the piety about the "only authorized version" of a popular song? Why is the song even popular? the movie? the book? So persuasive and agreeable is the *Exodus* formulation to so many in America that I am inclined to wonder if the burden that it is working to dislodge from the nation's consciousness (inasmuch as it exists there) is nothing less than the memory of the Holocaust itself, the murder of six million Jews, in all its raw, senseless, fiendish horror. As though, say, a popular song or movie were to come along some day soon to enable us to dispose of that other troublesome horror, the murder of the citizens of Hiroshima. In the case of Hiroshima, we might perhaps be given a song to sing about the beautiful modern city that has risen from the ashes of atomic annihilation, about how much more prosperous, healthy, and enterprising life is in the new city than it was in the Hiroshima that was obliterated. But be that as it may—and who in this go-getting land is to say that it may not be soon enough?—now there is Golden to assure us that even ghettoized Jews were really happy, optimistic, and warm (as opposed to aggrieved, pessimistic, fearful, and xenophobic), and there is Uris to say that you don't have to worry about Jewish vulnerability and victimization after all, the Jews can take care of themselves. They *have* taken care of themselves. One week *Life* magazine presents on its cover a picture of Adolf Eichmann; weeks later, a picture of Sal Mineo as a Jewish freedom fighter. A crime to which there is no adequate human response, no grief, no compassion, no vengeance that is sufficient seems, in part then, to have been avenged. And when the scales appear at last to begin to balance, there cannot but be a sigh of relief. The Jew is no longer looking out from the wings on the unending violence of our age, nor is he any longer its favorite victim; now he is a participant. Fine then. Welcome aboard. A man with a gun and a hand grenade, a man who kills for his God-given rights (in this case, as the song informs us, God-given *land*) cannot sit so easily in judgment of another man when he kills for what God has given *him*, according to his accounting and inventory and faith.

Mr. Uris's discovery that the Jews are fighters fills him with pride; it fills any number of his Jewish readers with pride as well, and his Gentile readers less perhaps with pride than with relief. The hero of *Dawn*, Elie Wiesel's novel about the Jewish terrorists, is visited with less comforting and buoyant emotions. He is overcome with shame and confusion and a sense that he is locked hopelessly and forever in a tragic nightmare. No matter how just he tells himself are the rights for which he murders, nothing in his or his people's past is able to make firing a bullet into another man anything less ghastly than it is. He has seen and suffered so much, in Buchenwald and Auschwitz, that it is with a final sense of the death of what he thought he was that he pulls the trigger on the British officer and becomes another of the executioners in our violent century. He is one of those Jews, like Job, who wonder why they were born.

Writing About Jews

I

EVER SINCE some of my first stories were collected in 1959 in a volume called *Goodbye, Columbus*, my work has been attacked from certain pulpits and in certain periodicals as dangerous, dishonest, and irresponsible. I have read editorials and articles in Jewish community newspapers condemning these stories for ignoring the accomplishments of Jewish life, or, as Rabbi Emanuel Rackman recently told the convention of the Rabbinical Council of America, for creating a "distorted image of the basic values of Orthodox Judaism," and even, he went on, for denying the non-Jewish world the opportunity of appreciating the "overwhelming contribution which Orthodox Jews are making in every avenue of modern endeavor. . . ." Among the letters I receive from readers, there have been a number written by Jews accusing me of being anti-Semitic and "self-hating," or, at least, tasteless; they argue or imply that the sufferings of the Jews throughout history, culminating in the murder of six million by the Nazis, have made certain criticisms of Jewish life insulting and trivial. It is charged that such criticism as I make of Jews—or apparent criticism—is taken by anti-Semites as justification, as "fuel" for their fires, particularly as it is a Jew himself who seemingly admits to habits and behavior in his Jewish characters that are not exemplary, or even normal and acceptable. When I speak before Jewish audiences, invariably there have been people who have come up to me afterward to ask, "Why don't you leave us alone? Why don't you write about the Gentiles?"—"Why must you be so critical?"—"Why do you disapprove of us so?"—this last question asked as often with incredulity as with anger; and often by people a good deal older than myself, asked as of an erring child by a loving but misunderstood parent.

This essay evolved from remarks delivered in 1962 and 1963 at the University of Iowa Hillel House, the Hartford, Conn., Jewish Community Center, and Yeshiva University (1963).

It is difficult, if not impossible, to explain to some of the people claiming to have felt my teeth sinking in that in many instances they haven't been bitten at all. Not always, but frequently, what such readers have taken to be my disapproval of the lives lived by Jews seems to have to do more with their own moral perspective than with the one they would ascribe to me: at times they see wickedness where I myself had seen energy or courage or spontaneity; they are ashamed of what I see no reason to be ashamed of, and defensive where there is no cause for defense.

Not only do they seem to me often to have cramped and untenable notions of right and wrong, but looking at fiction as they do—in terms of "approval" and "disapproval" of Jews, "positive" and "negative" attitudes toward Jewish life—they are likely not to see what it is that a story is really about.

To give an example. A story I wrote called "Epstein" tells of a sixty-year-old man who has an adulterous affair with the lady across the street. In the end, Epstein, who is the hero, is caught—caught by his family, and caught and struck down by all of which he had set out to make a final struggle against. There are Jewish readers, I know, who cannot figure out why I found it necessary to tell this story about a Jewish man: don't other people commit adultery too? Why is it the Jew who must be shown cheating?

But there is more to adultery than cheating: for one thing, there is the adulterer himself. For all that some people may experience him as a cheat and nothing else, he usually experiences himself as something more. And generally speaking, what draws most readers and writers to literature is this "something more"—all that is beyond simple moral categorizing. It is not my purpose in writing a story of an adulterous man to make it clear how right we all are if we disapprove of the act and are disappointed in the man. Fiction is not written to affirm the principles and beliefs that everybody seems to hold, nor does it seek to guarantee the appropriateness of our feelings. The world of fiction, in fact, frees us from the circumscriptions that society places upon feeling; one of the greatnesses of the art is that it allows both the writer and the reader to respond to experience in ways not always available in day-to-day conduct;

or, if they are available, they are not possible, or manageable, or legal, or advisable, or even necessary to the business of living. We may not even know that we have such a range of feelings and responses *until* we have come into contact with the work of fiction. This does not mean that either reader or writer no longer brings any judgment to bear upon human action. Rather, we judge at a different level of our being, for not only are we judging with the aid of new feelings but without the necessity of having to act upon judgment. Ceasing for a while to be upright citizens, we drop into another layer of consciousness. And this expansion of moral consciousness, this exploration of moral fantasy, is of some value to a man and to society.

I do not care to go at length here into what a good many readers take for granted are the purposes and devices of fiction. I do want to make clear to those whose interests may not lead them to speculate much on the subject, a few of the assumptions a writer may hold—assumptions such as lead me to say that I do not write a story to make evident whatever disapproval I may feel for adulterous men. I write a story of a man who is adulterous to reveal the condition of such a man. If the adulterous man is a Jew, then I am revealing the condition of an adulterous man who is a Jew. Why tell that story? Because I seem to be interested in how—and why and when—a man acts counter to what he considers to be his "best self," or what others imagine it to be, or would prefer it to be. The subject is hardly "mine"; it interested readers and writers for a long time before it became my turn to be engaged by it too.

One of my readers, a man in Detroit, posed several questions which I believe, in their very brevity, were intended to disarm me. I quote from his letter without his permission.

The first question: "Is it conceivable for a middle-aged man to neglect business and spend all day with a middle-aged woman?" The answer is yes.

Next he asks: "Is it a Jewish trait?" I take it he is referring to adultery and not facetiously to the neglecting of business. The answer is: "Who said it was?" Anna Karenina commits adultery with Vronsky, with consequences more disastrous than those Epstein precipitates. Who thinks to ask, "Is it a Russian trait?" It is a human possibility. Even though the most famous injunction against it is reported as being issued, for God's own reasons, to the Jews, adultery has been one of the ways by which people of *all* faiths have sought pleasure—or freedom, or vengeance, or power, or love, or humiliation . . .

The next in the gentleman's series of questions to me is: "Why so much *shmutz?*" Is he asking, Why is there dirt in the world? Why disappointment? Why hardship, ugliness, evil, death? It would be nice to think these were the questions he had in mind. But all he is really asking is, "Why so much *shmutz* in that story?" An old man discovers the fires of lust still burning in him? *Shmutz!* Disgusting! Who wants to hear that kind of stuff! Struck as he is by nothing but the dirty aspects of Epstein's troubles, the gentleman from Detroit concludes that I am narrow-minded.

As do others. Narrow-mindedness, in fact, was the charge that a New York rabbi, David Seligson, was reported in *The New York Times* recently as having brought against me and other Jewish writers who, he told his congregation, dedicated themselves "to the exclusive creation of a melancholy parade of caricatures." Rabbi Seligson also disapproved of *Goodbye, Columbus* because I described in it a "Jewish adulterer . . . and a host of other lopsided schizophrenic personalities." Of course, adultery is not a symptom of schizophrenia, but that the rabbi should see it this way indicates to me that we have different notions as to what mental health is. After all, it may be that *life* produces a melancholy middle-aged businessman like Lou Epstein, who in Dr. Seligson's eyes looks like another in a parade of caricatures. I myself find Epstein's adultery an unlikely solution to his problems, a pathetic, even doomed response, and a comic one too, since it does not even square with the man's own conception of himself and what he wants; but none of this *unlikeliness* leads me to despair of his sanity, or humanity. I suppose it is tantamount to a confession from me of lopsided schizophrenia to admit that the character of Epstein happened to have been conceived with considerable affection and sympathy. As I see it, the rabbi cannot recognize a bear hug when one is being administered right in front of his eyes.

The *Times* report continues: "The rabbi said he could only 'wonder about' gifted writers, 'Jewish by birth, who can see so little in the tremendous saga of Jewish history.'" But I don't imagine the rabbi "wonders" about me any more than I wonder about him: that wondering business is the voice of wisdom making itself heard, always willing to be shown the light, if, of course, there is any; but I don't buy it. Pulpit fair-mindedness only hides the issue—as it does here in the rabbi's conclusion, quoted by the *Times*: "'That they [the Jewish writers in question] must be free to write, we would affirm most vehemently; but that they would know their own people and tradition, we would fervently wish.'"

However, the issue is not knowledge of one's "people." It is not a question of who has more historical data at his fingertips, or is more familiar with Jewish tradition, or which of us observes more customs and rituals. The story of Lou Epstein stands or falls not on how much I know about tradition but on how much I know about Lou Epstein. Where the history of the Jewish people comes down in time and place to become the old man whom I called Epstein, that is where my knowledge must be sound. But I get the feeling that Rabbi Seligson wants to rule Lou Epstein *out* of Jewish history. I find his predicament too touching to dismiss, even if he is something of a *grubber yung* and probably more ignorant of history than the rabbi believes me to be.

Epstein is pictured not as a learned rabbi, after all, but as the owner of a small paper-bag company; his wife is not learned either, and neither is his mistress; consequently, a reader should not expect to find in this story knowledge on my part, or the part of the characters, of the *Sayings of the Fathers*; he has every right to expect that I be close to the truth as to what might conceivably be the attitudes of a Jewish man with Epstein's history toward marriage, family life, divorce, and fornication. This story is called "Epstein" because Epstein, not the Jews, is the subject.

Obviously, though, the rabbi's interest is not in the portrayal of character; what he is looking for in my fiction is, in his words, a "balanced portrayal of Jews as we know them." I even suspect that something called "balance" is what the rabbi would advertise as the fundamental characteristic of Jewish life; what Jewish history comes down to is that at long last we have in our ranks one of everything. In his sermon Rabbi

Seligson says of Myron Kaufmann's novel *Remember Me to God* that it can "hardly be said to be recognizable as a Jewish sociological study." But Mr. Kaufmann had no intention of writing a sociological study, or—for this seems more like what the rabbi really yearns for in reading fiction about Jews—a nice positive sampling. *Madame Bovary* is hardly recognizable as a sociological study either, having at its center only a single, dreamy, provincial Frenchwoman, and not one of every other kind of provincial Frenchwoman too; this does not diminish its brilliance as an exploration of Emma Bovary. Literary works do not take as their subjects characters who have impressed a writer primarily by the *frequency* of their appearance in the population. How many Jewish men, as we know them, have come to the brink of plunging a knife into an only son because they believed God demanded it of them? The story of Abraham and Isaac derives its meaning from something other than its being an everyday occurrence. The test of any literary work is not how broad is its range of representation—for all that breadth may be characteristic of a kind of narrative—but the veracity with which the writer reveals what he has chosen to represent.

To confuse a "balanced portrayal" with a novel is to be led into absurdities. "Dear Fyodor Dostoevsky—The students in our school feel that you have been unfair to us. Do you call Raskolnikov a balanced portrayal of students as we know them? Of Russian students? Of poor students? What about those of us who have never murdered anyone and who do our schoolwork every night?" "Dear Mark Twain—None of the slaves on our plantation has ever run away. But what will our owner think when he reads of Nigger Jim?" "Dear Vladimir Nabokov—The girls in our class . . ." and so on. What fiction does and what the rabbi would like it to do are entirely antithetical. The goals of fiction are not those of a statistician—or of a public-relations firm. The novelist asks himself, "What do people think?"; the PR man asks, "What *will* people think?" And I believe this is what is actually troubling the rabbi when he calls for his "balanced portrayal of Jews": What will people think?

To be exact: What will the goyim think?

2

This was the question raised—and urgently so—when another story of mine, "Defender of the Faith," appeared in *The New Yorker* in April 1959. The story is told by Nathan Marx, an army sergeant just rotated back to Missouri from combat duty in Germany, where the war has ended. As soon as he arrives, he is made first sergeant in a training company, and immediately is latched on to by a young recruit who tries to use his attachment to the sergeant to receive kindnesses and favors. The attachment, as he sees it, is that they are both Jews. As the story progresses, what the recruit, Sheldon Grossbart, comes to demand are not mere considerations but privileges to which Marx does not think he is entitled. The story is about one man who uses his own religion, and another's uncertain conscience, for selfish ends; but mostly it is about this other man, the narrator, Marx who, because of the complexities of being a member of his religion, is involved in a taxing, if perhaps mistaken, conflict of loyalties.

I don't now and didn't while writing, see Marx's problem as nothing more than "Jewish": confronting the limitations of charity and forgiveness in one's nature—having to draw a line between what is merciful and what is just—trying to distinguish between apparent evil and the real thing, in one's self and others—these are problems for most people, regardless of the level at which they are perceived or dealt with. Yet, though the moral complexities are not exclusively a Jew's, I never for a moment considered that the characters in the story should be anything other than Jews. Someone else might have written a story embodying the same themes, and similar events perhaps, and had at its center Negroes or Irishmen; for me there was no choice. Nor was it a matter of making Grossbart a Jew and Marx a Gentile, or vice versa; telling half the truth would have been much the same as telling a lie. Most of those jokes beginning "Two Jews were walking down the street" lose a little of their punch if one of the Jews, or both, is disguised as an Englishman. Similarly, to have made any serious alteration in the Jewish factuality of "Defender of the Faith," as it began to fill itself out in my imagination, would have so unsprung the tensions I felt in the story that I would no longer have had left a story that I wanted to tell.

Some of my critics must wish that this had happened, for in going ahead and writing this story about Jews, what else did I do but confirm an anti-Semitic stereotype? But to me the story confirms something different, if no less painful, to its readers. To me Grossbart is not something we can dismiss solely as an anti-Semitic stereotype; he is a Jewish fact. If people of bad intention or weak judgment have converted certain facts of Jewish life into a stereotype of The Jew, that does not mean that such facts are no longer important in our lives, or that they are taboo for the writer of fiction. Literary investigation may even be a way to redeem the facts, to give them the weight and value that they should have in the world, rather than the disproportionate significance they obviously have for some misguided or vicious people.

Sheldon Grossbart, the character I imagined as Marx's antagonist, has his seed in fact. He is not meant to represent The Jew, or Jewry, nor does the story indicate that the writer intends him to be understood that way. Grossbart is depicted as a single blundering human being, self-righteous, cunning, and, on occasion, even a little charming; he is depicted as a young man whose lapses of integrity seem to him so necessary to his survival as to convince him that such lapses are actually committed in the name of integrity. He has been able to work out a personal ethic whereby his own sense of responsibility can suspend operation, what with the collective guilt of the others having become so immense as to have seriously altered the conditions of trust in the world. He is represented not as the stereotype of The Jew, but as a Jew who acts like the stereotype, offering back to his enemies their vision of him, answering the punishment with the crime. Given the history of humiliation and persecution that the nations have practiced on the Jews, it argues for far too much nobility to deny not only that Jews like Grossbart exist but that the temptations to Grossbartism exist in many who perhaps have more grace, or willpower, or are perhaps only more cowed, than the simple frightened soul that I imagined weeping with fear and disappointment at the end of the story. Grossbart is not The Jew;

but he is a fact of Jewish experience and well within the range of its moral possibilities.

And so is his adversary, Marx, who is, after all, the story's central character, its consciousness and its voice. He is a man who calls himself a Jew more tentatively than does Grossbart; he is not sure what it means—means for *him*—though he is not unintelligent or without conscience; he is dutiful to the point of obsession, and confronted by what are represented to him as the dire needs of another Jew, he does not for a while know what exactly to do. He moves back and forth from feelings of righteousness to feelings of betrayal, and only at the end, when he truly does betray the trust that Grossbart tries to place in him, does he commit what he has hoped to all along: an act he believes to be honorable.

Marx does not strike me, nor any of the readers I heard from, as unlikely, incredible, "made-up"; the verisimilitude of the characters and their situation was not what was called into question. In fact, the air of convincingness that the story was believed to have caused a number of people to write to me, and *The New Yorker*, and the Anti-Defamation League, protesting its publication.

Here is one of the letters I received after the story was published:

> Mr. Roth:
>   With your one story, "Defender of the Faith," you have done as much harm as all the organized anti-Semitic organizations have done to make people believe that all Jews are cheats, liars, connivers. Your one story makes people—the general public—forget all the great Jews who have lived, all the Jewish boys who served well in the armed services, all the Jews who live honest hard lives the world over. . . .

Here is one received by *The New Yorker*:

> Dear Sir:
>   . . . We have discussed this story from every possible angle and we cannot escape the conclusion that it will do irreparable damage to the Jewish people. We feel that this story presented a distorted picture of the average Jewish soldier and are at a loss to understand why a magazine of your fine reputation should publish such a work which lends fuel to anti-Semitism.

Clichés like "this being Art" will not be acceptable. A reply will be appreciated.

Here is a letter received by the officials of the Anti-Defamation League, who, because of the public response, telephoned to ask if I wanted to talk to them. The strange emphasis of the invitation, I thought, indicated the discomfort they felt at having to pass on messages such as this one:

Dear ———,
What is being done to silence this man? Medieval Jews would have known what to do with him. . . .

The first two letters I quoted were written by Jewish laymen, the last by a rabbi and educator in New York City, a man of prominence in the world of Jewish affairs.

The rabbi was later to communicate directly with me. He did not mention that he had already written to the Anti-Defamation League to express regret over the decline of medieval justice, though he was careful to point out at the conclusion of his first letter his reticence in another quarter. I believe I was supposed to take it as an act of mercy: "I have not written to the editorial board of *The New Yorker*," he told me. "I do not want to compound the sin of informing. . . ."

Informing. There was the charge so many of the correspondents had made, even when they did not want to make it openly to me, or to themselves. I had informed on the Jews. I had told the Gentiles what apparently it would otherwise have been possible to keep secret from them: that the perils of human nature afflict the members of our minority. That I had also informed them it was possible for there to be such a Jew as Nathan Marx did not seem to bother anybody; if I said earlier that Marx did not strike my correspondents as unlikely, it is because he didn't seem to strike them at all. He might as well not have been there. Of the letters that I read, just one mentioned Marx, and only to point out that I was no less blameworthy for portraying the Sergeant as a "white Jew," as he was described by my correspondent, a kind of Jewish Uncle Tom.

But even if Marx were that and only that, a white Jew, and Grossbart a black one, did it in any way follow that because I

had examined the relationship between them—another concern central to the story which drew barely a comment from
my correspondents—that I had then advocated that Jews be
denationalized, deported, persecuted, murdered? Well, no.
Whatever the rabbi may believe privately, he did not indicate
to me that he thought I was an anti-Semite. There was a suggestion, however, a grave one, that I had acted like a fool. "You
have earned the gratitude," he wrote, "of all who sustain their
anti-Semitism on such conceptions of Jews as ultimately led to
the murder of six million in our time."

Despite the sweep there at the end of the sentence, the
charge made is actually up at the front: I "earned the gratitude . . ." But of whom? I would put it less dramatically but
more exactly: of those who are predisposed to misread the
story—out of bigotry, ignorance, malice, or even innocence. If
I did earn their gratitude, it was because they failed to see, even to
look for, what I was talking about. Such conceptions of Jews as
anti-Semites hold, then, and as they were able to confirm by
misunderstanding my story, are the same, the rabbi goes on to
say, as those which "ultimately led to the murder of six million
in our time."

"Ultimately"? Is that not a gross simplification of the history
of the Jews and the history of Hitler's Germany? People hold
serious grudges against one another, vilify one another, deliberately misunderstand one another, but they do not always, as
a consequence, *murder* one another, as the Germans murdered
the Jews, and as other Europeans allowed the Jews to be murdered, or even helped the slaughter along. Between prejudice
and persecution there is usually, in civilized life, a barrier constructed by the individual's convictions and fears, and the
community's laws, ideals, values. What "ultimately" caused this
barrier to disappear in Germany cannot be explained only in
terms of anti-Semitic misconceptions; surely what must also be
understood here is the intolerability of Jewry, on the one hand,
and its usefulness, on the other, to the Nazi ideology and
dream.

By simplifying the Nazi-Jewish relationship, by making
prejudice appear to be the primary cause of annihilation, the
rabbi is able to make the consequences of publishing "Defender of the Faith" in *The New Yorker* seem very grave indeed.

He doesn't appear to be made at all anxious by the consequences of his own position. For what he is suggesting is that
some subjects must not be written about, or brought to public
attention, because it is possible for them to be misunderstood
by people with weak minds or malicious instincts. Thus he
consents to put the malicious and weak-minded in a position
of determining the level at which open communication on
these subjects will take place. This is not fighting anti-Semitism
but submitting to it: submitting to a restriction of consciousness as well as communication, because being conscious and
being candid are too risky.

In his letter the rabbi calls my attention to that famous
madman who shouts "Fire!" in a "crowded theater." He leaves
me to complete the analogy myself: by publishing "Defender
of the Faith" in *The New Yorker*: (1) I am shouting; (2) I am
shouting "Fire!"; (3) there is no fire; (4) all this is happening in
the equivalent of a "crowded theater." The crowded theater:
there is the risk. I should agree to sacrifice the freedom essential to my vocation, and even, by my lights, to the general
well-being of the culture, because—because of what? The
"crowded theater" has no relevance to the situation of the Jew
in America today. It is a grandiose delusion. It is not a metaphor describing a cultural condition but a revelation of the
nightmarish visions that plague people as fearful as the rabbi
appears to be. No wonder he says to me finally, "Your story—
in Hebrew—in an Israeli magazine or newspaper—would have
been judged exclusively from a literary point of view." That is,
ship it off to Israel. But please don't tell it here, now.

Why? So that "they" will not commence persecuting Jews
again? If the barrier between prejudice and persecution col-
lapsed in 1930s Germany, this is hardly reason to contend that
no such barrier exists in our country today. And if it should
ever begin to appear to be crumbling, then we must do what is
necessary to strengthen it. But not by putting on a good face;
not by refusing to admit to the complexities of Jewish lives; not
by pretending that Jews have existences less deserving of honest attention than the lives of their neighbors; not by making
Jews invisible.

Jews are people who are not what anti-Semites say they are.
That was once a statement out of which a man might begin to

construct an identity for himself; now it does not work so well, for it is difficult to act counter to the ways people expect you to act when fewer and fewer people define you by such expectations. The success of the struggle against the defamation of Jewish character in this country has itself made more pressing the need for a Jewish self-consciousness that is relevant to this time and place, where neither defamation nor persecution is what it was elsewhere in the past. For those Jews who choose to continue to call themselves Jews, and find reason to do so, there are courses to follow to prevent it from ever being 1933 again that are more direct, reasonable, and dignified than beginning to act as though it already is 1933—*or as though it always is*. But the death of all those Jews seems to have taught my correspondent, a rabbi and a teacher, little more than to be discreet, to be foxy, to say this but not that. It has taught him nothing other than how to remain a victim in a country where he does not have to live like one if he chooses. How pathetic. And what an insult to the dead. Imagine: sitting in New York in the 1960's and piously summoning up the "six million" to justify one's own timidity.

Timidity—and paranoia. It does not occur to the rabbi that there are Gentiles who will read the story intelligently. The only Gentiles the rabbi can imagine looking into *The New Yorker* are those who hate Jews and those who don't know how to read very well. If there are others, they can get along without reading about Jews. For to suggest that one translate one's stories into Hebrew and publish them in Israel is to say, in effect: "There is nothing in our lives we need to tell the Gentiles about, unless it has to do with how well we manage. Beyond that, it's none of their business. We are important to no one but ourselves, which is as it should be (or better be) anyway." But to indicate that moral crisis is something to be hushed up is not, of course, to take the prophetic line; nor is it a rabbinical point of view that Jewish life is of no significance to the rest of mankind.

Even given his own kind of goals, the rabbi is not very farsighted or imaginative. What he fails to see is that the stereotype as often arises from ignorance as from malice; deliberately keeping Jews out of the imagination of Gentiles, for fear of the bigots and their stereotyping minds, is really to invite the invention of stereotypical ideas. A book like Ralph Ellison's *Invisible Man*, for instance, seems to me to have helped many whites who are not anti-Negro, but who do hold Negro stereotypes, to surrender their simpleminded notions about Negro life. I doubt, however, that Ellison, describing as he does not just the squalor Negroes must put up with but certain bestial aspects of his Negro characters as well, has converted one Alabama redneck or one United States senator to the cause of desegregation; nor could the novels of James Baldwin cause Governor Wallace to conclude anything more than that Negroes are just as hopeless as he's always known them to be. As novelists, neither Baldwin nor Ellison are (to quote Mr. Ellison on himself) "cogs in the machinery of civil rights legislation." Just as there are Jews who feel that my books do nothing for the Jewish cause, so there are Negroes, I am told, who feel that Mr. Ellison's work has done little for the Negro cause and probably has harmed it. But that many blind people are still blind does not mean that Ellison's book gives off no light. Certainly those of us who are willing to be taught, and who needed to be, have been made by *Invisible Man* less stupid than we were about Negro lives, including those lives that a bigot would point to as affirming his own half-baked, inviolable ideas.

3

But it is the treachery of the bigot that the rabbi appears to be worried about and that he presents to me, to himself, and probably to his congregation, as the major cause for concern. Frankly, I think those are just the old words coming out, when the right buttons are pushed. Can he actually believe that on the basis of my story anyone is going to start a pogrom, or keep a Jew out of medical school, or even call some Jewish schoolchild a kike? The rabbi is entombed in his nightmares and fears; but that is not the whole of it. He is also hiding something. Much of this disapproval of "Defender of the Faith" because of its effect upon Gentiles seems to me a coverup for what is really objected to, what is immediately painful—and that is its direct effect upon certain Jews. "You have hurt a lot of people's feelings because you have revealed something they are ashamed of." That is the letter the rabbi did not write but should have. I would have argued then that there are things of more importance—even to these Jews—than those feelings that have been hurt, but at any rate he would have confronted me with a genuine fact, with something I was actually responsible for, and which my conscience would have had to deal with, as it does.

For the record, all the letters I saw that came in about "Defender of the Faith" were from Jews. Not one of those people whose gratitude the rabbi believes I earned wrote to say, "Thank you," nor was I invited to address any anti-Semitic organizations. When I did begin to receive speaking invitations, they were from Jewish ladies' groups, Jewish community centers, and from all sorts of Jewish organizations, large and small.

And I think this bothers the rabbi too. Some Jews are hurt by my work; but some are interested. At the rabbinical convention I mentioned earlier, Rabbi Emanuel Rackman, a professor of political science at Yeshiva University, reported to his colleagues that certain Jewish writers were "assuming the mantle of self-appointed spokesmen and leaders for Judaism." To support his remark he referred to a symposium held in Israel this last June at which I was present; as far as I know, Rabbi Rackman was not. If he had been there, he would have heard me make it quite clear that I did not want to, did not intend to, and was not able to speak *for* American Jews; I surely did not deny, and no one questioned the fact, that I spoke *to* them, and I hope to others as well. The competition that Rabbi Rackman imagines himself to be engaged in hasn't to do with who will presume to lead the Jews; it is really a matter of who, in addressing them, is going to take them more seriously—strange as that may sound—with who is going to see them as something more than part of the mob in a crowded theater, more than helpless and threatened and in need of reassurance that they are as "balanced" as anyone else. The question really is, who is going to address men and women like men and women, and who like children. If there are Jews who have begun to find the stories the novelists tell more provocative and pertinent than the sermons of some of the rabbis, perhaps it is because there are regions of feeling and consciousness in them which cannot be reached by the oratory of self-congratulation and self-pity.

On Portnoy's Complaint

Would you say something about the genesis of Portnoy's Complaint? *How long has the idea of the book been in mind?*

Some of the ideas that went into the book have been in my mind ever since I began writing, particularly ideas about style and narration. The book proceeds by means of what I began to think of while writing as "blocks of consciousness," chunks of material of varying shapes and sizes piled atop one another and held together by association rather than chronology. I tried something vaguely like this in *Letting Go*, and have wanted to come at a narrative in this way again—or break down a narrative this way—ever since.

Then there's the matter of language and tone. Beginning with *Goodbye, Columbus*, I've been attracted to prose that has the spontaneity and ease of spoken language at the same time that it is solidly grounded on the page, weighted with the irony, precision, and ambiguity associated with a more traditional written rhetoric. I'm not the only one who wants to write like this nor is it a particularly new aspiration on the planet; but that's the kind of literary idea, or ideal, I was pursuing in this book.

I was thinking more in terms of the character and his predicament when I asked how long you had in mind the "idea of the book."

I know. That's partly why I answered as I did.

But surely you don't intend us to believe that this volatile novel of sexual confession, among other things, had its conception in purely literary motives?

No, I don't. But the conception is really nothing, you know, beside the delivery. My point is that until my "ideas"—about

---

The interviewer is George Plimpton (1969).

sex, guilt, childhood, about Jewish men and their Gentile women—were absorbed by an overall fictional strategy, they were ideas not unlike anybody else's. Everybody has "ideas" for novels; the subway is jammed with people hanging from the straps, their heads full of ideas for novels they cannot begin to write. I am often one of them.

Given the book's openness, however, about intimate sexual matters, as well as its frank use of obscenity, do you think you would have embarked upon such a book in a climate unlike today's?

As long ago as 1958, in *The Paris Review*, I published a story called "Epstein" that some people found offensive in its intimate sexual revelations; and my conversation has never been as refined as it should be. I think that many people in the arts have been living in a "climate like today's" for some time now; the mass media have just caught up, and with them, the general public. Obscenity as a usable and valuable vocabulary, and sexuality as a subject, have been available to us since Joyce, Henry Miller, and Lawrence, and I don't think there's a serious American writer in his thirties who has felt restricted by the times particularly, or suddenly feels liberated because these have been advertised as the "swinging sixties." In my writing lifetime the use of obscenity has, by and large, been governed by literary taste and tact and not by the mores of the audience.

What about the audience? Don't you write for an audience? Don't you write to be read?

If you mean by an audience a particular readership which can be described in terms of its education, politics, religion, or even by its literary sophistication, the answer is no. When I'm at work I don't really have any group of people in mind whom I want to communicate with; what I want is for the work to communicate itself as fully as it can, in accordance with its own intentions. Precisely so that it *can* be read, *but on its own terms.* If one can be said to have an audience in mind, it is not any special-interest group whose beliefs and demands one either accedes to or challenges, but that ideal reader whose sensibilities have been totally given over to the writer, in exchange for his seriousness.

My new book, *Portnoy's Complaint*, is full of dirty words and dirty scenes; my last novel, *When She Was Good*, had none. Why is that? Because I've suddenly become a "swinger"? But then I was "swinging" all the way back in the fifties, with "Epstein." And what about the dirty words in *Letting Go*? No, the reason there is no obscenity, or blatant sexuality either, in *When She Was Good* is that it would have been disastrously beside the point.

When She Was Good is, above all, a story about small-town Middle Westerners who more than willingly experience themselves as conventional and upright people; and it is their conventional and upright style of speech that I chose as my means of narration—rather, a heightened, more flexible version of their language, but one that drew freely upon their habitual locutions. It was not, however, to satirize them, in the manner, say, of Ring Lardner's "Haircut," that I settled eventually on this modest style, but rather to communicate, by their way of saying things, their way of seeing things and judging them. As for obscenity, I was careful, even when I had Roy Bassart, the young ex-G.I. in the novel, *reflecting*—had him safely walled-up in his head—to show that the furthest he could go in violating a taboo was to think "f. this and f. that." Roy's inability to utter more than the initial of the famous four-letter word, even to himself, was the small point I was making.

Discussing the purposes of his art, Chekhov distinguishes between "the solution of the problem and a correct presentation of the problem"—and adds, "only the latter is obligatory for the artist." Using "f. this and f. that," instead of The Word Itself, was part of the attempt to make a correct presentation of the problem.

Are you suggesting, then, that in Portnoy's Complaint *a "correct presentation of the problem" requires a frank revelation of intimate sexual matters, as well as an extensive use of obscenity?*

Yes. Obscenity is not only a kind of language that is used in *Portnoy's Complaint*, it is very nearly the issue itself. The book isn't full of dirty words because "that's the way people talk"; that's one of the least persuasive reasons for using the obscene in fiction, and besides, few people actually talk the way Portnoy does in this book—this is a man speaking out of an overwhelming obsession: he is obscene because he wants to be saved. An odd, maybe mad way to go about seeking personal salvation; but, nonetheless, the investigation of this passion, and of the combat that it precipitates with his conscience, is what's at the center of the novel. Portnoy's pains arise out of his refusal to be bound any longer by taboos which, rightly or wrongly, *he* experiences as unmanning. The joke on Portnoy is that for him breaking the taboo turns out to be as unmanning in the end as honoring it.

So, I wasn't simply after verisimilitude here; I wanted to raise obscenity to the level of a subject. You may remember that, at the conclusion of the novel, the Israeli girl soldier says to him, with loathing, "Tell me, please, *why* must you use that word all the time?" I gave her this question to ask him—and to ask at the end of this novel—deliberately: Why he must is what the book is about.

Do you think there will be Jews who will be offended by this book?

I think there will even be Gentiles who will be offended by this book.

I was thinking of the charges that were made against you by certain rabbis after the appearance of Goodbye, Columbus. *They said you were "anti-Semitic" and "self-hating," did they not?*

In "Writing About Jews," an essay I published in *Commentary*, in December 1963, I replied at length to those charges. Some critics also said that my work furnished "fuel" for anti-Semitism. I'm sure these charges will be made again—though the fact is that I have always been far more pleased by my good fortune in being born a Jew than my critics may imagine. It's a complicated, interesting, morally demanding, singular experience, and I like that. I find myself in the historic predicament of being Jewish, with all its implications. Who could ask for more? But as for those charges you mention

—yes, they probably will be leveled again. Because of the U.N. condemnation of Israeli "aggression," and anti-Semitic rage flaring up in the black community, many American Jews must be feeling more alienated than they have in a long time; I don't think it's a moment when I can expect a book as unrestrained as this one to be indulged or even tolerated, especially in those quarters where I was not hailed as the Messiah to begin with. The temptation from the pulpit to pluck single lines to quote out of the fictional context will be just about overwhelming on upcoming Saturday mornings. The rabbis have got their indignation to stoke, just as I do. And there are sentences in that book upon which a man could construct a pretty indignant sermon.

I have heard some people suggest that your book was influenced by the nightclub act of Lenny Bruce. Would you consider Bruce, or other stand-up comics such as Shelley Berman or Mort Sahl, or even The Second City comics, an influence upon the comic methods you employ in Portnoy's Complaint?

Not really. I was more strongly influenced by a sit-down comic named Franz Kafka and a very funny bit he does called "The Metamorphosis." The only time Lenny Bruce and I ever met and talked was in his lawyer's office, where it occurred to me that he was just about ripe for the role of Joseph K. He looked gaunt and driven, still determined but also on the wane, and he wasn't interested in being funny—all he could talk about and think about was his "case." I never saw Bruce perform, though I've heard tapes and records, and since his death I've watched a movie of one of his performances and read a collection of his routines. I recognize in him what I used to enjoy about The Second City company at its best, that joining of precise social observation with extravagant and dreamlike fantasy.

What about the influence of Kafka that you mention?

Well, of course, I don't mean I modeled my book after any work of his, or tried to write a Kafka-*like* novel. At the time I was beginning to play with the ideas for what turned out to be

Portnoy's Complaint, I was teaching a lot of Kafka in a course I gave at the University of Pennsylvania. When I look back now on the reading I assigned, I realize that the course might have been called "Studies in Guilt and Persecution"—"The Metamorphosis," *The Castle*, "In the Penal Colony," *Crime and Punishment*, "Notes from Underground," *Death in Venice*, *Anna Karenina* . . . My own previous two novels, *Letting Go* and *When She Was Good*, were about as gloomy as the gloomiest of these blockbusters, and fascinated as I still was by these dark books, I was looking for a way to get in touch with another side of my talent. Particularly after several years spent on *When She Was Good*, with its unfiery prose, its haunted heroine, its unrelenting concern with banality, I was aching to write something freewheeling and funny. It had been a long time between laughs. My students may have thought I was simply being entertaining when I began to describe the movie that could be made of *The Castle*, with Groucho Marx as K. and Chico and Harpo as the two "assistants." But I meant it. I thought of writing a story about Kafka writing a story. I had read somewhere that he used to giggle to himself while he worked. Of course! It was all so *funny*, this morbid preoccupation with punishment and guilt. Hideous, but funny.

Now—the road from these random ideas to *Portnoy's Complaint* was more winding and eventful than I can describe here; there is certainly a personal element in the book, but not until I had got hold of guilt as a comic idea did I begin to feel myself lifting free and clear of my last book and my old concerns.

In Response to Those Who Have Asked Me: How Did You Come to Write That Book, Anyway?

Portnoy's Complaint took shape out of the wreckage of four abandoned projects on which I had spent considerable effort—wasted, it seemed then—in the years 1962–7. Only now do I see how each was a building block for what was to come, and how each was abandoned in turn because it emphasized to the exclusion of all else what eventually would become an element of *Portnoy's Complaint* but was less than the whole story.

The first project, begun a few months after the publication of *Letting Go*, was a dreamy, humorous manuscript of about two hundred pages titled *The Jewboy*, which treated growing up in Newark as a species of folklore. This draft tended to cover with a patina of wacky inventiveness material quite interesting in itself and, as in certain types of dreams and folktales, intimated much more than I knew how to confront head-on in a fiction. Yet there were things that I liked and, when I abandoned the book, hated to lose: the graphic starkness with which the characters were presented and which accorded with my sense of what the impressions of childhood had felt like; the jokey comedy and dialogues that had the air of vaudeville turns; and a few scenes I was particularly fond of, like the grand finale where the Dickensian orphan-hero (first found in a shoebox by an aged *mohel* and circumcised, hair-raisingly, on the spot) runs away from his loving stepparents at age twelve and on ice skates sets off across a Newark lake after a blond little shiksa in a skating costume whose name, he thinks, is Thereal McCoy. "Don't!" his taxi-driver father calls after him (taxi driver because fathers I knew of invariably had cried out from behind the wheel at one exasperated moment or another, "That's all I am to this family—a taxi driver!"). "Oh, watch it, sonny"— calls the father—"you're skating on thin ice!" Whereupon the adventurous son in hot pursuit of the desirable exotic calls

Written in 1974.

back, "Oh, you dope, Daddy, that's only an expression," even as the ice begins to groan and give beneath his eighty-odd pounds.

The second abandoned project was a play entitled *The Nice Jewish Boy*. Still more about a Jewish family, their son, and his intrigue with the shiksa—in its way a less comforting, more aggressive *Abie's Irish Rose*. A draft of the play was read as a workshop exercise at the American Place Theatre in 1964, with Dustin Hoffman, then an off-Broadway actor, in the title role. The trouble was that the dramatic conventions I had adopted rather unthinkingly didn't provide the room I needed to get to the character's secret life. My unfamiliarity and timidity with the form, and the collaborative effort itself, wholly conventionalized my sense of things, and so rather than proceeding to a production, I decided after the reading to cut my losses. Again sadly. The comic surface of the play seemed to me accurate and funny; yet the whole enterprise lacked the inventive exuberance that had given *The Jewboy* whatever quality it had.

So: the struggle that was to be at the source of Alexander Portnoy's difficulties, and motivate his complaint, was in those early years of work still so out of focus that all I could do was recapitulate his problem *technically*, telling first the dreamy and fantastic side of the story, then the story in more conventional terms and by relatively measured means. Not until I found, in the person of a troubled analysand confiding to his psychoanalyst, the voice that could speak in behalf of both the "Jewboy" (with all that word signifies about aggression, appetite, and marginality) and the "nice Jewish boy" (and what that epithet implies about repression, respectability, and social acceptance) was I able to complete a fiction that was expressive, instead of symptomatic, of the character's dilemma.

While making abortive forays into what was going to emerge years later as *Portnoy's Complaint*, I was intermittently writing equally shadowy drafts of a novel that was variously titled—as theme and emphasis shifted—*Time Away*, *In the Middle of America*, and *Saint Lucy*, and that was published in 1967 as *When She Was Good*. This continuous movement back and forth from one partially realized project to another is fairly typical of how my work evolves and the way I deal with workaday frustration, and serves as a means of both checking and indulging "inspiration." The idea is to keep alive fictions that draw their energy from different sources, so that when circumstances combine to rouse one or another of the sleeping beasts, there is a carcass around for it to feed on.

After the manuscript of *When She Was Good* was completed midway through 1966, I almost immediately began to write a longish monologue, beside which the fetid indiscretions of *Portnoy's Complaint* would appear to be the work of Louisa May Alcott. I did not have any idea where I was going, and playing (in the mud) more accurately describes my activity than does writing, or "experimenting," that much-used catch-all with its flattering implication of courageous pioneering and disinterested self-abandonment.

This monologue was delivered by one of those lecturers who used to go around to schools, churches, and social groups showing slides of natural wonders. My slide show, delivered in the dark and with a pointer, and accompanied by running commentary (including humorous anecdotes), consisted of full-color enlargements of the private parts, fore and aft, of the famous. Actors and actresses, of course, but primarily—since the purpose was educational—distinguished authors, statesmen, scientists, etc. It was mean, bizarre, scatological, tasteless, and, largely out of self-disgust, remained unfinished . . . except that buried somewhere in the sixty or seventy pages were several thousand words on the subject of adolescent masturbation, a personal interlude by the lecturer, that seemed to me on re-reading to be worth saving, if only because it was the only sustained piece of writing on the subject that I could remember reading.

Not that at the time I could have deliberately set out to write about masturbating and come up with anything so pointedly intimate. Rather, it would seem to have required all that reckless roughhousing for me just to approach the subject. Knowing that what I was writing about President Johnson's testicles, Jean Genet's anus, Mickey Mantle's penis, Margaret Mead's breasts, and Elizabeth Taylor's pubic bush was simply unpublishable—nasty hijinks that might just as well never see the light of day—was precisely what allowed me to drop my guard and go on at some length about the solitary activity that is so difficult to talk about aloud and yet so near at hand. For me writing about the act had, at the outset at least, to be as secretive as the act itself.

More or less in tandem with this untitled exercise in voyeurism—which purported to enlarge and examine upon an illuminated screen the sexual parts of others—I began to write an autobiographical piece of fiction based upon my own upbringing in New Jersey. Simply as a genre title, it was called in its first rough draft of several hundred pages *Portrait of the Artist*. By sticking closely to the facts, and narrowing the gap between the actual and the invented, I thought I could come up with a story that would go to the heart of the particular ethos I'd come out of. But the more I stuck to the actual and the strictly verifiable, the less resonant the narrative became. Once again (as I now see it) I was oscillating between the extremes of hyperbolic fable or fantasy and realistic documentation, and thereby holding at bay what was still trying to come alive as my subject, if only I would let it. I had already described it, unknowingly, in the antipodal titles of the two projects previously abandoned: the argument between the Cain and Abel of my own respectable middle-class background, the Jewboy and the nice Jewish boy.

Somewhere along the way in *Portrait of the Artist*, in order to broaden the scope and relieve the monotony, I invented some relatives to live upstairs from the family, modeled upon my own, who were to have been at the center of the book. These upstairs relatives of "ours" I called the Portnoys. In the beginning the Portnoys were modeled loosely upon two or three families in whose apartments I used to play and snack and sometimes sleep overnight when I was a boy. In fact, an old boyhood friend of mine, who was interviewed by his local newspaper at the time of my book's publication, was quoted as saying that my family certainly did not seem to *him* to resemble the Portnoys; "but," he added, "I suppose Phil didn't see it that way." That there was a family which in certain important aspects Phil did see that way, and, I suspect, which this old boyhood friend of mine sometimes saw that way as well, he did not, for reasons of filial discretion, let on to the reporter.

Though actually the family the Portnoys looked most like to me, as I began to allow them to overtake the novel, was a family I had described in passing in an essay published in *American Judaism* some five years earlier. The essay had grown out of a talk I had given at a B'nai B'rith Anti-Defamation League symposium in Chicago in 1961, in which I had attacked what I took to be the unreality and silliness of images of Jews being popularized around that time in books by Harry Golden and Leon Uris. The family was not called the Portnoys then, nor were they as yet the product of my own imagination. Rather, I had come upon them, in various disguises and incarnations, in my reading. Here (abridged somewhat) is what I said at the A.D.L. symposium in 1961:

> . . . There are several Jewish graduate students in a class I teach at the Writing Workshop of the State University of Iowa, and during this last semester three of them wrote stories about a Jewish childhood . . . Curiously, or perhaps not so curiously, in each story the hero is a Jewish boy, somewhere between ten and fifteen, who gets excellent grades in school and is always combed and courteous . . . [This] Jewish boy . . . is watched—he is watched at bedtime, at study time, and especially at mealtime. Who he is watched by is his mother. The father we rarely see, and between him and the boy there seems to be little more than a nodding acquaintance. The old man is either working or sleeping or across the table, silently stowing it away. Still there is a great deal of warmth in these families—especially when compared to the Gentile . . . family [in the story]—and almost all of it is generated by the mother . . . [But] the fire that warms can also burn and asphyxiate: what the hero envies the Gentile boy is his parents' *indifference*, and largely, it would seem, because of the opportunities it affords him for sexual adventure . . . I hasten to point out that in these short stories the girls to whom the Gentile friend leads the young narrator are never Jewish. The Jewish women are mothers and sisters. The sexual yearning is for the Other . . .

Here then was the folktale—transmitted to me by my students—that began to enlarge my sense of who these Portnoys might become. Now it even made a nice kind of sense that in the draft of *Portrait of the Artist* I had imagined them to be "relatives" living "upstairs": here were the fallible, oversized, anthropomorphic gods who had reigned over the households of my neighborhood, that legendary Jewish family dwelling on high, whose squabbles over French-fried potatoes, synagogue attendance, and shiksas were of Olympian magnitude and splendor, and by whose terrifying kitchen lightning storms were illuminated the dreams, fears, and aspirations by which we mortal Jews lived somewhat less vividly down below.

This time, rather than choosing as I had in *The Jewboy* to treat this folklore *as* folklore—emphasizing the fantastic, the quaint, the magical—I took off in the opposite direction. Under the sway of the autobiographical impulse that had launched *Portrait of the Artist*, I began to ground the mythological in the locally recognizable. Though they might *derive* from Mt. Olympus (by way of Mt. Sinai), these Portnoys were going to live in a Newark and at a time and in a way whose realistic authenticity I could vouch for.

(With this sleight-of-hand, I seemed to have succeeded all too well. Among the several hundred letters I received after the book's publication, there was one from a woman in East Orange, New Jersey, who claimed to have known my sister when she and my correspondent's daughter were classmates together at Weequahic High in Newark, where the Portnoy children went to school. She remembered what a sweet, lovely, polite girl my sister was, and was shocked that I should be so thoughtless as to write about her intimate life, especially to make jokes about her unfortunate tendency to gain weight. Since, unlike Alexander Portnoy, I happen never to have had a sister, I assumed it was someone else's sister with a tendency to gain weight to whom my correspondent was mistakenly alluding.)

However, it was to be a while yet before I began to feel so constrained by the conventions I had imposed upon myself in *Portrait of the Artist* that I next abandoned that manuscript in its turn—and thus finally released the Portnoys from their role as supporting actors in another family's drama. The family Portnoy would not enjoy genuine star billing until sometime later, when out of the odds and ends of *Portrait of the Artist* I liked best, I began to write "A Jewish Patient Begins His Analysis," a brief story narrated by the Portnoys' son, Alexander, purportedly his introductory remarks to his psychoanalyst. And who was this Alexander Portnoy? None other than that Jewish boy who used to turn up time after time in the stories written by my Jewish graduate students back in the Iowa Writers' Workshop: the watched-over Jewish son with his sexual dream of The Other. The true writing of *Portnoy's Complaint* began with discovering Portnoy's mouth—and, along with it, the listening ear of the silent Dr. Spielvogel. The psychoanalytic monologue—a narrative technique whose unbuttoned rhetorical possibilities I'd been availing myself of for several years, only not on paper—was to furnish the means by which I might convincingly draw together the phantasmagoria of *The Jewboy* and the realistic documentation of *Portrait of the Artist* and *The Nice Jewish Boy*. And a means, too, of legitimizing the obscene preoccupations of the untitled slide show on the blasphemous subject of sexual parts. Instead of the projection screen (and the gaping), the Freudian couch (and the unveiling); instead of gleeful, sadistic voyeurism—brash, shameful, euphoric, conscience-ridden confession. Now I could perhaps to begin.

Imagining Jews

I. PORTNOY'S FAME—AND MINE

ALAS, IT wasn't exactly what I'd had in mind. Particularly as I was one of those students of the fifties who came to books by way of a rather priestly literary education in which writing poems and novels was assumed to eclipse all else in what we called "moral seriousness." As it happened, our use of that word "moral"—in private conversation about our daily affairs as easily as in papers and classroom discussions—tended often to camouflage and dignify vast reaches of naïveté, and served frequently only to restore at a more prestigious cultural level the same respectability that one had imagined oneself in flight from in (of all places) the English department.

The emphasis upon literary activity as a form of ethical conduct, as *the* way to the good life, certainly suited the times: the postwar onslaught of a mass electronically amplified philistine culture did look to some young literary people like myself to be the work of the Devil's legions, and High Art in turn the only refuge of the godly, a 1950's version of the pietistic colony established three centuries earlier in Massachusetts Bay. Also, the idea that literature was the domain of the virtuous would seem to have suited my character, which, though not exactly puritanical at heart, seemed that way in some key reflexes. So, inasmuch as I thought about Fame when I was starting out as a writer in my early twenties, I only naturally assumed that if and when it ever came my way, it would arrive as it had for Mann's Aschenbach, as Honor. *Death in Venice*, page 10: "But he had attained to honour, and honour, he used to say, is the natural goal towards which every considerable talent presses with whip and spur. Yes, one might put it that his whole career had been one conscious and overweening ascent to honour, which left in the rear all the misgivings or self-derogation which might have hampered him."

Written in 1974.

In the case of Aschenbach it was not his lustful fantasies (replete with mythological illusions but masturbatory at bottom) for which he is to be remembered by the "shocked and respectful world [that] received the news of his decease," but for powerful narratives like "*The Abject*, which taught a whole grateful generation that a man can still be capable of moral resolution even after he has plumbed the depths of knowledge. . . ." Now *that* is something like the reputation I'd had in mind for myself. But, as it was to turn out, the narrative of mine that elicited a strong response from a part of a generation, at least, "taught" less about the capacity for moral resolve than about moral remission and its confusions —and about those masturbatory fantasies that generally don't come decked out in adolescence (and in Newark) in classical decor.

Instead of taking an honorific place in the public imagination à la Gustave von Aschenbach, with the publication of *Portnoy's Complaint*, in February 1969, I found myself famous for being everything that Aschenbach had suppressed and kept a shameful secret right down to his morally resolute end. Jacqueline Susann, discussing her colleagues one night with Johnny Carson, tickled ten million Americans by saying that she'd like to meet me but didn't want to shake my hand. Didn't want to shake my hand—she, of all people? And from time to time the columnist Leonard Lyons had a ten-word tidbit about my fiery romance with Barbra Streisand: "Barbra Streisand has no complaints about her dates with Philip Roth." Dot dot dot. True enough, since, as it happened, the famous Jewish girl celebrity and the newly minted Jewish boy celebrity had and still have never met.

There was to be a considerable amount of this media myth-making, sometimes benign and silly enough, and sometimes, for me at least, unsettling. In order to be out of the direct line of fire I had decided to leave my New York apartment just after publication day, and so while "Philip Roth" began boldly to put in public appearances where I myself had not yet dared to tread, or twist, I took up residence for four months at the Yaddo retreat for writers, composers, and artists in Saratoga Springs.

Mostly, news about my *Doppelgänger*'s activities, of which the foregoing is but a tiny sample, came to me through the mail: anecdotes in letters from friends, clippings from the columnists, communications (and gentle, amused admonitions) from my lawyer on inquiries from me about libel and defamation of character. One evening in the second month of my Yaddo stay, I received a phone call from an editor (and friend) in a New York publishing house. He apologized for intruding on me, but at work that afternoon he had heard that I had suffered a breakdown and been committed to a mental hospital; he was phoning just to be sure it wasn't so. In only a matter of weeks news of the breakdown and commitment had spread westward, across the Continental Divide, out to California, where they do things in a big way. There, preparatory to a discussion of *Portnoy's Complaint* at a temple book program, announcement of Philip Roth's misfortune was made to the audience from the platform; having thus placed the author in a revealing light, they apparently went on to an objective discussion of the book.

In May, finally, at about the time I was considering returning to New York, I telephoned down to Bloomingdale's one day to try to correct an error that had turned up in my charge account for several months in succession. At the other end, the woman in the charge department gasped and said, "Philip Roth? *The* Philip Roth?" Tentatively: "Yes." "But *you're* supposed to be in an insane asylum!" "Oh, am I?" I replied lightheartedly, trying, as they say, to roll with the punch, but knowing full well that the charge department at Bloomingdale's wouldn't talk that way to Gustave von Aschenbach if he called to report an error in *his* charge account. Tadzio-lover though he was, it would still be, "Yes, Herr von Aschenbach; we're terribly sorry for any inconvenience, Herr von Aschenbach —do forgive us, Maestro, please."

Which was, as I have said, more like what I'd had in mind upon starting out on my own overweening ascent to honor.

Why was *Portnoy's Complaint* at once such a hit and such a scandal? To begin, a novel in the guise of a confession was received and judged by any number of readers as a confession in the guise of a novel. That sort of reading, wherein a work is dwarfed in significance by the personal circumstance which is imagined to have generated it, is nothing new; however, just such an interest in fiction was intensified in the late sixties by a passion for spontaneity and candor that colored even the drabbest lives and expressed itself in the pop rhetoric with phrases like "Tell it like it is," "Let it all hang out," etc. There were, of course, good solid reasons for this yearning for raw truth during the last years of the Vietnam War, but nonetheless its roots in individual consciousness were sometimes shallow, and had to do with little more than conforming to the cliché of the moment.

An example from the world of "bookchat" (as Gore Vidal has nicely named it): in what he charitably called his "thoughts" for the "end of the year," the *New York Times* lead book reviewer Christopher Lehmann-Haupt, who twice in 1969 had gone on record as an admirer of *Portnoy's Complaint*, announced himself to be a no-holds-barred kind of reviewer with this bold and challenging endorsement of first-person narration and the confessional approach: "I want the novelist," wrote Lehmann-Haupt, "to bare his soul, to stop playing games, to cease sublimating." Bold, challenging, and inevitably to be contradicted when the *Times* reviewer caught hold of the pendulum of received opinion as it swung the other way in the ensuing years, toward disguise, artifice, fantasy, montage, and complicated irony. By 1974, Lehmann-Haupt could disapprove of Grace Paley's personal-*seeming* (in fact, highly stylized) short stories in *Enormous Changes at the Last Minute* for precisely the reasons he had given to praise such a book five years earlier—and without the slightest understanding that for a writer like Grace Paley (or Mark Twain or Henry Miller), as for an actor like Marlon Brando, creating the illusion of intimacy and spontaneity is not just a matter of letting your hair down and being yourself but of inventing a whole new idea of what "being yourself" sounds like and looks like.

"You can see Mrs. Paley getting closer and closer to autobiography," Lehmann-Haupt writes about *Enormous Changes*, "leaning increasingly on a fictional self she calls Faith, and revealing more and more the sources of her imagination. In short, it now seems as if she no longer had the strength or the will to transmute life into art. . . . What has gone wrong, then? What has sapped the author of her will to turn experience into fiction—if that in fact is the trouble?" The trouble? Wrong? Well, mindlessness marches on. Still, by keeping track of the "thoughts" of a Lehmann-Haupt, one can over the years see which hand-me-down, uncomprehended literary dogma is at work, in a given cultural moment, making fiction "important" to insensate readers like himself.

In the case of my own "confession," it did not diminish the voyeuristic kick to remember that the novelist who was assumed to be baring his soul and ceasing to sublimate had formerly drawn a rather long, serious, even solemn, face in his first two novels. Nor did it hurt that the subject which this supposed confession focused on at some length was known to one and all and publicly disowned by just as many: masturbation. That this shameful, solitary addiction was described in graphic detail, and with gusto, must have done much to attract to the book an audience that previously had shown little interest in my writing. Till *Portnoy's Complaint*, no novel of mine had sold more than twenty-five thousand hardcover copies, and the hardcover edition of my first book of stories had sold just twelve thousand copies (and hadn't yet gained nationwide attention by way of the Ali McGraw movie, which was released after the publication of *Portnoy's Complaint*). For *Portnoy's Complaint*, however, 420,000 people—or seven times as many as had purchased my three previous books combined—stepped up to the bookstore cash register with $6.95, plus tax, in hand, and half of them within the first ten weeks the book was on sale.

It would seem then that masturbation was a dirtier little secret than even Alexander Portnoy had imagined. Indeed, the same highly charged preoccupation that prompted so many people who never buy a book to buy one that encouraged them to laugh at a "cunt crazy" masturbator of the respectable classes also revealed itself in the coast-to-coast rumor disclosing that for his excesses the author himself had had to be carted off to that lunatic asylum to which folklorists have been consigning unregenerate onanists since self-abuse began.

To be sure, the farcical treatment of masturbation does not explain entirely the avidity with which this particular bestseller was purchased and apparently even read. The moment when it was published—perhaps unlike any since the early days of

World War II for sustained social disorientation—had much to do, I think, with their avidity and my own subsequent notoriety. Without the disasters and upheavals of 1968, coming as they did at the end of a decade that had been marked by blasphemous defiance of authority and loss of faith in the public order, I doubt that a book like mine would have achieved such attention in 1969. Even three or four years earlier, a realistic novel that treated family authority with comical impiety and depicted sex as the farcical side of a seemingly respectable citizen's life would probably have been a good deal less acceptable —and comprehensible—to the middle-class Americans who bought the book, and would have been treated much more marginally (and hostilely) by the media that publicized it. But by the final year of the sixties, the national education in the irrational and the extreme had been so brilliantly conducted by our Dr. Johnson, with help from both enemies and friends, that, for all its tasteless revelations about everyday sexual obsession and the unromantic side of the family romance, even something like *Portnoy's Complaint* was now within the range of the tolerable. Finding that they *could* tolerate it may even have been a source of the book's appeal to a number of its readers.

However: the unseemly in *Portnoy's Complaint* would still not have been quite so alluring (and, to many, so offensive) if it weren't for the other key element which worked to make the untoward hero a more interesting case than he might otherwise have been at that moment for those Americans whose own psychic armor had been battered by the sixties: the man confessing to forbidden sexual acts and gross offenses against the family order and ordinary decency was a Jew. That was true whether you read the novel as a novel or as a thinly veiled autobiography.

What gave those acts and offenses the special meaning they had for Portnoy, what made them so rich for him with danger and shame, and so comically inappropriate even in his estimation, is very like what I now believe made Portnoy himself as intriguing as apparently he was to the book's large audience of Jews and Gentiles alike. In brief: going wild in public is the last thing in the world that a good Jew is expected to do— by himself, his family, his fellow Jews, and by the larger

community of Christians whose tolerance for him may be ten-
uous to begin with, and whose code of respectability he flaunts
at his own psychological risk, and perhaps at the risk of his
fellow Jews' well-being. Or so history and ingrained fear argue.
He is not expected to make a spectacle of himself, either by
shooting off his mouth or by shooting off his semen, and certainly not by shooting off his mouth about shooting off his
semen.

"As the paradigmatic outsiders of Western society, Jews
have, of course, been masters of social adaptation," writes David
Singer, in an essay on the subject of "The Jewish Gangster"
published in the winter 1974 issue of *Judaism*. It is no wonder
then, says Singer, that "the American Jewish establishment
—the defense agencies, the scholars, the historical societies"
along with "American Jews [generally] have systematically
denied any awareness of [this] important aspect of their history," whose major figures, according to Singer, constitute
". . . a veritable *Who's Who* in the annals of American crime,
comparable to that contributed by any other ethnic group."

Of course an Arnold Rothstein, a Lepke Buchalter, a Bugsy
Siegel, a Meyer Lansky (to name the supervillains on Singer's
list) Portnoy is not. Yet *his* sense of himself as a Jewish criminal
is a recurrent motif in his comic seizures of self-excoriation;
witness the book's last pages where, in concluding his manic
aria, he imagines the cops out of a grade-B movie closing in on
him, a grade-B racketeer named Mad Dog. It needs no Jewish
"defense agencies" other than his own to impugn Portnoy for
his conduct, and to make it seem to him that a preoccupation
with the flesh is as compromising to the safety and interests of
a Jew in America as was Arnold Rothstein's fixing—of all the
stupid things for a Jewish boy to go and fix—a whole World
Series.

That not even a Jew—believed to be society's most outstanding proponent of negotiation, whose most valued possession, envied even by his enemies, is his Kissingerian *sechel*—that
not even a Jew could put up a successful fight any longer
against non-negotiable demands of crude antisocial appetite
and aggressive fantasy . . . this may well have been precisely
what engaged the attention of any number of middle-class

readers whose own mastery of social adaptation had been seri-ously disturbed by the more unsettling experiences of the de-cade. Surely to many it must have come as a revelation of sorts to hear a Jew, of all people, and one whose public life as a civil rights attorney had entirely to do with enforcing social justice and legal controls, admit in italics and caps that, rather than shoring up his defenses and getting on with the business of being better (in all senses of the word), his secret desire was really to give way and be bad—or at the least, worse. That in particular was something they may not have heard or read much about recently in American novels written by Jews about Jews.

2. HEROES JEWISH WRITERS IMAGINE

To see just how strongly the Jew in the post-Holocaust decades has been identified in American fiction with righteousness and restraint, with the just and measured response rather than with those libidinous and aggressive activities that border on the socially acceptable and may even constitute criminal transgres-sion, it might be well to begin with the novels of Saul Bellow, by now the grand old man of American-Jewish writers, and to my mind the country's most accomplished working novelist. And reading Bellow, what does one find? That almost invari-ably his heroes are Jewish in vivid and emphatic ways when they are actors in dramas of conscience, but are by comparison only faintly marked by their Jewishness, if they are Jews at all, when appetite and libidinous adventure is at the heart of a novel.

Bellow's first Jewish (as distinguished from non-Jewish) Jew was Asa Leventhal in his second book, *The Victim*. Bellow himself now judges this excellent novel a "proper" book, by which I take him to mean, among other things, that it did not bear his particular stamp so much as convention's. To be Jew-ish in this novel is to be accessible, morbidly so, to claims made upon the conscience, to take upon oneself, out of a kind of gruff human sympathy and a responsiveness bordering danger-ously at times on paranoia, responsibility for another man's pain and misfortune. Being a Jew, to Asa Leventhal, is a burden at most, an irritation at least—and writing about such a Jew would appear after the fact to have been something of both to Bellow too, as though the enclosure of a victimized Jewish conscience happened also to constrain his inventiveness, and to exclude from imaginative consideration much that was pleasurable and exciting, involving appetite and the exuberant, rather than the ethical, life.

There is Bellow's own word "proper" to argue for this, and there is the next book, *The Adventures of Augie March*, where surely the least important ingredient in the lively and seductive hero's make-up is his sense of himself as a Jew. You could, in fact, take the Jew out of the adventurous Augie March without doing much harm to the whole of the book, whereas the same could not be said for taking Chicago out of the boy. (Whereas the same couldn't be said for taking the Jew out of the Levantine-looking Leventhal.) One can only speculate about how much writing *The Victim* may have served to settle the author's own conscience about touchy matters of survival and success (the bedeviling issue for Leventhal, right along with the issue of Jewish self-defense) and to open the way for the loquacious delight in his own winning attractiveness that is Augie's charm. But what couldn't be clearer is that, while Bellow seems largely to locate in Leventhal's Jewishness the roots of his morbidity, gloom, uncertainty, touchiness, and moral responsiveness, he connects Augie's health, cheeriness, vigor, stamina, and appetite, as well as his enormous appeal to just about everyone in Cook County, if not in all creation, to his rootedness in a Chicago that is *American* to the core, a place where being Jewish makes of a boy nothing more special in the Virtue Department than any other immigrant mother's child. Though it might be argued that it is the sensibility and verbal energy that in some essential way encompass the book's "Jewishness," this is an argument that would probably be given shortest shrift by Augie himself: "Look at me," he cries triumphantly at the book's conclusion, "going everywhere!" Essentially the sensibility and the energy are those of an exuberant and greedy eclectic, a "Columbus of those near-at-hand," as he describes himself, perpetually outward-bound.

The movement away from the obsessively Jewish Jew Leventhal to the relatively non-Jewish Jew Augie, away from claustrophobic bondage to the Chosen People toward heady, delight-filled choosing, culminates in Bellow's next big novel, *Henderson the Rain King*, whose hoggish and greedy hero, hearty in an altogether different sense from Leventhal, is so much a creature possessed by strange ravenous hungers of the senses and the spirit that Bellow cannot see his way to making him even the most attenuated of Jews. To hang from his Jewishness by no more than a thread—that will do very nicely for *Seize the Day*'s Tommy (*né* Adler) Wilhelm, who wants more than anything his daddy. But it will not do at all for a hero who wants, in the way he wants it, what this titanic clown Henderson is seeking.

Which is? To do good, to be just? No, that would be more like Leventhal's ambition, and one that seems to have less to do with "heart" than with a deal he has made to square it with the vengeful gods. What then? To be adopted, abducted, and adored? No, that is more in brainy, handsome, egotistic Augie's line (Augie, who is, when you stop to think about it, everything that Tommy Wilhelm had in mind but hadn't the Chicago in him to pull off; his is the story of ego quashed). What then is Henderson after? "I want!" Exclamation point. "I want!" And that is it—raw, untrammeled, uncompromising, insatiable, unsocialized desire.

"I want." In a Bellow novel only a goy can talk like that and get away with it. As indeed Henderson does, for by the conclusion of the book he is said actually to have been regenerated by this quest he has been on for intensity and orgasmic release. Is there anyone happier in all of Bellow's books? No punishment or victimization for this unchosen person. To the contrary, what makes *Henderson the Rain King* a full-scale comedy is that what the clown seeks he gets. What he had not enough of, if he had any, he now gets more of than he knows what to do with. He is the king of rain, of gush, of geyser.

If the goy gets more than enough to burst his spirit's sleep, Bellow's next two heroes, very Jewish Jews indeed, get far less than they *deserve*. Desire or appetite has nothing to do with it. What is denied here are *ethical* hopes and expectations. Others should act otherwise, they don't, and the Jewish hero suffers. With Moses Herzog and Artur Sammler, Bellow moves from satiated Henderson all the way back to the world of the victim—and, ineluctably, it would seem, back to the Jew, the man of acutely developed sensibilities and a great sense of personal dignity and inbred virtue, whose sanity in the one book, and whose sympathies in the other, are continuously tried by the libidinous greed of the willful, the crazed, and the criminal.

Henderson's hoggish "I want!" is in fact something like the rallying cry of those others who make Herzog moan, "I fail to understand," and cause Sammler, who has seen and survived nearly everything hideous, to admit at last in 1968 in New York City, "I am horrified." The pig-farmer goy as a noble Yahoo in black Africa—the ethically elegant Jew as a maimed and grieving Houyhnhnm on a darkening Upper West Side. Augie, the Chicago adventurer, returns as a bleeding, punished Herzog, the irresistible egoist who has been bitten by what he has chewed off—the Moses-trainer Madeleine having had better luck with her high-flying bird in the Berkshires than the eagle-trainer Thea in Mexico—and Leventhal, he of the bilious temper and the brooding conscience, is reincarnated as the moral magistrate Sammler, whose New York is no longer simply "as hot as Bangkok" on some nights, but has *become* a barbarous Bangkok, even on the Broadway bus and in the Columbia University lecture hall. "Most outdoor telephones were smashed, crippled. They were urinals, also. New York was getting worse than Naples or Salonika. It was like an Asian or an African town. . . ."

How remote, how diminished—how "proper" indeed—Leventhal's suffering seems beside Mr. Sammler's. And what a mild, mild nuisance is Allbee, the insinuating down-and-out goy who ruins Leventhal's summer solitude, who sullies his marriage bed and embarrassingly strokes his Jewish hair—how temperate he is compared to the lordly and ominous dude of a black pickpocket, whose uncircumcised member and "great oval testicles" are unveiled in all their iridescent grandeur for consideration by the superego's man in Manhattan. And yet, despite the difference in degree (and context and meaning) between the assault in the early book and in the later one, it is still the Jew who is aggressed *against*, the Jew who is on the receiving end when appetite and rage run wild: "the soul in its vehemence," as Sammler calls what horrifies him most, or, labels less delicately and more angrily, "sexual niggerhood." As opposed to what might be described as "ethical Jewhood."

Now, there are obviously other ways to go about reading Saul Bellow: the intention here is not to diminish his achievement by reducing his novels to just this pile of bare bones but rather to trace the characteristic connection made in his work (and, in Bernard Malamud's as well) between the Jew and conscience, and the Gentile and appetite—and thereby to point up how conditioned readers had become (one might say, how *persuaded*, given the authority of the writers in question) to associate the sympathetic Jewish hero with victimization as opposed to vengeful aggression, with dignified survival rather than euphoric or gloating triumph, with sanity and renunciation as opposed to excessive desire—except the excessive desire to be good and to do good.

To the degree that Saul Bellow has been a source of pride to what David Singer calls the "American Jewish establishment," I would suggest that it has had more to do with these bare bones I've laid out here than with the brimming novels themselves, which are too densely rendered and reflective to be vehicles of ethnic propaganda or comfort. The fact is that Bellow's ironic humanism coupled as it is with his wide-ranging sympathy for odd and dubious characters, for regular Chicago guys, for the self-mockery and self-love of the down-on-his-luck dauphin-type, has made him a figure of far more importance to other Jewish writers than he is to the Jewish cultural audience—unlike, say, Elie Wiesel or Isaac Bashevis Singer, who, as they relate to the Jewish past, have a somewhat awesome spiritual meaning for the community-at-large that is not necessarily of pressing literary interest to their fellow writers. But Bellow, by closing the gap, as it were, between Damon Runyon and Thomas Mann—or to use loosely Philip Rahv's categories, between redskin and paleface—has, I believe, inspired all sorts of explorations into immediate worlds of experience that American-born Jewish writers who have come after him might otherwise have overlooked or dumbly stared at for years without the ingenious example of *this* Columbus of those near-at-hand.

If Saul Bellow's longer works* tend generally to associate the
Jewish Jew with the struggles of ethical Jewhood and the
non-Jewish Jew and the Gentile with the release of appetite
and aggression (Gersbach, the Buber-booster and wife-stealer
in *Herzog*, is really no great exception, since he is a *spurious*
Jewish Jew who can't even pronounce his Yiddish right; and
Madeleine, that Magdalene, has of course worn a cross and
worked at Fordham), in the work of Bernard Malamud these
tendencies are so sharply, so schematically present as to give
Malamud's novels the lineaments of moral allegory. For Malamud, generally speaking, the Jew is innocent, passive, virtuous,
and this to the degree that he defines himself or is defined by
others as a Jew; the Gentile, on the other hand, is characteristically corrupt, violent, and lustful, particularly when he enters
a room or a store or a cell with a Jew in it.

   Now, on the face of it, it would seem that a writer could
not get very far with such evangelistic simplifications. And yet
that is not at all the case with Malamud (as it isn't with Jerzy

---

*I say "longer works" because the hard and ugly facts of life in a short story
like "The Old System," published first in *Playboy* in 1967, are of the sort that
have been known to set the phones ringing at the Anti-Defamation League.
Baldly put (which is how these things tend to be put when the lines are
drawn), it is a story of rich Jews and their money: first, how they make it big
in the world with under-the-table payoffs (a hundred thousand delivered to
an elegant old Wasp for lucrative countryclub acreage—and delivered by a
Jew Bellow depicts as an orthodox religious man); and then it is about how
Jews cheat and finagle one another out of the Almighty Dollar: a dying Jewish
woman, with a dirty mouth no less, demands twenty thousand in cash from
her businessman brother for the privilege of seeing her before she expires in
her hospital bed. This scene of sibling hatred and financial cunning in a Jewish
family is in fact the astonishing climax to which the story moves.
   One wonders about the reception the defense agencies would have given to
this story, especially appearing as it did in *Playboy* magazine, had it been the
work of some unknown Schwartz or Levy instead of the celebrated author of
Herzog. Indeed, in the aftermath of sixties' political radicalism and the trau-
matic shock upon Jews of the October 1973 war, one wonders what position
the Jewish press and cultural journals would take if a first novel like *Dangling
Man* were suddenly to be published, wherein the thoroughly deracinated and
depressive hero seems to dislike no one quite so much as his Jewish brother's
bourgeois family, or if out of the blue a book like *The Victim* were now to
appear, in which the hero's Jewishness is at times made to resemble a species
of psychopathology.

Kosinski in *The Painted Bird*), for so instinctively do the figures of a good Jew and a bad goy emerge from an imagination
essentially folkloric and didactic that his fiction is most convincing the more strictly he adheres to these simplifications,
and diminishes in conviction and narrative drive to the extent
that he surrenders them, or tries, however slyly, to undo their
hold on him.

His best book—containing as it does the classic Malamudian
moral arrangement—is still *The Assistant*, which proposes that
an entombed and impoverished grocer named Morris Bober
shall by the example of his passive suffering and his goodness
of heart transform a young thieving Italian drifter named
Frank Alpine into another entombed, impoverished, and suffering Jewish grocer, and that this shall constitute an act of *assistance*, and set Alpine on the road to redemption—or so the
stern morality of the book argues.

Redemption from what? Crimes of violence and deceit
against a good Jewish father, crimes of lust against the father's
virginal daughter, whom the goy has spied upon naked and
then raped. But oh how punitive is this redemption! We might
almost take what happens to the bad goy when he falls into the
hands of the good Jews as an act of enraged Old Testament
retribution visited upon him by the wrathful Jewish author—if
it weren't for the pathos and gentle religious coloration with
which Malamud invests the tale of conversion; and also the
emphasis that is clear to the author throughout—that it is the
good Jews who have fallen into the hands of the bad goy. It has
occurred to me that a less hopeful Jewish writer than Malamud
—Kosinski, say, whose novels don't put much stock in the capacity for redemption but concentrate on the persistence of
brutality and malice—might not have understood Alpine's
transformation into Jewish grocer and Jewish father (with all
that those roles entail in this book) as a sign of personal redemption but as the realization of Bober's revenge. "Now suffer,
you goy bastard, the way I did."

To see how still another sort of Jewish writer, Norman
Mailer, might have registered the implications of a story like
The Assistant, we can look to his famous essay "The White
Negro," published first in *Dissent* magazine in 1957, the very year
Malamud's novel appeared. Imagining all of this independently

of Malamud, Mailer nonetheless comes up with a scenario
startlingly similar to the one with which *The Assistant* begins. In
the Mailer version there are also two hoodlums who beat a defenseless shopkeeper over the head and take his money; however, quite characteristically for Mailer—and it is this that so
distinguishes his concerns from Malamud's or Bellow's—he ap-
praises the vicious act as it affects the physical well-being and
mental health of the violator rather than the violated.

"It can of course be suggested," writes Mailer parentheti-
cally, about "encourag[ing] the psychopath in oneself," "that
it takes little courage for two strong eighteen-year-old hoodlums, let us say, to beat in the brains of a candy-store keeper,
and indeed the act—even by the logic of the psychopath—is
not likely to prove very therapeutic, for the victim is not an
immediate equal. Still, courage of a sort is necessary, for one
murders not only a weak fifty-year-old man but an institution
as well, one violates private property, one enters into a new
relation with the police and introduces a dangerous element
into one's life. The hoodlum is therefore daring the unknown,
and so no matter how brutal the act, it is not altogether
cowardly."

These few lines on the positive value homicide has for the
aspiring psychopath should make it clear why Jewish cultural
audiences, which are generally pleased to hear Saul Bellow and
Bernard Malamud identified as Jewish writers, are perfectly
content that by and large Norman Mailer, with all his considerable influence and stature, should go forth onto the lecture
platform and the television talk shows as a writer, *period*. This
is obviously okay too with the author of *The Deer Park* and *An
American Dream*, to name just two of his books with heroes
he chooses not to call Cohen. It is pointless to wonder what
Jews (or Gentiles) would have made of those two books if the
author had had other than an O'Shaughnessy as the libidinous
voyager or a Rojack as the wife-murderer in his American Go-
morrah, for that an identifiably Jewish hero could perpetrate
such spectacular transgressions with so much gusto and so little
self-doubt or ethical disorientation turns out to be as incon-
ceivable to Norman Mailer as it is to Bernard Malamud. And
maybe for the same reason: it is just the Jew in one that says,

"No, no, *restrain* yourself" to such grandiose lusts and anti-social inclinations.

I cannot imagine Mailer having much patience with the conclusion of the violent hoodlum–defenseless shopkeeper scenario as Malamud realizes it in *The Assistant*. Some other lines from "The White Negro" might in fact stand as Mailer's description of just what is happening to Frank Alpine, who dons Morris Bober's apron, installs himself for eighteen hours a day behind his cash register, and from the tomb of a dying grocery store takes responsibility for the college education (rather than the orgasmic, no-holds-barred, time-of-her-timish education) of Morris's Jewish daughter: ". . . new kinds of victories," Mailer writes, "increase one's power for new kinds of perception; and defeats, the wrong kind of defeats, attack the body and imprison one's energy until one is jailed in the prison air of other people's habits, other people's defeats, boredom, quiet desperation, and muted icy self-destroying rage. . . ."

It is precisely with an attack upon the body—upon the very organ of offense with which Alpine had ravaged Bober's daughter—that Malamud concludes *The Assistant*. Whether Malamud sees it as something more like cruel and unusual punishment than poetic justice is another matter; given the novel's own signposts, it would appear that the reader is expected to take the last paragraph in the book as describing the conclusive act of Frank's redemption, the final solution to his Gentile problem.

> One day in April Frank went to the hospital and had himself circumcised. For a couple of days he dragged himself around with a pain between his legs. The pain enraged and inspired him. After Passover he became a Jew.

So penance for the criminal penis has been done. No cautionary folktale on the dangers of self-abuse could be any more vivid or pointed than this, nor could those connections that I have tried to trace in Bellow's novels be more glaringly apparent than they are here: Renunciation is Jewish and renunciation is All. By comparison to the tyrannical Yahweh who rules over *The Assistant*, the Bellow of *Mr. Sammler's Planet* seems like a doting parent who asks only for contraceptive common sense and no hard drugs. *The Assistant* is a manifestation of ethical Jewhood with what one might legitimately call a vengeance. Beneath the austerity and the pathos, Malamud has a fury all his own.

Malamud's *The Fixer*, page 69: "The fixer readily confessed he was a Jew. Otherwise he was innocent." Page 80: "I'm an innocent man. . . . I've had little in my life." Page 98: "I swear to you I am innocent of any serious crime. . . . It's not my nature." *What* isn't his nature? Ritual murder and sexual assault—vengeful aggression and brutal lust. So it is for the crimes of Frank Alpine and Ward Minogue, the hoodlum goyim who prey upon the innocent, helpless Jewish family of *The Assistant*, that Yakov Bok, the helpless, innocent Russian-Jewish handyman of *The Fixer*, is arrested and imprisoned, and in something far worse even than a dungeon of a grocery store. In fact, I know of no serious authors whose novels have chronicled physical brutality and fleshly mortification in such detail and at such length, and who likewise have taken a single defenseless innocent and constructed almost an entire book out of the relentless violations suffered by that character at the hands of perverse and savage captors, other than Malamud, the Marquis de Sade, and the pseudonymous author of *The Story of O. The Fixer*, the opening of Chapter V:

> The days were passing and the Russian officials were waiting impatiently for his menstrual period to begin. Grubeshov and the army general often consulted the calendar. If it didn't start soon they threatened to pump blood out of his penis with a machine they had for that purpose. The machine was a pump made of iron with a red indicator to show how much blood was being drained out. The danger of it was that it didn't always work right and sometimes sucked every drop of blood out of the body. It was used exclusively on Jews; only their penises fitted it.

The careful social and historical documentation of *The Fixer* —which Malamud's instinctive feel for folk material is generally able to transform from fiction researched into fiction imagined—envelops what is at its center a relentless work of violent pornography in which the pure and innocent Jew,

whose queasiness at the sight of blood is at the outset almost
maidenly, is ravished by the sadistic goyim, "men," a knowledgeable ghost informs him, as if any Jew needed informing,
"who [are] without morality."

To be sure, a few paragraphs from the end of the book, the
defenseless Jew who has been falsely accused of murdering a
twelve-year-old boy and drinking his blood, and has been unjustly brutalized for that crime for almost three hundred pages,
has his revenge offered him suddenly on a silver platter—*and
he takes it*. If it's murder they want, it's murder they'll get.
With his revolver he shoots the Czar! "Yakov pressed the trigger. Nicholas"—the italics are mine—"*in the act of crossing
himself*, overturned his chair, and fell, to his surprise, to the
floor, the stain spreading on his breast." And there is no remorse or guilt in Yakov, not after what he has been through at
the hands of Czar Nicholas's henchmen. "Better him than us,"
he thinks, dismissing with a commonplace idiom of four simple
words the crime of crimes: regicide, the murder of the Christian King.

Only it happens that all of this takes place in Yakov's imagination. It is a vengeful and heroic daydream that he is having
on the way to the trial at which it would seem he is surely
doomed. Which is as it must be in Malamud's world: for it is
not in Yakov's nature, any more than it is in Morris Bober's (or
Moses Herzog's), to press a real trigger and shed real blood.
Remember Herzog with his pistol? "It's not everyone who
gets the opportunity to kill with a clear conscience. They had,"
Herzog tells himself, "opened the way to justifiable murder."
But at the bathroom window, peering in at his treacherous,
wife-stealing enemy Gersbach bathing his precious daughter
Junie, Herzog cannot pull the trigger. "Firing this pistol,"
writes Bellow in *Herzog* (though it could as well be Malamud
at the conclusion of *The Fixer*), "was nothing but a thought."
Vengeance then must come in other forms for these victimized
Jewish men, if it comes at all. That vengeance *isn't* in his nature
is a large part of what makes him heroic to the author
himself.

In *Pictures of Fidelman* Malamud sets out to turn the tables
on himself, and, gamely, to take a holiday from his own pervasive mythology: he imagines as a hero a Jewish man living

without shame and even with a kind of virile, if shlemielish, forcefulness in a world of Italian gangsters, thieves, pimps, whores, and bohemians, a man who eventually finds love face-down with a Venetian glassblower who is the husband of his own mistress—and most of it has no more impact than the bullet that Yakov Bok fired in his imagination had on the real Czar of Russia. And largely, I think, because it has been conceived as a similar kind of compensatory daydream; in *Fidelman* a genuine sense of what conversions cost is dissolved in rhetorical flourishes rather than through the sort of extended struggle that Malamud's own deeply held sense of things calls forth in *The Assistant* and *The Fixer*. It's no accident that this of all the longer works generates no internal narrative tension (whereby it might test its own assumptions) and is without the continuous sequential progression that comes to this type of storyteller so naturally and acts in him as a necessary counterforce to runaway fantasy. This playful daydream of waywardness, criminality, transgression, and lust, simply could not have withstood the challenge of a fully developed narrative.

There are of course many winning pages along the way—there is a conversation between Fidelman and a talking light bulb in the section called "Pictures of the Artist" that is Malamud the folk comic at his best—but after the first section, "Last Mohican," the bulk of the book has an air of unchecked and unfocused indulgence, freewheeling about a libidinous and disordered life more or less to the extent that nothing much is at stake. What distinguishes "Last Mohican" from all that comes after is that *its* Fidelman, so meticulous about himself, so very cautious and constrained, is not at all the same fellow who turns up later cleaning out toilets in a whorehouse, shacking up with prostitutes, and dealing one-on-one with a pimp; the author may have convinced himself that it was the experience with Susskind he undergoes in "Last Mohican" that liberates Fidelman for what follows, but, if so, that comes under the category, as much does here, of magical thinking. Wherever the unconstraining processes, the hard-won struggles toward release, might appropriately be dramatized, there is a chapter break, and when the narrative resumes, the freedom is a *fait accompli*.

Of "Last Mohican"'s Fidelman it is written: "He was, at odd hours in certain streets, several times solicited by prostitutes, some heartbreakingly pretty, one a slender, unhappy-looking girl with bags under her eyes whom he desired mightily, but Fidelman feared for his health." *This* Fidelman desires unhappy-looking girls bearing the saddest signs of wear and tear. *This* Fidelman fears for his health. And that isn't all he fears for. But then this Fidelman is not just a Jew in name only. "To be un-masked as a hidden Jew," which is what frightens Yakov Bok in the early stages of *The Fixer*, could in fact serve to describe just what happens to "Last Mohican"'s Fidelman, with the assistance of his own imitable Bober, the wily shnorring refugee Susskind. "Last Mohican" is a tale of conscience tried and human sympa-thy unclotted, arising out of very different motives from the fiction that follows—and it abounds with references, humble, comic, and solemn, to Jewish history and life. But that is it, by and large, for the Jews: enter sex in Chapter 2, called "Still Life," and exit Susskind and Fidelman, the unmasked Jew. What is henceforth to be revealed in Fidelman—in this book which would, if it could, be a kind of counter-*Assistant*—is the hidden goy, a man whose appetites are associated elsewhere with the lust-ridden "uncircumcised dog" Alpine.

And if there should be any doubt as to how fierce and reflex-ive is the identification in Malamud's imagination between re-nunciation and Jew, and appetite and goy, one need only compare the pathetic air of self-surrender that marks the end-ing of "Last Mohican"—

> "Susskind, come back," he shouted, half sobbing. "The suit is yours. All is forgiven."
>
> He came to a dead halt but the refugee ran on. When last seen he was still running.

—to the comic and triumphant ending of "Still Life." The second chapter concludes with Fidelman's first successful pen-etration, which he is able, after much frustration, to accomplish upon a strong-minded Italian *pittrice* by inadvertently disguis-ing himself in a priest's vestments. There is both more and less to this scene than Malamud may have intended:

> She grabbed his knees. "Help me, Father, for Christ's sake."
> Fidelman, after a short tormented time, said in a quavering voice, "I forgive you, my child."
> "The penance," she wailed, "first the penance."
> After reflecting, he replied, "Say one hundred times each, Our Father and Hail Mary."
> "More," Annamaria wept. "More, more. Much more."
> Gripping his knees so hard they shook she burrowed her head into his black-buttoned lap. He felt the surprised beginnings of an erection.

But really it should not have come as such a surprise, this erection that arrives while dressed in priest's clothing. What would have been surprising is if Fidelman had disguised himself as a Susskind, say, and found that working like an aphrodisiac, maybe even on a Jewish girl like Helen Bober. Then would something have been at stake, then would something have been challenged. But as it is written, with Fidelman copulating in a priest's biretta rather than a skull-cap, the scene moves the novel nowhere, particularly as the final line seems to me to get entirely backward the implications of the joke that is being played here. "Pumping slowly," the chapter ends, "he nailed her to her cross." But isn't it rather the Jew who is being nailed, if not to his cross, to the age-old structure of his inhibitions?

The trouble with lines like the last one in that chapter is that they settle an issue with a crisp rhetorical flourish before it has even been allowed to have much of a narrative life. At the very moment that the writer appears to be most forceful and candid, he is in fact shying away and suppressing whatever is psychologically rich or morally daunting with a clever, essentially evasive, figure of speech. Here, for instance, is Fidelman's detumescence described earlier. Premature ejaculation has just finished him off, much to the *pittrice*'s dismay, and though he hasn't as yet stumbled unwittingly upon the clerical disguise that will make him fully potent and desirable, we note that the figure for erotic revitalization is, as usual, Christian; also noteworthy is that, generally speaking in *Fidelman*, where the sex act is, there shall whimsical metaphor be. "Although he mightily willed resurrection, his wilted flower bit the dust." And here is the hero discovering himself to be a homosexual.

"Fidelman had never in his life said 'I love you' without reservation to anyone. He said it to Beppo. If that's the way it works, that's the way it works." But that isn't the way it works at all. That is a dream of the way it works, and all of it neatly koshered with the superego and other Jewish defense agencies, with that most reassuring and comforting of all succoring words, "love."

"Think of love," says Beppo, as he leaps on naked Fidelman from behind. "You've run from it all your life." And, magically, one might say, just by *thinking* of it, Fidelman instantaneously loves, so that between the homosexual act of anal intercourse —an act which today's society still generally considers a disgusting transgression indeed—and its transformation into ideal behavior, there is not even time for the reader to say ouch. Or for Fidelman to think whatever perplexing thoughts might well accompany entry into the world of the taboo by the tight-assed fellow who at the outset, in the marvelous "Last Mohican" chapter, would barely give the refugee Susskind the time of day.

One wonders why the taboo must be idealized quite so fast. Why must Fidelman dress up as a priest merely to get himself laid right, and not only think of love but *fall* in love, the very first time he gets buggered? Why not think of lust, of base, unseemly desire? And surrender himself to *that*. People, after all, have been known to run from it too all their lives, just as fast and as far. And when last seen were still running. "In America," the book concludes, "he worked as a craftsman in glass and loved men and women."

Recall the last lines of *The Assistant*. Frank Alpine should have it so easy with *his* appetites. But whereas in *The Assistant* the lusting goy's passionate and aggressive act of *genuinely* loving desire for the Jewish girl takes the terrible form of rape, and requires penance (or retribution) of the harshest kind, in *Pictures of Fidelman*, the Jew's most wayward sexual act is, without anything faintly resembling Alpine's enormous personal struggle, converted on the spot into love. And if this is still insufficiently consoling about a Jew and sexual appetite, the book manages by the end to have severed the bisexual Fidelman as thoroughly from things Jewish as *The Assistant*, by its conclusion, has marked the sexually constrained, if not

desexed, Alpine as a Jew forevermore. Of all of Malamud's
Jewish heroes, is there any who is by comparison so strikingly
un-Jewish (after Chapter 1 is disposed of), who insists upon it
so little, and is so little reminded of it by the Gentile world?
And is there any who, at the conclusion, is happier?

In short, Fidelman is Malamud's Henderson, Italy his Africa,
and "love" the name that Malamud, for reasons that by now
should be apparent, gives in this book to getting finally what
you want the way you want it. Suggesting precisely the dis-
junction between act and self-knowledge that accounts for the
light-headed dreaminess of *Fidelman*, and that differentiates it
so sharply from those tough-minded, wholly convincing novels, *The Assistant* and *The Fixer*, where no beclouding ambiva-
lence stands between the author's imagination and the object
of his fury.

And now to return to *Portnoy's Complaint* and the hero imagined by this Jewish writer. Obviously the problem for Alexander Portnoy is that, unlike Arthur Fidelman, nothing *inflames*
his Jewish self-consciousness so much as setting forth on a
wayward libidinous adventure—that is, nothing makes it seem
quite so wayward than that a Jewish man like himself should
be wanting all he wants. The hidden Jew is unmasked in *him*
by the sight of his own erection. He cannot suppress the one
in the interest of the other, nor can he imagine them living
happily in peaceful coexistence. Like the rest of us, he too has
read Saul Bellow, Bernard Malamud, and Norman Mailer. His
condition might be compared to Frank Alpine's, if, after his
painful circumcision—with all that it means to him about
virtuous renunciation—Alpine had all at once found his old
disreputable self, the Maileresque hoodlum of the forbidden
desires, emerging from solitary confinement to engage his
freshly circumcised and circumscribed Jewish self in hand-to-
hand combat. In Portnoy the disapproving moralist who says
"I am horrified" will not disappear when the libidinous slob
shows up screaming "I want!" Nor will the coarse, antisocial
Alpine in him be permanently subdued by whatever of Morris
Bober, or of his own hard-working, well-intentioned Boberish
father, there may be in his nature. This imaginary Jew also

drags himself around with a pain between his legs, only it inspires him to acts of frenzied lust.

A lusting Jew. A Jew as sexual defiler. An odd type, as it
turns out, in recent Jewish fiction, where it is usually the goy
who does the defiling; also, it has been forcefully alleged, one
of the "crudest and most venerable stereotypes of anti-Semitic
lore." I am quoting from a letter written by Marie Syrkin—a
well-known American Zionist leader and daughter of one of
Socialist Zionism's outstanding organizers and polemicists in
the first quarter of the century—and published in *Commentary*
in March 1973. The letter constituted her improvement on two
separate attacks that had appeared several months earlier in
Commentary, one by Irving Howe directed at my work (most
specifically *Goodbye, Columbus* and *Portnoy's Complaint*), and
the other by the magazine's editor, Norman Podhoretz, directed
at what is assumed by him to be my cultural position and reputation. (*Commentary* associate editor Peter Shaw had already
attacked *Portnoy's Complaint* for "fanaticism in the hatred of
things Jewish" in the review he wrote when the novel first appeared and which, to be sure, turned up in *Commentary* too.)

The historical references Syrkin employs to identify what is
repugnant to her about *Portnoy's Complaint* suggest that to
some I had exceeded even the reductive "vulgarity" which
Howe said "deeply marred" my fiction here as elsewhere, and
had entered into the realm of the most wicked pathology.
Here is Syrkin's characterization of Portnoy's lustful, even
vengefully lustful, designs upon the Gentile world and its
women—and particularly of the gratifications he seeks, and to
some degree obtains, from a rich and pretty Wasp girl, a shiksa
whom he would have perform fellatio upon him, if only she
could master the skill without asphyxiating herself. It is of no
interest to Syrkin that Portnoy goes about tutoring his "tender
young countess" in techniques of breathing rather more like a
patient swimming instructor with a timid ten-year-old at a
summer camp than in the manner of the Marquis de Sade or
even Sergius O'Shaughnessy, nor does she give any indication
that oral intercourse may not necessarily constitute the last
word in human degradation, even for the participants themselves: "a classic description," writes Syrkin, "of what the Nazis

called *rassenschande* (racial defilement)"; ". . . straight out of the Goebbels-Streicher script . . ."; "the anti-semitic indictment straight through Hitler is that the Jew is the defiler and destroyer of the Gentile world."

Hitler, Goebbels, Streicher. Had she not presumably been constrained by limitations of space, Syrkin might eventually have had me in the dock with the entire roster of Nuremberg defendants. On the other hand, it does not occur to her that sexual entanglements between Jewish men and Gentile women might themselves be marked by the history of anti-Semitism that so obviously determines her own rhetoric and point of view in this letter. Nor is she about to allow the most obvious point of all: that this Portnoy can no more enter into an erotic relationship unconscious of his Jewishness and his, if you will, assistant's Gentileness than a Bober could enter into a relationship on terms less charged than these with Alpine, or Leventhal with Allbee. Rather, to Syrkin, for a Jew to have the kind of sexual desires Alexander Portnoy has is unimaginable to anyone but a Nazi.

Now, arguing as she does for what a Jew is not and could not be, other than to a pathological Nazi racist, Syrkin leaves little doubt that she herself has strongly held ideas as to what a Jew in fact is, or certainly ought to be. As did Theodor Herzl; as did Weizmann, Jabotinsky, and Nahman Syrkin; as did Hitler, Goebbels, and Streicher; as do Jean-Paul Sartre, Moshe Dayan, Meir Kahane, Leonid Brezhnev, and the Union of American Hebrew Congregations. In an era which had witnessed the brilliant Americanization of millions of uprooted Jewish immigrants and refugees, the annihilation as human trash of millions of European Jews, and the establishment and survival in the ancient holy land of a spirited, defiant modern Jewish state, it can safely be said that imagining what Jews are and ought to be has been anything but the marginal activity of a few American-Jewish novelists. The novelistic enterprise—particularly in books like *The Victim*, *The Assistant*, and *Portnoy's Complaint*—might itself be described as imagining Jews *being* imagined, by themselves and by others. Given all those projections, fantasies, illusions, programs, dreams, and solutions that the existence of the Jews has given rise to, it is no wonder that these three books, whatever may be their differences in literary merit and approach, are largely nightmares of bondage, each informed in its way by a mood of baffled, claustrophobic struggle.

As I see it, the task for the Jewish novelist has not been to go forth to forge in the smithy of his soul the *un*created conscience of his race, but to find inspiration in a conscience that has been created and undone a hundred times over in this century alone. Similarly, out of this myriad of prototypes, the solitary being to whom history or circumstance has assigned the designation "Jew" has had to imagine what *he* is and is not, must and must not do. If he can, with conviction, assent to that identity and imagine himself being such a thing at all. And that is not always so easy to accomplish. For, as the most serious of our novelists seem to indicate—in those choices of subject and emphasis that lead to the heart of what a writer thinks—there are passionate ways of living that not even imaginations seemingly as unfettered as theirs are able to attribute to a character forthrightly presented as a Jew.

Writing and the Powers That Be

Tell us first of all about your adolescence—its relationship with the type of American society you have represented in Goodbye, Columbus; *your rapport with your family; and if and how you felt the weight of paternal power.*

Far from being the classic period of explosion and tempestuous growth, my adolescence was more or less a period of suspended animation. After the victories of an exuberant and spirited childhood—lived out against the dramatic background of America's participation in World War II—I was to cool down considerably until I went off to college in 1950. There, in a respectable Christian atmosphere hardly less restraining than my own particular Jewish upbringing, but whose strictures I could ignore or oppose without feeling bedeviled by long-standing loyalties, I was able to reactivate a taste for inquiry and speculation that had been all but immobilized during my high school years. From age twelve, when I entered high school, to age sixteen, when I graduated, I was by and large a good, responsible, well-behaved boy, controlled (rather willingly) by the social regulations of the orderly lower-middle-class neighborhood where I had been raised, and mildly constrained still by the taboos that had filtered down to me, in attenuated form, from the religious orthodoxy of my immigrant grandparents. I was probably a "good" adolescent partly because I understood that in our Jewish section of Newark there was nothing much else to be, unless I wanted to steal cars or flunk courses, both of which were beyond me. Rather than becoming a sullen malcontent or a screaming rebel—or flowering, as I had in the prelapsarian days at elementary school—I obediently served my time in what was, after all, only a minimum-security institution, and enjoyed the latitude and privileges awarded to the inmates who make no trouble for their guards.

An interview conducted by the Italian critic Walter Mauro, for his collection of interviews with writers on the subject of power (1974).

The best of adolescence was the intense male friendships—
not only because of the camaraderie they afforded boys coming
unstuck from their close-knit families, but because of the opportunity they provided for uncensored talk. These marathon
conversations, characterized often by raucous discussions of
hoped-for sexual adventure and by all sorts of anarchic joking,
were typically conducted in the confines of a parked car—two,
three, four, or five of us in a single steel enclosure just about
the size and shape of a prison cell, and similarly set apart from
ordinary human society.

The greatest freedom and pleasure I knew in those years
may well have derived from what we said to one another for
hours on end in those automobiles. And how we said it. My
closest adolescent companions—clever, respectful Jewish boys
like myself, all four of whom have gone on to be successful
doctors—may not look back in the same way on those bull
sessions, but for my part I associate that amalgam of mimicry,
reporting, kibbitzing, disputation, satire, and legendizing from
which we drew so much sustenance with the work I now do,
and I consider what we came up with to amuse one another in
those cars to have been something like the folk narrative of a
tribe passing from one stage of human development to the
next. Also, those thousands of words were the means by which
we either took vengeance on or tried to hold at bay the forces
that were impeding us. Instead of stealing cars from strangers,
we sat in the cars we had borrowed from our fathers and said
the wildest things imaginable, at least in our neighborhood.
Which is where we were parked.

"The weight of paternal power," in its traditional oppressive
guises, was something I had hardly to contend with in adolescence. My father had little aside from peccadilloes to quarrel
with me about, and if anything weighed upon me, it was not
dogmatism, unswervingness, or the like, but his limitless pride
in me. When I tried not to disappoint him, or my mother, it was
never out of fear of the mailed fist or the punitive decree, but of
the broken heart; even in post-adolescence, when I began to
find reasons to emancipate myself from them, it never occurred
to me that as a consequence I might lose their love.

What may have encouraged my cooling down in adolescence
was the grave financial setback my father suffered at about the

time I was entering high school. The struggle back to solvency was arduous, and the determination and reserves of strength that it called forth from him in his mid-forties made him all at once a figure of considerable pathos and heroism in my eyes, a cross between Captain Ahab and Willy Loman. Half-consciously I wondered if he might not collapse, carrying us under with him—instead he proved to be undiscourageable, if not something of a stone wall. But as the outcome was in doubt during my early adolescence, it could be that my way in those years of being neither much more nor much less than "good" had to do with contributing what I could to family order and stability. To allow paternal power to weigh what it *should*, I would postpone until a later date my career as classroom conquistador, and suppress for the duration all rebellious and heretical inclinations. This is largely a matter of conjecture, certainly so by this late date—but the fact remains that I did little in adolescence to upset whatever balance of power enabled our family to come as far as it had and to work as well as it did.

Sex as an instrument of power and subjection. You develop this theme in Portnoy's Complaint *and achieve a desecration of pornography, at the same time recognizing the obsessive character of sexual concerns and their enormous conditioning power. Tell us in what real experience this dramatic fable originated or from what adventure of the mind or the imagination.*

Do I "achieve a desecration of pornography"? I never thought of it that way before, since generally pornography is itself considered a desecration of the acts by which men and women are imagined to consecrate their profound attachment to one another. I think of pornography more as the projection of an altogether human preoccupation with the genitalia *in and of themselves*—a preoccupation excluding all emotions other than those elemental feelings that the contemplation of genital functions arouses.

I don't think that I "desecrated" pornography but, rather, excised its central obsession with the body as an erotic contraption or plaything—with orifices, secretions, tumescence, friction, discharge, and all the abstruse intricacies of sex-tectonics—and then set that obsession into an utterly mundane family setting, where issues of power and subjection, among other things, can be seen in their broad everyday aspect rather than through the narrow lens of pornography. Now, perhaps it is just in this sense that I could be charged with having desecrated, or profaned, what pornography, by its exclusiveness and obsessiveness, does actually elevate into a kind of sacred, all-encompassing religion, whose solemn rites it ritualistically enacts: the religion of Fuckism (or, as in a movie like *Deep Throat*, Suckism). As in any religion these devotions are a matter of the utmost seriousness, and there is little more room for individual expressiveness or idiosyncrasy, for human error or mishap, than there is in the celebration of the Mass. In fact, the comedy of *Portnoy's Complaint* arises largely out of the mishaps that bedevil one would-be celebrant as he tries desperately to make his way to the altar and remove his clothes.

You want to know whether I have firsthand knowledge of "sex as an instrument of power and subjection." How could I not? I too have appetite, genitals, imagination, drive, inhibition, frailties, will, and conscience. Moreover, the massive late-sixties assault upon sexual customs—the Great War Against Repression—came nearly twenty years after I myself hit the beach and began fighting for a foothold on the erotic homeland held in subjugation by the enemy. I sometimes think of my generation of men as the first wave of determined D-day invaders over whose bloody, wounded carcasses the flower children subsequently stepped ashore to advance triumphantly toward that libidinous Paris we had dreamed of liberating as we inched inland on our bellies, firing into the dark. "Daddy," the youngsters ask, "what did you do in the war?" I humbly submit they could do worse than read *Portnoy's Complaint* to find out.

The relationship in your work between reality and imagination. Have the forms of power we have mentioned (family, religion, politics) influenced your style, your mode of expression? Or has writing served increasingly to free you from these forms of power?

Inasmuch as subject might be considered an aspect of "style," the answer to the first question is yes: family and religion as coercive forces have been a recurrent subject in my fiction, particularly in the work up to and including *Portnoy's*

Complaint; and the menacing appetites of the Nixon Administration were very much to the point of *Our Gang*. Of course the subjects themselves "influence" their treatment and my "mode of expression," but so does much else. Certainly, aside from the Nixon satire, I have never written anything intentionally destructive. Polemical or blasphemous assault upon the powers that be has served me more as a *theme* than as a purpose.

"The Conversion of the Jews," for instance, a story I wrote when I was twenty-three, reveals at its most innocent stage of development a budding concern with the oppressiveness of family feeling and with the binding ideas of religious exclusiveness which I had experienced first-hand in ordinary American-Jewish life. A good boy named Freedman brings to his knees a bad rabbi named Binder (and various other overlords) and then takes wing from the synagogue into the vastness of space. Primitive as this story seems to me now—it might better be called a prose daydream—it nonetheless evolved out of the same preoccupations that led me, years later, to invent Alexander Portnoy, an older incarnation of claustrophobic little Freedman, who cannot cut loose from what binds and inhibits him quite so magically as the hero I imagined humbling his mother and his rabbi in "The Conversion of the Jews." Ironically, where the boy in the early story is subjugated by figures of real stature in his world, whose power he for the moment at least is able to subvert, Portnoy is less oppressed by these people—who have little real say in his life any longer—than he is imprisoned by a rancor that persists against them. That his most powerful oppressor is himself makes for the farcical pathos of the book—and also connects it with my preceding novel, *When She Was Good*, where the focus is on a grown child's fury against long-standing authorities believed by her to have misused their power.

The question of whether *I* can ever free myself from these forms of power assumes that I experience family and religion as power and nothing else. It is much more complicated than that. I have never really tried, through my work or in my life, to sever all that binds me to my background. I am probably right now as devoted to my origins as I ever was in the days when I was indeed as powerless as little Freedman and, more or less, had no other sane choice. But this has come about only after subjecting these ties and connections to considerable scrutiny. In fact, the affinities that I continue to feel toward the forces that first shaped me, having withstood to the degree that they have the explorations of imagination and the inquiry of psychoanalysis (with all the cold-bloodedness *that* entails), would seem by now to be here to stay. Of course I have greatly refashioned my attachments through the effort of testing them, and over the years have developed my strongest attachment to the test itself.

Our Gang is a desecration of President Nixon and it takes its theme from a statement on abortion. In what period of your life have you most strongly felt the weight of political power as a moral coercion and how did you react to it? Do you feel that the element of the grotesque, which you often use, is the only means by which one can rebel and fight against such power?

I suppose I most strongly felt political power as moral coercion while growing up in New Jersey during World War II. Little was asked of an American schoolchild other than his belief in the "war effort," but that I gave with all my heart. I worried over the welfare of older cousins who were off in the war zone and wrote them long newsy letters to keep up their morale. I sat by the radio with my parents listening to Gabriel Heatter every Sunday, hoping upon hope that he had good news that night. I followed the battle maps and front-line reports in the evening paper, and on weekends I participated in the neighborhood collection of paper and tin cans. I was twelve when the war ended, and during the next few years my first political allegiances began to take shape. My entire clan— parents, aunts, uncles, cousins—were devout New Deal Democrats. In part because they identified him with Roosevelt, and also because they were by and large lower-middle-class people sympathetic to labor and the underdog, a number of them voted for Henry Wallace, the Progressive Party candidate for President in 1948. I'm proud to say that Richard Nixon was known as a crook in our kitchen some twenty-odd years before this dawned on the majority of Americans as a possibility. I was in college during Joe McCarthy's heyday—I reacted by campaigning for Adlai Stevenson and writing a long angry free-verse poem about McCarthyism for the college literary magazine.

The Vietnam War years were the most "politicized" of my life. I spent my days during this war writing fiction, none of which on the face of it would appear to connect to politics. But by being "politicized" I mean something other than writing about politics or even taking direct political action. I mean something akin to what ordinary citizens experience in countries like Czechoslovakia or Chile: a daily awareness of government *as a coercive force*, its continuous presence in one's thoughts as far more than just an institutionalized system of regulations and controls. In sharp contrast to Chileans or Czechs, we hadn't personally to fear for our safety and could be as outspoken as we liked, but this did not diminish the sense of living in a country with a government out of control and wholly in business for itself. Reading the morning *New York Times* and the afternoon *New York Post*, watching the seven and then the eleven o'clock TV news—all of which I did ritualistically—became for me like living on a steady diet of Dostoevsky. Rather than fearing for the well-being of my own kin and country, I now felt toward America's war mission as I had toward the Axis goals in World War II. One even began to use the word "America" as though it was the name not of the place where one had been raised and to which one had a patriotic attachment, but of a foreign invader that had conquered the country and with whom one refused, to the best of one's strength and ability, to collaborate. Suddenly America had turned into "them"—and with this sense of dispossession came the virulence of feeling and rhetoric that often characterized the anti-war movement.

I don't think—to come to your last question—that *Our Gang* uses the "element of the grotesque." Rather, it tries to objectify in a style of its own that element of the grotesque that is distinctive to Richard Nixon. He, not the satire, is what is grotesque. Of course there have been others as venal and lawless in American politics, but even a Joe McCarthy was more identifiable as human clay than this guy is. The wonder of Nixon (and contemporary America) is that a man so transparently fraudulent, if not on the edge of mental disorder, could ever have won the confidence and approval of a people who generally require at least a *little* something of the "human touch" in their leaders. It's strange that someone so unlike the types most admired by the average voter—in any Norman Rockwell drawing, Nixon would have been cast as the fuddy-duddy floorwalker or the prissy math teacher school kids love to tease; never the country judge, the bedside doctor, or the trout-fishin' dad—could have passed himself off to this *Saturday Evening Post* America as, of all things, an *American*.

Finally: "rebelling" or "fighting" against *outside* forces isn't what I take to be at the heart of my writing. *Our Gang* is one of eight disparate works of fiction I've written in the past fifteen years, and even there what most engaged me had to do with *expressiveness*, with problems of presentation, rather than bringing about change or "making a statement." Over the years, whatever rebelliousness I may have as a novelist has been directed far more at my own imagination's demonstrated habits of expression than at the powers that vie for control in the world.

After Eight Books

Your first book, Goodbye, Columbus, *won the most distinguished American literary honor—the National Book Award—in 1960; you were twenty-seven years old at that time. A few years later, your fourth book,* Portnoy's Complaint, *achieved a critical and popular success—and notoriety—that must have altered your personal life, and your awareness of yourself as a writer with a great deal of public "influence." Do you believe that your sense of having experienced life, its ironies and depths, has been at all intensified by your public reputation? Have you come to know more* because *of your fame? Or has the experience of enduring the bizarre projections of others been at times more than you can reasonably handle?*

My public reputation—as distinguished from the reputation of my work—is something I try to have as little to do with as I can. I know it's out there—a concoction spawned by *Portnoy's Complaint* and compounded out of the fantasies that book gave rise to because of its confessional strategy and its financial success. There isn't much else it can be based on, since outside of print I lead virtually no *public* life at all. I don't consider this a sacrifice, because I never much wanted one. Nor have I the temperament for it. Writing in a room by myself is practically my whole life. I enjoy solitude the way some people enjoy parties. It gives me an enormous sense of personal freedom and a sharp sense of being alive—and it provides me with the quiet and the breathing space I need to get my imagination going and my work done. I take no pleasure in being a creature of fantasy in the minds of those who don't know me—which is largely what the fame you're talking about consists of.

For the solitude (and the birds and the trees), I have lived mostly in the country for the last five years, right now more than half of each year in a wooded rural region a hundred miles from New York. I have some six or eight friends scattered within a twenty-mile radius of my house, and I see them a few

---

The interviewer is Joyce Carol Oates (1974).

times a month for dinner. Otherwise I write during the day, walk at the end of the afternoon, and read at night. Almost the whole of my public life takes place in a classroom—I teach one semester of each year. I began to earn my living teaching full-time in 1956, and though for now I can live on my writing income, I have stayed with teaching more or less ever since. In recent years my public reputation has sometimes accompanied me into the classroom, but usually after the first few sessions, when the students observe that I have neither exposed myself nor set up a stall to interest them in purchasing my latest book, whatever illusions about me they may have had begin to recede and I am allowed to be a literature teacher instead of Famous.

Since you have become fairly well established (I hesitate to use that unpleasant word "successful"), have less-established writers tried to use you, to manipulate you into endorsing their work? Do you feel you have received any especially unfair or inaccurate critical treatment? I am also interested in whether you have come to feel more communal now than you did when you were beginning as a writer.

No, I haven't felt, nor have I been, "manipulated" into endorsing the work of less-established writers. In 1972, *Esquire*, for a feature they were planning, asked four "older writers" (as they called them), Isaac Bashevis Singer, Leslie Fiedler, Mark Schorer, and me, each to write a brief essay about a writer under thirty-five he admired. I chose to write about Alan Lelchuk. I'd met him when we were both guests over a long stretch at Yaddo, and afterwards had read in manuscript his novel *American Mischief*, which I admired. I restricted myself to a description and analysis of the book, which, though it hardly consisted of unqualified praise, nonetheless caused some consternation among the Reputation Police. One prominent newspaper reviewer wrote in his column that "one would have to go into the Byzantine feuds and piques of the New York literary scene" to be able to figure out why I had written my fifteen-hundred-word essay, which led the reviewer to describe me as a "blurb writer." That I might simply have enjoyed a new writer's novel, and like Singer, Schorer, and Fiedler, taken

Esquire's invitation as an occasion to talk about his work, never occurred to him. Too unconspiratorial.

In recent years I've run into somewhat more of this kind of "manipulation"—malicious hallucination mixed with childish naïveté and disguised as Inside Dope—from marginal "literary" journalists (the "lice of literature," Dickens called them) than from working writers, young *or* established. In fact, I don't think there's been a time since graduate school when literary fellowship has been such a necessary part of my life. Contact with writers I admire or toward whom I feel a kinship is precisely my way *out* of isolation and furnishes me with whatever sense of community I have. I seem almost always to have had at least one writer I could talk to turn up wherever I happened to be teaching or living. These novelists I've met along the way—in Chicago, Rome, London, Iowa City, at Yaddo, in New York, in Philadelphia—are by and large people I continue to correspond with, exchange finished manuscripts with, try out ideas on, listen to, and visit, if I can, once or twice a year. By now, some of us whose friendships go back a ways may have fallen out of sympathy with the direction the other's work has taken, but since we seem not to have lost faith in one another's good will, the opposition tends to be without the superiority or condescension or the competitive preening that sometimes tends to characterize criticism written by professionals for *their* public. Novelists are, as a group, the most interesting readers of novels that I know.

In a sharp and elegantly angry little essay called "Reviewing," Virginia Woolf once suggested that book journalism ought to be abolished (because 95 percent of it was worthless) and that the serious critics who do reviewing should put themselves out to hire to the novelists, who have a strong interest in knowing what an honest and intelligent reader thinks about their work. For a fee the critic—to be called a "consultant, expositor or expounder"—would meet privately and with some formality with the writer, and "for an hour," writes Virginia Woolf, "they would consult upon the book in question. . . . The consultant would speak honestly and openly, because the fear of affecting sales and of hurting feelings would be removed. Privacy would lessen the shop-window temptation to cut a figure, to pay off scores. . . . He could thus concentrate upon the book itself, and upon telling the author why he likes or dislikes it. The author would profit equally. . . . He could state his case. He could point to his difficulties. He would no longer feel, as so often at present, that the critic is talking about something that he has not written. . . . An hour's private talk with a critic of his own choosing would be incalculably more valuable than the five hundred words of criticism mixed with extraneous matter that is now allotted him."

A very good idea. It surely would have seemed to me worth a hundred dollars to sit for an hour with Edmund Wilson and hear everything he had to say about a book of mine—nor would I have objected to paying to hear whatever Virginia Woolf might have had to say to me about *Portnoy's Complaint*, if she had been willing to accept less than all the tea in China to undertake that job. Nobody minds swallowing his medicine if it is prescribed by a real doctor. One beneficial side effect of this system is that since nobody wants to throw away his hard-earned money, the quacks would be driven out of business.

As for "especially unfair critical treatment"—yes, my blood has been drawn, my anger aroused, my feelings hurt, my patience tried, and in the end, I have wound up enraged most of all with myself, for allowing blood to be drawn, anger aroused, *etc*. When the "unfair critical treatment" has been associated with charges too serious to ignore—accusations against me, say, of "anti-Semitism"—then, rather than fuming to myself, I have answered the criticism at length and in public. Otherwise I fume and forget it; and keep forgetting it, until actually— miracle of miracles—I *do* forget it.

Lastly: who gets "critical treatment" anyway? Why dignify with such a phrase most of what is written about fiction? What one gets, as far as I can see, is what Edmund Wilson describes as a "collection of opinions by persons of various degrees of intelligence who have happened to have some contact with [the writer's] book."

What Edmund Wilson says is true, ideally, yet many writers are influenced by the "critical treatment" they receive. The fact that Goodbye, Columbus *was singled out for extraordinarily high praise must have encouraged you, to some extent; and the critics,*

*certainly, guided a large number of readers in your direction. I
began reading your work in 1959 and was impressed from the start
by your effortless (effortless-seeming, perhaps) synthesis of the colloquial, the comic, the near-tragic, the intensely moral . . . within
wonderfully readable structures that had the feel of being traditional stories, while being at the same time rather revolutionary.
I am thinking of "The Conversion of the Jews," "Eli, the Fanatic,"
and the novella, "Goodbye, Columbus," among others.*

*One of the prominent themes in your writing seems to be the
hero's recognition of a certain loss in his life, along with a regret
for the loss, and finally an ironic "acceptance" of this regret (as if
the hero had to go this way, fulfill this aspect of his destiny, no
matter how painful it might be). Consider the young girl in*
Goodbye, Columbus *and her twin in* My Life as a Man, *both of
whom are eventually rejected. But the loss might have broader
emotional and psychological implications as well—that is, the
beautiful too-young girl must have represented qualities that
were also trans-personal.*

1. You correctly spot the return of an old character in a new
incarnation. The *Goodbye, Columbus* heroine, inasmuch as she
existed as a character at all or "represented" an alternative of
consequence to the hero, is reconstituted in *My Life as a Man*
as Tarnopol's Dina Dornbusch, the "rich, pretty, protected,
smart, sexy, adoring, young, vibrant, clever, confident, ambitious" Sarah Lawrence girl he gives up because she's not what
the young literary fellow, in his romantic ambitiousness, recognizes as a "woman"—by which he means a knocked-around,
on-her-own, volatile, combative, handful like Maureen.

Furthermore, Dina Dornbusch (incidental character that
she is) is herself reconstituted and reappraised by Tarnopol, in
the two short stories preceding his own autobiographical narrative (the "useful fictions"). First in "Salad Days," she appears
as the nice suburban Jewish girl whom he besieges under her
family ping-pong table, and then, in "Courting Disaster," as the
altogether attractive, astute, academically ambitious college senior
who tells Professor Zuckerman, after he has severed relations with
her—to take up with his own brand of "damaged" woman—
that under all his flamboyant "maturity" he is "just a crazy little
boy."

Both these characters are called Sharon Shatzky, and together stand in relation to Dina Dornbusch as fictional distillations do to their models in the unwritten world. These Sharons are what can happen to a Dina when a Tarnopol sets her free from his life to play the role such a woman does in his personal mythology. This mythology, this legend of the self (the useful fiction frequently taken by readers for veiled autobiography), is a kind of idealized architect's drawing for what one may have constructed—or is yet to construct—out of the materials actuality makes available. In this way, a Tarnopol's fiction is his *idea* of his fate.

Or, for all I know, the process works the other way around and the personal myth meant to *reveal* the secret workings of an individual destiny actually makes even *less* readable the text of one's own history. Thereby increasing bewilderment—causing one to tell the story once again, meticulously reconstructing the erasures on what may never have been a palimpsest to begin with.

Sometimes it seems to me that only the novelists and the nuts carry on in quite this way about living what is, after all, only a life—making the transparent opaque, the opaque transparent, the obscure obvious, the obvious obscure, etc. Delmore Schwartz, from "Genesis": "'Why must I tell, hysterical, this story/ And must, compelled, speak of such secrecies?/ . . . Where is my freedom, if I cannot resist/So much speech blurted out . . . ?/How long must I endure this show and sight/Of all I lived through, all I lived in: Why?'"

2. ". . . loss, along with a regret for the loss, and finally an ironic 'acceptance' of this regret." You point to a theme I hadn't thought of as such before—and that I'd prefer to qualify some. Of course Tarnopol is relentlessly kicking himself for his mistake, but it is just those kicks (and the accompanying screams) that reveal to him how strongly determined by character that mistake was. He is his mistake and his mistake is him. "This me who is me being me and none other!" The last line of *My Life as a Man* is meant to point up a harsher attitude toward the self, and the history it has necessarily compiled, than "ironic 'acceptance'" suggests.

To my mind it is Bellow, in his last two pain-filled novels, who has sounded the theme of "loss . . . regret for the loss, and . . . ironic 'acceptance' of the regret"—as he did early on (and less convincingly, I thought) at the conclusion to *Seize the Day*, whose final event I always found a little forced with its sudden swell of *Urn-Burial* prose to elevate Tommy Wilhelm's misery. I prefer the conclusion of "Leaving the Yellow House," with its moving, ironic *rejection* of loss—no "sea-like music" necessary there to make the elemental felt. If there is an ironic acceptance of anything at the conclusion of *My Life as a Man* (or even along the way), it is of *the determined self*. And angry frustration, a deeply vexing sense of characterological enslavement, is strongly infused in that ironic acceptance. Thus the exclamation mark.

I have always been drawn to a passage that comes near the end of *The Trial*, the chapter where K., in the cathedral, looks up toward the priest with a sudden infusion of hope—that passage is pertinent to what I'm trying to say here, particularly by the word "determined," which I mean in both senses: driven, resolute and purposive—yet utterly fixed in position. "If the man would only quit his pulpit, it was not impossible that K. could obtain decisive and acceptable counsel from him which might, for instance, point the way, not toward some influential manipulation of the case, but toward a circumvention of it, a breaking away from it altogether, a mode of living completely outside the jurisdiction of the Court. This possibility must exist, K. had of late given much thought to it."

As who hasn't of late? Enter Stern Irony when the man in the pulpit turns out to be oneself. If only one *could* quit one's pulpit, one might well obtain decisive and acceptable counsel. How to devise a mode of living completely outside the jurisdiction of the Court when the Court is of one's own devising? It is the sense of loss that follows *that* struggle that I would point to as a theme of *My Life as a Man*.

Was it you, or someone more or less imitating you, who wrote about a boy who turned into a girl . . . ? How would that strike you, as a nightmare possibility? (I don't mean The Breast: *that seems to me a literary work, rather than a real psychological excursion, like other writings of yours.) Could you—can you— comprehend, by any extension of your imagination or your unconscious, a life as a woman?—a writing life as a woman? I know this is speculative but had you the choice, would you have wanted to live your life as a man, or as a woman (you could also check "other").*

Answer: Both. Like the hero-heroine of *Orlando*. That is, sequentially rather than simultaneously. It wouldn't be much different from what it's like now, if I weren't able to measure the one life against the other. It would also be interesting not to be Jewish, after having spent a lifetime as a Jew. Arthur Miller imagines the reverse of this as a "nightmare possibility" in *Focus*, where an anti-Semite is taken by the world for the very thing he hates. However, I'm not talking about mistaken identity or skin-deep conversions, but, as I think you are, magically becoming *totally* the other, all the while retaining knowledge of what it was to have been one's original being, wearing one's original badges of identity. In the early sixties I wrote (and shelved) a one-act play called *Buried Again*, about a dead Jewish man who, when given the chance to be reincarnated as a goy, refuses and is consigned forthwith to oblivion. I understand perfectly how he felt, though, if in the netherworld I am presented with this particular choice, I doubt that I will act similarly. I know this will produce a great outcry in *Commentary*, but I shall have to learn to live with that the second time around as I did the first.

Sherwood Anderson wrote "The Man Who Turned Into a Woman," one of the most beautifully sensuous stories I've ever read, where the boy at one point sees himself in a barroom mirror as a girl, but I doubt if that's the piece of fiction you're referring to. Anyway, it wasn't I who wrote about such a sexual transformation, unless you're thinking of *My Life as a Man*, where the hero puts on his wife's undergarments one day, but just to take a sex *break*.

Of course I have written *about* women, some of whom I identified with strongly and imagined myself into while I was working. In *Letting Go*, Martha Reganhart and Libby Herz; in *When She Was Good*, Lucy Nelson and her mother; and in *My Life as a Man*, Maureen Tarnopol and Susan McCall (and Lydia Ketterer and the Sharon Shatzkys). However much or little I am able to extend my imagination to "comprehend . . . life as a woman" is demonstrated in those books.

I never did much with Brenda in *Goodbye, Columbus*, which seems to me apprentice work and weak on character invention all around. Maybe I didn't get very far with her because she was cast as a pretty imperturbable type, a girl who knew how to get what she wanted and how to take care of herself, and as it happened, that, at the time, didn't stir my imagination much. Besides, the more I saw of young women who had flown the family nest—just what Brenda Patimkin decides *not* to do— the less imperturbable they seemed. Beginning with *Letting Go*, where I began to write about female vulnerability, and to see this vulnerability not only as it determined the lives of the women—who felt it frequently at their core—but the men to whom they looked for love and support, the women became characters my imagination could take hold of and enlarge upon. How this vulnerability shapes their relations with men (each vulnerable in the manner of *his* gender) is really at the heart of whatever story I've told about these woman characters.

In parts of Portnoy's Complaint, Our Gang, The Breast, *and most recently in your baseball extravaganza,* The Great American Novel, *you seem to be celebrating the sheer playfulness of the artist, an almost egoless condition in which, to use Thomas Mann's phrase, irony glances on all sides. There is a Sufi saying to the effect that the universe is "endless play and endless illusion"; at the same time, most of us experience it as deadly serious—and so we feel the need, indeed we cannot not feel the need, to be "moral" in our writing. Having been intensely "moral" in* Letting Go *and* When She Was Good, *and in much of* My Life as a Man, *and even in such a marvelously demonic work as the novella "On the Air," do you think your fascination with comedy is only a reaction against this other aspect of your personality, or is it something permanent? Do you anticipate (but no: you could not) some violent pendulum-swing back to what you were years ago, in terms of your commitment to "serious" and even Jamesian writing?*

Sheer Playfulness and Deadly Seriousness are my closest friends; it is with them that I take my walk at the end of the day. I am also on good terms with Deadly Playfulness, Playful

Playfulness, Serious Playfulness, Serious Seriousness, and Sheer Sheerness. From the last, however, I get nothing; it just wrings my heart and leaves me speechless.

I don't know whether the works you call comedies are so egoless. Isn't there really more *self* in the ostentatious display and assertiveness of *The Great American Novel* than in a book like *Letting Go*, say, where a devoted effort at self-removal is necessary for the investigation of self that goes on there? I think that the comedies may be the most ego-ridden of the lot; at least they aren't exercises in self-abasement. What made writing *The Great American Novel* such a pleasure for me was precisely the self-assertion that it entailed—or, if there is such a thing, self-pageantry. All sorts of impulses that I might once have put down as excessive, frivolous, or exhibitionistic I allowed to surface and proceed to their destination. The idea was to see what would emerge if everything that was "a little too" at first glance was permitted to go all the way. I understood that a disaster might ensue (I have been informed by some that it did), but I tried to put my faith in the fun that I was having. *Writing as pleasure*. Enough to make Flaubert spin in his grave.

I don't know what to expect next. *My Life as a Man*, which I finished a few months ago, is a book I'd been abandoning and returning to ever since I published *Portnoy's Complaint*. Whenever I gave up on it I went to work on one of the "playful" books—maybe my despair over the difficulties with the one book accounted for why I wanted to be so playful in the others. At any rate, all the while that *My Life as a Man* was simmering away on the back burner, I wrote *Our Gang*, *The Breast*, and *The Great American Novel*. Right now nothing is cooking. *For the moment* this isn't distressing; I feel (again, for the moment) as though I've reached a natural break of sorts in my work, nothing as yet pressing to be begun—only bits and pieces, fragmentary obsessions, bobbing into view, then sinking, for now, out of sight. Book ideas usually have come at me with all the appearance of pure accident or chance, though by the time I am done I can generally see how what has taken shape was spawned by the interplay between my previous fiction, recent undigested personal history, the circumstances of my immediate, everyday life, and the books I've been reading and teaching. The shifting relationship of these elements of experience brings the subject into focus, and then, by brooding, I find out how to take hold of it. I use "brooding" to describe what this activity apparently looks like; inside I am actually feeling very Sufisticated indeed.

Interview with Le Nouvel Observateur

Before Portnoy's Complaint, *you had become a well-known writer.* Portnoy *made you famous all over the world, and in America you became a star. I even read that, while living in seclusion in the countryside, you were reported in the press to be going around Manhattan with Barbra Streisand. What does it mean to be a celebrity in a media-dominated country like the United States?*

It's likely to mean that your income is going up, at least for a while. You may have become a celebrity just because your income has gone up. What distinguishes the merely famous from a celebrity or a star has usually to do with money, sex, or, as in my case, with both. I was said to have made a million dollars, and I was said to be none other than Portnoy himself. To become a celebrity is to become a brand name. There is Ivory soap, Rice Krispies, and Philip Roth. Ivory is the soap that floats; Rice Krispies the breakfast cereal that goes snap-crackle-pop; Philip Roth the Jew who masturbates with a piece of liver. And makes a million out of it. It isn't much more interesting, useful, or entertaining than that, not after the first half hour. The elevation to celebrity that's thought to bring a writer a wider readership is just another obstacle that most readers have to overcome to achieve a direct perception of the work.

In the late sixties, sex was being touted as the *thing: the heart of life, the redeemer, et cetera.* Portnoy's Complaint, *with its obscene language and erotomaniacal candor, appeared to many to be in sympathy with that viewpoint. But then, in subsequent works, you have seemed to withdraw from this "advanced" position. Instead of Sade or Bataille you refer in essays and interviews to such sexually restrained authors as James, Chekhov, Gogol, Babel, Kafka. Do you mean to disappoint sex worshipers or to regain credibility in respectable society?*

The interviewer is Alain Finkielkraut, a French journalist and author (1981).

I haven't withdrawn from a position because I never held a position. I would never have written a book as farcical as *Portnoy's Complaint* if I had any devotion to the cause of sex; causes don't thrive on self-satire. Nor was I a soldier in the cause of obscenity. Portnoy's obscenity is intrinsic to his predicament, not to my style. I have no case to make for dirty words, in or out of fiction—only for the right of access to them when they seem to the point.

Three years after *Portnoy's Complaint*, I published a novella about a man who turns into a female breast. I imagined scenes more lurid and less lighthearted than anything in *Portnoy's Complaint* but not necessarily to the satisfaction of "sex worshipers." *The Breast* has even been read as a critique of sexual salvationism.

Several of your novels are written in the first person. And their heroes have a lot in common with you. Portnoy is brought up in Newark, much as you were; David Kepesh in The Professor of Desire *is a professor and teaches the same literature courses that you have taught at the University of Pennsylvania. Your recent book* The Ghost Writer *begins some twenty years ago with a young writer's search for a spiritual father who will validate his art. This young writer, Nathan Zuckerman, has just published a group of stories that remind us necessarily of your first work,* Goodbye, Columbus. *Does all this mean that we should read your books as confession, as autobiography barely disguised?*

You should read my books as fiction, demanding the pleasures that fiction can yield. I have nothing to confess and no one I want to confess to. As for my autobiography, I can't begin to tell you how dull it would be. My autobiography would consist almost entirely of chapters about me sitting alone in a room looking at a typewriter. The uneventfulness of my autobiography would make Beckett's *The Unnamable* read like Dickens.

This is not to say that I haven't drawn from my general experience to feed my imagination. But this isn't because I care to reveal myself, exhibit myself, or even express myself. It's so that I can invent myself. My selves. My worlds. To label books like mine "autobiographical" or "confessional" is not only to falsify their suppositional nature but, if I may say so, to slight whatever artfulness leads some readers to think that they must be autobiographical.

These words *confessional* and *autobiographical* constitute yet another obstacle between the reader and the work—in this case, by strengthening the temptation, all too strong in a distracted audience anyway, to trivialize fiction by turning it into gossip.

Not that this is anything new. Rereading Virginia Woolf these last few months, I came across this passage of dialogue in *The Voyage Out*, her 1915 novel. The words are spoken by a character who wants to write books. "Nobody cares. All you read a novel for is to see what sort of person the writer is, and, if you know him, which of his friends he's put in. As for the novel itself, the whole conception, the way one's seen the thing, felt about it, made it stand in relation to other things, not one in a million cares for that."

"L'art, c'est une idée qu'on exagère," said Gide. One exaggeration gave birth to Portnoy, and we know his destiny: this character has become an archetype. Another exaggeration produced Maureen, the majestically deranged woman, the Fury of jealousy and paranoia in My Life as a Man. *But it is as if Portnoy had exhausted the curiosity of the reader in France.* My Life as a Man, *a book of yours that I much admire, is virtually unknown here. How was it received in America—for instance, by women's lib?*

I can only tell you that a few years after the appearance of *My Life as a Man*, a front-page article by a woman activist appeared in the influential Manhattan weekly *The Village Voice*, bearing this two-fisted headline: WHY DO THESE MEN HATE WOMEN? Beneath were photographs of Saul Bellow, Norman Mailer, Henry Miller, and me. *My Life as a Man* was the most damaging evidence brought against me by the prosecution.

Why? Because in 1974 the world had just recently discovered that women were good and only good, persecuted and only persecuted, exploited and only exploited, and I had depicted a woman who was not good, who persecuted others and who exploited others—and that spoiled everything. A woman without conscience, a vindictive woman with limitless cunning and wild, unfocused hatred and rage—and to depict such a woman was contrary to the new ethics and to the revolution that espoused them. It was antirevolutionary. It was on the wrong side of the cause. It was taboo.

Of course, My Life as a Man *is more than a challenge to feminist piety. In one scene Maureen buys a sample of urine from a pregnant black woman in order to pass the rabbit test and trick Peter Tarnopol into marriage. In another scene—their last brutal fight—when beaten by him, Maureen defecates in her pants, thus depriving them both of tragedy at the most painful moment of their marriage. Surely this novel is intended as a challenge to the pieties of American culture in general, to the moralizing and corny sentimentality so pervasive there. Do you agree with this interpretation?*

That it was intended, conceived, realized, as a challenge? No. You may be further describing the way it was received, however. The book was reviewed harshly, sold poorly, and went out of print in a mass paperback edition shortly after it was published, the first book of mine ever to disappear like that. If it's any comfort to you as a Frenchman, the book is almost as unknown in my country as in yours.

You seem deeply concerned with the obstacles that our society places between a work of art and its readers. We have talked about fame and the media's distortion of the writer's purpose. We have talked about gossip, the middlebrow distortion that reduces reading to voyeurism. We have talked about piety, the activist distortion that would exploit literature as propaganda. But there is yet another obstacle, is there not? The structuralist cliché, which is criticized in his introductory lecture by David Kepesh, your professor of desire: "You will discover (and not all will approve) that I do not hold with certain of my colleagues who tell us that literature, in its most valuable and intriguing moments, is fundamentally non-referential. I may come before you in my jacket and tie, I may address you as madam and sir, but I am going to request nonetheless that you restrain yourself from talking about 'structure,' 'form,' and 'symbols' in my presence." What makes the principles of the literary avant-garde so pernicious?

I don't think of the words *structure*, *form*, and *symbol* as the property of the avant-garde. In America they are usually the stock-in-trade of the most naive high school literature teachers. When I teach, I am not so gentle as my professor of desire, Mr. Kepesh: I *forbid* my students to use those words, on pain of expulsion. This results in a charming improvement in their English and even, sometimes, in their thinking.

As for structuralism: It really hasn't played any part in my life. I can't satisfy you with a vituperative denunciation.

I was not expecting a vituperative denunciation. I was just interested in what your idea of reading is.

I read fiction to be freed from my own suffocatingly boring and narrow perspective on life and to be lured into imaginative sympathy with a fully developed narrative point of view not my own. It's the same reason that I write.

How would you assess the sixties now? Was it a decade of liberation that gave permission to write as one felt and to live the life one wanted, or an era of arrogance, of narrow new dogmas to which you had better pay tribute if you didn't want to get into trouble?

As an American citizen I was appalled and mortified by the war in Vietnam, frightened by the urban violence, sickened by the assassinations, confused by the student uprisings, sympathetic to the liberationist pressure groups, delighted by the pervasive theatricality, disheartened by the rhetoric of the causes, excited by the sexual display, and enlivened by the general air of confrontation and change. During the last years of the decade, I was writing *Portnoy's Complaint*, a raucous, aggressive, abrasive book whose conception and composition were undoubtedly influenced by the mood of the times. I don't think I would or could have written that book in that way a decade earlier, not only because of the social, moral, and cultural attitudes that prevailed in the fifties but because, as a younger writer still strongly involved with literary studies, I had pledged my loyalty to a more morally earnest line of work.

But by the mid-sixties, I had already written two indisputably earnest books—*Letting Go* and *When She Was Good*—and was dying to turn my attention to something else, something that would call forth a more playful side of my talent. I now had the confidence to reveal that side in my fiction, in part because I was into my thirties and no longer had to work so hard as I did in my twenties at establishing my maturity credentials, and in part because of the infectious volatility of a moment that was inspiring feats of self-transformation and self-experimentation in virtually everyone.

You are known to us here in France as an American-Jewish writer—even as a member (along with Bellow and Malamud) of a so-called New York–Jewish school. Do you accept this label?

Only Malamud, of the three of us, comes from New York and spent his childhood there, in a poor neighborhood in Brooklyn. Virtually all of Malamud's adult life has been spent far away from New York, teaching at colleges in Oregon and Vermont. Bellow was born in Montreal and has lived almost all of his life in Chicago, eight hundred miles west of New York, a city as different from New York as Marseilles is from Paris. The book that brought him his first popular recognition, *Adventures of Augie March*, doesn't begin "I am a Jew, New York–born" but "I am an American, Chicago-born."

I was born in Newark, New Jersey, in my childhood an industrial port city of about 430,000, mostly white and working class and, during the thirties and forties, still very much the provinces. The Hudson River, separating New York from New Jersey, could as easily have been the channel separating England from France—the anthropological divide was that great, at least for people in our social position. I lived in a lower-middle-class Jewish neighborhood in Newark until I was seventeen and went off to a small college in rural Pennsylvania that had been founded by Baptists in the mid-nineteenth century and still required of its students weekly attendance at chapel services. You couldn't have gotten further from the spirit of New York or of my Newark neighborhood. I was eager to find out what the rest of "America" was like. America in quotes—because it was still almost as much of an idea in my mind as it had been in Franz Kafka's. I was, at sixteen and seventeen, strongly under the sway of Thomas Wolfe and his rhapsodic take on American life. I was still under the influence of the populist rhetoric that had risen out of the Depression and had been transformed by the patriotic fervor of World War II into the popular national myth about the "vastness" of the "land," the "rich diversity" of the "people." I'd read Sinclair Lewis and Sherwood Anderson and Mark Twain, and none of them led me to think that I would find "America" in New York City or even at Harvard.

So I chose an ordinary college in a pretty little town in a beautiful farming valley in central Pennsylvania about which I knew practically nothing, where I went to chapel once a week with the Christian boys and girls who were my classmates, youngsters from conventional backgrounds with predominantly philistine interests. My attempt to throw myself wholeheartedly into the traditional college life of that era lasted about six months, though chapel I could never stomach and I made it a habit conspicuously to be reading Schopenhauer in my pew during the sermon.

I spent the year after college in graduate school at the University of Chicago which was more my style, then went to Washington, D.C., where I served my stint in the Army. In 1956 I returned to Chicago to teach at the university for two years. I began to write the stories that were collected in my first book, *Goodbye, Columbus*. When the book was accepted for publication in the summer of 1958, I resigned my job at the university to move to Manhattan to pursue the life of a young writer instead of a young instructor. I lived on the Lower East Side for about six months, quite unhappily: I didn't like the "literary" scene; I wasn't interested in the publishing world; I couldn't master the mode of sexual

combat in vogue there in the late fifties; and as I wasn't employed in merchandising, manufacturing, or finance, I didn't
see much reason to stay. In the years that followed I lived in
Rome, London, Iowa City, and Princeton. When I returned
to New York in 1963, it was to get away from a marriage fifty
miles south in Princeton, where I was teaching at the University, and, later, to be psychoanalyzed. When the analysis was
over—and the sixties were over—I left for the countryside,
where I've lived ever since.

*So New York is wrong. But the Jewish background is a major
source of inspiration in your work. And what strikes me, from*
Goodbye, Columbus *to* The Ghost Writer, *is that as a novelist
you are drawn to the Jewish world for all the comic possibilities it
offers you, but not for the tragic ones, as might be expected. How
do you explain that?*

By my biography.
Like Bellow and Malamud, I was born to Jewish parents and
raised self-consciously as a Jew. I don't mean that I was strictly
raised according to Jewish traditions or brought up to be an
observant Jew but that I was born into the situation of being a
Jew, and it did not take long to be aware of its ramifications.
I lived in a predominantly Jewish neighborhood and attended public schools where about 90 percent of the pupils
and the teachers were Jewish. To live in an ethnic or cultural
enclave like this wasn't unusual for an urban American child of
my generation. Newark, a prosperous, thriving city during my
childhood, is now a predominantly black city with a reduced
population in a nightmarish state of decay. Until the late fifties
it was demographically divided up like any number of American industrial cities that had been heavily settled in the late
nineteenth and early twentieth centuries by waves of immigration from Germany, Ireland, Italy, Eastern Europe, and Russia.
As soon as they could climb out of the slums where most of
them began in America, more or less penniless, the immigrants
formed neighborhoods within the cities where they could have
the comfort and security of the familiar while undergoing the
arduous transformations of a new way of life. These neighbor-

hoods became rivalrous, competing, somewhat xenophobic subcultures within the city; each came to have an Americanized style of its own, and rather than dissolving when immigration virtually ceased, with the onset of World War I, they were transformed, over the decades, by their own growing affluence and stability into a permanent feature of American life.

My point is that my America in no way resembled the France or the England I would have grown up in as a Jewish child. It was not a matter of a few of us and all of them. What I saw was a few of *everyone*. Rather than growing up intimidated by the monolithic majority—or in defiance of it or in awe of it—I grew up feeling a part of the majority composed of the competing minorities, no one of which impressed me as being in a more enviable position than our own. By the time I was ready for college, it was no wonder that I chose as I did: I had never really known at first hand any of these so-called Americans who were also said to be living in our country.

I had simultaneously been surrounded from birth with a *definition* of the Jew of such stunning emotional and historical proportions that I couldn't but be enveloped by it, distant though it was to my own experience. This was the definition of the Jew as sufferer, the Jew as an object of ridicule, disgust, scorn, contempt, derision, of every heinous form of persecution and brutality, including murder. If the definition was not supported by my own experience, it was by the experience of my grandparents and their forebears, and by the experience of our European contemporaries. The disparity between this tragic dimension of Jewish life in Europe and the actualities of our daily lives as Jews in New Jersey was something that I had to puzzle over myself, and indeed, it was in the vast discrepancy between the two Jewish conditions that I found the terrain for my first stories and later for *Portnoy's Complaint*.

And let me say something about "school," the last word in that label.

Obviously, Bellow, Malamud, and I do not constitute a New York school of anything. If we constitute a Jewish school, it is only in the sense of having each found his own means of transcending the immediate parochialism of his Jewish background and transforming what once had been the imaginative property of anecdotal local colorists—and of apologists, nostalgists, publicists, and propagandists—into a fiction having entirely different intentions, but which nonetheless remains grounded in the specificity of the locale. And even this similarity amounts to little when you think about all that must follow from our differences in age, upbringing, regional origin, class, temperament, education, intellectual interests, literary antecedents, and artistic aims and ambitions.

Of course, The Ghost Writer *is not only about Jews. One of its subjects is what you have called "writing about Jews": young Nathan is accused, at the very outset of his career, of informing, of collaborating with the enemy, the anti-Semite. What makes writing about Jews so problematical?*

What makes it problematical is that Jews who register strong objections to what they see as damaging fictional portrayals of Jews are not necessarily philistine or paranoid. If their nerve endings are frayed, it is not without cause or justification. They don't want books that they believe will give comfort to anti-Semites or confirm anti-Semitic stereotypes. They don't want books that will wound the feelings of Jews already victimized, if not by anti-Semitic persecution in one form or another, by the distaste for Jews still endemic in pockets of our society. They don't want books that, as they see it, offend Jewish self-esteem and that do little, if anything, to increase the prestige of Jews in the non-Jewish world. In the aftermath of the horrors that have befallen so many millions of Jews in this century, it isn't difficult to understand their concern. It's the *ease* with which one understands it that presents a problem of conflicting loyalties that's difficult to resolve. For however much I may loathe anti-Semitism, however enraged I may be when faced with the slightest real manifestation of it, however much I might wish to console its victims, my job in a work of fiction is not to offer succor to Jewish sufferers or to mount an attack upon their persecutors or to make the Jewish case to the undecided. My Jewish critics, and in America there are many, would tell you that I bend over backward not to make the Jewish case. After more than twenty years of heated disagreement with them on this subject, I can only say again that that is the way they see it and not the way I see it. It's a fruitless conflict—which is exactly what makes it so problematical to write about Jews.

Having read The Ghost Writer *before our talk, I took it for granted that you were the young writer Nathan Zuckerman and that Lonoff—the austere, ascetic older writer Zuckerman so much admires—was an imaginary amalgam of Malamud and Singer. But I see now that, not unlike Lonoff, you live like a semi-recluse in New England; you seem to write and read most of the time— in other words, to spend most of your life, in Lonoff's self-descriptive phrase, "turning sentences around." Are you Lonoff? Or, to put it less bluntly: Do you share the ideal of the writer as hermit, a self-ordained monk who must remain secluded from life for the sake of art?*

Art is life too, you know. Solitude is life, meditation is life, pretending is life, supposition is life, contemplation is life, language is life. Is there less life in turning sentences around than in manufacturing automobiles? Is there less life in reading *To the Lighthouse* than in milking a cow or throwing a hand grenade? The isolation of a literary vocation—the isolation that involves far more than sitting alone in a room for most of one's waking existence—has as much to do with life as accumulating sensations or multinational corporations out in the great hurly-burly.

Am I Lonoff? Am I Zuckerman? Am I Portnoy? I could be, I suppose. I may be yet. As of now I am nothing like so sharply delineated as a character in a book. I am still amorphous Roth.

You seem to me to be made particularly rebellious by the strain of sentimental moralizing in American culture. At the same time, you strenuously claim your American heritage. My last question is very simple, if not simplistic: What does America mean to you?

America allows me the greatest possible freedom to practice my vocation. America has the only literary audience that I can ever imagine taking any sustained pleasure in my fiction. America is the place I know best in the world. It's the *only* place I know in the world. My consciousness and my language were shaped by America. I'm an American writer in ways that a plumber isn't an American plumber or a miner an American miner or a cardiologist an American cardiologist. Rather, what the heart is to the cardiologist, the coal to the miner, the kitchen sink to the plumber, America is to me.

Interview with The London Sunday Times

I imagine you get annoyed when critics read this trilogy as straight confession. Zuckerman as Philip Roth. Yet sometimes it's hard not to read it this way.

It's very easy to read it this way. This is the easiest possible way to read it. It makes it just like reading the evening paper. I get annoyed because it isn't the evening paper. Shaw wrote to Henry James, "People don't want works of art from you, they want help." They also want confirmation of their beliefs, including their beliefs about you.

But surely the journalistic approach is inescapable—unless the reader forgets everything he knows or has read about you, Philip Roth.

If my books are so persuasive that they are utterly convinced, these readers, that I give them life red hot, untransformed, as it's lived, well, I suppose that's not the worst cross any novelist has had to bear. Better than their not believing me at all. The fashion now is to praise books you don't believe in. "This is really a great book—I don't believe in it at all." But I *want* belief, and I work to try to get it. If all these readers see in my work is my biography, then they are numb to fiction—to impersonation, to ventriloquism, to irony, numb to the thousand observations on which a book is built, numb to all the devices by which novels create the illusion of a reality more like the real than our own. End of lecture. Or shall we pursue this further?

Since you're enjoying it so, why not a little further? In The Anatomy Lesson *there is the character Milton Appel, a distinguished and powerful literary critic. Reviewers have confidently identified him as Irving Howe. I won't ask you to confirm or deny this. I do think, though, that once the identification is made, it becomes*

The interviewer is the English poet, critic, and biographer Ian Hamilton (1984).

hard for the reader not to pursue the biographical interest (i.e.,
Roth versus Howe) at the expense, sometimes, of the fictional clash
between Zuckerman and Appel.

I wouldn't write a book to win a fight. I'd rather go 15
rounds with Sonny Liston. At least it would be over in an hour
and I could go back to bed, perhaps for good. But a book takes
me two years, if I'm lucky. Eight hours a day, seven days a week,
365 days a year. You have to sit alone in a room with only a tree
out the window to talk to. You have to sit there churning out
draft after draft of crap, waiting like a neglected baby for just
one drop of mother's milk.

Anybody who did this to win a fight would have to be even
crazier than I am. Angrier too. Milton Appel is not in this book
because I was once demolished in print by Irving Howe. Appel
is in this book because half of being a writer is being indignant.
And being *right*. If you only knew how *right* we are. Show me a
writer who isn't furious about being misrepresented, misread, or
unread, and who isn't sure he's right.

My trilogy is about the vocation of an American writer, who
is a Jew, to boot. If I left out the feuds and the paranoia and
the indignation, if I left out the fact that *they are wrong and we
are right*, I would not be telling the whole unpretty truth
about what goes on inside the heads of even Nobel Prize winners. I happen to know a couple of Nobel Prize winners, and
let me assure you, they too might not object if their critics
were pelted with offal while being drawn down Fifth Avenue
in cages.

Appel does come out of their argument rather well—better than
Zuckerman, in fact. In their showdown telephone conversation
one rather squirms for Zuckerman.

Of course you give the other guy the best lines. Otherwise
it's a mug's game.

That old magnanimity.

Yes, my strong suit. But it happens also to be a necessity.
Tilting at yourself is *interesting*, a lot more interesting than

winning. Let the vituperation flow and the mouth froth, but underestimate the opposition and you weaken the book. For me the work, the writing work, is transforming the I-madness into he-madness. Last point about Appel. Zuckerman's rage against Appel has less to do with Appel than with Z.'s physical condition. As if the willed self-absorption of the writer isn't imprisoning enough, there is the forced self-absorption kindled by his chronic pain.

If it weren't for Zuckerman's physical pain, there'd be no Appel in this book. Zuckerman wouldn't have his harem of Florence Nightingales. Wouldn't decide at forty to become a doctor and bolt for Chicago, oozing Percodan at every pore. Forget Appel. This book is about physical pain and the havoc it wreaks on one's human credentials. If Zuckerman were in good fighting shape, why would he even contend with his literary enemies on the Jewish magazine he calls *Foreskin*? He wouldn't bother.

But because the pain isn't diagnosed, because it's a mystery pain, we might tend to view it as symbolic pain, as pain visited upon him by *the Appels, by the less than first-rate women, by the state of Zuckerman's career, and so on.*

Symbolic pain? Could be for all I know. But in a real shoulder. What hurts is a real neck and shoulder. They're killing him. The trouble with pains is they don't feel symbolic, except maybe to literature professors.

What is your diagnosis?

My diagnosis is that these things happen. When I was writing, I said to myself, "I want someone who has known chronic pain to be able to read this book and say, "That's it, that's what it's like." I wanted to be as realistic and *un*symbolic as possible. Not knowing the source of one's pain doesn't make it symbolic: it just makes the suffering worse. Not that it would be a comfort to Zuckerman if he knew, say, that he had cancer. Sometimes knowing is worse, sometimes not knowing is worse. My book is about not knowing. Look, diagnoses abound in this book. Everybody *else* knows. They've all got him pegged, just like Appel. All his women know what's wrong with him. Even the trichologist who treats his baldness knows why he's losing his hair: "undue pressure." This book is *crammed* with people who know what's wrong with Zuckerman. I leave the diagnosing to his comforters. I try to stay out of it.

Of course Zuckerman ends the book in an advanced state of metaphor, with his mouth wired shut by surgery.

He breaks his jaw falling on a tombstone in a snowbound Jewish cemetery, after overdosing on painkillers and booze. What's so metaphorical about that? Happens all the time.

But he's silenced, completely. He can't write because of his agonising shoulder, and he can't speak because of his broken mouth.

Back in 1957 I published, in *The New Yorker*, a short story called "Defender of the Faith." I was twenty-four and I was pretty excited about it. Then the story came out and it enraged a lot of Jewish readers of *The New Yorker*. Among them was an eminent New York rabbi who wrote a letter of protest to the Anti-Defamation League of the B'nai B'rith—a worthy organisation, by the way, that's fought anti-Semitic discrimination in the U.S. courts for decades. One line of the rabbi's letter I never forgot. "What is being done to silence this man?" Well, to their credit, they never tried it. Free country, the U.S.A., and nobody appreciates that better than the Jews. But I remembered that line. What is being done to silence this man? It came to me when I was writing this book. That's why I broke Zuckerman's jaw. I did it for the rabbi.

So the charge of defamation started early on?

It started when I started. It has somewhat distinguished my career from most of my American colleagues. I was taken to be a dangerous fellow when I was still in my swaddling clothes. In its own strange way, the furor coming right at the outset probably has given my writing a direction and emphasis that it might not have had otherwise. It's difficult to ignore such an assault, particularly at twenty-four. Back then I did two stupid things: began to explain myself and began to defend myself. Obviously I'm still at it.

How did you make your case?

I was invited to speak at synagogues and temples and Jewish community centres, and I went out and spoke. People stood up and shouted at me during the question periods. In the end it was a good thing. They dragged me screaming out of the Department of English. There were real people out there who got inflamed. They didn't write papers about what they read—they got mad. What a surprise.

So by the time you wrote Portnoy's Complaint, *you already had an inflamed Jewish readership, so to speak?*

I also had an appreciative Jewish readership. Even a few Gentiles reading me, too. But as for my Jewish detractors, no, they wouldn't stop. They wouldn't let up, no matter what I wrote. So I thought finally, "Well, you want it, I'll give it to you." And out came Portnoy, apertures spurting.

What about your own family? How did they respond?

To the attacks on me? They were stunned. They were hurt. They heard a lot about my inadequacies from their neighbours. They would go to a lecture about me at their temple, expecting a star to be pinned on their boy just like back in grade school. Instead they'd hear from the platform that sleeping in my bedroom all those years, and eating with them at their table, was a self-hating anti-Semitic Jew. My mother had to hold my father down in his seat, he'd get so angry. No, they were all right. They recognised too many folks they knew to think such people as I'd described in fiction had never walked around New Jersey.

Your own father then isn't like Zuckerman's father, who on his deathbed curses his son for the books he writes?

I never said he was. You're confusing me with all those astute book reviewers who are sure that I am the only novelist in the history of literature who has never made anything up.

In each of these last two books, Zuckerman suffers a bereavement. In the second book, Zuckerman Unbound, *his father dies calling him "Bastard." In* The Anatomy Lesson, *Zuckerman's mother dies, and Zuckerman is left with a piece of paper on which his mother has written the word "Holocaust."*

She's dying of a brain tumor. Her neurologist comes to her hospital room to ascertain just how far gone she is and asks her to write her name for him on a piece of paper. This is in Miami Beach in 1970. She's a woman whose writings otherwise consist of recipes on index cards, knitting instructions, and thank-you notes. When the doctor puts the pen in her hand and asks her to write her name, instead of writing "Selma" she writes "Holocaust," perfectly spelled. The doctor can't throw it away and after her death he gives it to Zuckerman. Zuckerman can't throw it away either and carries it around in his wallet.

Why can't he throw it away?

Who can? Zuckerman isn't the only one who can't throw this word away and is carrying it with him all the time, whether he knows it or not. Without this word there would be no Nathan Zuckerman, not in Zuckerman's fix. No chiropodist father and his deathbed curse, no dentist brother with his ferocious chastisement. There'd of course be no Amy Bellette, the young woman in *The Ghost Writer* who he likes to imagine could have been Anne Frank. There'd be no Milton Appel with his moral ordinances and high-minded imperatives. And Zuckerman wouldn't be in his cage. If you take away that word—and with it the historical fact—none of these Zuckerman books would exist.

But you're not saying that your subject in these books has been the Holocaust?

Of course not—certainly not in the way it's the subject at the center of Styron's novel *Sophie's Choice*. I think for a writer like myself there's not the same impetus, or, oddly, even the necessity, that there is for a Christian American, like Styron, to take the Holocaust up so nakedly as a subject, to unleash upon it so much moral and philosophical speculation, so much harrowing, furious invention. It works through Jewish lives less visibly and in less spectacular ways. And that's the way I prefer to deal with it in fiction. For most reflective Jews, I would think, it is simply there, hidden, submerged, emerging, disappearing, unforgotten. You don't make use of it—it makes use of you. It certainly makes use of Zuckerman. There is a certain thematic architecture to these three books that I hope will make itself felt when they're published in one volume. I don't mean that everyone is going to be knocked off his feet by my conceptual grandeur. I just mean that the little piece of paper in Zuckerman's wallet might not seem quite so small.

Interview with The Paris Review

How do you get started on a new book?

Beginning a book is unpleasant. I'm entirely uncertain about the character and the predicament, and a character in his predicament is what I have to begin with. Worse than not knowing your subject is not knowing how to treat it, because that's finally everything. I type out beginnings and they're awful, more of an unconscious parody of my previous book than the breakaway from it that I want. I need something driving down the center of a book, a magnet to draw everything to it—that's what I look for during the first months of writing something new. I often have to write a hundred pages or more before there's a paragraph that's alive. Okay, I say to myself, that's your beginning, start there; that's the first paragraph of the book. I'll go over the first six months of work and underline in red a paragraph, a sentence, sometimes no more than a phrase, that has some life in it, and then I'll type all these out on one page. Usually it doesn't come to more than one page, but if I'm lucky, that's the start of page one. I look for the liveliness to set the tone. After the awful beginning come the months of freewheeling play, and after the play come the crises, turning against your material and hating the book.

How much of a book is in your mind before you start?

What matters most isn't there at all. I don't mean the solutions to problems, I mean the problems themselves. You're looking, as you begin, for what's going to resist you. You're looking for trouble. Sometimes in the beginning uncertainty arises not because the writing is difficult, but because it isn't difficult enough. Fluency can be a sign that nothing is happening; fluency can actually be my signal to stop, while being in the dark from sentence to sentence is what convinces me to go on.

The interviewer is the biographer Hermione Lee.

Must you have a beginning? Would you ever begin with an ending?

For all I know I *am* beginning with the ending. My page one can wind up a year later as page two hundred, if it's still even around.

What happens to those hundred or so pages that you have left over? Do you save them up?

I generally prefer never to see them again.

Do you work best at any particular time of the day?

I work all day, morning and afternoon, just about every day. If I sit there like that for two or three years, at the end I have a book.

Do you think other writers work such long hours?

I don't ask writers about their work habits. I really don't care. Joyce Carol Oates says somewhere that when writers ask each other what time they start working and when they finish and how much time they take for lunch, they're actually trying to find out "Is he as crazy as I am?" I don't need that question answered.

Does your reading affect what you write?

I read all the time when I'm working, usually at night. It's a way of keeping the circuits open. It's a way of thinking about my *line* of work while getting a little rest from the work at hand. It helps inasmuch as it fuels the overall obsession.

Do you show your work-in-progress to anyone?

It's more useful for my mistakes to ripen and burst in their own good time. I give myself all the opposition I need while I'm writing, and praise is meaningless to me when I know something isn't even half finished. Nobody sees what I'm doing until I absolutely can't go any further and might even like to believe that I'm done.

Do you have a Roth reader in mind when you write?

No. I occasionally have an anti-Roth reader in mind. I think, "How he is going to hate this!" That can be just the encouragement I need.

You spoke of the last phase of writing a novel being a "crisis" in which you turn against the material and hate the work. Is there always this crisis, with every book?

Always. Months of looking at the manuscript and saying, "This is wrong—but what's wrong?" I ask myself, "If this book were a dream, it would be a dream of what?" But when I'm asking this I'm also trying to *believe* in what I've written, to forget that it's writing and to say, "This *has* taken place," even if it hasn't. The idea is to perceive your invention as a reality that can be understood as a dream. The idea is to turn flesh and blood into literary characters and literary characters into flesh and blood.

Can you say more about these crises?

In *The Ghost Writer* the crisis—one among many—had to do with Zuckerman, Amy Bellette, and Anne Frank. It wasn't easy to see that Amy Bellette *as* Anne Frank was Zuckerman's own creation. Only by working through numerous alternatives did I decide that not only was she his creation, but that she might possibly be her own creation too, a young woman inventing herself *within* Zuckerman's invention. To enrich his fantasy without obfuscation or muddle, to be ambiguous *and* clear— well, that was my writing problem through one whole summer and fall. In *Zuckerman Unbound* the crisis was a result of failing to see that Zuckerman's father shouldn't already be dead when the book begins. I eventually realized that the death should come at the conclusion of the book, allegedly as a consequence of the son's blasphemous best-seller. But, starting off, I'd got the thing back to front, and then I stared at it dumbly for months, seeing nothing. I knew that I wanted the book to veer away from Alvin Pepler—I like to be steamrolling along in one direction and then to spring my surprise—but I couldn't give up the premise of my earliest drafts until I saw that the novel's obsessive concern with assassinations, death threats, funerals, and funeral homes, was leading up to, rather than away from, the death of Zuckerman's father. How you juxtapose the events can tie you in knots and rearranging the sequence can free you suddenly to streak for the finish line. In *The Anatomy Lesson* the discovery I made—having banged the typewriter with my head far too long—was that Zuckerman, in the moment that he takes flight for Chicago to try to become a doctor, should begin to impersonate a pornographer. There had to be willed extremism at either end of the moral spectrum, each of his escape-dreams of self-transformation subverting the meaning and mocking the intention of the other. If he had gone off solely to become a doctor, driven only by that high moral ardor, or, if he had just gone around impersonating a pornographer, spewing only that anarchic and alienating rage, he wouldn't have been my man. He has two dominant modes: his mode of self-abnegation, and his fuck-'em mode. You want a bad Jewish boy, that's what you're going to get. He rests from one by taking up the other, though, as we see, it's not much of a rest. The thing about Zuckerman that interests me is that everybody's split, but few so openly as this. Everybody is full of cracks and fissures, but usually we see people trying very hard to hide the places where they're split. Most people desperately want to heal their lesions, and keep trying to. Hiding them is sometimes taken for healing them (or for not having them). But Zuckerman can't successfully do either, and by the end of the trilogy has proved it even to himself. What's determined his life and his work are the lines of fracture in what is by no means a clean break. I was interested in following those lines.

What happens to Philip Roth when he turns into Nathan Zuckerman?

Nathan Zuckerman is an act. It's all the art of impersonation, isn't it? That's the fundamental novelistic gift. Zuckerman is a writer who wants to be a doctor impersonating a pornographer. I am a writer writing a book impersonating a writer who wants to be a doctor impersonating a pornographer—who then, to compound the impersonation, to barb the edge, pretends he's a well-known literary critic. Making fake biography, false history, concocting a half-imaginary existence out of the actual drama of my life *is* my life. There has to be some pleasure in this job, and that's it. To go around in disguise. To act a character. To pass oneself off as what one is not. To *pretend*. The sly and cunning masquerade. Think of the ventriloquist. He speaks so that his voice appears to proceed from someone at a distance from himself. But if he weren't in your line of vision you'd get no pleasure from his art at all. His art consists of being present *and* absent; he's most himself by simultaneously being someone else, neither of whom he "is" once the curtain is down. You don't necessarily, as a writer, have to abandon your biography completely to engage in an act of impersonation. It may be more intriguing when you don't. You distort it, caricature it, parody it, you torture and subvert it, you exploit it—all to give the biography that dimension that will excite your verbal life. Millions of people do this all the time, of course, and not with the justification of making literature. They *mean* it. It's amazing what lies people can sustain behind the mask of their real faces. Think of the art of the adulterer: under tremendous pressure and against enormous odds, ordinary husbands and wives, who would freeze with self-consciousness up on a stage, yet in the theater of the home, alone before the audience of the betrayed spouse, they act out roles of innocence and fidelity with flawless dramatic skill. Great, great performances, conceived with genius down to the smallest particulars, impeccably meticulous naturalistic acting, and all done by rank amateurs. People beautifully pretending to be "themselves." Make-believe can take the subtlest forms, you know. Why should a novelist, a pretender by profession, be any less deft or more reliable than a stolid unimaginative suburban accountant cheating on his wife? Jack Benny used to pretend to be a miser, remember? Called himself by his own good name and claimed that he was stingy and mean. It excited his comic imagination to do this. He probably wasn't all that funny as just another nice fellow writing checks to the U.J.A. and taking his friends out to dinner. Céline pretended to be a rather indifferent, even irresponsible physician when he seems in fact to have worked hard at his practice and to have been conscientious about his patients. But that wasn't interesting.

But it is. Being a good doctor is interesting.

For William Carlos Williams maybe, but not for Céline. Being a devoted husband, an intelligent father, and a dedicated family physician in Rutherford, New Jersey, might have seemed as admirable to Céline as it does to you, or to me for that matter, but *his* writing drew its vigor from the demotic voice and the dramatization of his outlaw side (which was considerable), and so he created the Céline of the great novels in somewhat the way Jack Benny, also flirting with the taboo, created himself as a miser. You have to be awfully naïve not to understand that a writer is a performer who puts on the act he does best—not least when he dons the mask of the first-person singular. That may be the best mask of all for a second self. Some (many) pretend to be more lovable than they are and some pretend to be less. Beside the point. Literature isn't a moral beauty contest. Its power arises from the authority and audacity with which the impersonation is pulled off; the belief it inspires is what counts. The question to ask about the writer isn't "Why does he behave so badly?" but "What does he gain by wearing this mask?" I don't admire the Genet that Genet presents as himself any more than I admire the unsavory Molloy impersonated by Beckett. I admire Genet because he writes books that won't let me forget who that Genet is. When Rebecca West was writing about Augustine, she said that his *Confessions* was too subjectively true to be objectively true. I think this is so in the first-person novels of Genet and Céline, as it is in Colette, books like *The Shackle* and *The Vagabond*. Gombrowicz has a novel called *Pornografia* in which he introduces himself as a character, using his own name—the better to implicate himself in certain highly dubious proceedings and bring the moral terror to life. Konwicki, another Pole, in his last two novels, *The Polish Complex* and *A Minor Apocalypse*, works to close the gap between the reader and the narrative by introducing "Konwicki" as the central character. He strengthens the illusion that the novel is true—and not to be discounted as "fiction"—by impersonating himself. It all goes back to Jack Benny. Need I add, however, that it's hardly a disinterested undertaking? Writing for me isn't a natural thing that I just keep doing, the way fish swim and birds fly. It's something that's done under a certain kind of provocation, a particular urgency. It's the transformation, through an elaborate impersonation, of a personal emergency into a public act (in both senses of that word). It can be a very trying spiritual exercise to siphon through your being qualities that are alien to your moral makeup—as trying for the writer as for the reader. You can wind up feeling more like a sword-swallower than a ventriloquist or impersonator. You sometimes use yourself very harshly in order to reach what is, literally speaking, beyond you. The impersonator can't afford to indulge the ordinary human instincts which direct people in what they want to present and what they want to hide.

If the novelist is an impersonator, then what about the autobiography? What is the relationship, for example, between the deaths of the parents, which are so important in the last two Zuckerman novels, and the death of your own parents?

Why not ask about the relationship between the death of my parents and the death of Gabe Wallach's mother, the germinating incident in my 1962 novel, *Letting Go*? Or ask about the death and funeral of the father, at the heart of my first published story, "The Day It Snowed," which appeared in the *Chicago Review* in 1955? Or ask about the death of Kepesh's mother, wife of the owner of a Catskill hotel, which is the turning point in *The Professor of Desire*? The terrible blow of the death of a parent is something I began writing about long before any parent of mine had died. Novelists are frequently as interested in what hasn't happened to them as in what has. What may be taken by the innocent for naked autobiography is, as I've been suggesting, more than likely mock-autobiography or hypothetical autobiography or autobiography grandiosely enlarged. We know about the people who walk into the police station and confess to crimes they haven't committed. Well, the false confession appeals to writers, too. Novelists are even interested in what happens to other people and, like liars and con men everywhere, will pretend that something dramatic or awful or hair-raising or splendid that happened to someone else actually happened to them. The physical particulars and moral circumstances of Zuckerman's mother's death have practically nothing to do with the death of my own mother. The death of the mother of one of my dearest friends—whose account of her suffering stuck in my mind long after he'd told me about it—furnished the most telling details for the mother's death in *The Anatomy Lesson*. The black cleaning woman who commiserates with Zuckerman in Miami Beach about his mother's death is modeled on the housekeeper of old friends in Philadelphia, a woman I haven't seen for ten years and who never laid eyes on anybody in my family but me. I was always entranced by her tangy style of speech, and when the right moment came, I used it. But the words in her mouth I invented. Olivia, the black eighty-three-year-old Florida cleaning woman, *c'est moi*.

As you well know, the intriguing biographical issue—and critical issue, for that matter—isn't that a writer will write about some of what has happened to him, but *how* he writes about it, which, when understood properly, takes us a long way to understanding *why* he writes about it. A more intriguing question is why and how he writes about what hasn't happened —how he feeds what's hypothetical or imagined into what's inspired and controlled by recollection, and how what's recollected spawns the overall fantasy. I suggest, by the way, that the best person to ask about the autobiographical relevance of the climactic death of the father in *Zuckerman Unbound* is my own father, who lives in Elizabeth, New Jersey. I'll give you his phone number.

Then what is the relationship between your experience of psychoanalysis and the use of psychoanalysis as a literary stratagem?

If I hadn't been analyzed I wouldn't have written *Portnoy's Complaint* as I wrote it, or *My Life as a Man* as I wrote it, nor would *The Breast* resemble itself. Nor would I resemble myself. The experience of psychoanalysis was probably more useful to me as a writer than as a neurotic, although there may be a false distinction there. It's an experience that I shared with tens of thousands of baffled people, and anything that powerful in the private domain that joins a writer to his generation, to his class, to his moment, is tremendously important for him, providing that afterwards he can separate himself enough to examine the experience objectively, imaginatively, in the writing clinic. You have to be able to become your doctor's doctor, even if only to write about patienthood, which was, certainly in part, a subject in *My Life as a Man*. Why patienthood interested me—and as far back as *Letting Go*, written four or five years before my own analysis—was because so many enlightened contemporaries had come to accept the view of themselves as patients, and the ideas of psychic disease, cure, and recovery. You're asking me about the relationship between art and life? It's like the relationship between the eight hundred or so hours that it took to be psychoanalyzed, and the eight or so hours that it would take to read *Portnoy's Complaint* aloud. Life is long and art is shorter.

Can you talk about your marriage?

It took place so long ago that I no longer trust my memory of it. The problem is complicated further by *My Life as a Man*, which diverges so dramatically in so many places from its origin in my own nasty situation that I'm hard put, some twenty-five years later, to sort out the invention of 1975 from the facts of 1959. You might as well ask the author of *The Naked and the Dead* what happened to him in the Philippines. I can only tell you that that was my time as an infantryman, and that *My Life as a Man* is the war novel I wrote some years after failing to receive the Distinguished Service Cross.

Do you have painful feelings on looking back?

Looking back I see these as fascinating years—as people of fifty often do contemplating the youthful adventure for which they paid with a decade of their lives a comfortingly long time ago. I was more aggressive then than I am today, some people were even said to be intimidated by me, but I was an easy target, all the same. We're easy targets at twenty-five, if only someone discovers the enormous bull's-eye.

And where was it?

Oh, where it can usually be found in self-confessed budding literary geniuses. My idealism. My romanticism. My passion to capitalize the L in life. I wanted something difficult and dangerous to happen to me. I wanted a hard time. Well, I got it. I'd come from a small, safe, relatively happy provincial background —my Newark neighborhood in the thirties and forties was just a Jewish Terre Haute—and I'd absorbed, along with the ambition and drive, the fears and phobias of my generation of American Jewish children. In my early twenties, I wanted to prove to myself that I wasn't afraid of all those things. It wasn't a mistake to want to prove that, even though, after the ball was over, I was virtually unable to write for three or four years. From 1962 to 1967 is the longest I've gone, since becoming a writer, without publishing a book. Alimony and recurrent court costs had bled me of every penny I could earn by teaching and writing, and, hardly into my thirties, I was thousands of dollars in debt to my friend and editor, Joe Fox. The loan was to help pay for my analysis, which I needed primarily to prevent me from going out and committing murder because of the alimony and court costs incurred for having served two years in a childless marriage. The image that teased me during those years was of a train that had been shunted onto the wrong track. In my early twenties, I had been zipping right along there, you know—on schedule, express stops only, final destination clearly in mind; and then suddenly I was on the wrong track, speeding off into the wilds. I'd ask myself, "How the hell do you get this thing back on the right track?" Well, you can't. I've continued to be surprised, over the years, whenever I discover myself, late at night, pulling into the wrong station.

But not getting back on the same track was a great thing for you, presumably.

John Berryman said that for a writer any ordeal that doesn't kill him is terrific. The fact that his ordeal did finally kill him doesn't make what he was saying wrong.

What do you feel about feminism, particularly the feminist attack on you?

What is it?

The force of the attack would be, in part, that the female characters are unsympathetically treated, for instance that Lucy Nelson in When She Was Good *is hostilely presented.*

Don't elevate that by calling it a "feminist" attack. That's just stupid reading. Lucy Nelson is a furious adolescent who wants a decent life. She is presented as better than her world and conscious of being better. She is confronted and opposed by men who typify deeply irritating types to many women. She is the protector of a passive, defenseless mother whose vulnerability drives her crazy. She happens to be raging against aspects of middle-class American life that the new militant feminism was to identify as the enemy only a few years after Lucy's appearance in print—hers might even be thought of as a case of premature feminist rage. *When She Was Good* deals with Lucy's struggle to free herself from the terrible disappointment engendered in a daughter by an irresponsible father. It deals with her hatred of the father he was and her yearning for the father he couldn't be. It would be sheer idiocy, particularly if this *were* a feminist attack, to contend that such powerful feelings of loss and contempt and shame do not exist in the daughters of drunks, cowards, and criminals. There is also the helpless Mama's boy Lucy marries, and her hatred of his incompetence and professional innocence. Is there no such thing in the world as marital hatred? That will come as news to all the rich divorce lawyers, not to mention Thomas Hardy and Gustave Flaubert. By the way, is Lucy's father treated "hostilely" because he's a drunk and a petty thief who ends up in jail? Is Lucy's husband treated "hostilely" because he happens to be a big baby? Is the uncle who tries to destroy Lucy "hostilely" treated because he's a brute? This is a novel about a wounded daughter who has more than sufficient cause to be enraged with the men in her life. She is only "hostilely" presented if it's an act of hostility to recognize that young women can be wounded and young women can be enraged. I'd bet there are even some enraged and wounded women who are feminists. *When She Was Good* is not serving the cause—that's true. The anger of this young woman isn't presented to be endorsed with a hearty "Right on!" that will move the populace to action. The nature of the anger is examined, as is the depth of the wound. So are the consequences of the anger, for Lucy as for everyone. I hate to have to be the one to say it, but the portrait isn't without its poignancy. I don't mean by poignancy what the compassionate book reviewers call "compassion." I mean you see the suffering that real rage is.

But supposing I say to you that nearly all the women in the books are there to obstruct, or to help, or to console the male characters. There's the woman who cooks and consoles and is sane and calming, or the other kind of woman, the dangerous maniac, the obstructor. They occur as means of helping or obstructing Kepesh or Zuckerman or Tarnopol. And that could be seen as a limited view of women.

Let's face it, some women who are sane also happen to know how to cook. So do some of the dangerous maniacs. Let's leave out the sin of cooking. A great book on the order of *Oblomov* could be written about a man allying himself with woman after woman who gorge him with marvelous meals, but I haven't written it. If your description of the "sane," "calm," and "consoling" woman applies to anyone, it's to Claire Ovington in *The Professor of Desire*, with whom Kepesh establishes a tender liaison some years after the breakup of his marriage. Now, I'd have no objection to your writing a novel about this relationship from the point of view of Claire Ovington— I'd be intrigued to see how she saw it—so why do you take a slightly critical tone about my writing the novel from the point of view of David Kepesh?

There's nothing wrong with the novel's being written from David Kepesh's point of view. What might cause difficulties for some readers is that Claire, and the other women in the novel, are there to help or hinder him.

I'm not pretending to give you anything other than his

sense of his life with this young woman. My book doesn't stand or fall on the fact that Claire Ovington is calm and sane, but on whether I am able to depict what calmness and sanity are like, and what it is to have a mate—and why it is one would want a mate—who possesses those and other virtues in abundance. She is also vulnerable to jealousy when Kepesh's ex-wife turns up uninvited, and she carries with her a certain sadness about her family background. She isn't there "as a means" of helping Kepesh. She *helps* him—and he helps her. *They are in love.* She is there because Kepesh has fallen in love with a sane and calm and consoling woman after having been unhappily married to a difficult and exciting woman he was unable to handle. Don't people do that? Someone more doctrinaire than you might tell me that the state of being in love, particularly of being passionately in love, is no basis for establishing permanent relationships between men and women. But people, even people of intelligence and experience, *will* do it—have done it and seem intent on going on doing it—and I am not interested in writing about what people *should* do for the good of the human race and pretending that's what they *do* do, but writing about what they do indeed do, lacking the programmatic efficiency of the infallible theorists. The irony of Kepesh's situation is that having found the calm and consoling woman he can live with, a woman of *numerous* qualities, he then finds his desire for her perversely seeping away, and realizes that unless this involuntary diminution of passion can be arrested, he'll become alienated from the best thing in his life. Doesn't that happen either? From what I hear this damn seeping away of desire happens all the time and is extremely distressing to the people involved. Look, I didn't invent the loss of desire, and I didn't invent the lure of passion, and I didn't invent sane companions, and I didn't invent maniacs. I'm sorry if my men don't have the correct feelings about women, or the universal range of feelings about women, or the feelings about women that it will be okay for men to have in 1995, but I do insist that there is some morsel of truth in my depiction of what it might be like for a man to be a Kepesh, or a Portnoy, or a breast.

Why have you never reused the character of Portnoy in another book, the way that you have used Kepesh and Zuckerman?

But I did use Portnoy in another book. *Our Gang* and *The Great American Novel* are Portnoy in another book. Portnoy wasn't a character for me, he was an explosion, and I wasn't finished exploding after *Portnoy's Complaint*. The first thing I wrote after *Portnoy's Complaint* was a long story called "On the Air" that appeared in Ted Solotaroff's *American Review*. John Updike was here a while ago and while we were all having dinner one night, he said, "How come you've never reprinted that story?" I said, "It's too disgusting." John laughed. He said, "It is, it's a truly disgusting story." And I said, "I didn't know what I was thinking about when I wrote it." And that is true to some degree—I didn't want to know; the idea was *not* to know. But I also did know. I looked in the arsenal and found another dynamite stick, and I thought, "Light the fuse and see what happens." I was trying to blow up more of myself. This phenomenon is known to students of literary survey courses as the writer changing his style. I was blowing up a lot of old loyalties and inhibitions, literary as well as personal. I think this may be why so many Jews were incensed by *Portnoy's Complaint*. It wasn't that they'd never heard about kids masturbating before, or about Jewish family fighting. It was, rather, that if they couldn't even control someone like me anymore, with all my respectable affiliations and credentials, all my Seriousness of Purpose, something had gone wrong. After all, I wasn't Abbie Hoffman or Lenny Bruce, I was a university teacher who had published in *Commentary*. But at the time it seemed to me that the next thing to be serious about was not being so goddamn serious. As Zuckerman reminds Appel, "Seriousness can be as stupid as anything else."

Weren't you also looking for a fight, writing Portnoy's Complaint?

I'd found a fight without looking for it long before that. They never really got off my ass for publishing *Goodbye, Columbus*, which was considered in some circles to be my *Mein Kampf*. Unlike Alexander Portnoy, my education in petit bourgeois morality didn't come at home, but after I'd left home and begun to publish my first short stories. My own household environment as a youngster was much closer to Zuckerman's than to Portnoy's. It had its constraints, but there was nothing resembling the censorious small-mindedness and shame-ridden xenophobia that I ran into from the official Jews who wanted me to shut up. The moral atmosphere of the Portnoy household, in its repressive aspects, owes a lot to the response of persistent voices within the official Jewish community to my debut. They did much to help make it seem auspicious.

You've been talking about the opposition to Portnoy's Complaint. *What about the recognition—how did its enormous success affect you?*

It was too big, on a larger and much crazier scale than I could begin to deal with, so I took off. A few weeks after publication, I boarded a bus at the Port Authority terminal for Saratoga Springs, and holed up at Yaddo, the writer's colony, for three months. Precisely what Zuckerman should have done after *Carnovsky*—but he hung around, the fool, and look what happened to him. He would have enjoyed Yaddo more than he enjoyed Alvin Pepler. But it made *Zuckerman Unbound* funnier keeping him in Manhattan, and it made my own life easier, not being there.

Do you dislike New York?

I lived there from 1962 until I moved to the country after *Portnoy's Complaint*, and I wouldn't trade those years for anything. New York *gave* me *Portnoy's Complaint* in a way. When I was living and teaching in Iowa City and Princeton, I didn't ever feel so free as I did in New York, in the sixties, to indulge myself in comic performance, on paper and with friends. There were raucous evenings with my New York friends, there was uncensored shamelessness in my psychoanalytic sessions, there was the dramatic, stagey atmosphere of the city itself in the years after Kennedy's assassination—all this inspired me to try out a new voice, a fourth voice, a less page-bound voice than the voice of *Goodbye, Columbus*, or of *Letting Go*, or of *When She Was Good*. So did the opposition to the war in Vietnam.

There's always something behind a book to which it has no seeming connection, something invisible to the reader which has helped to release the writer's initial impulse. I'm thinking about the rage and rebelliousness that were in the air, the vivid examples I saw around me of angry defiance and hysterical opposition. This gave me a few ideas for my act.

Did you feel you were part of what was going on in the sixties?

I felt the power of the life around me. I believed myself to be feeling the full consciousness of a place—this time New York—for the first time really since childhood. I was also, like others, receiving a stunning education in moral, political, and cultural possibilities from the country's eventful public life and from what was happening in Vietnam.

But you published a famous essay in Commentary *in 1960 called "Writing American Fiction" about the way that intellectuals or thinking people in America felt that they were living in a foreign country, a country in whose communal life they were not involved.*

Well, that's the difference between 1960 and 1968. (Being published in *Commentary* is another difference.) Alienated in America, a stranger to its pleasures and preoccupations—that was how many young people like me saw their situation in the fifties. It was a perfectly honorable stance, I think, shaped by our literary aspirations and modernist enthusiasms, the high-minded of the second post-immigrant generation coming into conflict with the first great eruption of postwar media garbage. Little did we know that some twenty years later the philistine ignorance on which we would have liked to turn our backs would infect the country like Camus's plague. Any satirist writing a futuristic novel who had imagined a President Reagan during the Eisenhower years would have been accused of perpetrating a piece of crude, contemptible, adolescent, anti-American wickedness, when, in fact, he would have succeeded, as prophetic sentry, just where Orwell failed; he would have seen that the grotesquerie to be visited upon the English-speaking world would not be an extension of the repressive Eastern totalitarian nightmare but a proliferation of the Western farce of media stupidity and cynical commercialism—American-style philistinism run amok. It wasn't Big Brother who'd be watching us from the screen, but we who'd be watching a terrifyingly powerful world leader with the soul of an amiable, soap opera grandmother, the values of a civic-minded Beverly Hills Cadillac dealer, and the historical background and intellectual equipment of a high school senior in a June Allyson musical.

What happened to you later, in the seventies? Did what was happening in the country continue to mean much to someone like you?

I have to remember what book I was writing and then I can remember what happened to me—though what was happening to me was largely the book I was writing. Nixon came and went in '73, and while Nixon was coming and going I was being driven quite crazy by *My Life as a Man*. In a way I had been writing that book on and off since 1964. I kept looking for a setting for the sordid scene in which Maureen buys a urine specimen from a poor pregnant black woman in order to get Tarnopol to think he's impregnated her. I thought of it first as a scene for *When She Was Good*, but it was all wrong for Lucy and Roy in Liberty Center. Then I thought it might go into *Portnoy's Complaint*, but it was too malevolent for that kind of comedy. Then I wrote cartons and cartons of drafts of what eventually turned out to be *My Life as a Man*—eventually, after I finally realized that my solution lay in the very problem I couldn't overcome: my inability to find the setting appropriate to the sordid event, rather than the sordid event itself, was really at the heart of the novel. Watergate made life interesting when I wasn't writing, but from nine to five every day I didn't think too much about Nixon or about Vietnam. I was trying to solve the problem of this book. When it seemed I never would, I stopped and wrote *Our Gang*; when I tried again and still couldn't write it, I stopped and wrote the baseball book; then while finishing the baseball book, I stopped to write *The Breast*. It was as though I were blasting my way through a tunnel to reach the novel that I couldn't write. Each of one's books *is* a blast, clearing the way for what's next. It's all one book you write anyway. At night you dream six dreams. But *are* they six dreams? One dream prefigures or anticipates the next, or somehow concludes what hasn't yet even been fully dreamed. Then comes the next dream, the corrective of the dream before—the alternative dream, the antidote dream—enlarging upon it, or laughing at it, or contradicting it, or trying just to get the dream *right*. You can go on trying all night long.

After Portnoy, *after leaving New York, you moved to the country. What about rural life? Obviously it was used as material in* The Ghost Writer.

I might never have become interested in writing about a reclusive writer if I hadn't first had my own small taste of E. I. Lonoff's thirty-five years of rural splendor. I need something solid under my feet to kick off my imagination. But aside from giving me a sense of the Lonoffs' lives, the country existence hasn't offered anything as yet in the way of subject. Probably it never will and I should get the hell out. Only I happen to love living there, and I can't make *every* choice conform to the needs of my work.

What about England, where you spend part of each year? Is that a possible source of fiction?

Ask me twenty years from now. That's about how long it took Isaac Singer to get enough of Poland out of his system—and to let enough of America in—to begin, little by little, as a writer, to see and depict his upper Broadway cafeterias. If you don't know the fantasy life of a country, it's hard to write fiction about it that isn't just description of the decor, human and otherwise. Little things trickle through when I see the country dreaming out loud—in the theater, at an election, during the Falklands crisis, but I know nothing really about what means what to people here. It's very hard for me to understand who people are, even when they tell me, and I don't even know if that's *because* of who they are or because of me. I don't know who is impersonating what, if I'm necessarily seeing the real thing or just a fabrication, nor can I easily see where the two overlap. My perceptions are clouded by the fact that I speak the language. I believe I know what's being said, you see, even if I don't. Worst of all, I don't hate anything here. What a relief it is to have no culture-grievances, not to have to hear the sound of one's voice taking positions and having opinions and recounting all that's wrong! What bliss—but for the writing that's no asset. Nothing drives me crazy here, and a writer *has* to be driven crazy to help him to *see*. A writer needs his poisons. The antidote to his poisons is often a book. Now if I *had* to live here, if for some reason I were forbidden ever to return to America, if my position and my personal well-being were suddenly to become permanently bound up with England, well, what was maddening and meaningful might begin to come into focus, and yes, in about the year 2005, maybe 2010, little by little I'd stop writing about Newark and I would dare to set a story at a table in a wine bar on Kensington Park Road. A story about an elderly exiled foreign writer, in this instance reading not the *Jewish Daily Forward* but the *Herald Tribune*.

In these last three books, the Zuckerman novels, there has been a reiteration of the struggle with Jewishness and Jewish criticism. Why do you think these books go over the past as much as they do? Why is that happening now?

In the early seventies, I began to be a regular visitor to Czechoslovakia. I went to Prague every spring and took a little crash course in political repression. I'd only known repression firsthand in somewhat more benign and covert forms—as psychosexual constraint or as social restriction. I knew less about anti-Semitic repression from personal experience than I did about the repressions Jews practiced upon themselves, and upon one another, as a consequence of the history of anti-Semitism. Portnoy, you remember, considers himself just such a practicing Jew. Anyway, I became highly attuned to the differences between the writer's life in totalitarian Prague and in freewheeling New York, and I decided, after some initial uncertainty, to focus on the unreckoned consequences of a life in art in the world that I knew best. I realized that there were already many wonderful and famous stories and novels by Henry James and Thomas Mann and James Joyce about the life of the artist, but none I knew of about the comedy that an artistic vocation can turn out to be in the U.S.A. When Thomas Wolfe tackled the subject he was rather rhapsodic. Zuckerman's struggle with Jewishness and Jewish criticism is seen in the context of his comical career as an American writer, ousted by his family, alienated from his fans, and finally at odds with his own nerve endings. The Jewish quality of books like mine doesn't really reside in their subject matter. Talking about Jewishness hardly interests me at all. It's a kind of sensibility that makes, say, *The Anatomy Lesson* Jewish, if anything does: the nervousness, the excitability, the arguing, the dramatizing, the indignation, the obsessiveness, the touchiness, the play-acting—above all the *talking*. The talking and the shouting. Jews will go on, you know. It isn't what it's talking *about* that makes a book Jewish—it's that the book won't shut up. The book won't leave you alone. Won't let up. Gets too close. "Listen, listen—that's only the half of it!" I knew what I was doing when I broke Zuckerman's jaw. For a Jew a broken jaw is a terrible tragedy. It was to avoid this that so many of us went into teaching rather than prizefighting.

Why is Milton Appel, the good, high-minded Jew who was a guru for Zuckerman in his early years, a punching-bag in The Anatomy Lesson, *someone that Zuckerman wants to desanctify?*

If I were not myself, if someone else had been assigned the role of being Roth and writing his books, I might very well, in this other incarnation, have been his Milton Appel.

Is Zuckerman's rage at Milton Appel the expression of a kind of guilt on your part?

Guilt? Not at all. As a matter of fact, in an earlier draft of the book, Zuckerman and his young girlfriend Diana took exactly opposite positions in their argument about Appel. She, with all her feisty inexperience, said to Zuckerman, "Why do you let him push you around, why do you take this shit sitting down?" and Zuckerman, the older man, said to her, "Don't be ridiculous, dear, calm down, he doesn't matter." There was the real autobiographical scene, and it had no life at all. I had to absorb the rage into the main character even if my own rage on this topic had long since subsided. By being true to life I was actually ducking the issue. So I reversed their positions, and had the twenty-year-old college girl telling Zuckerman to grow up, and gave Zuckerman the tantrum. Much more fun. I wasn't going to get anywhere with a Zuckerman as eminently reasonable as myself.

So your hero always has to be enraged or in trouble or complaining.

My hero has to be in a state of vivid transformation or radical displacement. "I am not what I am—I am, if anything, what I am not!" The litany begins something like that.

How conscious are you as you are writing of whether you are moving from a third- to a first-person narrative?

It's not conscious or unconscious—the movement is spontaneous.

But how does it feel, to be writing in the third person as opposed to the first person?

How does it feel looking through a microscope, when you adjust the focus? Everything depends upon how close you want to bring the naked object to the naked eye. And vice versa. Depends on what you want to magnify, and to what power.

But do you free yourself in certain ways by putting Zuckerman in the third person?

I free myself to say about Zuckerman what it would be inappropriate for him to say about himself in quite the same way. The irony would be lost in the first person, or the comedy; I can introduce a note of gravity that might be jarring coming from him. The shifting within a single narrative from the one voice to the other is how a reader's moral perspective is determined. It's something like this that we all want to do in ordinary conversation when we employ the indefinite pronoun "one" in speaking of ourselves. Using "one" places your observation in a looser relationship to the self that's uttering it. Look, sometimes it's more telling to let him speak for himself, sometimes it's more telling to speak about him; sometimes it's more telling to narrate obliquely, sometimes not. *The Ghost Writer* is narrated in the first person, probably because what's being described is largely a world Zuckerman's discovered outside of himself, the book of a young explorer. The older and more scarred he gets, the more *inward*-looking he gets, the further out *I* have to get. The crisis of solipsism he suffers in *The Anatomy Lesson* is better seen from a bit of a distance.

Do you direct yourself as you are writing to make distinctions between what is spoken and what is narrative?

I don't "direct" myself. I respond to what seem the liveliest possibilities. There's no necessary balance to be achieved between what is spoken and what is narrated. You go with what's alive. Two thousand pages of narrative and six lines of dialogue may be just the ticket for one writer, and two thousand pages of dialogue and six lines of narrative the solution for another.

Do you ever take long chunks that have been dialogue and make them into narrative, or the other way around?

Sure. I did that with the Anne Frank section of *The Ghost Writer*. I had trouble getting that right. When I began, in the third person, I was somehow *revering* the material. I was taking a high elegiac tone in telling the story of Anne Frank surviving and coming to America. I didn't know where I was going so I began by doing what you're supposed to do when writing the life of a saint. It was the tone appropriate to hagiography. Instead of Anne Frank gaining new meaning within the context of my story, I was trying to draw from the ready store of stock emotions that everybody is supposed to have about her. It's what even good actors sometimes will do during the first weeks of rehearsing a play—gravitate to the conventional form of presentation, cling to the cliché while anxiously waiting for something authentic to take hold. In retrospect, my difficulties look somewhat bizarre, because just what Zuckerman was fighting against, I was in fact succumbing to—the officially authorized and most consoling legend. I tell you, no one who later complained that in *The Ghost Writer* I had abused the memory of Anne Frank would have batted an eye had I let those banalities out into the world. That would have been just fine; I might even have got a citation. But I couldn't have given myself any prizes for it. The difficulties of telling a Jewish story—How should it be told? In what tone? To whom should it be told? To what end? Should it be told at all?—was finally to become *The Ghost Writer*'s theme. But before it became a theme, it apparently had to be an ordeal. It often happens, at least with me, that the struggles that generate a book's moral life are naively enacted upon the body of the book during the early, uncertain stages of writing. That *is* the ordeal, and it ended when I took that whole section and recast it in the first person—Anne Frank's story told by Amy Bellette. The victim wasn't herself going to talk about her plight in the voice of "The March of Time." She hadn't in the *Diary*, so why should she in life? I didn't want this section to *appear* as first-person narration, but I knew that by passing it through the first-person sieve, I stood a good chance of getting rid of this terrible tone, which wasn't hers, but mine. I did get rid of it. The impassioned cadences, the straining emotions, the somber, overdramatized, archaic diction—I cleared it all out, thanks to Amy Bellette. Rather straightforwardly, I then cast the section *back* into the third person, and then I was able to get to work on it—to write rather than to rhapsodize or eulogize.

How do you think you have influenced the environment, the culture, as a writer?

Not at all. If I had followed my early college plans to become an attorney, I don't see where it would matter to the culture.

Do you say that with bitterness or with glee?

Neither. It's a fact of life. In an enormous commercial society that demands complete freedom of expression, the culture is a maw. Recently, the first American novelist to receive a special Congressional Gold Medal for his "contribution to the nation" was Louis L'Amour. It was presented to him at the White House

by the President. The only other country in the world where
such a writer would receive his government's highest award is
the Soviet Union. In a totalitarian state, however, *all* culture is
dictated by the regime; fortunately we Americans live in Reagan's and not Plato's Republic, and aside from their stupid
medal, culture is almost entirely ignored. And that is preferable
by far. As long as those on top keep giving the honors to Louis
L'Amour and couldn't care less about anything else, everything
will be just fine. When I was first in Czechoslovakia, it occurred
to me that I work in a society where as a writer everything goes
and nothing matters, while for the Czech writers I met in
Prague, nothing goes and everything matters. This isn't to say I
wished to change places. I didn't envy them their persecution
and the way in which it heightens their social importance. I
didn't even envy them their seemingly more valuable and serious
themes. The trivialization, in the West, of much that's deadly
serious in the East is itself a subject, one requiring considerable
imaginative ingenuity to transform into compelling fiction. To
write a serious book that doesn't signal its seriousness with the
rhetorical cues or thematic gravity that's traditionally associated
with seriousness is a worthy undertaking too. To do justice
to a spiritual predicament that is *not* blatantly shocking and
monstrously horrible, that does *not* elicit universal compassion,
or occur on a large historical stage, or on the grandest scale of
twentieth-century suffering—well, that's the lot that has fallen
to those who write where everything goes and nothing matters.
I recently heard the critic George Steiner, on English television,
denouncing contemporary Western literature as utterly worthless and without quality, and claiming that the great documents
of the human soul, the masterpieces, could only arise from souls
being crushed by regimes like those in Czechoslovakia. I wonder then why all the writers I know in Czechoslovakia loathe the
regime and passionately wish that it would disappear from the
face of the earth. Don't they understand, as Steiner does, that
this is their chance to be great? Sometimes one or two writers
with colossal brute strength do manage, miraculously, to survive
and, taking the system as their subject, to make art of a very
high order out of their persecution. But most of them who remain sealed up inside totalitarian states are, as writers, throttled

by the system. That system doesn't make masterpieces; it makes coronaries, ulcers, and asthma, it makes alcoholics, it makes depressives, it makes bitterness and desperation and insanity. The writers are intellectually disfigured, spiritually demoralized, physically sickened, and culturally bored. Frequently they are silenced completely. Nine-tenths of the best of them will never do their best work just because of the system. The writers nourished by this system are the party hacks. When such a system prevails for two or three generations, relentlessly grinding away at a community of writers for twenty, thirty, or forty years, the obsessions become fixed, the language grows stale, the readership slowly dies out from starvation, and the existence of a national literature of originality, variety, vibrancy (which is very different from the brute survival of a single powerful voice) is nearly impossible. A literature that has the misfortune of remaining isolated underground for too long will inevitably become provincial, backwards, even naive, despite the fund of dark experience that may inspire it. By contrast, our work here hasn't been deprived of authenticity because as writers we haven't been stomped on by a totalitarian government. I don't know of any Western writer, aside from George Steiner, who is so grandiosely and sentimentally deluded about human suffering—and "masterpieces"—that he's come back from behind the Iron Curtain thinking himself devalued because he hasn't had to contend with such a wretched intellectual and literary environment. If the choice is between Louis L'Amour and our literary freedom and our extensive, lively national literature on the one hand, and Solzhenitsyn and that cultural desert and crushing suppression on the other, I'll take L'Amour.

But don't you feel powerless as a writer in America?

Writing novels is not the road to power. I don't believe that, in my society, novels effect serious changes in anyone other than the handful of people who are writers, whose own novels are of course seriously affected by other novelists' novels. I can't see anything like that happening to the ordinary reader, nor would I expect it to.

What do novels do then?

To the ordinary reader? Novels provide readers with something to read. At their best writers change the *way* readers read. That seems to me the only realistic expectation. It also seems to me quite enough. Reading novels is a deep and singular pleasure, a gripping and mysterious human activity that does not require any more moral or political justification than sex.

But are there no other aftereffects?

You asked me if I thought my fiction had changed anything in the culture and the answer is no. Sure there's been some scandal, but people are scandalized all the time; it's a way of life for them. It doesn't mean a thing. If you ask if I *want* my fiction to change anything in the culture, the answer is still no. What I want is to possess my readers while they are reading my book—if I can, to possess them in ways that other writers don't. Then let them return, just as they were, to a world where everybody else is working to change, persuade, tempt, and control them. The best readers come to fiction to be free of all that noise, to have set loose in them the consciousness that's otherwise conditioned and hemmed in by all that *isn't* fiction. This is something that every child, smitten by books, understands immediately, though it's not at all a childish idea about the importance of reading.

Last question. How would you describe yourself? What do you think you are like, compared with those vividly transforming heroes of yours?

I am like somebody who is trying vividly to transform himself out of himself and into his vividly transforming heroes. I am very much like somebody who spends all day writing.

Interview on Zuckerman

Many critics and reviewers persist in writing about Roth rather than his fiction. Why this persistence after all these years?

If that's so, it may have to do with the intensity with which my fiction has focused upon the self-revealing dilemmas of a single central character whose biography, in certain obvious details, overlaps with mine and who is then assumed "to be" me.

The Ghost Writer was automatically described in the press as "autobiographical" because the narrator, Nathan Zuckerman, is an American-Jewish writer my age, born in Newark, whose earliest writing elicits a protest from some Jewish readers. But, as a matter of fact, that about constitutes the similarity between my history and Zuckerman's in that book. The unsettling opposition from his father that young Zuckerman confronts and that propels the moral plot of *The Ghost Writer* I happen to have been spared; the intelligent, fatherly interest taken in his work by a renowned older writer whose New England houseguest he's lucky enough to be at twenty-three resembles no experience of mine starting out in the fifties; nor have I ever met a woman to whom I have been drawn because she resembled Anne Frank or whom I mentally transformed into Anne Frank and endowed with her status in order to try to clear myself of Jewish charges of self-hatred and anti-Semitism.

Though some readers may have trouble disentangling my life from Zuckerman's, *The Ghost Writer*—along with the rest of *Zuckerman Bound* and *The Counterlife*—is an imaginary biography, an invention stimulated by themes in my experience but the result of a writing process a long way from the methods, let alone the purposes, of autobiography. If an avowed autobiographer transformed *his* personal themes into a detailed narrative distinct and independent from his own day-to-day history, peopled with imaginary characters conversing in words never spoken, given meaning by a sequence of events that had

An interview with Asher Z. Milbauer and Donald G. Watson for their book *Reading Philip Roth* (St. Martin's Press, 1988).

never taken place, we wouldn't be surprised if he was charged with representing as his real life what was an outright lie.

May I quote John Updike? Asked about my Zuckerman books, he said to an interviewer, "Roth's inventing what looks like a *roman-à-clef* but is not."

But if your books are misread, other than by John Updike, isn't that more or less the fate of most good writing? Don't you expect to be misread?

That novelists serve readers in ways that they can't anticipate or take into account while writing doesn't come as news to someone who spent eight years with *Zuckerman Bound*. That's the story told on nearly every one of its 800 pages, from the opening scene, when Nathan the budding writer enters Lonoff's living room seeking absolution from sins committed in his juvenilia against his family's self-esteem, to its conclusion on the day that, as an established writer in his forties, he is forced to surrender to the Prague police the wholly harmless Yiddish stories that they've decided to impound as subversive.

The only reading resembling the ideal reading that a writer yearns for is the writer's reading of himself. Every other reading is something of a surprise—to use your word, a "misreading," if what's meant isn't reading that's shallow and stupid but that's fixed in its course by the reader's background, ideology, sensibility, etc.

To be misread in any way that bears thinking about, however, a writer has to be *read* as well. But *those* misreadings, conferred by skillful, cultivated, widely read misreaders can be instructive, even when bizarre—witness Lawrence on American literature; or Freud, the all-time most influential misreader of imaginative literature. So are those misreaders the censors influential, though for other reasons. And *are* the Soviet censors necessarily misreading, in Solzhenitsyn's fiction, his political aims? Though censors may appear to be the most narrow-minded and perverse of all misreaders, at times they may be more discerning about the socially injurious implications of a book than the most tolerantly open-minded audience.

Serious misreading has little to do with a text's impenetrability; geniuses misread nursery rhymes—all that's required is for the genius to have his own fish to fry.

In the light of this, what about an audience? Do you think you have one, and, if so, what does it mean to you?

I've had two audiences, a general audience and a Jewish audience. I have virtually no sense of my impact on the general audience, nor do I really know who these people are. By a general audience I don't refer to anything vast. Despite the popularity of *Portnoy's Complaint*, the number of Americans who may have read, with real attention, half of my books—as opposed to those who have read one or two—can't number more than 50,000, if that. I don't think anymore about them when I'm at work than they think about me when they're at work. They're as remote as the onlookers are to a chess player concentrating on the board and his opponent's game. On the other hand, an unknowable audience of 50,000 judicious readers (or inventive misreaders) whose concentration I freely command is a great satisfaction. The enigmatic interchange between a silent book and a silent reader has struck me, ever since childhood, as a unique transaction. As far as I'm concerned, it's what the public side of the novelist's vocation comes down to. It's all that counts.

Counterbalancing the general audience has been a Jewish audience, affording me the best of both worlds. With my Jewish audience I feel intensely their expectations, disdain, delight, criticism, their wounded self-love, their healthy curiosity, their outrage—what I imagine the writer's awareness of an audience is in the capital of a small country where culture is thought to mean as much as politics, where culture *is* politics: some little nation perpetually engaged in evaluating its purpose, contemplating its meaning, joking away its oddities, and continually sensing itself imperiled in one way or another.

Why do you irritate Jews so much?

Do I any longer? Certainly "so much" must be an exaggeration by now. After fifteen books I may have become much less irritating than the Zuckerman I've depicted, largely because the Jewish generation that didn't go for me is by now less influential and the rest are no longer ashamed, if they ever were, of how Jews behave in my fiction.

Because it *was* shame—theirs—that had a lot to do with that conflict. But now that everybody's more confident about the right of Jews to have sexual thoughts and engage in authorized and even unauthorized erotic practices, I think that stuff is over. On the whole, Jewish readers aren't quite so responsive any longer to other people's ideas (real or imaginary) of what constitutes socially acceptable Jewish behavior and don't appear to be obsessively worried that damaging perceptions of them can be indelibly imprinted on the public mind through a work of fiction and that these will set off an anti-Semitic reaction. American Jews are far less intimidated by Gentile disapproval than they were when I began publishing in the 1950s, more sophisticated about anti-Semitism and its causes, and less hedged in by suffocating concepts of normalcy.

This is because they are not so preoccupied as they once were with the problematic nature of assimilation and are justifiably less troubled by ethnic disparities in the new American society of the last fifteen years—a society created by a massive influx of over twenty million people far less assimilable than themselves, about eighty-five percent of them non-Europeans, whose visible presence has reestablished polygenesis as a glaring and unalterable fact of our national life. When the cream of Miami is the Cuban bourgeoisie, and the best students at M.I.T. are Chinese, and not a candidate can stand before a Democratic presidential convention without flashing his racial or ethnic credentials—when *everybody* sticks out and doesn't seem to mind—perhaps Jews are less likely to worry about *their* sticking out, less likely *to* stick out.

In addition to the shame I fomented there was the menace I was said to pose by confirming the beliefs of the committed Jew-hater and mobilizing the anti-Semitism latent in the Gentile population generally. Some years ago, the eminent scholar of Jewish mysticism Gershom Scholem published an attack on *Portnoy's Complaint* in an Israeli newspaper, predicting that not I but the Jews would pay the price for that book's impudence. I learned about Scholem's article only recently in Israel—a university professor from Tel Aviv summarized Scholem's argument for me and asked what I thought of it. I said that history had proved Scholem wrong: more than fifteen years had passed since the publication of *Portnoy's Complaint* and not a single Jew had paid for the book anything other than the few dollars it cost in the bookstore. The professor's reply? "Not yet," he said, "but the Gentiles will make use of it when the time is right."

The Jews I still irritate are for the most part like the Israeli professor; for them the danger of abetting anti-Semitism overrides every other consideration.

Of course there must be many Jews as well as Gentiles who don't care for my books because they think that I don't know how to write fiction. Nothing wrong with that. I'm pointing rather to a psychological or ideological orientation that *had* to make *Portnoy's Complaint* anathema to a certain group of readers. Though the example of the Israeli professor might seem to suggest otherwise, this particular Jewish orientation seems to me to be disappearing just *because* of the existence of Israel and its effect upon American Jewish self-confidence.

I'm not referring to the pride that may be inspired in American Jews by Israeli military might. It's not images of Israel triumphant or naïve notions of Israeli infallibility that have signaled to American Jews that they needn't any longer be too tightly constrained by protective self-censorship, but just the opposite, their awareness of Israel as an openly discordant, divisive society with conflicting political goals and a self-questioning conscience, a Jewish society that makes no effort to conceal its imperfections from itself and that couldn't conceal them from the world if it wanted to. The tremendous publicity to which Israeli Jews are exposed—and to which they're not unaddicted—has many causes, not all of them benign, but certainly one effect of unashamed Israeli self-divulging has been to lead American Jews to associate a whole spectrum of behavior with which they themselves may have preferred not to be publicly identified, with people perceived as nothing if *not* Jews.

To move to a more general subject, do you think of fiction as a way of knowing the world or of changing the world?

As a way of knowing the world as it's not otherwise known. A lot can be known about the world without the help of fiction, but nothing engenders fiction's kind of knowing because nothing makes the world *into* fiction. What you know from Flaubert or Beckett or Dostoyevsky is never a great deal more than you may have known before about adultery or loneliness or murder—what you know is *Madame Bovary*, *Molloy*, and *Crime and Punishment*. Fiction derives from that unique mode of scrutiny, imagination, and its wisdom is inseparable *from* imagination. The intelligence of even the most intelligent novelist is often debased, and at the least distorted, when it's isolated from the novel that embodies it; without intending to, the novel is made to address the mind alone rather than suffusing a wider consciousness, and however much prestige it may be accorded as "thought," it ceases to be a way of knowing the world as it's not otherwise known. Detached from the fiction, a novelist's wisdom can even be just so much talk.

Novels *do* influence behavior, shape opinion, alter conduct—a book can, of course, change somebody's life—but that's because of a choice made by the reader to use the fiction for purposes of his own (purposes that might appal the novelist) and not because the novel is incomplete without the reader's taking action.

You sound as though you really prefer that fiction should change nothing.

Everything changes everything—nobody argues with that. My point is that whatever changes fiction may appear to inspire have usually to do with the goals of the reader and not of the writer.

There is something that writers do have the power to change and that they work to change every day, and that's writing. A writer's responsibility is to the integrity of his own kind of discourse.

Do you feel that the importance, if not even the integrity, of fictional discourse is threatened by rivals like film and television and the headlines, which propose entirely different ways of knowing

*the world? Haven't the popular media all but usurped the scruti-
nizing function that you attribute to the literary imagination?*

Fiction that has a scrutinizing function isn't merely threatened, it's been all but swept away in America as a serious way
of knowing the world, almost as much within the country's
small cultural elite as among the tens of millions for whom
television is almost the only source of knowing anything. Animated talk about tenth-rate movies by first-rate people has
practically displaced discussion of any comparable length or
intensity about a book. Talking about movies in the relaxed,
impressionistic way that movies invite being talked about is
not only the unliterate man's literary life but the literary life of
the literate as well. It appears to be easier for even the
best-educated people to articulate how they know the world
from a pictured story than for them to confidently tell you
what they make of a verbal narrative.

The popular media have usurped literature's scrutinizing
function—usurped it and trivialized it. The momentum of the
bulk of American mass media is toward the trivialization of
everything. The trivialization of everything is of no less importance for Americans than repression is for Eastern Europeans,
and if the problem has not achieved the same notoriety at PEN
as political repression, it's because it flows out of political *freedom*. The threat to a civilized America isn't the censorship of
this or that book in some atypical school district somewhere;
it's not the government's attempt to suppress or falsify this or
that piece of information. It's the *superabundance* of information, the circuits *burgeoning* with information—it's the censorship of *nothing*. The trivialization of everything results from
exactly what they do *not* have in Eastern Europe or the Soviet
Union—the freedom to say anything and to sell anything
however one chooses.

There are now even writers in the West tempted to think
that it might really be better for their work if they were oppressed in Moscow or Warsaw rather than free in London or
Paris. It's as though without an authoritarian environment
imaginative possibilities are curtailed and one's literary seriousness is open to question. Unfortunately for writers who may
be afflicted with such longings, the intellectual situation for

thinking Americans in no telling way mirrors, parallels, or resembles what is horrifying for thoughtful people in the Soviet orbit. There is, however, a looming American menace that evokes its own forms of deprivation, and that's the creeping trivialization of everything ("dumbing down" it's sometimes loosely called) in a society where freedom of expression is anything but compressed.

The Czech writer Josef Škvorecký, who now lives in Toronto, has said, "To be a bad writer in Eastern Europe, you *really* have to be bad." He means that in those countries the political origins of people's suffering are plainly visible in everyday life and the predicament is constantly staring them in the face; personal misfortune is inevitably colored by politics and history, and no individual drama is seemingly without wider social implications. What Škvorecký wryly suggests is that there is almost a chemical affinity between the consequences of oppression and the genre of the novel; what I'm saying is that in the less graspable consequences of our unprecedented Western freedom there may well be a subject for imaginative scrutiny of no less gravity. Our society doesn't lack for imaginative possibilities because it isn't plagued by the secret police. That it isn't always as easy to be interesting in our part of the world as it is in Škvorecký's occupied country may only mean that to be a good writer in the West and of the West you *really* have to be good.

Was it not a problem for your generation of writers to establish the seriousness of your fiction without resorting to or falling back upon the established conventions of seriousness, be they the realism of James or the modernism of Joyce?

That's a problem for every generation. Ambitious young writers are often tempted to imitate those verified by authority; the influence of an established writer on a beginning writer has usually to do with the search for credentials. Finding a voice and a subject of one's own, however, entails making fiction that may well prompt the writer's first readers to think, "But he can't be serious," as opposed to "This is very serious indeed." The lesson of modernism isn't encapsulated in a technique that's "Joycean" or a vision that's "Kafkaesque"; it

originates in the revolutionary sense of seriousness that's exemplified in the fiction of Joyce, Kafka, Beckett, Céline, fiction
that to an unknowing reader probably bears the earmark less
of seriousness than of high eccentricity and antic obsession. By
now the methods of these outlandish writers have themselves
become the conventions of seriousness, but that in no way di-
lutes their message, which isn't "Make it new," but "Make it
serious in the least likely way."

Has the "least likely way" for you been your kind of comedy?

Comedy has often been my most likely way, though it did require time to work up confidence to take the instinct for comedy
seriously, to let it contend with my earnestness and finally get a
hearing. It's not that I don't trust my uncomic side or that I don't
have one; it's that the uncomic side more or less resembles everyone else's. Up to now, it's usually been through the expressive
gradations of comedy that I can best imagine what I know.

Yet isn't Zuckerman, in The Anatomy Lesson, *afraid that he is
not "serious" enough, afraid that for all his physical ailments he
is not "suffering" sufficiently? Isn't that why he wants to enroll in
medical school and, in* The Prague Orgy, *travels to Eastern
Europe?*

His comic predicament results from the repeated attempts to
escape his comic predicament. Comedy is what Zuckerman is
bound by—what's laughable in *Zuckerman Bound* is his insatiable desire to be a serious man taken seriously by all the serious men like his father and his brother and Milton Appel. A
stage direction that appears in *The Prague Orgy* could have
been the trilogy's title: *Enter Zuckerman, a serious person.*
Coming to terms with the profane dimension of what he had
assumed to be one of the world's sacred professions is for him
a terrible ordeal. His quest for superseriousness is what the
comedy's *about.*
Zuckerman Bound opens with a pilgrimage to the patron
saint of seriousness, E. I. Lonoff; it ends, as you point out, at
the shrine of suffering, Kafka's occupied Prague. Imagining
himself married to Anne Frank is the earliest escape that he

attempts to contrive from what first challenges his youthful illusions about a dignified role in the world. Judge Leopold Wapter, Alvin Pepler, the Czech secret police, a crippling, unexplained pain in the neck—all are examples of impious life encroaching upon that seriousness he had once believed inherent to his calling. But what most successfully subverts the calling's esteem is his own sizeable talent for depicting the impious: it's Zuckerman the *writer* who repeatedly gives his dignity a hard time.

The denouement of the trilogy begins midway through the third volume, when, on the way to Chicago to become a doctor —for those Jews who most disapprove of him, the embodiment of professional seriousness—Zuckerman adopts the disguise of a professional pornographer and, abandoning whatever claim he believes he still may have to be taken seriously, transforms himself into a vessel of the profane. It's a long way from pretending to be affianced to Anne Frank in E. I. Lonoff's sanctum sanctorum to proclaiming himself publisher of *Lickety Split*.

I realize that this sort of ordeal, as suffered by my high-minded heroes, looks like an old, obsessional theme if you think of Gabe Wallach in *Letting Go* or David Kepesh in *The Breast* and *The Professor of Desire*. The ordeal of an unhallowed existence is also what Portnoy's complaining about.

Are you complaining about it—is that why it's an old, obsessional theme?

Obsessional themes evolve from astonishment as much as anything else. A writer is beset not so much by the theme as by an underlying *naïveté* in the face of it. The novelist suffers from genuine ignorance of his obsessional theme. He lays siege to it time and again because the obsessional theme is the one he least understands.

We realize that you are reluctant to appear to be explicating a book prior to its publication. However, without "explaining" it away, can you comment generally on the unusual form for The Counterlife, *which is certainly unlike anything you've done before?*

Normally there is a contract between the author and the reader that gets torn up at the end of the book. In this book the contract gets torn up at the end of each chapter: a character who is dead and buried is suddenly alive, a character who is assumed to be alive is, in fact, dead. This is not the ordinary Aristotelian narrative that readers are accustomed to reading or that I am accustomed to writing. It isn't that the book lacks a beginning, middle, and ending; there are too *many* beginnings, middles, and endings. It is a book where you never get to the bottom of things—rather than concluding with all the questions answered, it leaves everything suddenly open to question. Because one's original reading is always being challenged and the book progressively undermines its own fictional assumptions, the reader is constantly cannibalizing his own reactions.

In many ways it's everything that people don't want in a novel. Primarily what they want is a story in which they can be made to believe; otherwise they don't wish to be bothered. They agree, in accordance with the standard author-reader contract, to believe in the story they are being told—and then in *The Counterlife* they are being told a contradictory story. "I'm interested in what's going on," says the reader, "only now, suddenly, there are three things going on. Which is real and which is false? Which are you asking me to believe in? Why do you bother me like this?"

Which is real and which is false? All are equally real and equally false.

Which are you asking me to believe in? All/none.

Why do you bother me like this? Because there is nothing unusual about somebody's changing his story. People constantly change their story—one runs into that every day. There is nothing "modernist," "postmodernist," or the least bit avant-garde about it: we are writing fictitious versions of our lives all the time, contradictory but mutually entangling stories that, however subtly or grossly falsified, constitute our hold on reality and are the closest thing we have to the truth.

Why do I bother you like this? Because life doesn't necessarily have a course, a simple sequence, a predictable pattern. The bothersome approach is intended to dramatize just that. The narratives are all awry but they have a unity; it is expressed in the title—the idea of a counterlife, of counterlives, counter-living. Life, like the novelist, has a powerful transforming urge.

TWO

SHOP TALK

A Writer and His Colleagues and Their Work

For my friend C. H. Huvelle
1916–2000

CONTENTS

Primo Levi

[1986]

O N THE Friday in September 1986 that I arrived in Turin to renew a conversation with Primo Levi that we had begun one afternoon in London the spring before, I asked to be shown around the paint factory where he'd been employed as a research chemist and, afterward, until retirement, as manager. Altogether the company employs fifty people, mainly chemists who work in the laboratories and skilled laborers on the floor of the plant. The production machinery, the row of storage tanks, the laboratory building, the finished product in man-sized containers ready to be shipped, the reprocessing facility that purifies the wastes—all of it is encompassed in four or five acres seven miles from Turin. The machines that are drying resin and blending varnish and pumping off pollutants are never distressingly loud, the yard's acrid odor—the smell, Levi told me, that clung to his clothing for two years after his retirement—is by no means disgusting, and the thirty-yard Dumpster loaded to the brim with the black sludgy residue of the antipolluting process isn't particularly unsightly. It is hardly the world's ugliest industrial environment, but a long way nonetheless from those sentences suffused with mind that are the hallmark of Levi's autobiographical narratives.

However far from the spirit of the prose, the factory is clearly close to his heart; taking in what I could of the noise, the stink, the mosaic of pipes and vats and tanks and dials, I remembered Faussone, the skilled rigger in *The Monkey's Wrench*, saying to Levi, who calls Faussone "my alter ego," "I have to tell you, being around a work site is something I enjoy."

As we walked through the open yard to the laboratory, a simply designed two-story building constructed during Levi's managerial days, he told me, "I have been cut off from the factory for twelve years. This will be an adventure for *me*." He said he believed that nearly everybody once working with him was now retired or dead, and indeed, those few still there whom he ran into seemed to strike him as specters. "It's another ghost," he whispered to me after someone from the central office that had once been his emerged to welcome him back. On our way to the section of the laboratory where raw materials are scrutinized before moving to production, I asked Levi if he could identify the chemical aroma faintly permeating the corridor: I thought it smelled like a hospital corridor. Just fractionally he raised his head and exposed his nostrils to the air. With a smile he told me, "I understand and can analyze it like a dog."

He seemed to me inwardly animated more in the manner of some quicksilver little woodland creature enlivened by the forest's most astute intelligence. Levi is small and slight, though not so delicately built as his unassuming demeanor makes him at first appear, and seemingly as nimble as he must have been at ten. In his body, as in his face, you see—as you don't in most men—the face and the body of the boy that he was. The alertness is nearly palpable, keenness trembling within like his pilot light.

It is not as surprising as one might initially think to find that writers divide like the rest of mankind into two categories: those who listen to you and those who don't. Levi listens, and with his entire face, a precisely modeled face that, tipped with its white chin beard, looks at sixty-seven youthfully Panlike and professorial as well, the face of irrepressible curiosity and of the esteemed *dottore*. I can believe Faussone when he says to Primo Levi early in *The Monkey's Wrench*, "You're quite a guy, making me tell these stories that, except for you, I've never told anybody." It's no wonder that people are always telling him things and that everything is already faithfully recorded before it is written down: when listening he is as focused and as still as a chipmunk spying something unknown from atop a stone wall.

In a large, substantial-looking apartment house built a few years before he was born—indeed the house where he *was* born, for formerly this was the home of his parents—Levi lives with his wife, Lucia; except for his year in Auschwitz and the adventurous months immediately after his liberation, he has lived in this apartment all his life. The building, whose bourgeois solidity has begun slightly to give way to time, is on a wide boulevard of apartment buildings that struck me as the northern Italian counterpart of Manhattan's West End Avenue:

a steady stream of auto and bus traffic, trolley cars speeding by on their tracks, but also a column of big chestnut trees stretching all along the narrow islands at either side of the street, and the green hills bordering the city visible from the intersection. The famous arcades at the commercial heart of the city are an unswerving fifteen-minute walk straight through what Levi has called "the obsessive Turin geometry."

The Levis' large apartment is shared, as it has been since the couple met and married after the war, with Primo Levi's mother. She is ninety-one. Levi's ninety-five-year-old mother-in-law lives not far away; in the apartment next door lives his twenty-eight-year-old son, a physicist; and a few streets farther on is his thirty-eight-year-old daughter, a botanist. I don't know of another contemporary writer who has voluntarily remained, over so many decades, intimately entangled and in such direct, unbroken contact with his immediate family, his birthplace, his region, the world of his forebears, and, particularly, the local working environment, which in Turin, the home of Fiat, is largely industrial. Of all the intellectually gifted artists of the twentieth century—and Levi's uniqueness is that he is more the artist-chemist than the chemist-writer—he may well be the most thoroughly adapted to the totality of the life around him. Perhaps in the case of Primo Levi, a life of communal interconnectedness, along with his masterpiece on Auschwitz, constitutes his profoundly spirited response to those who did all they could to sever his every sustained connection and tear him and his kind out of history.

In *The Periodic Table*, beginning with the simplest of sentences a paragraph that describes one of chemistry's most satisfying processes, Levi writes, "Distilling is beautiful." What follows is a distillation too, a reduction to essential points of the lively, wide-ranging conversation we conducted, in English, over the course of a long weekend, mostly behind the door of the quiet study off the entrance foyer to the Levis' apartment. His study is a large, simply furnished room. There is an old flowered sofa and a comfortable easy chair; on the desk is a shrouded word processor; neatly shelved behind the desk are Levi's variously colored notebooks; on shelves all around the room are books in Italian, German, and English. The most evocative object is one of the smallest: an unobtrusively hung sketch of a half-destroyed barbed-wire fence at Auschwitz. Displayed more prominently on the walls are playful constructions skillfully twisted into shape by Levi himself out of insulated copper wire—that is, wire coated with the varnish developed for that purpose in his own laboratory. There is a big wire butterfly, a wire owl, a tiny wire bug, and high on the wall behind the desk are two of the largest constructions: one the wire figure of a bird-warrior armed with a knitting needle and the other, as Levi explained when I couldn't make out what the figure was meant to represent, "a man playing his nose." "A Jew," I suggested. "Yes, yes," he said, laughing, "a Jew, of course."

Roth: In *The Periodic Table*, your book about "the strong and bitter flavor" of your experience as a chemist, you tell about Giulia, your attractive young colleague in a Milan chemical factory in 1942. Giulia explains your "mania about work" by the fact that in your early twenties you are shy with women and don't have a girlfriend. But she was mistaken, I think. Your real mania about work derives from something deeper. Work would seem to be your chief subject, not just in *The Monkey's Wrench* but even in your first book, about your incarceration at Auschwitz.

Arbeit Macht Frei—"Work Makes Freedom"—are the words inscribed by the Nazis over the Auschwitz gate. But work in Auschwitz is a horrifying parody of work, useless and senseless —labor as punishment leading to agonizing death. It's possible to view your entire literary labor as dedicated to restoring to work its humane meaning, reclaiming the word *Arbeit* from the derisive cynicism with which your Auschwitz employers had disfigured it. Faussone says to you, "Every job I undertake is like a first love." He enjoys talking about his work almost as much as he enjoys working. Faussone is Man the Worker made truly free through his labors.

Levi: I do not believe that Giulia was wrong in attributing my frenzy for work to my shyness at that time with girls. This shyness, or inhibition, was genuine, painful, and heavy—much more important for me than devotion to work. Work in the Milan factory I described in *The Periodic Table* was mock work that I did not trust. The catastrophe of the Italian armistice of September 8, 1943, was already in the air, and it would have been foolish to ignore it by digging oneself into a scientifically meaningless activity.

I have never seriously tried to analyze this shyness of mine, but no doubt Mussolini's racial laws played an important role. Other Jewish friends suffered from it, some "Aryan" school-mates jeered at us, saying that circumcision was nothing but castration, and we, at least at an unconscious level, tended to believe it, with the help of our puritanical families. I think that *at that time* work was for me a sexual compensation rather than a real passion.

However, I am fully aware that after the camp my work, or rather my two kinds of work (chemistry and writing), did play, and still play, an essential role in my life. I am persuaded that normal human beings are biologically built for an activity that is aimed toward a goal and that idleness, or aimless work (like Auschwitz's *Arbeit*), gives rise to suffering and to atrophy. In my case, and in the case of my alter ego, Faussone, work is identical with "problem solving."

At Auschwitz I quite often observed a curious phenomenon. The need for *lavoro ben fatto*—"work properly done"—is so strong as to induce people to perform even slavish chores "properly." The Italian bricklayer who saved my life by bring-ing me food on the sly for six months hated Germans, their food, their language, their war; but when they set him to erect walls, he built them straight and solid, not out of obedience but out of professional dignity.

Roth: *Survival in Auschwitz* concludes with a chapter enti-tled "The Story of Ten Days," in which you describe, in diary form, how you endured from January 18 to January 27, 1945, among a small remnant of sick and dying patients in the camp's makeshift infirmary after the Nazis had fled westward with some twenty thousand "healthy" prisoners. What's recounted there reads to me like the story of Robinson Crusoe in hell, with you, Primo Levi, as Crusoe, wrenching what you need to live from the chaotic residue of a ruthlessly evil island. What struck me there, as throughout the book, was the extent to which thinking contributed to your survival, the thinking of a practical, humane scientific mind. Yours doesn't seem to me a survival that was determined by either brute biological strength or incredible luck. It was rooted in your professional character:

the man of precision, the controller of experiments who seeks the principle of order, confronted with the evil inversion of everything he values. Granted you were a numbered part in an infernal machine, but a numbered part with a systematic mind that has always to understand. At Auschwitz you tell yourself, "I think too much" to resist, "I am too civilized." But to me the civilized man who thinks too much is inseparable from the survivor. The scientist and the survivor are one.

Levi: Exactly—you hit the bull's eye. In those memorable ten days, I truly did feel like Robinson Crusoe, but with one important difference. Crusoe set to work for his individual survival, whereas I and my two French companions were consciously and happily willing to work at last for a just and human goal, to save the lives of our sick comrades.

As for survival, this is a question that I put to myself many times and that many have put to me. I insist there was no general rule, except entering the camp in good health and knowing German. Barring this, luck dominated. I have seen the survival of shrewd people and silly people, the brave and the cowardly, "thinkers" and madmen. In my case, luck played an essential role on at least two occasions: in leading me to meet the Italian bricklayer and in my getting sick only once, but at the right moment.

And yet what you say, that for me thinking and observing were survival factors, is true, although in my opinion sheer luck prevailed. I remember having lived my Auschwitz year in a condition of exceptional spiritedness. I don't know if this depended on my professional background, or an unsuspected stamina, or on a sound instinct. I never stopped recording the world and people around me, so much that I still have an unbelievably detailed image of them. I had an intense wish to understand, I was constantly pervaded by a curiosity that somebody afterward did, in fact, deem nothing less than cynical: the curiosity of the naturalist who finds himself transplanted into an environment that is monstrous but new, monstrously new.

I agree with your observation that my phrase "I think too much . . . I am too civilized" is inconsistent with this other frame of mind. Please grant me the right to inconsistency: in the camp our state of mind was unstable, it oscillated from hour to hour between hope and despair. The coherence I think one notes in my books is an artifact, a rationalization a posteriori.

Roth: *Survival in Auschwitz* was originally published in English as *If This Is a Man*, a faithful rendering of your Italian title, *Se questo è un uomo* (and the title that your first American publishers should have had the good sense to preserve). The description and analysis of your atrocious memories of the Germans' "gigantic biological and social experiment" are governed precisely by a quantitative concern for the ways in which a man can be transformed or broken down and, like a substance decomposing in a chemical reaction, lose his characteristic properties. *If This Is a Man* reads like the memoir of a theoretician of moral biochemistry who has himself been forcibly enlisted as the specimen organism to undergo laboratory experimentation of the most sinister kind. The creature caught in the laboratory of the mad scientist is himself the epitome of the rational scientist.

In *The Monkey's Wrench*, which might accurately have been titled *This Is a Man*, you tell Faussone, your blue-collar Scheherazade, that "being a chemist in the world's eyes, and feeling . . . a writer's blood in my veins" you consequently have "two souls in my body, and that's too many." I'd say there's one soul, enviably capacious and seamless; I'd say that not only are the survivor and the scientist inseparable but so are the writer and the scientist.

Levi: Rather than a question, this is a diagnosis, which I accept with thanks. I lived my camp life as rationally as I could, and I wrote *If This Is a Man* struggling to explain to others, and to myself, the events I had been involved in, but with no definite literary intention. My model (or, if you prefer, my style) was that of the "weekly report" commonly used in factories: it must be precise, concise, and written in a language comprehensible to everybody in the industrial hierarchy. And certainly not written in scientific jargon. By the way, I am not a scientist, nor have I ever been. I did want to become one, but war and the camp prevented me. I had to limit myself to being a technician throughout my professional life.

I agree with you about there being only "one soul . . . and seamless," and once more I feel grateful to you. My statement

that "two souls . . . is too many" is half a joke but half hints
at serious things. I worked in a factory for almost thirty years,
and I must admit that there is no incompatibility between
being a chemist and being a writer—in fact, there is a mutual
reinforcement. But factory life, and particularly factory managing, involves many other matters, far from chemistry: hiring
and firing workers; quarreling with the boss, customers, and
suppliers; coping with accidents; being called to the telephone,
even at night or when at a party; dealing with bureaucracy; and
many more soul-destroying tasks. This whole trade is brutally
incompatible with writing, which requires a fair amount of
peace of mind. Consequently I felt hugely relieved when I
reached retirement age and could resign, and so renounce my
soul number one.

Roth: Your sequel to *If This Is a Man* (*The Reawakening*,
also unfortunately retitled by one of your early American publishers) was called in Italian *La tregua*, "the truce." It's about
your journey from Auschwitz back to Italy. There is a legendary dimension to that tortuous journey, especially to the story
of your long gestation period in the Soviet Union, waiting to
be repatriated. What's surprising about *The Truce*, which might
understandably have been marked by a mood of mourning and
inconsolable despair, is its exuberance. Your reconciliation
with life takes place in a world that sometimes seemed to you
like the primeval Chaos. Yet you are engaged by everyone, so
highly entertained as well as instructed that I wonder if, despite the hunger and the cold and the fears, even despite the
memories, you've ever really had a better time than during
those months you call "a parenthesis of unlimited availability, a
providential but unrepeatable gift of fate."

You appear to be someone who requires, above all, rootedness—in his profession, his ancestry, his region, his language—
and yet when you found yourself as alone and uprooted as a
man can be, you considered that condition a gift.

Levi: A friend of mine, an excellent doctor, told me many
years ago: "Your remembrances of before and after are in black
and white; those of Auschwitz and of your travel home are in
Technicolor." He was right. Family, home, factory are good
things in themselves, but they deprived me of something that I

still miss: adventure. Destiny decided that I should find adventure in the awful mess of a Europe swept by war.

You are in the business, so you know how these things happen. *The Truce* was written fourteen years after *If This Is a Man*; it is a more "self-conscious" book, more methodical, more literary, the language much more profoundly elaborated. It tells the truth, but filtered truth. It was preceded by countless verbal versions. I mean, I had recounted each adventure many times, to people at widely different cultural levels (to friends mainly, and to high school boys and girls), and I had retouched it en route so as to arouse their most favorable reactions. When *If This Is a Man* began to achieve some success, and I began to see a future for my writing, I set out to put these adventures on paper. I aimed at having fun in writing and at amusing my prospective readers. Consequently I gave emphasis to strange, exotic, cheerful episodes—mainly to the Russians seen close up—and I relegated to the first and last pages the mood, as you put it, "of mourning and inconsolable despair."

I must remind you that the book was written around 1961; these were the years of Khrushchev, of Kennedy, of Pope John, of the first thaw and of great hopes. In Italy, for the first time, you could speak of the USSR in objective terms without being called a philo-Communist by the right wing and a disruptive reactionary by the powerful Italian Communist Party.

As for "rootedness," it is true that I have deep roots and that I had the luck of not losing them. My family was almost completely spared by the Nazi slaughter. The desk here where I write occupies, according to family legend, exactly the spot where I first saw light. When I found myself as "uprooted as a man can be," certainly I suffered, but this was far more than compensated for afterward by the fascination of adventure, by human encounters, by the sweetness of "convalescence" from the plague of Auschwitz. In its historical reality, my Russian "truce" turned to a "gift" only many years later, when I purified it by rethinking it and by writing about it.

Roth: You begin *The Periodic Table* by speaking of your Jewish ancestors, who arrived in Piedmont from Spain, by way of Provence, in 1500. You describe your family roots in

Piedmont and Turin as "not enormous, but deep, extensive, and fantastically intertwined." You supply a brief lexicon of the jargon these Jews concocted and used primarily as a secret language from the Gentiles, an argot composed of words derived from Hebrew roots but with Piedmontese endings. To an outsider your rootedness in this Jewish world of your forebears seems not only intertwined but, in an essential way, identical with your rootedness in the region. However, in 1938, when the racial laws were introduced restricting the freedom of Italian Jews, you came to consider being Jewish an "impurity," though, as you say in *The Periodic Table*, "I began to be proud of being impure."

The tension between your rootedness and your impurity makes me think of something that Professor Arnaldo Momigliano wrote about the Jews of Italy, that "the Jews were less a part of Italian life than they thought they were." How much a part of Italian life do you think *you* are? Do you remain an impurity, "a grain of salt or mustard," or has that sense of distinctness disappeared?

Levi: I see no contradiction between "rootedness" and being (or feeling) "a grain of mustard." To feel oneself a catalyst, a spur to one's cultural environment, a something or a somebody that confers taste and sense to life, you don't need racial laws or anti-Semitism or racism in general; however, it is an advantage to belong to a (not necessarily racial) minority. In other words, it can prove useful not to be pure. If I may return to the question: don't you feel yourself, you, Philip Roth, "rooted" in your country and at the same time "a mustard grain"? In your books I perceive a sharp mustard flavor.

I think this is the meaning of your quotation from Arnaldo Momigliano. Italian Jews (but the same can be said of the Jews of many other nations) made an important contribution to their country's cultural and political life without renouncing their identity, in fact by keeping faith with their cultural tradition. To possess two traditions, as happens to Jews but not only to Jews, is a richness—for writers but not only for writers.

I feel slightly uneasy replying to your explicit question. Yes, sure, I am a part of Italian life. Several of my books are read and discussed in high schools. I receive lots of letters—

intelligent, silly, senseless—of appreciation, less frequently dissenting and quarrelsome. I receive useless manuscripts by would-be writers. My "distinctness" has changed in nature: I don't feel an *emarginato*, ghettoized, an outlaw, anymore, as in Italy there is actually no anti-Semitism. In fact, Judaism is viewed with interest and mostly with sympathy, although with mixed feelings toward Israel.

In my own way I have remained an impurity, an anomaly, but now for reasons other than before: not especially as a Jew but as an Auschwitz survivor and as an outsider-writer, coming not from the literary or university establishment but from the industrial world.

Roth: *If Not Now, When?* is like nothing else of yours that I've read in English. Though pointedly drawn from actual historical events, the book is cast as a straightforward picaresque adventure tale about a small band of Jewish partisans of Russian and Polish extraction harassing the Germans behind their Eastern frontlines. Your other books are perhaps less "imaginary" as to subject matter but strike me as more imaginative in technique. The motive behind *If Not Now, When?* seems more narrowly tendentious—and consequently less liberating to the writer—than the impulse that generates the autobiographical works.

I wonder if you agree with this: if in writing about the bravery of the Jews who fought back, you felt yourself doing something you *ought* to do, responsible to moral and political claims that don't necessarily intervene elsewhere, even when the subject is your own markedly Jewish fate.

Levi: *If Not Now, When?* is a book that followed an unforeseen path. The motivations that drove me to write it are manifold. Here they are, in order of importance.

I had made a sort of bet with myself: After so much plain or disguised autobiography, are you or are you not a fully fledged writer, capable of constructing a novel, shaping character, describing landscapes you have never seen? Try it!

I intended to amuse myself by writing a "Western" plot set in a landscape uncommon in Italy. I intended to amuse my readers by telling them a substantially optimistic story, a story of hope, even occasionally cheerful, although projected onto a background of massacre.

I wished to assault a commonplace still prevailing in Italy: a Jew is a mild person, a scholar (religious or profane), unwarlike, humiliated, who tolerated centuries of persecution without ever fighting back. It seemed to me a duty to pay homage to those Jews who, in desperate conditions, found the courage and the skill to resist.

I cherished the ambition to be the first (perhaps the only) Italian writer to describe the Yiddish world. I intended to "exploit" my popularity in my country in order to impose upon my readers a book centered on the Ashkenazi civilization, history, language, and frame of mind, all of which are virtually unknown in Italy, except by some sophisticated readers of Joseph Roth, Bellow, Singer, Malamud, Potok, and of course you.

Personally, I am satisfied with this book, mainly because I had good fun planning and writing it. For the first and only time in my life as a writer, I had the impression (almost a hallucination) that my characters were alive, around me, behind my back, suggesting spontaneously their feats and their dialogues. The year I spent writing was a happy one, and so, whatever the result, for me this was a liberating book.

Roth: Let's talk about the paint factory. In our time many writers have worked as teachers, some as journalists, and most writers over fifty, in the East or the West, have been employed, for a while at least, as somebody or other's soldier. There is an impressive list of writers who have simultaneously practiced medicine and written books and of others who have been clergymen. T. S. Eliot was a publisher, and as everyone knows Wallace Stevens and Franz Kafka worked for large insurance companies. To my knowledge, only two writers of importance have been managers of paint factories: you in Turin, Italy, and Sherwood Anderson in Elyria, Ohio. Anderson had to leave the paint factory (and his family) to become a writer; you seem to have become the writer you are by staying and pursuing your career there. I wonder if you think of yourself as actually more fortunate—even better equipped to write—than those of us who are without a paint factory and all that's implied by that kind of connection.

Levi: As I have already said, I entered the paint industry by chance, but I never had very much to do with the general run of paints, varnishes, and lacquers. Our company, immediately after it began, specialized in the production of wire enamels, insulating coatings for copper electrical conductors. At the peak of my career, I numbered among the thirty or forty specialists in the world in this branch. The animals hanging here on the wall are made out of scrap enameled wire.

Honestly, I knew nothing of Sherwood Anderson till you spoke of him. No, it would never have occurred to me to quit family and factory for full-time writing, as he did. I'd have feared the jump into the dark, and I would have lost any right to a retirement allowance.

However, to your list of writer–paint manufacturers I must add a third name, Italo Svevo, a converted Jew of Trieste, the author of *The Confessions of Zeno*, who lived from 1861 to 1928. For a long time Svevo was the commercial manager of a paint company in Trieste, the Società Venziani, that belonged to his father-in-law and that dissolved a few years ago. Until 1918 Trieste belonged to Austria, and this company was famous because it supplied the Austrian navy with an excellent antifouling paint, preventing shellfish incrustation, for the keels of warships. After 1918 Trieste became Italian, and the paint was delivered to the Italian and British navies. To be able to deal with the Admiralty, Svevo took lessons in English from James Joyce, at the time a teacher in Trieste. They became friends and Joyce assisted Svevo in finding a publisher for his works. The trade name of the antifouling paint was Moravia. That it is the same as the nom de plume of the novelist is not fortuitous: both the Trieste entrepreneur and the Roman writer derived it from the family name of a mutual relative on the mother's side. Forgive me this hardly pertinent gossip.

No, as I've hinted already, I have no regrets. I don't believe I have wasted my time in managing a factory. My factory *militanza* —my compulsory and honorable service there—kept me in touch with the world of real things.

Aharon Appelfeld

[1988]

A HARON APPELFELD lives a few miles west of Jerusalem in a mazelike conglomeration of attractive stone dwellings next to an "absorption center," where immigrants are temporarily housed, schooled, and prepared for life in their new society. The arduous journey that landed Appelfeld on the beaches of Tel Aviv in 1946, at the age of fourteen, seems to have fostered an unappeasable fascination with all uprooted souls, and at the local grocery where he and the absorption center's residents do their shopping, he will often initiate an impromptu conversation with an Ethiopian, or a Russian, or a Rumanian Jew still dressed for the climate of a country to which he or she will never return.

The living room of the two-story apartment is simply furnished: some comfortable chairs, books in three languages on the shelves, and on the walls impressive adolescent drawings by the Appelfelds' son Meir, who is now twenty-one and, since finishing his military duty, has been studying art in London. Yitzak, eighteen, recently completed high school and is in the first of his three years of compulsory army service. Still at home is twelve-year-old Batya, a clever girl with the dark hair and blue eyes of her Argentinean Jewish mother, Appelfeld's youthful, good-natured wife, Judith. The Appelfelds appear to have created as calm and harmonious a household as any child could hope to grow up in. During the four years that Aharon and I have been friends, I don't think I've ever visited him at home in Mevasseret Zion without remembering that his own childhood—as an escapee from a Nazi work camp, on his own in the primitive wilds of the Ukraine—provides the grimmest possible antithesis to this domestic ideal.

A portrait photograph that I've seen of Aharon Appelfeld, an antique-looking picture taken in Chernovtsy, Bukovina, in 1938, when Aharon was six—a picture brought to Palestine by surviving relatives—shows a delicately refined bourgeois child seated alertly on a hobbyhorse and wearing a beautiful sailor suit. You cannot imagine this child, only twenty-four months on, confronting the exigencies of surviving for years as a hunted and parentless little boy in the woods. The keen intelligence is certainly there, but where is the robust cunning, the feral instinct, the biological tenacity it took to endure that terrifying adventure?

As much is secreted away in that child as in the writer he's become. At fifty-five, Aharon is a small, bespectacled, compact man with a perfectly round face and a perfectly bald head and the playfully thoughtful air of a benign wizard. He'd have no trouble passing for a magician who entertains children at birthday parties by pulling doves out of a hat—it's easier to associate his gently affable and kindly appearance with that job than with the responsibility by which he seems inescapably propelled: responding, in a string of elusively portentous stories, to the disappearance from Europe—while he was outwitting peasants and foraging in the forests—of just about all the continent's Jews, his parents among them.

His literary subject is not the Holocaust, however, or even Jewish persecution. Nor, to my mind, is what he writes Jewish fiction or, for that matter, Israeli fiction. Nor, since he is a Jewish citizen of a Jewish state composed largely of immigrants, is his an exile's fiction. And, despite the European locale of many of his novels and the echoes of Kafka, these books written in the Hebrew language aren't European fiction. Indeed, all that Appelfeld is not adds up to what he is, and that is a dislocated writer, a deported writer, a dispossessed and uprooted writer. Appelfeld is a displaced writer of displaced fiction, who has made of displacement and disorientation a subject uniquely his own. His sensibility—marked almost at birth by the solitary wanderings of a little bourgeois boy through an ominous nowhere—appears to have spontaneously generated a style of sparing specificity, of out-of-time progression and thwarted narrative drives, that is an uncanny prose realization of the displaced mentality. As unique as the subject is a voice that originates in a wounded consciousness pitched somewhere between amnesia and memory and that situates the fiction it narrates midway between parable and history.

Since we met in 1984, Aharon and I have talked together at great length, usually while walking through the streets of

London, New York, and Jerusalem. I've known him over these years as an oracular anecdotalist and folkloristic enchanter, as a wittily laconic kibitzer and an obsessive dissector of Jewish states of mind—of Jewish aversions, delusions, remembrances, and manias. Yet as is often the case in friendships between writers, during these peripatetic conversations we had never really touched on each other's work—that is, not until last month, when I traveled to Jerusalem to discuss with him the six of his fifteen published books that are now in English translation.

After our first afternoon together we disencumbered ourselves of an interloping tape recorder and, though I took some notes along the way, mostly we talked as we've become accustomed to talking—wandering along city streets or sitting in coffee shops where we'd stop to rest. When finally there seemed to be little left to say, we sat down together and tried to synthesize on paper—I in English, Aharon in Hebrew—the heart of the discussion. Aharon's answers to my questions have been translated by Jeffrey Green.

Roth: I find echoes in your fiction of two Middle European writers of a previous generation: Bruno Schulz, the Polish Jew who wrote in Polish and was shot and killed at fifty by the Nazis in Drohobycz, the heavily Jewish Galician city where he taught high school and lived at home with his family, and Kafka, the Prague Jew who wrote in German and also lived, according to Max Brod, "spellbound in the family circle" for most of his forty-one years. You were born 500 miles east of Prague, 125 miles southeast of Drohobycz, in Chernovtsy. Your family—prosperous, highly assimilated, German-speaking—bore certain cultural and social similarities to Kafka's, and, like Schulz, you, along with your family, suffered personally the Nazi horror. The affinity that interests me, however, isn't biographical but literary, and though I see signs of it throughout your work, it's particularly clear in *The Age of Wonders*. The opening scene, for instance, depicting a mother and her adoring twelve-year-old luxuriating on a train journey home from their idyllic summer vacation, reminds me of similar scenes in Schulz stories. And only a few pages on, there is a Kafkaesque surprise when the train stops unexpectedly by a dark old sawmill and the security forces request that "all Austrian passengers who are not Christians by birth" register at the sawmill's office. I'm reminded of *The Trial*—of *The Castle* as well—where there is at the outset an ambiguously menacing assault on the legal status of the hero. Tell me, how pertinent to your imagination do you consider Kafka and Schulz to be?

Appelfeld: I discovered Kafka here in Israel during the 1950s, and as a writer he was close to me from my first contact. He spoke to me in my mother tongue, German—not the German of the Germans but the German of the Hapsburg Empire, of Vienna, Prague, and Chernovtsy, with its special tone, which, by the way, the Jews worked hard to create.

To my surprise he spoke to me not only in my mother tongue but also in another language that I knew intimately, the language of the absurd. I knew what he was talking about. It wasn't a secret language for me and I didn't need any explications. I had come from the camps and the forests, from a world that embodied the absurd, and nothing in that world was foreign to me. What was surprising was this: how could a man who had never been there know so much, in precise detail, about that world?

Other surprising discoveries followed: the marvel of his objective style, his preference for action over interpretation, his clarity and precision, the broad, comprehensive view laden with humor and irony. And, as if that weren't enough, another discovery showed me that behind the mask of placelessness and homelessness in his work stood a Jewish man, like me, from a half-assimilated family, whose Jewish values had lost their content and whose inner space was barren and haunted.

The marvelous thing is that the barrenness brought him not to self-denial or self-hatred but rather to a kind of tense curiosity about every Jewish phenomenon, especially the Jews of Eastern Europe, the Yiddish language, the Yiddish theater, Hasidism, Zionism, and even the ideal of moving to Mandate Palestine. This is the Kafka of his journals, which are no less gripping than his works. I found a palpable embodiment of Kafka's Jewish involvement in his Hebrew handwriting, for he had studied Hebrew and knew it. His handwriting is clear and amazingly beautiful, showing his effort and concentration as in his German handwriting, but his Hebrew handwriting has an additional aura of love for the isolated letter.

Kafka revealed to me not only the plan of the absurd world but also the charms of its art, which I needed as an assimilated Jew. The fifties were years of search for me, and Kafka's works illuminated the narrow path that I tried to blaze for myself. Kafka emerges from an inner world and tries to get some grip on reality, and I came from a world of detailed, empirical reality, the camps and the forests. My real world was far beyond the power of imagination, and my task as an artist was not to develop my imagination but to restrain it, and even then it seemed impossible to me, because everything was so unbelievable that one seemed oneself to be fictional.

At first I tried to run away from myself and from my memories, to live a life that was not my own and to write about a life that was not my own. But a hidden feeling told me that I was not allowed to flee from myself and that if I denied the experience of my childhood in the Holocaust, I would be spiritually deformed. Only when I reached the age of thirty did I feel the freedom to deal as an artist with those experiences.

To my regret, I came to Bruno Schulz's work years too late, after my literary approach was rather well formed. I felt and still feel a great affinity with his writing, but not the same affinity I feel with Kafka.

Roth: Of your six books translated now into English, *The Age of Wonders* is the one in which an identifiable historical background is most sharply delineated. The narrator's writer-father is an admirer of Kafka's; in addition, the father is party, we are told, to an intellectual debate about Martin Buber; we're also told that he's a friend of Stefan Zweig's. But this specificity, even if it doesn't develop much beyond these few references to an outside world, is not common in the books of yours I've read. Hardship generally fells your Jews the way the overpowering ordeal descends on Kafka's victims: inexplicably, out of nowhere, in a society seemingly without history or politics. "What do they want of us?" asks a Jew in *Badenheim 1939*, after he's gone to register as a Jew at, of all places, the Badenheim Sanitation Department. "It's hard to understand," another Jew answers.

There's no news from the public realm that might serve as a warning to an Appelfeld victim, nor is the victim's impending doom presented as part of a European catastrophe. The historical focus is supplied by the reader, who understands, as the victims cannot, the magnitude of the enveloping evil. Your reticence as a historian, when combined with the historical perspective of a knowing reader, accounts for the peculiar impact your work has, for the power that emanates from stories that are told through such modest means. Also, dehistoricizing the events and blurring the background, you probably approximate the disorientation felt by people who were unaware that they were on the brink of a cataclysm.

It's occurred to me that the perspective of the adults in your fiction resembles in its limitations the viewpoint of a child, who has no historical calendar in which to place unfolding events and no intellectual means of penetrating their meaning. I wonder if your own consciousness as a child at the edge of the Holocaust isn't mirrored in the simplicity with which the imminent horror is perceived in your novels.

Appelfeld: You're right. In *Badenheim 1939* I completely ignored the historical explanation. I assumed that the historical facts were known to readers and that they would fill in what was missing. You're also correct, it seems to me, in assuming that my description of the Second World War has something in it of a child's vision, but I'm not sure whether the ahistorical quality of *Badenheim 1939* derives from the child's vision that's preserved within me. Historical explanations have been alien to me ever since I became aware of myself as an artist. And the Jewish experience in the Second World War was not "historical." We came into contact with archaic mythical forces, a kind of dark subconscious the meaning of which we did not know, nor do we know it to this day. This world appears to be rational (with trains, departure times, stations, and engineers), but in fact these were journeys of the imagination, lies and ruses, which only deep, irrational drives could have invented. I didn't understand, nor do I yet understand, the motives of the murderers.

I was a victim, and I try to understand the victim. That is a broad, complicated expanse of life that I've been trying to deal with for thirty years now. I haven't idealized the victims. I don't think that in *Badenheim 1939* there's any idealization either. By the way, Badenheim is a rather real place, and spas like that were scattered all over Europe, shockingly petit bourgeois and idiotic in their formalities. Even as a child I saw how ridiculous they were.

It is generally agreed, to this day, that Jews are deft, cunning, and sophisticated creatures, with the wisdom of the world stored up in them. But isn't it fascinating to see how easy it was to fool the Jews? With the simplest, almost childish tricks they were gathered up in ghettos, starved for months, encouraged with false hopes, and finally sent to their deaths by train. That ingenuousness stood before my eyes while I was writing *Badenheim*. In that ingenuousness I found a kind of distillation of humanity. Their blindness and deafness, their obsessive preoccupation with themselves, is an integral part of their ingenuousness. The murderers were practical, and they knew just what they wanted. The ingenuous person is always a shlemazl, a clownish victim of misfortune, never hearing the danger signals in time, getting mixed up, tangled up, and finally falling in the trap. Those weaknesses charmed me. I fell in love with them. The myth that the Jews run the world with their machinations turned out to be somewhat exaggerated.

Roth: Of all your translated books, *Tzili* depicts the harshest reality and the most extreme suffering. Tzili, the simple child of a poor Jewish family, is left alone when her family flees the Nazi invasion. The novel recounts her horrendous adventures in surviving and her excruciating loneliness among the brutal peasants for whom she works. The book strikes me as a counterpart to Jerzy Kosinski's *Painted Bird*. Though less grotesque, *Tzili* portrays a fearful child in a world even bleaker and more barren than Kosinski's, a child moving in isolation through a landscape as uncongenial to human life as any in Beckett's *Molloy*.

As a boy you wandered alone like Tzili after your escape, at eight, from the camp. I've been wondering why, when you came to transform your own life in an unknown place, hiding out among the hostile peasants, you decided to imagine a girl as the survivor of this ordeal. And did it occur to you ever *not* to fictionalize this material but to present your experiences as you remember them, to write a survivor's tale as direct, say, as Primo Levi's depiction of his Auschwitz incarceration?

Appelfeld: I have never written about things as they happened. All my works are indeed chapters from my most personal experience, but nevertheless they are not "the story of my life." The things that happened to me in my life have already happened, they are already formed, and time has kneaded them and given them shape. To write things as they happened means to enslave oneself to memory, which is only a minor element in the creative process. To my mind, to create means to order, sort out, and choose the words and the pace that fit the work. The materials are indeed materials from one's life, but ultimately the creation is an independent creature.

I tried several times to write "the story of my life" in the woods after I ran away from the camp. But all my efforts were in vain. I wanted to be faithful to reality and to what really happened. But the chronicle that emerged proved to be a weak scaffolding. The result was rather meager, an unconvincing imaginary tale. The things that are most true are easily falsified.

Reality, as you know, is always stronger than the human imagination. Not only that, reality can permit itself to be unbelievable, inexplicable, out of all proportion. The created work, to my regret, cannot permit itself all that.

The reality of the Holocaust surpassed any imagination. If I remained true to the fact, no one would believe me. But the moment I chose a girl, a little older than I was at that time, I removed "the story of my life" from the mighty grip of memory and gave it over to the creative laboratory. There memory is not the only proprietor. There one needs a causal explanation, a thread to tie things together. The exceptional is permissible only if it is part of an overall structure and contributes to its understanding. I had to remove those parts that were unbelievable from "the story of my life" and present a more credible version.

When I wrote *Tzili* I was about forty years old. At that time I was interested in the possibilities of naiveness in art. Can there be a naive modern art? It seemed to me that without the naiveté still found among children and old people and, to some extent, in ourselves, the work of art would be flawed. I tried to correct that flaw. God knows how successful I was.

Roth: *Badenheim 1939* has been called fablelike, dreamlike, nightmarish, and so on. None of these descriptions makes the book less vexing to me. The reader is asked—pointedly, I think —to understand the transformation of a pleasant Austrian resort for Jews into a grim staging area for Jewish "relocation" to Poland as being somehow analogous to events preceding Hitler's Holocaust. At the same time your vision of Badenheim and its Jewish inhabitants is almost impulsively antic and indifferent to matters of causality. It isn't that a menacing situation develops, as it frequently does in life, without warning or logic, but that about these events you are laconic, I think, to the point of inscrutability. Do you mind addressing my difficulties as a reader with this highly praised novel, which is perhaps your most famous book in America? What is the relation between the fictional world of *Badenheim* and historical reality?

Appelfeld: Rather clear childhood memories underlie *Badenheim 1939*. Every summer we, like all the other petit-bourgeois families, would set out for a resort. Every summer we tried to find a restful place where people didn't gossip in the corridors, didn't confess to one another in corners, didn't interfere with you, and, of course, didn't speak Yiddish. But every summer, as though we were being spited, we were once again surrounded by Jews, and that left a bad taste in my parents' mouths, and no small amount of anger.

Many years after the Holocaust, when I came to retrace my childhood from before the Holocaust, I saw that these resorts occupied a particular place in my memories. Many faces and bodily twitches came back to life. It turned out that the grotesque was etched in, no less than the tragic. Walks in the woods and the elaborate meals brought people together in Badenheim—to speak to one another and to confess to one another. People permitted themselves not only to dress extravagantly but also to speak freely, sometimes picturesquely. Husbands occasionally lost their lovely wives, and from time to time a shot would ring out in the evening, a sharp sign of disappointed love. Of course I could arrange these precious scraps of life to stand on their own artistically. But what was I to do? Every time I tried to reconstruct those forgotten resorts, I had visions of the trains and the camps, and my most hidden childhood memories were spotted with the soot from the trains.

Fate was already hidden within those people like a mortal illness. Assimilated Jews built a structure of humanistic values and looked out on the world from it. They were certain that they were no longer Jews and that what applied to "the Jews" did not apply to them. That strange assurance made them into blind or half-blind creatures. I have always loved assimilated Jews, because that was where the Jewish character, and also perhaps Jewish fate, was concentrated with the greatest force.

In *Badenheim* I tried to combine sights from my childhood with sights of the Holocaust. My feeling was that I had to remain faithful to both realms. That is, that I must not prettify the victims but rather depict them in full light, unadorned, but at the same time that I had to point out the fate hidden within them, though they do not know it.

That is a very narrow bridge, without a railing, and it's very easy to fall off.

Roth: Not until you reached Palestine, in 1946, did you come in contact with Hebrew. What effect do you think this had on your Hebrew prose? Are you aware of any special connection between how you came to Hebrew and how you write in Hebrew?

Appelfeld: My mother tongue was German. My grandparents spoke Yiddish. Most of the inhabitants of Bukovina, where I lived as a child, were Ruthenians and so they all spoke Ruthenian. The government was Rumanian, and everyone was required to speak that language as well. When the Second World War broke out, and I was eight, I was deported to a camp in Transmistria. After I ran away from the camp I lived among the Ukrainians, and so I learned Ukrainian. In 1944 I was liberated by the Russian army and I worked for them as a messenger boy, and that's how I came by my knowledge of Russian. For two years, from 1944 to 1946, I wandered all over Europe and picked up other languages. When I finally reached Palestine in 1946, my head was full of tongues, but the truth of the matter is that I had no language.

I learned Hebrew by dint of much effort. It is a difficult language, severe and ascetic. Its ancient basis is the proverb from the Mishna: "Silence is a fence for wisdom." The Hebrew language taught me how to think, to be sparing with words, not to use too many adjectives, not to intervene too much, and not to interpret. I say that it "taught me." In fact, those are the demands it makes. If it weren't for Hebrew, I doubt whether I would have found my way to Judaism. Hebrew offered me the heart of the Jewish myth, its way of thinking and its beliefs, from the days of the Bible to Agnon. This is a thick strand of five thousand years of Jewish creativity, with all its rises and falls: the poetic language of the Bible, the juridical language of the Talmud, and the mystical language of the Kabala. This richness is sometimes difficult to cope with. Sometimes one is stifled by too many associations, by the multitude of worlds hidden in the single word. But never mind, those are marvelous resources. Ultimately you find in them even more than you were looking for.

Like most of the other kids who came to this country as Holocaust survivors, I wanted to run away from my memories, from my Jewishness, and to build up a different image for myself. What didn't we do to change, to be tall, blond, and strong, to be goyim, with all the outer trappings. The Hebrew language also sounded like a Gentile language to us, which is perhaps why we fell in love with it so easily.

But then something amazing happened. That very language, which we saw as a means of melting into self-forgetfulness and merging with the Israeli celebration of the land and heroism, that language tricked me and brought me, against my will, to the most secret storehouses of Judaism. Since then I haven't budged from there.

Roth: Living in this society you are bombarded by news and political disputation. Yet, as a novelist, you have by and large pushed aside the Israeli daily turbulence to contemplate markedly different Jewish predicaments. What does this turbulence mean to a novelist like yourself? How does being a citizen of this self-revealing, self-asserting, self-challenging, self-legendizing society affect your writing life? Does the news-producing reality ever tempt your imagination?

Appelfeld: Your question touches on a matter that is very important to me. True, Israel is full of drama from morning to night, and there are people who are overcome by that drama to the point of inebriation. This frenetic activity isn't only the result of pressure from the outside. Jewish restlessness contributes its part. Everything is buzzing here, and dense. There's a lot of talk, the controversies rage. The Jewish shtetl has not disappeared.

At one time there was a strong anti-Diaspora tendency here,

a recoiling from anything Jewish. Today things have changed a bit, though this country is restless and tangled up in itself, living with ups and downs. Today we have redemption, tomorrow darkness. Writers are also immersed in this tangle. The occupied territories, for example, are not only a political issue but also a literary matter.

I came here in 1946, still a boy but burdened with life and suffering. In the daytime I worked on kibbutz farms and at night I studied Hebrew. For many years I wandered about this feverish country, lost and lacking any orientation. I was looking for myself and for the face of my parents, who had been lost in the Holocaust. During the 1940s one had a feeling that one was being reborn here as a Jew, and one would therefore turn out to be quite a wonder. Every utopian view produces that kind of atmosphere. Let's not forget that this was after the Holocaust. To be strong was not merely a matter of ideology. "Never again like sheep to the slaughter" thundered from loudspeakers at every corner. I very much wished to fit into that great activity and take part in the adventure of the birth of a new nation. Naively I believed that action would silence my memories and I would flourish like the natives, free of the Jewish nightmare, but what could I do? The need, you might say the necessity, to be faithful to myself and to my childhood memories made me a distant, contemplative person. My contemplation brought me back to the region where I was born and where my parents' home stood. That is my spiritual history, and it is from there that I spin the threads.

Artistically speaking, settling back there has given me an anchorage and a perspective. I'm not obligated to rush out to meet current events and interpret them immediately. Daily events do indeed knock on every door, but they know that I don't let such agitated guests into my house.

Roth: In *To the Land of the Cattails*, a Jewish woman and her grown son, the offspring of a Gentile father, are journeying back to the remote Ruthenian countryside where she was born. It's the summer of 1938. The closer they get to her home, the more menacing is the threat of Gentile violence. The mother says to her son: "They are many, and we are few." Then you write: "The word *goy* rose up from within her. She smiled as if hearing a distant memory. Her father would sometimes, though only occasionally, use that word to indicate hopeless obtuseness."

The Gentile with whom the Jews of your books seem to share their world is usually the embodiment of hopeless obtuseness and of menacing, primitive social behavior—the goy as drunkard, wife beater, as the coarse, brutal semi-savage who is "not in control of himself." Though obviously there's more to be said about the non-Jewish world in those provinces where your books are set—and about the capacity of Jews, in their own world, also to be obtuse and primitive—even a non-Jewish European would have to recognize that the power of this image over the Jewish imagination is rooted in real experience. Alternatively the goy is pictured as an "earthy soul . . . overflowing with health." *Enviable* health. As the mother in *Cattails* says of her half-Gentile son, "He's not nervous like me. Other, quiet blood flows in his veins."

I'd say that it's impossible to know anything about the Jewish imagination without investigating the place that the goy has occupied in the folk mythology that's been exploited, in America, at one level by comedians like Lenny Bruce and Jackie Mason and, at quite another level, by Jewish novelists. American fiction's most single-minded portrait of the goy is in *The Assistant* by Bernard Malamud. The goy is Frank Alpine, the down-and-out thief who robs the failing grocery store of the Jew, Bober, later attempts to rape Bober's studious daughter, and eventually, in a conversion to Bober's brand of suffering Judaism, symbolically renounces goyish savagery. The New York Jewish hero of Saul Bellow's second novel, *The Victim*, is plagued by an alcoholic Gentile misfit named Allbee, who is no less of a bum and a drifter than Alpine, even if his assault on Leventhal's hard-won composure is intellectually more urbane. The most imposing Gentile in all of Bellow's work, however, is Henderson—the self-exploring rain king who, to restore his psychic health, takes his blunted instincts off to Africa. For Bellow no less than for Appelfeld, the truly "earthy soul" is not the Jew, nor is the search to retrieve primitive energies portrayed as the quest of a Jew. For Bellow no less than for Appelfeld, and, astonishingly, for Mailer no less than for Appelfeld—we all know that in Mailer when a man is a sadistic sexual aggressor his name is Sergius O'Shaughnessy, when he is a wife killer his name is

Stephen Rojack, and when he is a menacing murderer he isn't Lepke Buchalter or Gurrah Shapiro, he's Gary Gilmore.

Appelfeld: The place of the non-Jew in the Jewish imagination is a complex affair growing out of generations of Jewish fear. Which of us dares to take up the burden of explanation? I will hazard only a few words, something from my personal experience.

I said fear, but the fear wasn't uniform, and it wasn't of all Gentiles. In fact, there was a sort of envy of the non-Jew hidden in the heart of the modern Jew. The non-Jew was frequently viewed in the Jewish imagination as a liberated creature without ancient beliefs or social obligation who lived a natural life on his own soil. The Holocaust, of course, altered somewhat the course of the Jewish imagination. In place of envy came suspicion. The feelings that had walked in the open descended to the underground.

Is there some stereotype of the non-Jew in the Jewish soul? It exists, and it is frequently embodied in the word *goy*, but that is an undeveloped stereotype. The Jews have had imposed on them too many moral and religious strictures to express such feelings utterly without restraint. Among the Jews there was never the confidence to express verbally the depths of hostility they may well have felt. They were, for good or bad, too rational. What hostility they permitted themselves to feel was, paradoxically, directed at themselves.

What has preoccupied me, and continues to perturb me, is this anti-Semitism directed at oneself, an ancient Jewish ailment which in modern times has taken on various guises. I grew up in an assimilated Jewish home where German was treasured. German was considered not only a language but also a culture, and the attitude toward German culture was virtually religious. All around us lived masses of Jews who spoke Yiddish, but in our home Yiddish was absolutely forbidden. I grew up with the feeling that anything Jewish was blemished. From my earliest childhood my gaze was directed at the beauty of non-Jews. They were blond and tall and behaved naturally. They were cultured, and when they didn't behave in a cultured fashion, at least they behaved naturally.

Our housemaid illustrated that theory well. She was pretty and buxom, and I was attached to her. She was, in my eyes, the eyes of a child, nature itself, and when she ran off with my mother's jewelry, I saw that as no more than a forgivable mistake.

From my earliest youth I was drawn to non-Jews. They fascinated me with their strangeness, their height, their aloofness. Yet the Jews seemed strange to me too. It took years to understand how much my parents had internalized all the evil they attributed to the Jew, and, through them, I did also. A hard kernel of revulsion was planted within each of us.

The change took place in me when we were uprooted from our house and driven into the ghettos. Then I noticed that all the doors and windows of our non-Jewish neighbors were suddenly shut, and we walked alone in the empty streets. None of our many neighbors, with whom we had connections, was at the window when we dragged along our suitcases. I say "the change," and that isn't the entire truth. I was eight years old then, and the whole world seemed like a nightmare to me. Afterward too, when I was separated from my parents, I didn't know why. All during the war I wandered among the Ukrainian villages, keeping my hidden secret: my Jewishness. Fortunately for me, I was blond and didn't arouse suspicion.

It took me years to draw close to the Jew within me. I had to get rid of many prejudices within me and to meet many Jews in order to find myself in them. Anti-Semitism directed at oneself was an original Jewish creation. I don't know of any other nation so flooded with self-criticism. Even after the Holocaust, Jews did not seem blameless in their own eyes. On the contrary, harsh comments were made by prominent Jews against the victims, for not protecting themselves and fighting back. The ability of Jews to internalize any critical and condemnatory remark and castigate themselves is one of the marvels of human nature.

The feeling of guilt has settled and taken refuge among all the Jews who want to reform the world, the various kinds of socialists, anarchists, but mainly among Jewish artists. Day and night the flame of that feeling produces dread, sensitivity, self-criticism, and sometimes self-destruction. In short, it isn't a particularly glorious feeling. Only one thing may be said in its favor: it harms no one except those afflicted with it.

Roth: In *The Immortal Bartfuss*, Bartfuss asks "irreverently" of his dying mistress's ex-husband, "What have we Holocaust survivors done? Has our great experience changed us at all?" This is the question the novel somehow engages itself with on virtually every page. We sense in Bartfuss's lonely longing and regret, in his baffled effort to overcome his own remoteness, in his avidity for human contact, in his mute wanderings along the Israeli coast and his enigmatic encounters in dirty cafés, the agony that life can become in the wake of a great disaster. Of the Jewish survivors who wind up smuggling and black-marketeering in Italy right after the war, you write, "No one knew what to do with the lives that had been saved."

My last question, growing out of this preoccupation in *The Immortal Bartfuss*, is perhaps preposterously comprehensive. From what you observed as a homeless youngster wandering in Europe after the war, and from what you've learned during four decades in Israel, do you discern distinguishing patterns in the experience of those whose lives were saved? What *have* the Holocaust survivors done and in what ways *were* they ineluctably changed?

Appelfeld: True, that is the painful point of my latest book. Indirectly I tried to answer your question there. Now I'll try to expand somewhat. The Holocaust belongs to the type of enormous experience that reduces one to silence. Any utterance, any statement, any "answer" is tiny, meaningless, and occasionally ridiculous. Even the greatest of answers seems petty.

With your permission, two examples. The first is Zionism. Without doubt, life in Israel gives the survivors not only a place of refuge but also a feeling that the entire world is not evil. Though the tree has been chopped down, the root has not withered—despite everything, we continue living. Yet that satisfaction cannot take away the survivor's feeling that he or she must do something with this life that was saved. The survivors have undergone experiences that no one else has undergone, and others expect some message from them, some key to understanding the human world—a human example. But they, of course, cannot begin to fulfill the great tasks imposed upon them, so theirs are clandestine lives of flight and hiding. The trouble is that no more hiding places are available. One has a feeling of guilt that grows from year to year and becomes, as in Kafka, an accusation. The wound is too deep and bandages won't help. Not even a bandage such as the Jewish state.

The second example is the religious stance. Paradoxically, as a gesture toward their murdered parents, not a few survivors have adopted religious faith. I know what inner struggles that paradoxical stance entails, and I respect it. But that stance is born of despair. I won't deny the truth of despair. But it's a suffocating position, a kind of Jewish monasticism and indirect self-punishment.

My book offers its survivor neither Zionist nor religious consolation. The survivor, Bartfuss, has swallowed the Holocaust whole, and he walks about with it in all his limbs. He drinks the "black milk" of the poet Paul Celan, morning, noon, and night. He has no advantage over anyone else, but he still hasn't lost his human face. That isn't a great deal, but it's something.

Ivan Klíma

[1990]

BORN IN Prague in 1931, Ivan Klíma has undergone what Jan Kott calls a "European education": during his adult years as a novelist, critic, and playwright his work was suppressed in Czechoslovakia by the Communist authorities (and his family members harried and punished right along with him), while during his early years, as a Jewish child, he was transported, with his parents, to the Terezin concentration camp by the Nazis. In 1968, when the Russians moved into Czechoslovakia, he was out of the country, in London, on the way to the University of Michigan to see a production of one of his plays and to teach literature. When his teaching duties ended in Ann Arbor in the spring of 1970, he returned to Czechoslovakia with his wife and two children to become one of the "admirable handful"—as a professor recently reinstated at Charles University described Klíma and his circle to me at lunch one day—whose persistent opposition to the regime made their daily lives extremely hard.

Of his fifteen or so novels and collections of stories, those written after 1970 were published openly only abroad, in Europe primarily; only two books—neither of them among his best—have appeared in America, where his work is virtually unknown. Coincidentally, Ivan Klíma's novel *Love and Garbage*, inspired in part by his months during the seventies as a Prague street cleaner, was published in Czechoslovakia on the very day in February 1990 that I flew there to see him. He arrived at the airport to pick me up after spending the morning in a Prague bookstore where readers who had just bought his book waited for him to sign their copies in a line that stretched from the shop into the street. (During my week in Prague, the longest lines I saw were for ice cream and for books.) The initial printing of *Love and Garbage*, his first Czech publication in twenty years, was 100,000 copies. Later in the afternoon, he learned that a second book of his, *My Merry Mornings*, a collection of stories, had been published that day as well, also in an edition of 100,000. In the three months since censorship

217

has been abolished, a stage play of his has been produced and a TV play has been broadcast. Five more of his books are to appear this year.

Love and Garbage is the story of a well-known, banned Czech writer "hemmed in by prohibition" and at work as a street cleaner, who for a number of years finds some freedom from the claustrophobic refuge of his home—from the trusting wife who wants to make people happy and is writing a study on self-sacrifice; from the two dearly loved growing children—with a moody, spooky, demanding sculptor, a married mother herself, who comes eventually to curse him and to slander the wife he can't leave. To this woman he is erotically addicted:

> There was a lot of snow that winter. She'd take her little girl to her piano lessons. I'd walk behind them, without the child being aware of me. I'd sink into the freshly fallen snow because I wasn't looking where I was going. I was watching her walking.

It is the story of a responsible man who guiltily yearns to turn his back on all the bitter injustices and to escape into a "private region of bliss." "My ceaseless escapes" is how he reproachfully describes the figure in his carpet.

At the same time, the book is a patchwork rumination on Kafka's spirit (the writer mentally works up an essay about Kafka while he's out cleaning streets); on the meaning of soot, smoke, filth, and garbage in a world that can turn even people into garbage; on death; on hope; on fathers and sons (a dark, tender leitmotif is the final illness of the writer's father); and, among other things, on the decline of Czech into "jerkish." Jerkish is the name of the language developed in the United States some years back for the communication between people and chimpanzees; it consists of 225 words, and Klíma's hero predicts that, after what has happened to his own language under the Communists, it can't be long before jerkish is spoken by all mankind. "Over breakfast," says this writer whom the state will not allow to be published, "I'd read a poem in the paper by the leading author writing in jerkish." The four banal little quatrains are quoted. "For this poem of 69 words," he says, "including the title, the author needed a mere 37 jerkish terms and no idea at all . . . Anyone strong enough to read the poem attentively will realize that for a jerkish poet even a vocabulary of 225 words is needlessly large."

Love and Garbage is a wonderful book, marred only by some distressing lapses into philosophical banality, particularly as the central story winds down, and (in the English version published by Chatto and Windus in London) by the translator's inability to imagine a pungent, credible demotic idiom appropriate to the argot of the social misfits in Klíma's street-cleaning detail. It is an inventive book that—aside from its absurdist title—is wholly unexhibitionistic. Klíma juggles a dozen motifs and undertakes the boldest transitions without hocus-pocus, as unshowily as Chekhov telling the story "Gooseberries"; he provides a nice antidote to all that magic in magic realism. The simplicity with which he creates his elaborate collage—harrowing concentration camp memories, ecological reflections, imaginary spats between the estranged lovers, and down-to-earth Kafkean analysis, all juxtaposed and glued to the ordeal of the exhilarating, exhausting adultery—is continuous with the disarming directness, verging on adolescent ingenuousness, with which the patently autobiographical hero confesses his emotional turmoil.

The book is permeated by an intelligence whose tenderness colors everything and is unchecked and unguarded by irony. Klíma is, in this regard, Milan Kundera's antithesis—an observation that might seem superfluous were it not for the correspondence of interests. The temperamental divide between the two is considerable, their origins diverge as sharply as the paths they've taken as men, and yet their affinity for the erotically vulnerable, their struggle against political despair, their brooding over social excreta, whether garbage or kitsch, a shared inclination for extended commentary and for mixing modes—not to mention their fixation on the fate of outcasts—create an odd, tense kinship, one not as unlikely as it might seem to both writers. I sometimes had the feeling while reading *Love and Garbage* that I was reading *The Unbearable Lightness of Being* turned inside out. The rhetorical contrast between the two titles indicates just how discordant, even adversarial, the perspectives can be of imaginations engaged similarly with similar themes—in this case, with what Klíma's hero calls "the most important of all themes . . . suffering resulting from a life deprived of freedom."

During the early seventies, when I began to make a trip to Prague each spring, Ivan Klíma was my principal reality instructor. He drove me around to the street-corner kiosks where writers sold cigarettes, to the public buildings where they mopped the floors, to the construction sites where they were laying bricks, and out of the city to the municipal waterworks where they slogged about in overalls and boots, a wrench in one pocket and a book in the other. When I got to talk at length with these writers, it was often over dinner at Ivan's house.

After 1976 I was no longer able to get a visa to enter Czechoslovakia and we corresponded through the West German or Dutch couriers who discreetly carried manuscripts and books in and out of the country for the people who were under close surveillance. By the summer of 1978, ten years after the Russian invasion, even Ivan, who had always seemed to me the most effervescent of those I'd met in the opposition, was sufficiently exhausted to admit, in a letter written in somewhat uneven English, "Sometime I hesitate if it is reasonable to remain in this misery for the rest of our life." He went on:

> Our life here is not very encouraging—the abnormality lasts too long and is depressing. We are persecuted the whole time, it is not enough that we are not allowed to publish a single word in this country—we are asked for interrogations, many of my friends were arrested for the short time. I was not imprisoned, but I am deprived of my driving license (without any reason of course) and my telephone is disconnected. But what is the worst: one of our colleagues . . .

Not uncharacteristically, he then described at much greater length a writer he considered to be in straits more dire than his own.

Fourteen years after I last saw him, Ivan Klíma's engaging blend of sprightliness and stolidness struck me as amazingly intact and his strength undiminished. Even though his Beatle haircut has been clipped back a bit since the seventies, his big facial features and mouthful of large carnivore teeth still make me sometimes think (particularly when he's having a good time) that I'm in the presence of a highly intellectually evolved

Ringo Starr. Ivan had been at the center of the activities known now in Czechoslovakia as "the revolution," and yet he showed not the least sign of the exhaustion that even the young students reading English literature, whose Shakespeare class I sat in on at the university, told me had left them numb with fatigue and relieved to be back quietly studying even something as abstruse to them as the opening scenes of *Macbeth*.

I got a reminder of the stubborn force in Ivan's temperament during dinner at his house one evening as he advised a writer friend of his and mine how to go about getting back the tiny two-room apartment that had been confiscated by the authorities in the late seventies, when the friend had been hounded by the secret police into an impoverished exile. "Take your wife," Ivan told him, "take your four children, and go down to the office of Jaroslav Koran." Jaroslav Koran was the new mayor of Prague, formerly a translator of poetry from English; as the week passed and I either met or heard about Václav Havel's appointees, it began to seem to me as though a primary qualification for joining the new administration was having translated into Czech the poems of John Berryman. Have there ever before been so many translators, novelists, and poets at the head of anything other than PEN?

"In Koran's office," Ivan continued, "lie down on the floor, all of you, and refuse to move. Tell them, 'I'm a writer, they took my apartment, and I want it back.' Don't beg, don't complain, just lie there and refuse to move. You'll have an apartment in twenty-four hours." The writer without an apartment —a very spiritual and mild person who, since I'd seen him last selling cigarettes in Prague, had aged in all the ways that Ivan had not—responded only with a forlorn smile suggesting, gently, that Ivan was out of his mind. Ivan turned to me and said, matter-of-factly, "Some people don't have the stomach for this."

Helena Klímová, Ivan's wife, is a psychotherapist who received her training in the underground university that the dissidents conducted in various living rooms during the Russian occupation. When I asked how her patients were responding to the revolution and the new society it had ushered in, she told me, in her precise, affable, serious way, "The psychotics are getting better and the neurotics are getting worse." "How do you explain that?" I asked. "With all this new freedom," she said, "the neurotics are terribly uncertain. What will happen now? Nobody knows. The old rigidity was detestable, even to them, of course, but also reassuring, dependable. There was a structure. You knew what to expect and what not to expect. You knew whom to trust and whom to hate. To the neurotics the change is very unsettling. They are suddenly in a world of choices." "And the psychotics? Is it really possible that they're getting better?" "I think so, yes. The psychotics suck up the prevailing mood. Now it's exhilaration. Everybody is happy, so the psychotics are even happier. They are euphoric. It's all very strange. Everybody is suffering from adaptation shock."

I asked Helena what she was herself having most difficulty adapting to. Without hesitation she answered that it was all the people who were nice to her who never had been before—not that long ago she and Ivan had been treated most warily by neighbors and associates looking to avoid trouble. Helena's expression of anger over the rapidity with which those once so meticulously cautious—or outright censorious—people were now amicable to the Klímas was a surprise to me, since during their hardest years she had always impressed me as a marvel of tolerance and equilibrium. The psychotics were getting better, the neurotics were getting worse, and, despite the prevailing mood of exhilaration, among the bravely decent, the admirable handful, some were beginning openly to seethe a little with those poisoned emotions whose prudent management fortitude and sanity had demanded during the decades of resistance.

On my first full day in Prague, before Ivan came to meet me to begin our talks, I went for a morning walk on the shopping streets just off Václavské náměstí, the big open boulevard where the crowds that helped to chant the revolution through to success first assembled in November 1989. In only a few minutes, outside a storefront, I encountered a loose gathering of some seventy or eighty people, laughing at a voice coming over a loudspeaker. From the posters and inscriptions on the building I saw that, unwittingly, I had found the headquarters of Civic Forum, the opposition movement led by Havel.

This crowd of shoppers, strollers, and office workers was standing around together listening, as best I could figure out, to a comedian who must have been performing in an auditorium inside. I don't understand Czech, but I guessed that it was a comedian—and a very funny one—because the staccato rhythm of his monologue, the starts, stops, and shifts of tone, seemed consciously designed to provoke the crowd into spasms of laughter, which ripened into a rich roar and culminated, at the height of their hilarity, with outbursts of applause. It sounded like the response you hear from the audience at a Chaplin movie. I saw through a passageway that there was another laughing crowd of about the same size on the other side of the Civic Forum building. It was only when I crossed over to them that I understood what I was witnessing. On two television sets above the front window of Civic Forum was the comedian himself: viewed in close-up, seated alone at a conference table, was the former general secretary of the Czech Communist Party, Milos Jakes. Jakes, who'd been driven from office early in December 1989, was addressing a closed meeting of party apparatchiks in the industrial city of Pilsen in October.

I knew it was Jakes at the Pilsen meeting because the evening before, at dinner, Ivan and his son, Michal, had told me all about this videotape, which had been made secretly by the staff of Czech TV. Now it played continuously outside the Prague headquarters of Civic Forum, where passersby stopped throughout the day to have a good laugh. What they were laughing at was Jakes's dogmatic, humorless party rhetoric and his primitive, awkward Czech—the deplorably tangled sentences, the ludicrous malapropisms, the euphemisms and evasions and lies, the pure jerkish that, only months earlier, had filled so many people with shame and loathing. Michal had told me that on New Year's Eve Radio Free Europe had played Jakes's Pilsen videotape as "the funniest performance of the year."

Watching people walk back out into the street grinning, I thought that this must be the highest purpose of laughter, its sacramental reason for being—to bury wickedness in ridicule. It seemed a very hopeful sign that so many ordinary men and women (and teenagers, and even children, who were in the crowd) should be able to recognize that the offense against their language had been as humiliating and atrocious as anything else. Ivan told me later that at one point during the revolution a vast crowd had been addressed for a few minutes by a sympathetic young emissary from the Hungarian democratic movement, who concluded his remarks by apologizing to them for his imperfect Czech. Instantaneously, as one voice, a half million people roared back, "You speak better than Jakes."

Pasted to the window beneath the TV sets were two of the ubiquitous posters of the face of Václav Havel, whose Czech is everything that Jakes's is not.

Ivan Klíma and I spent our first two days together talking; then, in writing, we compressed the heart of our discussion into the exchange that follows.

Roth: What has it been like, all these years, publishing in your own country in samizdat editions? The surreptitious publication of serious literary works in small quantities must find an audience that is, generally speaking, more enlightened and intellectually more sophisticated than the wider Czech readership. Samizdat publication presumably fosters a solidarity between writer and reader that can be exhilarating. Yet because samizdat is a limited and artificial response to the evil of censorship, it remains unfulfilling for everyone. Tell me about the literary culture that was spawned here by samizdat publication.

Klíma: Your observation that samizdat literature fosters a special type of reader seems right. The Czech samizdat originated in a situation that is in its way unique. The Power, supported by foreign armies—the Power installed by the occupier and aware that it could exist only by the will of the occupier—was afraid of criticism. It also realized that any kind of spiritual life at all is directed in the end toward freedom. That's why it did not hesitate to forbid practically all Czech culture, to make it impossible for writers to write, painters to exhibit, scientists —especially in the social sciences—to carry out independent research; it destroyed the universities, appointing as professors for the most part docile clerks. The nation, caught unawares in this catastrophe, accepted it passively, at least for a time, looking on helplessly at the disappearance, one after another, of people whom it had so recently respected and to whom it had looked with hope.

Samizdat originated slowly. At the beginning of the seventies, my friends and fellow writers who were forbidden to publish used to meet at my house once a month. They included the leading creators of Czech literature: Václav Havel, Jiří Grusa, Ludvík Vaculík, Pavel Kohout, Alexandr Kliment, Jan Trefulka, Milan Uhde, and several dozen others. At these meetings we read our new work aloud to one another; some, like Bohumil Hrabal and Jaroslav Seifert, did not come personally but sent their work for us to read. The police got interested in these meetings; on their instructions television produced a short film that hinted darkly that dangerous conspiratorial conclaves were going on in my flat. I was told to cancel the meetings, but we all agreed that we would type out our manuscripts and sell them for the price of the copy. The "business" was taken on by one of the best Czech writers, Ludvík Vaculík. That's how we began, one typist and one ordinary typewriter.

The works were printed in editions of ten to twenty copies; the cost of one copy was about three times the price of a normal book. Soon what we were doing got about. People began to look out for these books. New "workshops" sprang up, which often copied the unauthorized copies. At the same time the standard of the layout improved. Somewhat deviously, we managed to have books bound at the state bookbindery; they were often accompanied by drawings by leading artists, also banned. Many of these books will be, or already are, the pride of bibliophiles' collections. As time went on, the numbers of copies increased, as did the titles and readers. Almost everyone "lucky" enough to own a samizdat was surrounded by a circle interested in borrowing it. The writers were soon followed by others: philosophers, historians, sociologists, nonconforming Catholics, as well as supporters of jazz, pop, and folk music, and young writers who refused to publish officially even though they were allowed to. Dozens of books in translation began to come out in this way, political books, religious books, often lyrical poetry or meditative prose. Whole editions came into being and remarkable feats of editing—for instance, the collected writings, with commentary, of our greatest contemporary philosopher, Jan Patocka.

At first the police tried to prevent samizdats, confiscating individual copies during house searches. A couple of times they arrested the typists who copied them, and some were even sentenced to imprisonment by the "free" courts, but the samizdat started to resemble, from the point of view of the

authorities, the many-headed dragon in the fairy tale, or a
plague. Samizdat was unconquerable.

There are no precise statistics yet, but I know there were
roughly two hundred samizdat periodicals alone and several
thousand books. Of course when we speak of thousands of
book titles we can't always expect high quality, but one thing
completely separated samizdat from the rest of Czech culture:
it was independent both of the market and of the censor. This
independent Czech culture strongly attracted the younger
generation, in part because it had the aura of the forbidden.
How widespread it really was will perhaps soon be answered
by scientific research; we've estimated that some books had
tens of thousands of readers, and we mustn't forget that a lot
of these books were published by Czech publishing houses in
exile and then returned to Czechoslovakia by the most devious
routes.

Nor should we pass over the great part played in propagat-
ing what was called "uncensored literature" by the foreign
broadcasting stations Radio Free Europe and the Voice of
America. Radio Free Europe broadcast the most important of
the samizdat books in serial form, and its listeners numbered
in the hundreds of thousands. (One of the last books that I
heard read on this station was Havel's remarkable *Long-Distance
Interrogation*, which is an account not only of his life but also
of his political ideas.) I'm convinced that this "underground
culture" had an important influence on the revolutionary
events of the autumn of 1989.

Roth: It always seemed to me that there was a certain
amount of loose, romantic talk in the West about "the muse of
censorship" behind the Iron Curtain. I would venture that
there were even writers in the West who sometimes envied the
terrible pressure under which you people wrote and the clarity
of the mission this burden fostered: in your society you were
virtually the only monitors of truth. In a censorship culture,
where everybody lives a double life—of lies and truth—literature
becomes a life preserver, the remnant of truth people cling to.
I think it's also true that in a culture like mine, where nothing
is censored but where the mass media inundate us with inane
falsifications of human affairs, serious literature is no less of a
life preserver, even if the society is all but oblivious of it.

When I returned to the United States from Prague after my first visit in the early seventies, I compared the Czech writers' situation to ours in America by saying, "There nothing goes and everything matters; here everything goes and nothing matters." But at what cost did everything you wrote matter so much? How would you estimate the toll that repression, which put such a high premium on literature, has taken on the writers you know?

Klíma: Your comparison of the situation of Czech writers and writers in a free country is one that I have often repeated. I'm not able to judge the paradox of the second half, but the first catches the paradox of our situation wonderfully. Writers had to pay a high price for these words that take on importance because of the bans and persecution—the ban on publishing was connected not only to a ban on all social activity but also, in most cases, to a ban on doing any work writers were qualified for. Almost all my banned colleagues had to earn their living as laborers. Window cleaners, as we know them from Kundera's novel [*The Unbearable Lightness of Being*], were not really typical among doctors, but there were many writers, critics, and translators who earned their living in this way. Others worked on the building sites of the underground, as crane operators, or digging at geological research sites. Now, it might seem that such work could provide an interesting experience for a writer. And that's true, so long as the work lasts for a limited time and there is some prospect of escape from blunting and exhausting drudgery. Fifteen or even twenty years of work like that, exclusion like that, affects one's whole personality. The cruelty and injustice completely broke some of those subjected to it; others were so exhausted that they were simply unable to undertake any creative work. If they did somehow manage to persevere, it was by sacrificing to this work everything: any claim to rest and often to any chance of a personal life.

Roth: Milan Kundera, I discover, is something of an obsession here among the writers and journalists I talk to. There appears to be a controversy over what might be called his "internationalism." Some people have suggested to me that, in his two books written in exile, *The Book of Laughter and Forgetting* and *The Unbearable Lightness of Being*, he is writing "for" the

French, "for" the Americans, and so on, and that this constitutes some sort of cultural misdemeanor or even betrayal. To me he seems rather to be a writer who, once he found himself living abroad, decided, quite realistically, that it was best not to pretend that he was a writer living at home, and who had then to devise for himself a literary strategy, one congruent not with his old but with his new complexities. Leaving aside the matter of quality, the marked difference of approach between the books written in Czechoslovakia, like *The Joke* and *Laughable Loves*, and those written in France does not represent to me a lapse of integrity, let alone a falsification of his experience, but a strong, innovative response to an inescapable challenge. Would you explain what problems Kundera presents to those Czech intellectuals who are so obsessed with his writing in exile?

Klíma: Their relation to Kundera is indeed complicated, and I would stress beforehand that only a minority of Czechs have any opinion about Kundera's writing, for one simple reason: his books have not been published in Czechoslovakia for more than twenty years. The reproach that he is writing for foreigners rather than for Czechs is only one of the many reproaches addressed to Kundera and only a part of the more substantial rebuke—that he has lost his ties to his native country. We can really leave aside the matter of quality because largely the allergy to him is not produced by the quality of his writing but by something else.

The defenders of Kundera—and there are many here— explain the animosity toward him among Czech intellectuals by what is not so rare an attitude toward our famous Czech compatriots: envy. But I don't see this problem so simply. I can mention many famous compatriots, even among the writers (Havel at home, Škvorecký abroad), who are very popular and even beloved by intellectuals here.

I have used the word *allergy*. Various irritants produce an allergy, and it's rather difficult to find the crucial ones. In my opinion the allergy is caused, in part, by what people take to be the simplified and spectacular way in which Kundera presents his Czech experience. What's more, the experience he presents is, they would say, at odds with the fact that he himself was an indulged and rewarded child of the Communist regime until 1968.

The totalitarian system is terribly hard on people, as Kundera recognizes, but the hardness of life has a much more complicated shape than we find in his presentation of it. Kundera's picture, his critics would tell you, is the sort of picture that you would see from a very capable foreign journalist who'd spent a few days in our country. Such a picture is acceptable to the Western reader because it confirms his expectations; it reinforces the fairy tale about good and evil, which a good child likes to hear again and again. But for these Czech readers our reality is no fairy tale. They expect a much more comprehensive and complex picture, a deeper insight into our lives from a writer of Kundera's stature. Kundera certainly has other aspirations for his writing than only to give a picture of Czech reality, but those attributes of his work may not be so relevant for the Czech audience I'm talking about.

Another reason for the allergy probably has to do with the prudery of some Czech readers. Although in their personal lives they may not behave puritanically, they are rather more strict about an author's morality.

Last but not least is an extraliterary reason, which may, however, be at the very core of the charge against him. At the time when Kundera was achieving his greatest world popularity, Czech culture was in a bitter struggle with the totalitarian system. Intellectuals at home as well as those in exile shared in this struggle. They underwent all sorts of hardships: they sacrificed their personal freedom, their professional positions, their time, their comfortable lives. For example, Josef Škvorecký and his wife virtually abandoned their personal lives to work from abroad on behalf of suppressed Czech literature. Kundera seems to many people to have stood apart from this kind of effort. Surely it was Kundera's right—why should every writer have to become a fighter?—and it certainly can be argued that he has done more than enough for the Czech cause by his writing itself. Anyway, I have tried to explain to you, quite candidly, why Kundera has been accepted in his own country with considerably more hesitation than in the rest of the world.

In his defense, let me say that there is a kind of xenophobia here with respect to the suffering of the last half century. The Czechs are by now rather possessive of their suffering, and though this is perhaps understandable and a natural enough

deformation, it has resulted, in my opinion, in an unjust deni-
gration of Kundera, who is, without a doubt, one of the great
Czech writers of this century.

Roth: The official, or officialized, writers are a bit of a mystery to me. Were they all bad writers? Were there any interesting opportunistic writers? I say opportunistic writers rather
than believing writers because, though there may well have
been believers among the writers in the first decade or so after
World War II, I assume that during the past decade the official
writers were opportunists and nothing more. Correct me if
I'm wrong about that. And then tell me, was it possible to remain a good writer and accept the official rulers and their
rules? Or was the work automatically weakened and compromised by this acceptance?

Klíma: It's quite true that there is a basic difference between
authors who supported the regime in the fifties and those who
supported it after the occupation in 1968. Before the war, what
was called leftist literature played a relatively important role. The
fact that the Soviet army liberated the greater part of the republic further strengthened this leftist tendency; so did the memory
of Munich and the Western powers' desertion of Czechoslovakia, despite all their treaties and promises. The younger generation especially succumbed to illusions of a new and more just
society that the Communists were going to build. It was precisely this generation that soon saw through the regime and
contributed enormously to setting off the '68 Prague Spring
movement and to demystifying the Stalinist dictatorship.

After 1968 there was no longer any reason for anyone, except perhaps a few frenzied fanatics, to share those postwar illusions. The Soviet army had changed in the eyes of the nation
from a liberating army to an army of occupation, and the regime that supported this occupation had changed into a band
of collaborators. If a writer didn't notice these changes, his
blindness deprived him of the right to count himself among
creative spirits; if he noticed them but pretended he knew
nothing about them, we may rightfully call him an opportunist
—it is probably the kindest word we can use.

Of course the problem lay in the fact that the regime did not
last just a few months or years but two decades. This meant that,

exceptions apart—and the regime persecuted these exceptions harshly—virtually a generation of protesters, from the end of the seventies on, was hounded into emigration. Everyone else had to accept the regime in some way or even support it. Television and radio had to function somehow, the publishing houses had to cover paper with print. Even quite decent people thought, "If I don't hold this job, someone worse will. If I do not write—and I shall try to smuggle at least a bit of truth through to the reader—the only people left will be those who are willing to serve the regime devotedly and uncritically."

I want to avoid saying that everyone who published anything over the past twenty years is necessarily a bad writer. It's true too that the regime gradually tried to make some important Czech writers their own and so began to publish some of their works. In this way it published at least a few works by Bohumil Hrabal and the poet Miroslav Holub (both of them made public self-criticisms) and also poems by the Nobel Prize winner Jaroslav Seifert, who signed Charter 77. But it can be stated categorically that the effort of publication, getting past all the traps laid by the censor, was a severe burden on the works of many of those who were published. I have carefully compared the works of Hrabal—who, to my mind, is one of the greatest living European prose writers—that came out in samizdat form and were published abroad and those that were published officially in Czechoslovakia. The changes he was evidently forced to make by the censor are, from the point of view of the work, monstrous in the true sense of the word. But much worse than this was the fact that many writers reckoned with censorship beforehand and deformed their own work, and so, of course, deformed themselves.

Only in the eighties did "angry young men" begin to appear, especially among young writers, theater people, and the authors of protest songs. They said exactly what they meant and risked their works not coming out or even losing their livelihoods. They contributed to our having a free literature today —and not only literature.

Roth: Since the Soviet occupation of Czechoslovakia a sizable sampling of contemporary Czech writers have been published in the United States: from among those living in exile,

Kundera, Pavel Kohout, Škvorecký, Jirí Grusa, and Arnost Lustig; from among those in Czechoslovakia, you, Vaculík, Hrabal, Holub, and Havel. This is an astonishing representation from a small European country—I, for one, can't think of ten Norwegian or ten Dutch writers who have been published in America since 1968. To be sure, the place that produced Kafka has special significance, but I don't think either of us believes that this accounts for the attention that your nation's literature has been able to command in the West. You have had the ear of many foreign writers. They have been incredibly deferential to your literature. You have been given a special hearing and your lives and works have absorbed a lot of their thinking. Has it occurred to you that this has now all changed and that in the future you're perhaps going to be talking not so much to us but to one another again?

Klíma: Certainly the harsh fate of the nation, as we have said, suggested many compelling themes. A writer was himself often forced by circumstances to have experiences that would otherwise have remained foreign to him and that, when he wrote about them, may have appeared to readers almost exotic. It's also true that writing—or work in the arts altogether—was the last place where one could still set up shop as an individual. Many creative people actually became writers just for this reason. All this will pass to some extent, even though I think that there is an aversion to the cult of the elite in Czech society and that Czech writers will always be concerned with the everyday problems of ordinary people. This applies to the great writers of the past as well as to contemporary ones: Kafka never ceased to be an office worker or Capek a journalist; Hasek and Hrabal spent a lot of their time in smoky pubs with beer-drinking buddies. Holub never left his job as a scientist and Vaculík stubbornly avoided everything that might drag him away from leading the life of the most ordinary of citizens. Of course as changes come in social life, so will changes in themes. But I'm not sure this will mean our literature will necessarily become uninteresting to outsiders. I believe that our literature has pushed open the gate to Europe and even to the world just a crack, not only because of its subject but because of its quality too.

Roth: And inside Czechoslovakia? Right now I know people are wildly hungry for books, but after the revolutionary fervor subsides, with the sense of unity in struggle dissipating, might you not come to mean far less to readers here than you did when you were fighting to keep alive for them a language other than that of the official newspapers, the official speeches, and the official government-sanctioned books?

Klíma: I agree that our literature will lose some of its extraliterary appeal. But many think that these secondary appeals were distracting both writers and readers with questions that should really have been answered by journalists, by sociologists, by political analysts. Let's go back to what I call the intriguing plots offered by the totalitarian system. Stupidity triumphant, the arrogance of power, violence against the innocent, police brutality, the ruthlessness that permeates life and produces labor camps and prisons, the humiliation of man, life based on lies and pretenses—these stories will lose their topicality, I hope, even though writers will probably return to consider them again after a while. But the new situation must bring new subjects. In the first place, forty years of the totalitarian system have left behind a material and spiritual emptiness, and filling this emptiness will involve difficulties, tension, disappointment, and tragedy.

It is also true that in Czechoslovakia a feeling for books has a deep tradition, reaching back to the Middle Ages, and even with television sets everywhere, it's hard to find a family that does not own a library of good books. Even though I don't like prophesying, I believe that at least for now the fall of the totalitarian system will not turn literature into an occasional subject with which to ward off boredom at parties.

Roth: The Polish writer Tadeusz Borowski said that the only way to write about the Holocaust was as the guilty, as the complicit and implicated; that is what he did in his first-person fictional memoir, *This Way for the Gas, Ladies and Gentlemen*. There Borowski may even have pretended to a dramatically more chilling degree of moral numbness than he felt as an Auschwitz prisoner, precisely to reveal the Auschwitz horror as the wholly innocent victims could not. Under the domination of Soviet Communism, some of the most original Eastern European writers I have read in English have positioned themselves similarly—Tadeusz Konwicki, Danilo Kis, and Kundera, say, to name only three K's who have crawled out from under Kafka's cockroach to tell us that there are no uncontaminated angels, that the evil is inside as well as outside. Still, this sort of self-flagellation, despite its ironies and nuances, cannot be free from the element of blame, from the moral habit of situating the source of the evil in the system even when examining how the system contaminates you and me. You are used to being on the side of truth, with all the risks entailed in becoming righteous, pious, didactic, dutifully counterpropagandistic. You are not used to living without that well-defined, recognizable, objective sort of evil. I wonder what will happen to your writing—and to the moral habits embedded in it—with the removal of the system: without them, with just you and me.

Klíma: That question makes me think back over everything I have said until now. I have found that I often do describe a conflict in which I am defending myself against an aggressive world, embodied by the system. But I have often written about the conflict between the system and me without necessarily supposing that the world is worse than I am. I should say that the dichotomy, I on the one side and the world on the other, is the way in which not only writers but all of us are tempted to perceive things.

Whether the world appears as a bad system or as bad individuals, bad laws, or bad luck is not really the point. We could both name dozens of works created in free societies in which the hero is flung here and there by a bad, hostile, misunderstanding society, and so assure each other that it is not only in our part of the world that writers succumb to the temptation to see the conflict between themselves—or their heroes—and the world around them as the dualism of good and evil.

I would imagine that those here in the habit of seeing the world dualistically will certainly be able to find some other form of external evil. On the other hand, the changed situation could help others to step out of the cycle of merely reacting to the cruelty or stupidity of the system and lead them to reflect anew on man in the world. And what will happen to my writing now? Over the past three months I have been swamped with so many other duties that the idea that someday I'll write a story in peace and quiet seems to me fantastic. But not to evade the question—for my writing, the fact that I shall no longer have to worry about the unhappy social system I regard as a relief.

Roth: Kafka. Last November, while the demonstrations that resulted in the new Czechoslovakia were being addressed by the outcast ex-convict Havel here in Prague, I was teaching a course on Kafka at a college in New York City. The students read *The Castle*, about K.'s tedious, fruitless struggle to gain recognition as a land surveyor from that mighty and inaccessible sleepyhead who controls the castle bureaucracy, Mr. Klamm. When the photograph appeared in the *New York Times* showing Havel reaching across a conference table to shake the hand of the old regime's prime minister, I showed it to my class. "Well," I said, "K. meets Klamm at last." The students were pleased when Havel decided to run for president—that would put K. in the castle, and as successor, no less, to Klamm's boss.

Kafka's prescient irony may not be the most remarkable attribute of his work, but it's always stunning to think about it. He is anything but a fantasist creating a dream or a nightmare world as opposed to a realistic one. His fiction keeps insisting that what seems to be unimaginable hallucination and hopeless paradox is precisely what constitutes one's reality. In works like "The Metamorphosis," *The Trial*, and *The Castle*, he chronicles the education of someone who comes to accept—rather too late, in the case of the accused Joseph K.—that what looks to be outlandish and ludicrous and unbelievable, beneath your dignity and concern, is nothing less than what is happening to you: that thing beneath your dignity turns out to be your destiny.

"It was no dream," Kafka writes only moments after Gregor Samsa awakens to discover that he is no longer a good son supporting his family but a repellent insect. The *dream*, according to Kafka, is of a world of probability, of proportion, of stability and order, of cause and effect—a dependable world of dignity and justice is what is absurdly fantastic to him. How amused Kafka would have been by the indignation of those dreamers who tell us daily, "I didn't come here to be insulted!" In Kafka's world—and not just in Kafka's world—life begins to make sense only when we realize that that is why we *are* here.

I'd like to know what role Kafka may have played in your

imagination during your years of being here to be insulted, tormented and debased. Kafka was banned by the Communist authorities from the bookstores, libraries, and universities in his own city and throughout Czechoslovakia. Why? What frightened them? What enraged them? What did he mean to the rest of you who know his work intimately and may even feel a strong affinity with his origins?

Klíma: Like you, I have studied Kafka's works—not too long ago I wrote an extensive essay about him and a play about his love affair with Felice Bauer. I would formulate my opinion on the conflict between the dream world and the real one in his work just a little bit differently. You say: "The dream, according to Kafka, is of a world of probability, of proportion, of stability and order, of cause and effect—a dependable world of dignity and justice is what is absurdly fantastic to him." I would replace the word *fantastic* with the word *unattainable*. What you call the dream world was rather for Kafka the real world, the world in which order reigned, in which people, at least as he saw it, were able to grow fond of one another, make love, have families, be orderly in all their duties—but this world was for him, with his almost sick truthfulness, unattainable. His heroes suffered not because they were unable to realize their dream but because they were not strong enough to enter properly into the real world, to properly fulfill their duty.

The question why Kafka was banned under Communist regimes is answered in a single sentence by the hero of my novel *Love and Garbage*: "What matters most about Kafka's personality is his honesty." A regime that is built on deception, that asks people to pretend, that demands external agreement without caring about the inner conviction of those to whom it turns for consent, a regime afraid of anyone who asks about the sense of his action, cannot allow anyone whose veracity attained such fascinating or even terrifying completeness to speak to the people.

If you ask what Kafka meant for me, we get back to the question we somehow keep circling. On the whole Kafka was an unpolitical writer. I like to quote the entry in his diary for August 21, 1914. It is very short. "Germany has declared war on Russia.—Swimming in the afternoon." Here the historic, world-shaking plane and the personal one are exactly level. I am sure that Kafka wrote only from his innermost need to confess his personal crises and so solve what was for him insoluble in his personal life—in the first place his relationship with his father and his inability to pass beyond a certain limit in his relationships with women. In my essay on Kafka I show that, for instance, his murderous machine in the short story "In the Penal Colony" is a wonderful, passionate, and desperate image of the state of being married or engaged. Several years after writing this story he confided to Milena Jesenska his feelings on thinking about their living together:

> You know, when I try to write down something [about our engagement] the swords whose points surround me in a circle begin slowly to approach the body, it's the most complete torture; when they begin to graze me it's already so terrible that I immediately at the first scream betray you, myself, everything.

Kafka's metaphors were so powerful that they far exceeded his original intentions. I know that *The Trial* as well as "In the Penal Colony" have been explained as ingenious prophesies of the terrible fate that befell the Jewish nation during World War II, which broke out fifteen years after Kafka's death. But it was no prophecy of genius. These works merely prove that a creator who knows how to reflect his most personal experiences deeply and truthfully also touches the suprapersonal or social spheres. Again I am answering the question about political content in literature. Literature doesn't have to scratch around for political realities or even worry about systems that come and go; it can transcend them and still answer questions that the system evokes in people. This is the most important lesson that I extracted for myself from Kafka.

Roth: Ivan, you were born a Jew and, because you were a Jew, you spent part of your childhood in a concentration camp. Do you feel that this background distinguishes your work—or that, under the Communists, it altered your predicament as a writer—in ways worth talking about? In the decade before the war, Central Europe without Jews as a pervasive cultural presence—without Jewish readers or Jewish writers, without Jewish journalists, playwrights, publishers, critics—was unthinkable. Now that the literary life in this part of Europe is about to be conducted once again in an intellectual atmosphere that harks back to prewar days, I wonder if—perhaps even for the first time—the absence of Jews will register with any impact on the society. Is there a remnant left in Czech literature of the prewar Jewish culture, or have the mentality and sensibility of Jews, which were once strong in Prague, left Czech literature for good?

Klíma: Anyone who has been through a concentration camp as a child—who has been completely dependent on an external power that can at any moment come in and beat or kill him and everyone around him—probably moves through life at least a bit differently from people who have been spared such an education. That life can be snapped like a piece of string—that was my daily lesson as a child. And the effect of this on my writing? An obsession with the problem of justice, with the feelings of people who have been condemned and cast out, the lonely and the helpless. The themes issuing from this, thanks to the fate of my country, have lost nothing of their topicality. And the effect on my life? Among friends I have always been known as an optimist. Anyone who survives being repeatedly condemned to death may suffer either from paranoia all his life or from a confidence not justified by reason that everything can be survived and everything will turn out all right in the end.

As for the influence of Jewish culture on our present culture —if we look back, we are apt to idealize the cultural reality in rather the same way that we idealize our own childhoods. If I look back at my native Prague, say at the beginning of this century, I am amazed by the marvelous mix of cultures and customs, by the city's many great men. Kafka, Rilke, Hasek, Werfel, Einstein, Dvořák, Max Brod . . . But of course the past of Prague, which I name here only as a symbol of Central Europe, consisted not only of a dazzling number of the greatly gifted, not only of a culture surge; it was also a time of hatred, of furious and petty and often bloody clashes.

If we speak of the magnificent surge of Jewish culture that Prague witnessed more than almost anywhere else, we must recognize also that there has never been a long period here without some sort of anti-Semitic explosion. To most people the Jews represented a foreign element, which they tried at the very least to isolate. There is no doubt that Jewish culture enriched Czech culture, by the very fact that, like German culture, which also had an important presence in Bohemia—and Jewish literature in Bohemia was largely written in German—it became for the developing Czech culture, whose evolution had been stifled for two hundred years, a bridge to Western Europe.

What has survived from that past? Seemingly nothing. But I'm convinced this is not the whole story. The present longing to overcome the nihilist past with tolerance, the longing to return to untainted sources, is this not a response to the almost forgotten warning call of the dead, and indeed the murdered, to us, the living?

Roth: Havel. A complicated man of mischievous irony and solid intellect like Havel, a man of letters, a student of philosophy, an idealist with strong spiritual inclinations, a playful thinker who speaks his native language with precision and directness, who reasons with logic and nuance, who laughs with gusto, who is enchanted with theatricality, who knows intimately and understands his country's history and culture—such a person would have even less chance of being elected president in America than Jesse Jackson or Geraldine Ferraro.

Just this morning I went to the Castle, to a press conference Havel held about his trips to the United States and Russia, and I listened with pleasure and some astonishment to a president composing, on the spot, sentences that were punchy, fluent, and rich with human observation, sentences of a kind that probably haven't been formulated so abundantly—and off the cuff—at our White House since Lincoln was shot.

When a German journalist asked whose company Havel had most preferred, the Dalai Lama's, George Bush's, or Mikhail Gorbachev's—all three of whom he's recently met—he began, "Well, it wouldn't be wise to make a hierarchy of sympathy . . ." When asked to describe Gorbachev, he said that one of Gorbachev's most attractive qualities is that "he is a man who doesn't hesitate to confess his embarrassment when he feels it." When he announced that he had scheduled the arrival of the West German president for March 15—the same day Hitler entered Prague in 1939—one of the reporters noted that Havel "liked anniversaries," whereupon Havel immediately corrected him. "No," he told him, "I did not say that I 'liked anniversaries.' I spoke about symbols, metaphors, and a sense of dramatic structures in politics."

How did this happen here? And why did it happen here to Havel? As he would probably be the first to recognize, he was not the only stubborn, outspoken person among you, nor was he alone imprisoned for his ideas. I'd like you to tell me why he has emerged as the embodiment of this nation's new idea of itself. I wonder if he was quite such a hero to large segments of the nation when, altogether quixotically—the very epitome of the foolish, high-minded intellectual who doesn't understand real life—he was writing long, seemingly futile letters of protest to his predecessor, President Husak. Didn't a lot of people think of him then as either a nuisance or a nut? For the hundreds of thousands who never really raised an objection to the Communist regime, isn't worshiping Havel a convenient means by which to jettison, practically overnight, their own complicity with what you call the nihilist past?

Klíma: Before I try to explain that remarkable phenomenon "Havel," I'll try to give my opinion on the personality named Havel. (I hope I won't be breaking the law, still extant, that virtually forbids criticism of the president.) I agree with your characterization of Havel. Only, as someone who has met him innumerable times over the past twenty-five years, I would supplement it. Havel is mainly known to the world as an important dramatist, then as an interesting essayist, and lastly as a dissident, an opponent of the regime so firm in his principles that he did not hesitate to undergo anything for his convictions, including a Czech prison—more exactly, a Communist prison. But in this list of Havel's skills or professions there is one thing missing, and in my opinion it's the fundamental one.

As a dramatist Havel is placed by world critics in the stream of the theater of the absurd. But back when it was still permissible to present Havel's plays in our theaters, the Czech public understood them primarily as political plays. I used to say, half jokingly, that Havel became a dramatist simply because at that time the theater was the only platform from which political opinions could be expressed. Right from the beginning, when I got to know him, Havel was, for me, in the first place a politician, in the second place an essayist of genius, and only last a dramatist. I am not ordering the value of his achievements but rather the priority of interest, personal inclination, and enthusiasm.

In the Czech political desert, where former representatives of the democratic regime had either emigrated, been locked up, or had completely disappeared from the political scene, Havel was for a long time really the only active representative of the line of thoroughly democratic Czech politics represented by Tomáš Masaryk. Today Masaryk lives in the national consciousness rather as an idol or as the author of the principles on which the First Republic was built. Few people know that he was an outstanding politician, a master of compromises and surprising political moves, of risky, ethically motivated acts. (One of these was the passionate defense of a poor, wandering young Jew from a well-to-do family, Leopold Hossner, who was accused and convicted of the ritual murder of a young dressmaker. This act of Masaryk's so enraged the Czech nationalist public that it looked for a while as if the experienced politician had committed political suicide—he must then have seemed to his contemporaries to be "a nuisance or a nut.") Havel brilliantly continued in Masaryk's line of "suicidal" ethical behavior, though of course he carried on his political activity under much more formidable conditions than those of old Austria-Hungary. His letter to Husak in 1975 was indeed an ethically motivated but expressly political—even suicidal—act, just like the signature campaigns that he instigated over and over again, for which he was always persecuted.

Like Masaryk, Havel was a master of compromises and alliances who never lost sight of the basic aim: to remove the totalitarian system and replace it with a renewed system of pluralist democracy. For that aim he did not hesitate in 1977 to join together all the antitotalitarian forces, whether they were reform Communists—all of them long since expelled from the party—members of the arts underground, or believing Christians. The greatest significance of Charter 77 lay precisely in this unifying act, and I haven't the slightest doubt that it was Václav Havel himself who was the author of this conception and that his was the personality that was able to link such absolutely heterogeneous political forces.

Havel's candidacy for president and his election were, in the first place, an expression of the precipitate, truly revolutionary course of events in this country. When I was returning from a meeting of one of the committees of Civic Forum one day toward the end of last November, my friends and I were saying to one another that the time was near when we should nominate our candidate for the office of president. We agreed then that the only candidate to consider, for he enjoyed the relatively wide support of the public, was Alexander Dubček. But it became clear a few days later that the revolution had gone beyond the point where any candidate who was connected, if only by his past, with the Communist Party was acceptable to the younger generation of Czechs. At that moment the only suitable candidate emerged—Václav Havel. Again it was an example of Havel's political instincts—and Dubček certainly remained the only suitable candidate for Slovakia—that he linked his candidacy with the condition that Dubček should be given the second-highest function in the state.

I explain the change of attitude toward him by the Czech public—because for a certain sector here Havel was, indeed, more or less unknown, or known as the son of a rich capitalist and even as a convict—by the revolutionary ethos that seized the nation. In a certain atmosphere, in the midst of a crowd, however civil and restrained the crowd may be, an individual suddenly identifies himself with the prevailing mood and state of mind and captures the crowd's enthusiasm. It's true that the majority of the country shared in the doings of the former system, but it's also true that the majority hated it at the same time just because it had made them complicit in its awfulness, and hardly anyone identified himself any longer with that regime which had so often humiliated, deceived, and cheated them. Within a few days Havel became the symbol of revolutionary change, the man who would lead society out of its crisis—nobody had any exact idea how—lead it out of evil to good. Whether the motivation for supporting him was basically metaphysical, whether this support will be maintained or eventually come to be based more on reason and practical concerns, time will tell.

Roth: Earlier we spoke about the future. May I close with a prophecy of my own? What I say may strike you as arrogantly patronizing—the freedom-rich man warning the freedom-poor man about the dangers of becoming rich. You have fought for something for so many years now, something that you needed like air, and what I am going to say is that the air you fought for is poisoned a little too. I assure you that I am not a sacred artist putting down the profane nor am I a poor little rich boy whining about his luxuries. I am not complaining. I am only making a report to the academy.

There is still a pre–World War II varnish on the societies that, since the forties, have been under Soviet domination. The countries of the satellite world have been caught in a time warp, with the result, for instance, that the McLuhanite revolution has barely touched your lives. Prague is still very much Prague and not a part of the global village. Czechoslovakia is still Czechoslovakia, and yet the Europe you are rejoining is a rapidly homogenizing Europe, a Europe whose very distinct nations are on the brink of being radically transformed. You live here in a society of prelapsarian racial innocence, knowing nothing of the great postcolonial migrations—your society, to my eyes, is astonishingly white. And then there is money and the culture of money that takes over in a market economy.

What are you going to do about money, you writers, about coming out from under the wing of a subsidized writers' union, a subsidized publishing industry, and competing in the marketplace and publishing profitable books? And what of this market economy that your new government is talking about— five, ten years from now, what are you going to make of the commercialized culture that it breeds?

As Czechoslovakia becomes a free, democratic consumer society, you writers are going to find yourselves bedeviled by a number of new adversaries from which, strangely enough, repressive, sterile totalitarianism protected you. Particularly unsettling will be the one adversary that is the pervasive, all-powerful archenemy of literature, literacy, and language. I can guarantee you that no defiant crowds will ever rally in Wenceslas Square to overthrow its tyranny nor will any playwright-intellectual be elevated by the outraged masses to redeem the national soul from the fatuity into which this adversary reduces virtually all of human discourse. I am speaking about that trivializer of everything, commercial television—not a handful of channels nobody wants to watch because it is controlled by an oafish state censor but a dozen or two channels of boring clichéd television that most everybody watches all the time because it is *entertaining*. At long last you and your writer colleagues have broken out of the intellectual prison of Communist totalitarianism. Welcome to the World of Total Entertainment. You don't know what you've been missing. Or do you?

Klíma: As a man who has, after all, lived for some time in the United States, and who for twenty years has been published only in the West, I am aware of the "danger" that a free society, and especially a market mechanism, brings to culture. Of course I know that most people prefer virtually any sort of kitsch to Cortázar or Hrabal. I know that the period will probably pass when even books of poetry in our country reach editions of tens of thousands. I suppose that a wave of literary and television garbage will break over our market—we can hardly prevent it. Nor am I alone in realizing that, in its newly won freedom, culture not only gains something important but also loses something. At the beginning of January one of our best Czech film directors was interviewed on television, and he gave a warning against the commercialization of culture. When he said that the censorship had protected us not only from the best works of our own and foreign culture but also from the worst of mass culture, he annoyed many people, but I understood him. A memorandum on the position of television recently appeared that states that

> television, owing to its widespread influence, is directly able to contribute to the greatest extent toward a moral revival. This of course presupposes . . . setting up a new structure, and not only in an organizational sense but in the sense of the moral and creative responsibility of the institution as a whole and of every single member of its staff, especially its leading ones. The times we are living through offer our television a unique chance to try for something that does not exist elsewhere in the world.

The memorandum does not of course ask for the introduction of censorship, but of a supraparty arts council, a group of independent authorities of the highest spiritual and moral standards. I signed this memorandum as the president of the Czech PEN club, although personally, for myself, I thought that the desire to structure the TV of a free society in this way was rather utopian. The language of the memorandum struck me as the kind of unrealistic and moralistic language that can emerge from the euphoria of revolution.

I have mentioned that, among intellectuals especially, utopian ideas have begun to surface about how this country will link the good points of both systems—something from the state-controlled system, something from the new market system. And these ideas are probably strongest in the realm of culture. The future will show to what extent they are purely utopian. Will there be commercial television in our country, or will we continue only with subsidized, centrally directed broadcasting? And if this last does remain, will it manage to resist the demands of mass taste? We'll know only in time.

I have already told you that in Czechoslovakia literature has always enjoyed not only popularity but esteem. This is borne out by the fact that in a country with fewer than twelve million inhabitants, books by good writers, both Czech and translated, were published in editions of hundreds of thousands. What's more, the system is changing in our country at a time when ecological thinking is growing tremendously (the environment in Czechoslovakia is one of the worst in Europe), and it surely makes no sense for us to strive to purify the environment and at the same time to pollute our culture. So it is not really such a utopian idea to try to influence the mass media to maintain standards and even educate the nation. If at least some part of that idea could be realized, it would certainly be, as the authors of the memorandum say, a unique event in the history of mass communications. And after all, impulses of a spiritual character really have, from time to time, come from this little country of ours in the center of Europe.

Isaac Bashevis Singer

[1976]

SOME MONTHS after I first read Bruno Schulz and decided to include him in the Penguin series "Writers from the Other Europe," I learned that when his autobiographical novel, *The Street of Crocodiles*, appeared in English fourteen years ago, it had been reviewed and praised by Isaac Bashevis Singer. Since Schulz and Singer were born in Poland of Jewish parents within twelve years of each other—Schulz in 1892 in the provincial Galician city of Drohobycz, Singer in Radzymin, near Warsaw, in 1904—I telephoned Singer, whom I had met socially once or twice, and asked if we might get together to talk about Schulz and about what life had been like for a Jewish writer in Poland during the decades when they were both coming of age there as artists. Our meeting took place in Singer's Manhattan apartment at the end of November 1976.

Roth: When did you first read Schulz, here or in Poland?

Singer: I read him in the United States for the first time. I must tell you, like many another writer I approach a book of fiction always with some kind of doubts; since the majority of writers are not really good writers, I assume when I am sent a book that it's going to be not too good a book. And I was surprised the moment I began to read Schulz. I said to myself, here is a first-class writer.

Roth: Had you known Schulz's name before?

Singer: No, I didn't even know Schulz's name. I left Poland in 1935. Schulz was not really known then—and if he was known, I didn't know about him. I never heard of him. My first impression was that this man writes like Kafka. There are two writers about whom they say they write like Kafka. One was Agnon. Agnon used to say that he never read Kafka, but people have some doubts about it. As a matter of fact he did read Kafka, there is no question about it. I wouldn't say he was influenced by Kafka; there is a possibility that two or three people write in the same kind of style, in the same spirit. Because not every person is completely unique. If God could

246

create one Kafka, He could have created three Kafkas, if He was in the mood to do so. But the more I read Schulz—maybe I shouldn't say it—but when I read him, I said he's better than Kafka. There is greater strength in some of his stories. Also he's very strong in the absurd, though not in a silly way but in a clever way. I would say that between Schulz and Kafka there is something that Goethe calls *Wahlverwandtschaft*, an affinity of souls that you have chosen for yourself. This might have been the case completely with Schulz, and it might also be to a degree with Agnon.

Roth: To me it seems as though Schulz could not keep his imagination away from anything, including the work of other writers, and particularly the work of someone like Kafka, with whom he does seem to have had important affinities of background and temperament. Just as in *The Street of Crocodiles* he reimagines his hometown of Drohobycz into a more terrifying and wonderful place than it actually was—partly, as he says, to be "liberated from the tortures of boredom"—so, in a way, he reimagines bits and pieces of Kafka for his own purposes. Kafka may have put some funny ideas into his head, but that they serve different purposes is probably best exemplified by the fact that in Schulz's book the character transformed into a cockroach isn't the son but the father. Imagine Kafka imagining that. Out of the question. Certain artistic predilections may be similar, but these predilections are in league with wildly different desires. As you know, Schulz translated *The Trial* into Polish in 1936. I wonder if Kafka was ever translated into Yiddish.

Singer: Not that I know of. As a young man I read many of the writers of the world in Yiddish; if Kafka would have been translated into Yiddish, this would have been in the thirties and I would have known about it. I'm afraid there is no Yiddish translation. Or maybe there is and I don't know about it, which is also possible.

Roth: Do you have any idea why Schulz wrote in Polish rather than in Yiddish?

Singer: Most probably he was brought up in a home that was already half assimilated. Probably his parents spoke Polish. Many Jews in Poland—after Poland became independent, and even before—brought up their children to speak Polish. That happened even in Russian Poland, but especially in Galicia, the part of Poland that belonged to Austria and where the Poles had a kind of autonomy and were not culturally suppressed. It was a natural thing that people who themselves spoke Polish brought up their children in this way. Whether it was good or bad I don't know. But since Polish was, so to say, his mother tongue, Schulz had no choice, since a real writer will write not in a learned language but in the language he knows from his childhood. And Schulz's strength, of course, is in the language. I read him first in English, and though the translation is a good one, when I read him later in Polish I saw this strength very clearly.

Roth: Schulz was born of Jewish parents in Poland in 1892. You were born in 1904. Was it unusual for a Polish Jew of that generation to write in Polish, or to write in Yiddish, as you did?

Singer: The Jews had a number of important writers who wrote in Polish, and all of them were born more or less at this time, in the 1890s. Antoni Slonimski, Julian Tuwim, Józef Wittlin—all these writers were about this age. They were good writers, talented writers, but nothing special. Some of them, however, were very strong in the Polish language. Tuwim was a master of Polish. Slonimski was a grandson of Chaim Zelig Slonimski, who was the founder of the Hebrew newspaper *Hatsefira* in Warsaw. Slonimski was converted to Catholicism by his parents when he was a child, while Tuwim and Wittlin remained Jews, though Jews only in name. They had very little to do with Yiddish writers. My older brother, Israel Joshua Singer, was born more or less at the same time and was a known Yiddish writer in Poland and had no association with either of these writers. I was still a beginner, in Poland, and I certainly had nothing to do with them. We Yiddish writers looked at them as people who had left their roots and culture and become a part of Polish culture, which we considered younger and perhaps less important than our culture. They felt that we Yiddish writers were writing for ignorant people, poor people, people without education, while they were writing for readers who went to universities. So we both had a good reason to despise each other. Though the truth is, they had no choice and we had no choice. They didn't know Yiddish, we didn't know Polish. Although I was born in Poland, Polish was not as close to me as Yiddish. And I spoke it with an accent. As a matter of fact, I speak all languages with an accent.

Roth: Not Yiddish, I take it.

Singer: Yes. The Litvaks say I speak Yiddish with an accent.

Roth: I want to ask you about Warsaw in the thirties. Schulz studied architecture in Lwów as a young man, and then, as far as I know, he returned to the Galician town of Drohobycz, where for the rest of his life he taught drawing in the high school. He did not leave Drohobycz for any significant length of time until his middle or late thirties, when he came to Warsaw. What kind of cultural atmosphere would he have found in Warsaw then?

Singer: There are two things to remember about Schulz. First of all, he was a terribly modest person. The very fact that he stayed in this town, which was far away from the center of everything, shows that he was highly modest, and also kind of afraid. He felt like a yokel who's afraid to come to the big city and to meet people who are already famous. He was afraid, most probably, that they would make fun of him or they would ignore him. I think this man was a bundle of nerves. He suffered from all the inhibitions that a writer can suffer. When you look at his picture you see the face of a man who never made peace with life. Tell me, Mr. Roth, he was not married. Did he have some girlfriends?

Roth: If his drawings are any indication, I would think he had strange relations with women. A recurring subject in the drawings that I've seen is female dominance and male submission. There is an eerie, almost tawdry erotic suggestiveness to some of these pictures—small, supplicating men looking not unlike Schulz himself and remote, half-naked adolescent girls or statuesque, painted shopgirls. They remind me a little of the "trashy" erotic world of another Polish writer, Witold Gombrowicz. Like Kafka, who also never married, Schulz is said to have had long and intense correspondences with women and to have lived a good deal of his erotic life through the mails. Jerzy Ficowski, his biographer, who wrote the introduction to the Penguin edition, says that *The Street of Crocodiles* began as a series of letters to a close woman friend. They must have been some letters. According to Ficowski, it was this woman

who urged Schulz—who was indeed a deeply inhibited person
—to see these letters as a work of literature. But to return to
Schulz and Warsaw—what was the cultural life like when he
got there in the middle thirties? What was the dominant mood
or ideology among writers and intellectuals?

Singer: I would say they had almost the same movement
that we have today—kind of leftist. This was true of the Jewish
writers who were writing in Polish. They were all leftist or
considered leftists by the old Polish writers, who looked upon
these Jewish writers, actually, as intruders.

Roth: Because they were writing in Polish?

Singer: Because they were writing in Polish. They might
have said, "Why the hell don't they write in their own jargon,
their own Yiddish—what do they want from us Poles?" Still, in
the thirties, these Jewish writers became very important despite their adversaries. First, because they were quite good
writers, though not great writers; second, because they were leftists, and that was the trend then; and third, because they were
energetic, they published often in the magazine *Wiadomosci Lit-
erackie*, they wrote for the variety theater, and so on. Sometimes these Jewish writers wrote things that sounded anti-Semitic
to the Jews. Of course I did not agree that it was anti-Semitism,
because some critics said the same thing about me. Although I
wrote in Yiddish, they said, "Why do you write about Jewish
thieves and Jewish prostitutes?" and I said, "Shall I write about
Spanish thieves and Spanish prostitutes? I write about the
thieves and prostitutes that I know."

Roth: When you wrote in praise of Schulz back in 1963, you
did have certain criticisms to make of him. You said, "If Schulz
had identified himself more with his own people, he might not
have expended so much energy on imitation, parody, and caricature." I wonder if you have any more to say about that.

Singer: I felt so when I wrote this and I think I feel so too
now. There is great mockery in the writing both of Schulz and
of Kafka, although in Kafka the mockery is more hidden. I
think that Schulz had enough power to write real serious novels but instead often wrote a kind of parody. And I think basically he developed this style because he was not really at home,
neither at home among the Poles nor at home among the
Jews. It's a style that's somewhat characteristic also of Kafka,

because Kafka also felt that he had no roots. He was a Jew who wrote in German and lived in Czechoslovakia, where the language was actually Czech. It is true that Kafka might have been more assimilated than Schulz—he didn't live in as Jewish a town as Drohobycz, which was full of Hasidim, and his father was maybe more of an assimilationist than Schulz's father, but the situation was basically the same, and as stylists the two writers were more or less of the same cut.

Roth: It's possible to think of Schulz's "rootlessness" another way: not as something that held him back from writing serious novels but as a condition upon which his particular talent and imagination thrived.

Singer: Yes, of course, that is true. If a genuine talent cannot be nourished directly from the soil, he will be nourished by something else. But from my point of view, I would rather have liked to have seen him as a Yiddish writer. He wouldn't have had all the time to be as negative and mocking as he was.

Roth: I wonder if it isn't negativism and mockery that drive Schulz so much as boredom and claustrophobia. Perhaps what sets him off on what he calls a "counteroffensive of fantasy" is that he is a man of enormous artistic gifts and imaginative riches living out his life as a high school teacher in a provincial town where his family are merchants. Also, he is his father's son, and his father, as he describes him, was, at least in his later years, a highly entertaining but terrifying madman, a grand "heresiarch," fascinated, Schulz says, "by doubtful and problematical forms." That last might be a good description of Schulz himself, who seems to me wholly conscious of just how close to madness, or heresy, his own agitated imagination could carry him. I don't think that with Schulz, any more than with Kafka, the greatest difficulty was an inability to be at home with this people or with that people, however much that may have added to his troubles. From the evidence of this book, it looks as though Schulz could barely identify himself with reality, let alone with the Jews. One is reminded of Kafka's remark on his communal affiliations: "What have I in common with the Jews? I have hardly anything in common with myself and should stand very quietly in the corner, content that I can breathe." Schulz needn't have remained in Drohobycz if he found it all that stifling. People can pick up and go. He could have stayed in Warsaw once he finally got there. But perhaps the claustrophobic environment that didn't suit the needs of the man was just what gave life to his kind of art. *Fermentation* is a favorite word of his. It may only have been in Drohobycz that Schulz's imagination fermented.

Singer: I think also that in Warsaw he felt he ought to get back to Drohobycz because in Warsaw everybody said, "Who is Schulz?" Writers are not really ready to see a young man from the provinces and immediately to say, "You are our brother, you are our teacher"—they are not inclined to do so. Most probably they said, "Another nuisance with a manuscript." Also, he was a Jew. And these Jewish writers in Poland, who were really the rulers of the literary field, they were cautious about the fact that they were Jews.

Roth: Cautious in what way?

Singer: They were called Jews by their adversaries, by those who did not like them. This was always the eternal reproach. "What are you doing, Mr. Tuwim, with your Hebrew name, writing in Polish? Why don't you go back to the ghetto with Israel Joshua Singer and the others?" That is the way it was. So when there came another Jew who writes Polish, they felt not really comfortable about it. Because there came another problem child.

Roth: I take it that it was easier to assimilate into artistic or intellectual circles than into the bourgeois world of Warsaw.

Singer: I would say that it was more difficult. I will tell you why. A Jewish lawyer, if he didn't like to be called Levin or Katz, could call himself Levinski or Kacinski and people didn't bother him. But about a writer they were always cautious. They would say, "You have nothing to do with us." I think that some small similarity exists even in this country with the Jewish writers who write in English and are at home in English. No writer here would say to Saul Bellow or to you, "Why don't you write in Yiddish, why don't you go back to East Broadway?" Yet some small part of that still exists. I would think that there are some conservative writers here or critics who would say that people like you are not really American writers. However, here the Jewish writers are not really ashamed of being Jewish and they don't apologize all the time. There, in Poland, there was an atmosphere of apologizing.

There they tried to show how Polish they were. And they tried of course to know Polish better than the Poles, in which they succeeded. But still the Poles said they have nothing to do with us . . . Let me make it clearer. Let's say if we would have now, here, a goy who would write in Yiddish, if this goy would be a failure, we would leave him in peace. But if he would be a great success, we would say, "What are you doing with Yiddish? Why don't you go back to the goyim, we don't need you."

Roth: A Polish Jew of your generation writing in Polish would have been as strange a creature as that?

Singer: Almost. And if there would be many such people, let's say there would be six goyim who would write in Yiddish, and there would come a seventh one . . .

Roth: Yes, it's clearer. You make it clearer.

Singer: I once was sitting in the subway with the Yiddish writer S, who had a beard, and at this time, forty years ago, very few people had beards. And he liked women, so he looked over and sitting across from him was a young woman, and he seemed to be highly interested. I sat on the side and I saw it—he didn't see me. Suddenly right near him came in another man also with a beard, and he began to look at the same woman. When S saw another one with a beard, he got up and left. He suddenly realized his own ridiculous situation. And this woman, as soon as this other man came in, she must have thought, What's going on here, already two beards?

Roth: You had no beard.

Singer: No, no. Do I need everything? A bald head *and* a beard?

Roth: You left Poland in the middle thirties, some years before the Nazi invasion. Schulz remained in Drohobycz and was killed there by the Nazis in 1942. Coming here to talk to you, I was thinking about how you, the Jewish writer from Eastern Europe most nourished by the Jewish world and most bound to it, left that world to come to America, while the other major Jewish writers of your generation—Jews far more assimilated, far more drawn toward the contemporary currents in the larger culture, writers like Schulz in Poland, and Isaac Babel in Russia, and, in Czechoslovakia, Jiří Weil, who wrote some of the most harrowing stories I've read about the Holocaust—were destroyed in one ghastly way or another, either by Nazism or Stalinism. May I ask who or what encouraged you to leave before the horrors began? After all, to be exiled from one's native country and language is something that nearly all writers would dread and probably be most reluctant to accomplish voluntarily. Why did you do it?

Singer: I had all the reasons to leave. First of all, I was very pessimistic. I saw that Hitler was already in power in 1935 and he was threatening Poland with invasion. Nazis like Göring came to Poland to hunt and to vacation. Second, I worked for the Yiddish press, and the Yiddish press was going down all the time—it has been ever since it has existed. And my way of living became very frugal—I could barely exist. And the main thing was that my brother was here; he had come about two years before. So I had all the reasons to run to America.

Roth: And, leaving Poland, did you have fears about losing touch with your material?

Singer: Of course, and the fear became even stronger when I got to this country. I came here and I saw that everybody speaks English. I mean, there was a Hadassah meeting, and so I went and expected to hear Yiddish. But I came in and there was sitting about two hundred women and I heard one word: "delicious, delicious, delicious." I didn't know what it was, but it wasn't Yiddish. I don't know what they gave them there to eat, but two hundred women were sitting and saying, "Delicious." By the way, this was the first English word I learned. Poland looked far away then. When a person who is close to you dies, in the first few weeks after his death he is as far from you, as far as a near person can ever be; only with the years does he become nearer, and then you can almost live with this person. This is what happened to me. Poland, Jewish life in Poland, is nearer to me now than it was then.

Milan Kundera

[1980]

THIS INTERVIEW is condensed from two conversations I had with Milan Kundera after reading a translated manuscript of his *Book of Laughter and Forgetting*—one conversation while he was visiting London for the first time, the other when he was on his first visit to the United States. He took these trips from France; since 1975 he and his wife have been living there as émigrés, in Rennes, where he taught at the university, and now in Paris. During our conversations, Kundera spoke sporadically in French but mostly in Czech, and his wife, Vera, served as his translator and mine. A final Czech text was translated into English by Peter Kussi.

Roth: Do you think the destruction of the world is coming soon?

Kundera: That depends on what you mean by the word *soon*.

Roth: Tomorrow or the day after.

Kundera: The feeling that the world is rushing to ruin is an ancient one.

Roth: So then we have nothing to worry about.

Kundera: On the contrary. If a fear has been present in the human mind for ages, there must be something to it.

Roth: In any event, it seems to me that this concern is the background against which all the stories in your latest book take place, even those that are of a decidedly humorous nature.

Kundera: If someone had told me as a boy, "One day you will see your nation vanish from the world," I would have considered it nonsense, something I couldn't possibly imagine. A man knows he is mortal, but he takes it for granted that his nation possesses a kind of eternal life. But after the Russian invasion of 1968, every Czech was confronted with the thought that his nation could be quietly erased from Europe, just as over the past five decades forty million Ukrainians have been quietly vanishing from the world without the world paying any heed. Or Lithuanians. Do you know that in the seventeenth

century Lithuania was a powerful European nation? Today the
Russians keep Lithuanians on their reservation like a half-
extinct tribe; they are sealed off from visitors to prevent knowledge about their existence from reaching the outside. I don't
know what the future holds for my own nation. It is certain
that the Russians will do everything they can to dissolve it
gradually into their own civilization. Nobody knows whether
they will succeed. But the possibility is there. And the sudden
realization that such a possibility exists is enough to change
one's whole sense of life. Nowadays I see even Europe as frag-
ile, mortal.

Roth: And yet, are not the fates of Eastern Europe and
Western Europe radically different matters?

Kundera: As a concept of cultural history, Eastern Europe is
Russia, with its quite specific history anchored in the Byzantine
world. Bohemia, Poland, Hungary, just like Austria, have never
been part of Eastern Europe. From the very beginning they
have taken part in the great adventure of Western civilization,
with its Gothic, its Renaissance, its Reformation—a movement
that has its cradle precisely in this region. It was there, in Central Europe, that modern culture found its greatest impulses:
psychoanalysis, structuralism, dodecaphony, Bartók's music,
Kafka's and Musil's new aesthetics of the novel. The postwar
annexation of Central Europe (or at least its major part) by
Russian civilization caused Western culture to lose its vital
center of gravity. It is the most significant event in the history
of the West in our century, and we cannot dismiss the possibility that the end of Central Europe marked the beginning of
the end for Europe as a whole.

Roth: During the Prague Spring, your novel *The Joke* and
your stories *Laughable Loves* were published in editions of
150,000. After the Russian invasion you were dismissed from
your teaching post at the film academy and all your books were
removed from the shelves of public libraries. Seven years later
you and your wife tossed a few books and some clothes in the
back of your car and drove off to France, where you've become
one of the most widely read of foreign authors. How do you
feel as an émigré?

Kundera: For a writer, the experience of living in a number
of countries is an enormous boon. You can only understand

the world if you see it from several sides. My latest book [*The Book of Laughter and Forgetting*], which came into being in France, unfolds in a special geographic space: those events that take place in Prague are seen through Western European eyes, while what happens in France is seen through the eyes of Prague. It is an encounter of two worlds. On one side, my native country: in the course of a mere half century, it experienced democracy, fascism, revolution, Stalinist terror as well as the disintegration of Stalinism, German and Russian occupation, mass deportations, the death of the West in its own land. It is thus sinking under the weight of history and looks at the world with immense skepticism. On the other side, France: for centuries it was the center of the world and nowadays it is suffering from the lack of great historic events. This is why it revels in radical ideological postures. It is the lyrical, neurotic expectation of some great deed of its own, which is not coming, however, and will never come.

Roth: Are you living in France as a stranger or do you feel culturally at home?

Kundera: I am enormously fond of French culture and I am greatly indebted to it. Especially to the older literature. Rabelais is dearest to me of all writers. And Diderot. I love his *Jacques le fataliste* as much as I do Laurence Sterne. Those were the greatest experimenters of all time in the form of the novel. And their experiments were, so to say, amusing, full of happiness and joy, which have by now vanished from French literature and without which everything in art loses its significance. Sterne and Diderot understood the novel as a great game. They discovered the humor of the novelistic form. When I hear learned arguments that the novel has exhausted its possibilities, I have precisely the opposite feeling: in the course of its history the novel missed many of its possibilities. For example, impulses for the development of the novel hidden in Sterne and Diderot have not been picked up by any successors.

Roth: *The Book of Laughter and Forgetting* is not called a novel, and yet in the text you declare: This book is a novel in the form of variations. So then, is it a novel or not?

Kundera: As far as my own quite personal aesthetic judgment goes, it really is a novel, but I have no wish to force this opinion on anyone. There is enormous freedom latent within the novelistic form. It is a mistake to regard a certain stereotyped structure as the inviolable essence of the novel.

Roth: Yet surely there is something that makes a novel a novel and that limits this freedom.

Kundera: A novel is a long piece of synthetic prose based on play with invented characters. These are the only limits. By the term *synthetic* I have in mind the novelist's desire to grasp his subject from all sides and in the fullest possible completeness. Ironic essay, novelistic narrative, autobiographical fragment, historical fact, flight of fantasy—the synthetic power of the novel is capable of combining everything into a unified whole like the voices of polyphonic music. The unity of a book need not stem from the plot but can be provided by the theme. In my latest book there are two such themes: laughter and forgetting.

Roth: Laughter has always been close to you. Your books provoke laughter through humor or irony. When your characters come to grief it is because they bump against a world that has lost its sense of humor.

Kundera: I learned the value of humor during the time of Stalinist terror. I was twenty then. I could always recognize a person who was not a Stalinist, a person whom I needn't fear, by the way he smiled. A sense of humor was a trustworthy sign of recognition. Ever since, I have been terrified by a world that is losing its sense of humor.

Roth: In *The Book of Laughter and Forgetting*, though, something else is involved. In a little parable you compare the laughter of angels with the laughter of the devil. The devil laughs because God's world seems senseless to him; the angels laugh with joy because everything in God's world has its meaning.

Kundera: Yes, man uses the same physiological manifestation —laughter—to express two different metaphysical attitudes. Someone's hat drops on the coffin in a freshly dug grave, the funeral loses its meaning and laughter is born. Two lovers race through the meadow, holding hands, laughing. Their laughter has nothing to do with jokes or humor; it is the serious laughter of angels expressing their joy of being. Both kinds of laughter belong among life's pleasures, but when it is carried to extremes it also denotes a dual apocalypse: the enthusiastic laughter of angel-fanatics, who are so convinced of their world's significance that they are ready to hang anyone not sharing their joy. And the other laughter, sounding from the opposite side, which proclaims that everything has become meaningless, that even funerals are ridiculous and group sex a mere comical pantomime. Human life is bounded by two chasms: fanaticism on one side, absolute skepticism on the other.

Roth: What you now call the laughter of angels is a new term for the "lyrical attitude to life" of your previous novels. In one of your books you characterize the era of Stalinist terror as the reign of the hangman and the poet.

Kundera: Totalitarianism is not only hell but also the dream of paradise—the age-old dream of a world where everybody lives in harmony, united by a single common will and faith, without secrets from one another. André Breton, too, dreamed of this paradise when he talked about the glass house in which he longed to live. If totalitarianism did not exploit these archetypes, which are deep inside us all and rooted deep in all religions, it could never attract so many people, especially during the early phases of its existence. Once the dream of paradise starts to turn into reality, however, here and there people begin to crop up who stand in its way, and so the rulers of paradise must build a little gulag on the side of Eden. In the course of time this gulag grows ever bigger and more perfect, while the adjoining paradise gets ever smaller and poorer.

Roth: In your book, the great French poet Éluard soars over paradise and gulag, singing. Is this bit of history that you mention in the book authentic?

Kundera: After the war, Paul Éluard abandoned surrealism and became the greatest exponent of what I might call the "poesy of totalitarianism." He sang for brotherhood, peace, justice, better tomorrows, he sang for comradeship and against isolation, for joy and against gloom, for innocence and against cynicism. When in 1950 the rulers of paradise sentenced Éluard's Prague friend, the surrealist Závis Kalandra, to death by hanging, Éluard suppressed his personal feelings of friendship for the sake of suprapersonal ideals and publicly declared his approval of his comrade's execution. The hangman killed while the poet sang.

And not just the poet. The whole period of Stalinist terror

was a period of collective lyrical delirium. This has by now been completely forgotten, but it is the crux of the matter. People like to say: Revolution is beautiful; it is only the terror arising from it that is evil. But this is not true. The evil is already present in the beautiful, hell is already contained in the dream of paradise, and if we wish to understand the essence of hell we must examine the essence of the paradise from which it originated. It is extremely easy to condemn gulags, but to reject the totalitarian poesy that leads to the gulag by way of paradise is as difficult as ever. Nowadays, people all over the world unequivocally reject the idea of gulags, yet they are still willing to let themselves be hypnotized by totalitarian poesy and to march to new gulags to the tune of the same lyrical song piped by Éluard when he soared over Prague like the great archangel of the lyre, while the smoke of Kalandra's body rose to the sky from the crematory chimney.

Roth: What is so characteristic of your prose is the constant confrontation of the private and the public. But not in the sense that private stories take place against a political backdrop or that political events encroach on private lives. Rather, you continually show that political events are governed by the same laws as private happenings, so that your prose is a kind of psychoanalysis of politics.

Kundera: The metaphysics of man is the same in the private sphere as in the public one. Take the other theme of the book, forgetting. This is the great private problem of man: death as the loss of the self. But what is this self? It is the sum of everything we remember. Thus, what terrifies us about death is not the loss of the future but the loss of the past. Forgetting is a form of death ever present within life. This is the problem of my heroine, in desperately trying to preserve the vanishing memories of her beloved dead husband. But forgetting is also the great problem of politics. When a big power wants to deprive a small country of its national consciousness it uses the method of organized forgetting. This is what is currently happening in Bohemia. Contemporary Czech literature, insofar as it has any value at all, has not been printed for twelve years; 200 Czech writers have been proscribed, including the dead Franz Kafka; 145 Czech historians have been dismissed from their posts, history has been rewritten, monuments have been demolished. A nation that loses awareness of its past gradually loses its self. And so the political situation has brutally illuminated the ordinary metaphysical problem of forgetting that we face all the time, every day, without paying any attention. Politics unmasks the metaphysics of private life, private life unmasks the metaphysics of politics.

Roth: In the sixth part of your book of variations the main heroine, Tamina, reaches an island where there are only children. In the end they hound her to death. Is this a dream, a fairy tale, an allegory?

Kundera: Nothing is more foreign to me than allegory, a story invented by the author in order to illustrate some thesis. Events, whether realistic or imaginary, must be significant in themselves, and the reader is meant to be naively seduced by their power and poetry. I have always been haunted by this image, and during one period of my life it kept recurring in my dreams: a person finds himself in a world of children, from which he cannot escape. And suddenly childhood, which we all lyricize and adore, reveals itself as pure horror. As a trap. This story is not allegory. But my book is a polyphony in which various stories mutually explain, illumine, complement one another. The basic event of the book is the story of totalitarianism, which deprives people of memory and thus retools them into a nation of children. All totalitarianisms do this. And perhaps our entire technical age does this, with its cult of the future, its cult of youth and childhood, its indifference to the past and mistrust of thought. In the midst of a relentlessly juvenile society, an adult equipped with memory and irony feels like Tamina on the isle of children.

Roth: Almost all your novels, in fact all the individual parts of your latest book, find their denouement in great scenes of coitus. Even that part which goes by the innocent name of "Mother" is but one long scene of three-way sex, with a prologue and epilogue. What does sex mean to you as a novelist?

Kundera: These days, when sexuality is no longer taboo, mere description, mere sexual confession, has become noticeably boring. How dated Lawrence seems, or even Henry Miller with his lyricism of obscenity! And yet certain erotic passages of Georges Bataille have made a lasting impression on me. Perhaps it is because they are not lyrical but philosophic. You are right that with me everything ends in great erotic scenes. I have the feeling that a scene of physical love generates an extremely sharp light that suddenly reveals the essence of characters and sums up their life situation. Hugo makes love to Tamina while she is desperately trying to think about lost vacations with her dead husband. The erotic scene is the focus where all the themes of the story converge and where its deepest secrets are located.

Roth: The last part, the seventh, actually deals with nothing but sexuality. Why does this part close the book rather than another, such as the much more dramatic sixth part, in which the heroine dies?

Kundera: Tamina dies, metaphorically speaking, amid the laughter of angels. Through the last section of the book, on the other hand, resounds the contrary kind of laugh, the kind heard when things lose their meaning. There is a certain imaginary dividing line beyond which things appear senseless and ridiculous. A person asks himself: Isn't it nonsensical for me to get up in the morning? to go to work? to strive for anything? to belong to a nation just because I was born that way? Man lives in close proximity to this boundary and can easily find himself on the other side. That boundary exists everywhere, in all areas of human life and even in the deepest, most biological of all: sexuality. And precisely because it is the deepest region of life, the question posed to sexuality is the deepest question. This is why my book of variations can end with no variation but this.

Roth: Is this, then, the furthest point you have reached in your pessimism?

Kundera: I am wary of the words *pessimism* and *optimism*. A novel does not assert anything; a novel searches and poses questions. I don't know whether my nation will perish and I don't know which of my characters is right. I invent stories, confront one with another, and by this means I ask questions. The stupidity of people comes from having an answer for everything. The wisdom of the novel comes from having a question for everything. When Don Quixote went out into the world, that world turned into a mystery before his eyes. That is the legacy of the first European novel to the entire subsequent history of the novel. The novelist teaches the reader to comprehend the world as a question. There is wisdom and tolerance in that attitude. In a world built on sacrosanct certainties the novel is dead. The totalitarian world, whether founded on Marx, Islam, or anything else, is a world of answers rather than questions. There the novel has no place. In any case, it seems to me that all over the world people nowadays prefer to judge rather than to understand, to answer rather than to ask, so that the voice of the novel can hardly be heard over the noisy foolishness of human certainties.

Edna O'Brien

[1984]

THE IRISH writer Edna O'Brien, who has lived in London now for many years, moved recently to a wide boulevard of imposing nineteenth-century façades, a street that in the 1870s, when it was built, was renowned, she tells me, for its mistresses and kept women. The real estate agents have taken to calling this corner of the Maida Vale district "the Belgravia of tomorrow"; at the moment it looks a little like a builder's yard because of all the renovation going on.

O'Brien works in a quiet study that looks out to the green lawn of an immense private garden at the rear of her flat, a garden probably many times larger than the farm village in County Clare where she attended mass as a child. There is a desk, a piano, a sofa, a rosy Oriental carpet deeper in color than the faint marbleized pink of the walls, and, through the French doors that open onto the garden, enough plane trees to fill a small park. On the mantel of the fireplace there are photographs of the writer's two grown sons from an early marriage—"I live here more or less alone"—and the famous lyrical photograph of the profile of a very young Virginia Woolf, the heroine of O'Brien's *Virginia: A Play*. On the desk, which is set to look out toward the church steeple at the far end of the garden, there's a volume of J. M. Synge's collected works open to a chapter in *The Aran Islands*; a volume of Flaubert's correspondence lies on the sofa, the pages turned to an exchange with George Sand. While waiting for me to arrive, she has been signing pages of a special edition of fifteen thousand copies of her selected stories and listening to a record of rousing choruses from Verdi operas in order to help her get through.

Because everything she's wearing for the interview is black, you cannot miss the white skin, the green eyes, the auburn hair. The coloring is dramatically Irish—as is the mellifluous fluency.

Roth: In *Malone Dies*, your compatriot Samuel Beckett writes: "Let us say before I go any further, that I forgive nobody. I wish them all an atrocious life in the fires of icy hell and in the execrable generations to come." This quotation stands as the epigraph of *Mother Ireland*, a memoir you published in 1976. Did you mean to suggest by this epigraph that your own writing about Ireland isn't wholly uncontaminated by such sentiments? Frankly, I don't feel such harshness in your work.

O'Brien: I picked the epigraph because I am, or was, especially at that time, unforgiving about lots of things in my life, and I picked somebody who said it more eloquently and more ferociously than I could say it.

Roth: The fact is that your fiction argues *against* your unforgivingness.

O'Brien: To some extent it does, but that is because I am a creature of conflicts. When I vituperate, I subsequently feel I should appease. That happens throughout my life. I am not a natural out-and-out hater any more than I am a natural, or thorough, out-and-out lover, which means I am often rather at odds with myself and others!

Roth: Who is *the* unforgiven creature in your imagination?

O'Brien: Up to the time he died, which was a year ago, it was my father. But through death a metamorphosis happens: within. Since he died I have written a play about him embodying all his traits—his anger, his sexuality, his rapaciousness, et cetera —and now I feel differently toward him. I do not want to relive my life with him or be reincarnated as the same daughter, but I do forgive him. My mother is a different matter. I loved her, overloved her, yet she visited a different legacy on me, an all-embracing guilt. I still have a sense of her over my shoulder, judging.

Roth: Here you are, a woman of experience, talking about forgiving your mother and father. Do you think that still worrying those problems has largely to do with your being a writer? If you weren't a writer, if you were a lawyer, if you were a doctor, perhaps you wouldn't be thinking about these people so much.

O'Brien: Absolutely. It's the price of being a writer. One is dogged by the past—pain, sensations, rejections, all of it. I do believe that this clinging to the past is a zealous, albeit hopeless, desire to reinvent it so that one could change it. Doctors, lawyers, and many other stable citizens are not afflicted by a persistent memory. In their way, they might be just as disturbed as you or I, except that they don't know it. They don't delve.

Roth: But not all writers feast on their childhood as much as you have.

O'Brien: I am obsessive, also I am industrious. Besides, the time when you are most alive and most aware is in childhood, and one is trying to recapture that heightened awareness.

Roth: From the point of view not of a daughter or of a woman but of a fiction writer, do you consider yourself fortunate in your origins—having been born in the isolated reaches of Ireland, raised on a lonely farm in the shadow of a violent father, and educated by nuns behind the latched gate of a provincial convent? As a writer, how much or how little do you owe to the primitive rural world you often describe in stories about the Ireland of your childhood?

O'Brien: There's no telling, really. If I had grown up on the steppes of Russia or in Brooklyn—my parents lived there when they were first married—my material would have been different but my apprehension might be just the same. I happened to grow up in a country that was and is breathlessly beautiful, so the feeling for nature, for verdure, and for the soil was instilled into me. Secondly, there was no truck with culture or literature, so that my longing to write sprung up of its own accord, was spontaneous. The only books in our house were prayer books, cookery books, and blood-stock reports. I was privy to the world around me, was aware of everyone's little history, the stuff from which stories and novels are made. On the personal level, it was pretty drastic. So all these things combined to make me what I am.

Roth: But are you surprised that you survived the isolated farm and the violent father and the provincial convent without having lost the freedom of mind to be able to write?

O'Brien: I am surprised by my own sturdiness, yes, but I do not think that I am unscarred. Such things as driving a car or swimming are quite beyond me. In a lot of ways I feel a cripple. The body was as sacred as a tabernacle and everything a potential occasion of sin. It is funny now, but not that funny—the body contains the life story just as much as the brain. I console myself by thinking that if one part is destroyed another flourishes.

Roth: Was there enough money around when you were growing up?

O'Brien: No—but there had been! My father liked horses and liked leisure. He inherited a great deal of land and a beautiful stone house, but he was profligate and the land got given away or squandered in archetypal Irish fashion. Cousins who came home from America brought us clothes, and I inherited from my mother a certain childish pleasure in these things. Our greatest excitement was these visits, these gifts of trinkets and things, these signals of an outside, cosmopolitan world, a world I longed to enter.

Roth: I'm struck, particularly in the stories of rural Ireland during the war years, by the vastness and precision of your recall. You seem to remember the shape, texture, color, and dimensions of every object your eye may have landed upon while you were growing up—not to mention the human significance of all you saw, heard, smelled, tasted, and touched. The result is prose like a piece of fine meshwork, a net of detail that enables you to contain all the longing and pain and remorse that surge through the fiction. What I want to ask is how you account for this ability to reconstruct with such passionate exactness an Irish world you haven't fully lived in for decades? How does your memory keep it alive, and why won't this vanished world leave you alone?

O'Brien: At certain times I am sucked back there, and the ordinary world and the present time recede. This recollection, or whatever it is, invades me. It is not something that I can summon up; it simply comes and I am the servant of it. My hand does the work and I don't have to think; in fact, were I to think, it would stop the flow. It's like a dam in the brain that bursts.

Roth: Do you visit Ireland to help along the recall?

O'Brien: When I visit Ireland, I always secretly hope that something will spark off the hidden world and the hidden stories waiting to be released, but it doesn't happen like that! It happens, as you well know, much more convolutedly, through one's dreams, through chance, and, in my case, through the welter of emotion stimulated by a love affair and its aftermath.

Roth: I wonder if you haven't chosen the way you live—living by yourself—to prevent anything emotionally too powerful from separating you from that past.

O'Brien: I'm sure I have. I rail against my loneliness but it is as dear to me as the thought of unity with a man. I have often said that I would like to divide my life into alternating periods of penance, cavorting, and work, but as you can see that would not strictly fit in with a conventional married life.

Roth: Most American writers I know would be greatly unnerved by the prospect of living away from the country that's their subject and the source of their language and the repository of their memories. Many Eastern European writers I know remain behind the Iron Curtain because the hardships of totalitarianism seem preferable to the dangers, for a writer, of exile. If ever there was a case for a writer's staying within earshot of the old neighborhood, it's been provided by two Americans who, to my mind, together constitute the spine of my country's literature in the twentieth century: Faulkner, who settled back in Mississippi after a brief period abroad, and Bellow, who, after his wanderings, returned to live and teach in Chicago. Now, we all know that neither Beckett nor Joyce seemed to want or to need a base in Ireland once they began experimenting with their Irish endowment, but do *you* ever feel that leaving Ireland as a very young woman and coming to London to make a life has cost you anything as a writer? Isn't there an Ireland other than the Ireland of your youth that might have been turned to your purposes?

O'Brien: To establish oneself in a particular place and to use it as the locale for fiction is both a strength to the writer and a signpost to the reader. But you have to go if you find your roots too threatening, too impinging. Joyce said that Ireland is the sow that eats its farrow. He was referring to its attitude toward its writers—it savages them. It is no accident that our two greatest illustrissimi, himself and Mr. Beckett, left and stayed away, though they never lost their particular Irish consciousness. In my own case, I do not think that I would have written anything if I had stayed. I feel I would have been watched, would have been judged (even more!), and would have lost that priceless commodity called freedom. Writers are always on the run, and I was on the run from many things.

Yes, I dispossessed myself and I am sure that I lost something, lost the continuity, lost the day-to-day contact with reality. However, compared with Eastern European writers, I have the advantage that I can always go back. For them it must be terrible, the finality of it, the utter banishment, like a soul shut out of heaven.

Roth: Will you go back?

O'Brien: Intermittently. Ireland is very different now, a much more secular land, where, ironically, both the love of literature and the repudiation of literature are on the wane. Ireland is becoming as materialistic and as callow as the rest of the world. Yeats's line—"Romantic Ireland's dead and gone"— has indeed come to fruition.

Roth: In my foreword to your book *A Fanatic Heart*, I quote what Frank Tuohy, in an essay about James Joyce, had to say about the two of you: that while Joyce, in *Dubliners* and *A Portrait of the Artist as a Young Man*, was the first Irish Catholic to make his experience and surroundings recognizable, "the world of Nora Barnacle [the former chambermaid who became Joyce's wife] had to wait for the fiction of Edna O'Brien." Can you tell me how important Joyce has been to you? A story of yours like "Tough Men," about the bamboozling of a scheming shopkeeper by an itinerant con man, seems to me right out of some rural *Dubliners*, and yet you don't seem to have been challenged by Joyce's linguistic and mythic extravagences. What has he meant to you, what if anything have you taken or learned from him, and how intimidating is it for an Irish writer to have as precursor this great verbal behemoth who has chewed up everything Irish in sight?

O'Brien: In the constellation of geniuses, he is a blinding light and father of us all. (I exclude Shakespeare because for Shakespeare no human epithet is enough.) When I first read Joyce, it was a little book edited by T. S. Eliot that I bought on the quays in Dublin, secondhand, for fourpence. Before that, I had read very few books and they were mostly gushing and outlandish. I was a pharmaceutical apprentice who dreamed of writing. Now here was "The Dead" and a section of *A Portrait of the Artist as a Young Man*, which stunned me not only by the bewitchment of style but because they were so true to life, they *were* life. Then, or rather later, I came to read *Ulysses*, but as a young girl I balked, because it was really too much for me, it was too inaccessible and too masculine, apart from the famous Molly Bloom section. I now think *Ulysses* is the most diverting, brilliant, intricate, and unboring book that I have ever read. I can pick it up at any time, read a few pages, and feel that I have just had a brain transfusion. As for his being intimidating, it doesn't arise—he is simply out of bounds, beyond us all, "the far Azores," as he might call it.

Roth: Let's go back to the world of Nora Barnacle, to how the world looks to the Nora Barnacles, those who remain in Ireland and those who take flight. At the center of virtually all your stories is a woman, generally a woman on her own, battling isolation and loneliness, or seeking love, or recoiling from the surprises of adventuring among men. You write about women without a taint of ideology or, as far as I can see, any concern with taking a correct position.

O'Brien: The correct position is to write the truth, to write what one feels regardless of any public consideration or any clique. I think an artist never takes a position either through expedience or umbrage. Artists detest and suspect positions because you know that the minute you take a fixed position you are something else—you are a journalist or you are a politician. What I am after is a bit of magic, and I do not want to write tracts or to read them. I have depicted women in lonely, desperate, and often humiliated situations, very often the butt of men and almost always searching for an emotional catharsis that does not come. This is my territory and one that I know from hard-earned experience. If you want to know what I regard as the principal crux of female despair, it is this: in the Greek myth of Oedipus and in Freud's exploration of it, the son's desire for his mother is admitted; the infant daughter also desires her mother but it is unthinkable, either in myth, in fantasy, or in fact, that that desire can be consummated.

Roth: Yet you can't be oblivious to the changes in "consciousness" that have been said to be occasioned by the women's movement.

O'Brien: Yes, certain things have been changed for the better—women are not chattel, they express their right to earn as much as men, to be respected, not to be "the second sex"—but in the mating area things have not changed. Attraction and sexual love are spurred not by consciousness but by instinct and passion, and in this men and women are radically different. The man still has the greater authority and the greater autonomy. It's biological. The woman's fate is to receive the sperm and to retain it, but the man's is to give it and in the giving he spends himself and then subsequently withdraws. While she is in a sense being fed, he is in the opposite sense being drained, and to resuscitate himself he takes temporary flight. As a result, you get the woman's resentment at being abandoned, however briefly; his guilt at going; and, above all, his innate sense of self-protection in order to refind himself so as to reaffirm himself. Closeness is therefore always only relative. A man may help with the dishes and so forth, but his commitment is more ambiguous and he has a roving eye.

Roth: Are there no women as promiscuous?

O'Brien: They sometimes are but it doesn't give them the same sense of achievement. A woman, I dare to say, is capable of a deeper and more lasting love. I would also add that a woman is more afraid of being left. That still stands. Go into any women's canteen, dress department, hairdresser's, gymnasium, and you will see plenty of desperation and plenty of competition. People utter a lot of slogans but they are only slogans and what we feel and do is what determines us. Women are no more secure in their emotions than they ever were. They simply are better at coming to terms with them. The only real security would be to turn away from men, to detach, but that would be a little death—at least for me it would.

Roth: Why do you write so many love stories? Is it because of the importance of the subject or because, like many others in our profession, once you grew up and left home and chose the solitary life of a writer, sexual love inevitably became the strongest sphere of experience to which you continued to have access?

O'Brien: First of all, I think love replaced religion for me in my sense of fervor. When I began to look for earthly love (i.e., sex), I felt that I was cutting myself off from God. By taking on the mantle of religion, sex assumed proportions that are rather far-fetched. It became the central thing in my life, the goal. I was very prone to the Heathcliff/Mr. Rochester syndrome and still am. The sexual excitement was to a great extent linked with pain and separation. My sexual life is pivotal to me, as I believe it is for everyone else. It takes up a lot of time both in the thinking and in the doing, the former often taking pride of place. For me, primarily, it is secretive and contains elements of mystery and plunder. My daily life and my sexual life are not of a whole—they are separated. Part of my Irish heritage!

Roth: What's most difficult about being both a woman and a writer? Are there difficulties you have writing as a woman that I don't have as a man? And do you imagine that there might be difficulties I have that you don't?

O'Brien: I think it is different being a man and being a woman—it is very different. I think you as a man have waiting for you in the wings of the world a whole cortege of women—potential wives, mistresses, muses, nurses. Women writers do not have that bonus. The examples are numerous: the Brontë sisters, Jane Austen, Carson McCullers, Flannery O'Connor, Emily Dickinson, Marina Tsvetayeva. I think it was Dashiell Hammett who said he wouldn't want to live with a woman who had more problems than he had. I think the signals men get from me alarm them.

Roth: You will have to find a Leonard Woolf.

O'Brien: I do not want a Leonard Woolf. I want Lord Byron and Leonard Woolf mixed in together.

Roth: But does the job fundamentally come down to the same difficulties then, regardless of gender?

O'Brien: Absolutely. There is no difference at all. You, like me, are trying to make something out of nothing and the anxiety is extreme. Flaubert's description of his room echoing with curses and cries of distress could be any writer's room. Yet I doubt that we would welcome an alternative life. There is something stoical about soldiering on all alone.

An Exchange with Mary McCarthy

141 rue de Rennes
75006 Paris
January 11, 1987

Dear Philip:

Thank you for sending me your book [*The Counterlife*], which I started reading with excitement and enthusiasm that continued to mount through the section in Israel and the El Al part, too, but that left me in England at Christmastime, not to return, and I don't know why exactly. Perhaps you have a better guess than I. It is probably never wise to give an author a negative or "qualified" opinion of his book, but I am moved to do so because I liked your last book, all the parts of it, very, very much and I guess because I assumed that if you sent me your book it was because you were interested in my opinion of it.

So I will try to say what I think. The high point, for me, was the Hebron chapter, brilliant in every way and laying the whole problem—Israel—out with honesty and clarity. As I read, I kept contrasting it with an imaginary novel by Bellow. I also liked the earlier, dentist's office parts, the bifurcation of the Zuckerman figure, and the independent existence, like an angleworm's, achieved by the separate pieces. It seems to me a pity that this idea (unless I failed to understand) seems to have been lost sight of in *Gloucestershire* and *Christendom*, which, on their own, wearied me. With what feels to me like pathology—a severe case of anti-anti-semitism.

I remember Philip Rahv saying that all Gentiles, without exception, were anti-semitic. If so, that is an awful problem for a Jewish novelist who wants to have Gentile characters in his work. Maybe the English sections of *The Counterlife* won't offend Jewish readers, but they irritated and offended. I'm not a Christian (I don't believe in God), but to the extent that I am and can't help being (just as a "nice Jewish boy" can't help being Jewish), I bridle at your picture of Christianity. There's more to Christmas, that is, to the idea of the Incarnation, than Jew-hatred. True, I've sometimes thought that all our Christmas-caroling must be offensive to non-sharers in the bliss of that wondrous occasion. But perhaps non-sharers, those outside the Law, can get the general idea or try to, as I hope I would try to get the idea of the Wailing Wall, repellent as it is to me, if I were taken to it. And I confess that the crib with angels and animals and a star is to me a more sympathetic idea than the Wailing Wall; as a non-believer, I greatly prefer it. The residual Christian in me probably looks forward happily to the millennium and the conversion of the Jews, including Philip Roth. Philip Rahv too.

Then all that circumcision business. Why so excited about making a child a Jew by taking a knife to him? I have nothing against circumcision; the men of my generation were all circumcised—a de rigueur pediatric procedure—and my son's generation, too. It must have been Freudian influences somehow that in the Forties persuaded educated people that circumcision was a superstition (I even heard it called a dirty Jewish superstition) which robbed the male of full sexual enjoyment in the pretended interest of hygiene. So then it became unchic to have a baby boy circumcised. Religion did not enter into any of this, any more than it did into the breast-feeding, anti-breast-feeding discussion. And if Nathan Zuckerman *isn't* a believing Jew, why is he so hung up on this issue?

Forgive me if all this is disagreeable to you. It is strange to *me* that *The Counterlife* should remind me so forcibly that I am a Christian whatever I choose to imagine. The last time in my adult life that I felt anything like that was in Hanoi in 1968 with U.S. bombers overhead when I reacted, in the privacy of my thoughts, against the Marxist-Buddhist orthodoxy that I felt in the local leaders.

I am sorry that we never got together with Leon [Botstein] this past fall. Next year, I hope. I last saw him at a Christmas-carol singing, just before we flew back here.

Happy New Year, sincerely,
Mary

15 Fawcett St.
London SW10
January 17, 1987

Dear Mary:
Thanks for writing at such length about the book. Of course I would want to know what you thought and that is indeed

why I sent you the book, and I'm delighted that you have been so candid with me.

To begin with, it sounds as though you were held by an awful lot of it, virtually everything up to the last two chapters. I won't go into a discussion of why the structural idea was not abandoned in the last two chapters but in fact sealed and reinforced, since I think that would take too long and probably sound like a lecture, which I don't intend to deliver to you, of all people.

I happen to be known (to Jews) for having "a severe case of anti-anti-Semitism," as you claim to have yourself, *as does Zuckerman*. I think here all these issues seem to have struck you *outside* the narrative context and the thematic preoccupations of the book.

Let me take up your points one at a time.

1. Rahv's statement that all Gentiles are anti-Semitic. This is, of course, exactly what Zuckerman hears at Agor [a Jewish settlement on Israel's West Bank]. He is hardly sympathetic to that assertion. How could he have married Maria Freshfield if he were? Though that's the least of it: it simply runs counter to his experience, period. The irony, it seemed to me, was that, having been exposed to a kind of rhetoric he finds profoundly unpersuasive, he then comes back to London and runs smack into Maria's sister, her hymn of [anti-Semitic] hate, and her insinuations about [the anti-Semitism of] Maria's mother. There is then the [anti-Semitic] incident at the restaurant and the conversation with Maria [about English anti-Semitism] that gets so hopelessly out of hand. None of this is evidence that all Gentiles are anti-Semitic. But it does force Zuckerman—the very same fellow so skeptical, to put it mildly, of Lippman's [Agor] manifesto—to have to deal with a phenomenon previously unknown to him, though hardly unknown in the world (or in England, for that matter). I wanted him astonished, caught off-balance, *educated*. I wanted him threatened with the loss of this woman he adores because of this stinking, hideous old problem that seems to have turned up right at the heart of the family into which he has married. Truly, I don't see what there is to be offended by there, and maybe it wasn't this that offended and irritated you.

2. "There's more to Christmas, that is, to the idea of the Incarnation, than Jew-hatred." But Zuckerman doesn't say there isn't. He does, however, articulate (for the first time anywhere in fiction, as far as I know) how many a Jew happens to feel when confronted with this stuff. Whether justified or not, he is mildly affronted, and what he says is not quite what you suggest he says. "But between me and *church devotion* [*not* the Incarnation] there is an unbridgeable world of feeling, a natural and thoroughgoing incompatibility—I have the emotions of a spy in the adversary's camp and feel I'm overseeing the very rites that *embody the ideology* that's been responsible for the persecution and mistreatment of Jews . . . I just find the religion . . . profoundly inappropriate, and never more so than when the congregants are observing the highest standards of liturgical decorum and the clerics most beautifully enunciating the doctrine of love." (I've added the italics.) Now, you may not think such reasoning is sound, but that even an intelligent Jew is capable of reasoning in just that way is a fact. I was trying to be truthful.

3. ". . . as a non-believer, I greatly prefer it," you say, meaning "the crib with angels and animals and a star" to "the Wailing Wall." That is again where you and Zuckerman part company. As a non-believer, he prefers neither. He finds little to recommend the sanctification of either set of icons or symbols or whatever they all are taken together. Furthermore, Zuckerman behaves beautifully at the carol service and therefore *looks* at least as you might look at the Wailing Wall, where you say you would try to get the idea, repellent as it is to you. I think you have—a word I hate—overreacted to these few observations, which he himself knows are determined by his Jewishness and nothing more. "Yet, Jewishly, I still thought, what *do* they need all this stuff for?" His objections really are aesthetic, aren't they? "Though frankly I've always felt that the place where Christianity gets dangerously, vulgarly obsessed with the miraculous is Easter, the Nativity has always struck me as a close second to the Resurrection in nakedly addressing the most childish need." You say you bridle at my picture of Christianity, and if you bridle at this, so be it. But you do see it has nothing to do, or not much to do, with "Jew-hatred."

Now to speak only as a novelist (which I am far more than I

am a Jew). If Zuckerman hadn't gone to [Agor in] Judea and heard what he heard there I would never have had this scene in the church or have had him think these thoughts. But it seemed to me only fair that—no, I don't mean that: it seemed to me simply that the one scene called forth the other. I didn't want all his skepticism focused on Jewish ritual and none of it on Christian. That would have had all the wrong implications and made him see what he is not, and that is a self-hating Jew who—to borrow a phrase—casts a cold eye only on his own.

4. "Why so excited about making a child a Jew by taking a knife to him?" Context, context, context. This is his response, his aggressive and angry response, to the suggestion that his child will have to be christened in order to please Maria's mother. The paean to circumcision arises out of that threat. If you won't listen to me on this subject, listen to Maria. In her letter (written in fact by Z., but that subject I'm not going into) she writes, "If it's this that establishes for you the truth of your paternity—that regains for you the truth of your *own* paternity—so be it." Here I was thinking thoughts the reader can hardly be expected to follow. I was thinking about Zuckerman and his own father, and the word *bastard* that the old man Zuckerman [in *Zuckerman Unbound*] whispers to Nathan from his deathbed. The circumcision of little English-American Z. is big American Z. settling that issue at last. That is my business, I suppose, but it figured in the thing.

I think you also fail to see how serious this circumcision business is to Jews. I am still hypnotized by uncircumcised men when I see them at my swimming pool locker room [in London]. The damn thing never goes unregistered. Most Jewish men I know have similar reactions, and when I was writing the book, I asked several of my equally secular Jewish male friends if they could have an uncircumcised son, and they all said no, sometimes without having to think about it and sometimes after the nice long pause that any rationalist takes before opting for the irrational. Why is N.Z. hung up on circumcision? I hope that's clearer now.

5. "Forgive me if all this is disagreeable to you." I would have had to forgive you if you had been "agreeable."

Yours,
Philip

Pictures of Malamud

"Mourning is a hard business," Cesare said. "If people knew, there'd be less death."
— From Malamud's "Life Is Better Than Death"

[1986]

IN FEBRUARY 1961 I traveled west from Iowa City, were I was teaching in the Writers' Workshop of the university and finishing a second book, to give a lecture at a small community college in Monmouth, Oregon. A buddy from my graduate school days was teaching there and had arranged the invitation. I accepted not only because of the opportunity the trip afforded me to see, for the first time in five years, my friends the Bakers, but because Bob Baker promised that if I came he'd arrange for me to meet Bernard Malamud.

Bern taught nearby at the state university in Corvallis. He'd been in Corvallis, Oregon (pop. 15,000), since leaving New York (pop. 8,000,000) and a night-school teaching job there in 1949—twelve years in the Far West instructing freshmen in the fundamentals of English composition and writing the unorthodox baseball novel *The Natural*; his masterpiece set in darkest Brooklyn, *The Assistant*; as well as four or five of the best American short stories I'd ever read (or I ever will). The other stories weren't bad either.

In the early fifties I was reading Malamud's stories, later collected in *The Magic Barrel*, as they appeared—the day they appeared—in *Partisan Review* and the old *Commentary*. He seemed to me to be doing no less for his lonely Jews and their peculiarly immigrant, Jewish forms of failure—for those Malamudians "who never stopped hurting"—than was Samuel Beckett, in his longer fiction, for misery-ridden Molloy and Malone. Both writers, while bound imaginatively (though not communally) to the common life of the clan, severed racial memories from the larger social and historical setting and then, focusing as narrowly as they could on the dismal daily round of resistance borne by the most helpless of their landsmen, created parables of frustration steeped in the gravity of the grimmest philosophers.

278

Not unlike Beckett, Malamud wrote of a meager world of pain in a language all his own, an English that appeared, even apart from the idiosyncratic dialogue, to have been pulled out of what one might have thought would be the most unmagical barrel around—the locutions, inversions, and diction of Jewish immigrant speech, a heap of broken verbal bones that looked, until he came along and made them dance to his sad tune, to be of use no longer to anyone other than a Borscht Belt comic or a professional nostalgist. Even when he pushed his parable prose to its limits, Malamud's metaphors retained a proverbial ring. At his most consciously original, when he sensed in his grimly told, impassioned tales the moment to sound his deepest note, he remained fixed to what seemed old and homely, emitting the most unadorned poetry to make matters even sadder than they already were: "He tried to say some sweet thing but his tongue hung in his mouth like dead fruit on a tree, and his heart was a black-painted window."

The forty-six-year-old man whom I met at the Bakers' little house in Monmouth, Oregon, in 1961 never let on that he could have written that or any such line. At first glance Bern looked to someone who'd grown up among such people like nothing so much as an insurance agent—he could have passed for one of my father's colleagues at the district office of Metropolitan Life. When Malamud entered the Bakers' hallway after having attended my lecture, when he stood there on the welcome mat removing his wet overshoes, I saw a conscientious, courteous workingman of the kind whose kibitzing and conversation had been the background music of my childhood, a stubborn, seasoned life insurance salesman who does not flee the snarling dog or alarm the children when he appears after dark at the top of the tenement stairwell. He doesn't frighten anyone but he doesn't make the place light up with laughter either: he is, after all, the insurance man, whom you can only beat by dying.

That was the other surprise about Malamud. So little laughter. No display at all of the playfulness that flickered on and off in those underheated, poorly furnished flats wherein were enacted the needs of his entombed. No sign from him of the eerie clowning that distinguishes *The Natural*. There were Malamud stories like "Angel Levine"—and later "The Jewbird" and

"Talking Horse"—where the joke seemed only an inch away from the art, where the charm of the art was how it humorously hovered at the edge of the joke, and yet, over twenty-five years, I remember him telling me two jokes. Jewish dialect jokes, expertly recounted, but that was it. For twenty-five years two jokes were enough.

There was no need to overdo anything other than the responsibility to his art. Bern didn't exhibit himself and didn't consider it necessary to exhibit his themes, certainly not casually to a stranger. He couldn't have exhibited himself had he even been foolish enough to try, and never being foolish was a small part of his larger burden. S. Levin, the Chaplinesque professor of *A New Life*, teaching his first college class with a wide-open fly, is hilariously foolish time and again, but not Bern. No more could Kafka have become a cockroach than could Malamud have metamorphosed into a Levin, comically outfoxed by an erotic mishap on the dark back roads of mountainous Oregon and sneaking homeward, half naked, at 3 A.M., beside him a sexually disgruntled barroom waitress dressed in only one shoe and a bra. Seymour Levin the ex-drunkard and Gregor Samsa the bug embody acts of colossal self-travesty, affording both authors a weirdly exhilarating sort of masochistic relief from the weight of sobriety and dignified inhibition that formed the cornerstone of their staid comportment. With Malamud, exuberant showmanship, like searing self-mockery, was to be revealed through what Heine called *Maskenfreiheit*, the freedom conferred by masks.

The sorrowing chronicler of need clashing with need, of need mercilessly resisted and abated only glancingly if at all, of blockaded lives racked with a need for the light, the lift, of a little hope—"A child throwing a ball straight up saw a bit of pale sky"—preferred to present himself as someone whose own need was nobody else's business. Yet his was a need so harsh that it makes one ache to imagine it. It was the need to consider long and seriously every last demand of a conscience torturously exacerbated by the pathos of need unabated. That was a theme of his that he couldn't hide entirely from anyone who thought at all about where the man who could have passed himself off as your insurance agent was joined to the parabolical moralist of the claustrophobic stories about "things you can't get past." In *The Assistant*, the petty criminal and drifter Frank Alpine, while doing penance behind the counter of a failing grocery store that he'd once helped to rob, has a "terrifying insight" about himself: "that all the while he was acting like he wasn't, he was a man of stern morality." I wonder if early in adult life Bern didn't have an insight about himself still more terrifying: that he was a man of stern morality who could act *only* like what he was.

Between our first meeting in Oregon in February 1961 and our last meeting in the summer of 1985 at his home in Bennington, Vermont, I rarely saw him more than a couple times a year, and for several years, after I'd published an essay about American Jewish writers in the *New York Review of Books* that examined *Pictures of Fidelman* and *The Fixer* from a perspective he didn't like—and couldn't have been expected to—we didn't see each other at all. In the mid-sixties, when I was a guest for long periods at the Yaddo artists' colony in Saratoga Springs, New York, a short drive from Bennington, he and his wife, Ann, would have me over when I felt like escaping for a few hours from the Yaddo solitude. In the seventies, when we were both members of the Yaddo corporation board, we'd see each other at the biannual meetings. When the Malamuds began to take refuge in Manhattan from the Vermont winters and I was still living in New York, we'd meet occasionally near their Gramercy Park apartment for dinner. And when Bern and Ann visited London, where I'd begun spending my time, they'd come to have dinner with Claire Bloom and me.

Though Bern and I ended up most evenings talking together about books and writing, we hardly ever alluded to each other's fiction and never seriously discussed it, observing an unwritten rule of propriety that exists among novelists, as among rival teammates in sports, who understand just how little candor can be sustained however deep the respect may run. Blake says, "Opposition is true friendship," and though that sounds admirably bracing, particularly to the argumentative, and subscribing to its wisdom probably works out well in the best of all possible worlds, among the writers in this world, where touchiness and pride can make for a potent explosive, one learns to settle for something a bit more amicable than outright opposition if one wants to have any true writer friends at all. Even those writers who adore opposition usually get about as much as they can stand from their daily work.

It was in London that we arranged to meet again after my 1974 *New York Review* essay and the exchange of letters about it that was to be the last communication between us for a couple of years. His letter had been characteristically terse and colloquial, a single sentence, sounding perhaps a little less fractious than it looked alone on that white sheet of typing paper inscribed above the tiny, measured signature. What I'd written about *Fidelman* and *The Fixer*, he informed me, "is your problem, not mine." I wrote right back to tell him that I'd probably done him a favor of precisely the kind William Blake advocated. I didn't have quite the gall to mention Blake, but that was more or less my tack: what I'd written would help him out. Not too awful as these exchanges go, but not one to ennoble either of us in the canon of literary correspondence.

The London reconciliation didn't take long for Bern and me to pull off. At 7:30 P.M. the doorbell rang and there, on the dot as always, were the Malamuds. Under the porch light I gave Ann a kiss and then, with my hand extended, plunged past her, advancing upon Bern, who with his own outstretched hand was briskly coming up the steps toward me. In our eagerness each to be the first to forgive—or perhaps to be forgiven—we wound up overshooting the handshake and kissing on the lips, rather like the poor baker Lieb and the even less fortunate Kobotsky at the conclusion of "The Loan." The two Jews in that Malamud tale, once immigrants together out of steerage, meet after many years of broken friendship and, at the back of Lieb's shop, listen to the stories of the afflictions in each other's lives, stories so affecting that Lieb forgets all about the bread in his oven, which goes up in smoke. "The loaves in the trays," the story ends, "were blackened bricks—charred corpses. Kobotsky and the baker embraced and sighed over their lost youth. They pressed mouths together and parted forever." We, on the other hand, remained friends for good.

In July 1985, just back from England, Claire and I drove north from Connecticut to have lunch and spend the afternoon with the Malamuds in Bennington. The summer before, they had made the two-and-a-half-hour trip down to us and then spent the night, but Bern wasn't equal to the journey now. The debilitating aftereffects of a stroke three years earlier were sapping his strength, and the effort not to submit without a fight to all the disabling physical problems had begun to beat even him down. I saw how weak he'd got as soon as we drove up. Bern, who always managed, regardless of the weather, to be waiting in the driveway to greet you and see you off, was out there all right in his poplin jacket, but as he nodded a rather grim welcome, he looked to be listing slightly to one side at the same time that he seemed to be holding himself, by dint of willpower alone, absolutely still, as though the least movement would send him crashing to the ground. The forty-six-year-old transplanted Brooklynite whom I'd met in the Far West, that undiscourageable round-the-clock worker with the serious, attentive face and the balding crown and the pitiless Corvallis haircut, whose serviceable surface mildness could have misled anyone about the molten obstinacy at the core—and probably was intended to—was now a frail and very sick old man, his tenacity about used up.

It was bypass surgery and the stroke and the medication that had done the job, but to a longtime reader of the man and his fiction it couldn't help but appear as if the pursuit of that unremitting aspiration that he shared with so many of his characters —to break through the iron limits of self and circumstance in order to live a better life—had finally taken its toll. Though he'd never said much to me about his childhood, from the little I knew about his mother's death when he was still a boy, about the father's poverty and the handicapped brother, I imagined that he'd had no choice but to forgo youth and accept adulthood at an early age. And now he looked it—like a man who'd had to be a man for just too long a time. I thought of his story "Take Pity," the most excruciating parable he ever wrote about life's unyieldingness even to—especially to—the most unyielding longings. When quizzed by Davidov, a heavenly census taker, about how a poor Jewish refugee died, Rosen, himself newly arrived among the dead, replies: "Broke in him something. That's how." "Broke what?" "Broke what breaks."

It was a sad afternoon. We tried talking in the living room before lunch, but concentration was a struggle for him, and though his was a will powerless to back away from any difficult task, it was disheartening to realize how imposing a challenge merely pursuing a friendly conversation had become.

As we were leaving the living room to have lunch outdoors on the back porch, Bern asked if he might read aloud to me later the opening chapters of a first draft of a novel. He'd never before asked my opinion of a work in progress, and I was surprised by the request. I was also perturbed and wondered throughout lunch what sort of book it could be, conceived and begun in the midst of all this hardship by a writer whose memory of even the multiplication tables had been clouded now for several years and whose vision, also impaired by the stroke, made shaving every morning what he'd wryly described to me as "an adventure."

After coffee Bern went to his study for the manuscript, a thin sheaf of pages meticulously typed and clipped together. Ann, whose back was bothering her, excused herself to take a rest, and when Bern settled himself again at the table it was to begin to read in his quiet, insistent way to Claire and me.

I noticed that around his chair, on the porch floor, were scattered crumbs from lunch. A tremor had made eating an adventure too, and yet he had driven himself to write these pages, to undertake once again the writer's ordeal. I remembered the opening of *The Assistant*, the picture of the aging grocer, Morris Bober, dragging the heavy milk cases in from the curb at six o'clock on a November morning; I remembered the exertion that kills him—already close to physical collapse, Bober nonetheless goes out at night to clear six inches of fresh March snow from the sidewalk in front of the imprisoning store. When I got home that evening, I reread the pages describing the grocer's last great effort to do his job.

> To his surprise the wind wrapped him in an icy jacket, his apron flapping noisily. He had expected, the last of March, a milder night . . . He flung another load of snow into the street. "A better life," he muttered.

It turned out that not many words were typed on each page and that the chapters Bern had written were extremely brief. I didn't dislike what I heard, because there was nothing yet to like or dislike—he hadn't got started, really, however much he wanted to think otherwise. Listening to what he read was like being led into a dark hole to see by torchlight the first Malamud story ever scratched upon a cave wall.

I didn't want to lie to him but, looking at those few typewritten pages shaking in his frail hands, I couldn't tell the truth, even if he was expecting it. Only a little evasively, I said that it seemed to me a beginning like all beginnings. That was truthful enough for a man of seventy-one who had published some of the most original works of fiction written by an American in my lifetime. Trying to be constructive, I suggested that the narrative opened too slowly and that he might better begin further along, with one of the later chapters. I asked where it was all going. "What comes next?" I said, hoping we could pass on to what it was he had in mind if not yet down on the page.

But he wouldn't let go of what he'd written, at such cost, as easily as that. Nothing was ever as easy as that, least of all the end of things. In a soft voice suffused with fury, he replied: "What's next isn't the point."

In the silence that followed, he was perhaps as angry at failing to master the need for assurance that he'd so nakedly displayed as he was chagrined with me for having nothing good to say. He wanted to be told that what he had painfully composed while enduring all his burdens was something more than he himself must have known it to be in his heart. He was suffering so, I wished that I could have said it *was* something more and that if I'd said it, he could have believed me.

Before I left for England in the fall I wrote him a note inviting him and Ann to come down to Connecticut the next summer—it was our turn to entertain them. The response that reached me in London some weeks later was pure, laconic Malamudese. They'd be delighted to visit, but, he reminded me, "next summer is next summer."

He died on March 18, 1986, three days before spring.

Pictures by Guston

"One time, in Woodstock," Ross Feld said, "I stood next to Guston in front of some of these canvases. I hadn't seen them before; I didn't really know what to say. For a time, then, there was silence. After a while, Guston took his thumbnail away from his teeth and said, 'People, you know, complain that it's horrifying. As if it's a picnic for me, who has to come in here every day and see them first thing. But what's the alternative? I'm trying to see how much I can stand.'"
—From *Night Studio: A Memoir of Philip Guston*
by Musa Mayer

[1989]

IN 1967, sick of life in the New York art world, Philip Guston left his Manhattan studio forever and took up permanent residence with his wife, Musa, in their Woodstock house on Maverick Road, where they had been living off and on for some twenty years. Two years later, I turned my back on New York to hide out in a small furnished house in Woodstock, across town from Philip, whom I didn't know at the time. I was fleeing the publication of *Portnoy's Complaint*. My overnight notoriety as a sexual freak had become difficult to evade in Manhattan, and so I decided to clear out—first for Yaddo, the upstate artists' colony, and then, beginning in the spring of 1969, for that small rented house tucked out of sight midway up a hillside meadow a couple of miles from Woodstock's main street. I lived there with a young woman who was finishing a Ph.D. and who for several years had been renting a tiny cabin, heated by a wood stove, in the mountainside colony of Byrd-cliffe, which some decades earlier had been a primitive hamlet of Woodstock artists. During the day I wrote on a table in the upstairs spare bedroom while she went off to the cabin to work on her dissertation.

Life in the country with a postgraduate student was anything but freakish, and it provided a combination of social seclusion and physical pleasure that, given the illogic of creation, led me to write, over a four-year period, a cluster of uncharacteristically freakish books. My new reputation as a crazed penis was what instigated the fantasy at the heart of *The Breast*, a book about a college professor who turns into a female breast; it had something to do as well with inspiring the farcical legend of homeless alienation in homespun America that evolved into *The Great American Novel*. The more simplehearted my Woodstock satisfactions, the more tempted I was in my work by the excesses of the Grand Guignol. I'd never felt more imaginatively polymorphous than when I would put two deck chairs on the lawn at the end of the day and we'd stretch out to enjoy the twilight view of the southern foothills of the Catskills, for me unpassable Alps through which no disconcerting irrelevancy could pass. I felt refractory and unreachable and freewheeling, and I was dedicated—perversely overdedicated, probably—to shaking off the vast newfound audience whose collective fantasies were not without their own transforming power.

Guston's situation in 1969—the year we met—was very different. At fifty-six, Philip was twenty years older than I and full of the doubt that can beset an artist of consequence in late middle age. He felt he'd exhausted the means that had unlocked him as an abstract painter, and he was bored and disgusted by the skills that had gained him renown. He didn't want to paint like that ever again; he tried to convince himself he shouldn't paint at all. But since nothing but painting could contain his emotional turbulence, let alone begin to deplete his self-mythologizing monomania, renouncing painting would have been tantamount to committing suicide. Although painting monopolized just enough of his despair and his seismic moodiness to make the anxiety of being himself something even he could sometimes laugh at, it never neutralized the nightmares entirely.

It wasn't supposed to. The nightmares were his not to dissipate with paint but, during the ten years before his death, to intensify with paint, to paint into nightmares that were imperishable and never before incarnated in such trashy props. That terror may be all the more bewildering when it is steeped in farce we know from what we ourselves dream and from what has been dreamed for us by Beckett and Kafka. Philip's discovery —akin to theirs, driven by a delight in mundane objects as

boldly distended and bluntly depoeticized as theirs—was of
the dread that emanates from the most commonplace appurte-
nances of the world of utter stupidity. The unexalted vision of
everyday things that newspaper cartoon strips had impressed
upon him when he was growing up in an immigrant Jewish
family in California, the American crumminess for which, even
in the heyday of his thoughtful lyricism, he always had an intellectual's soft spot, he came to contemplate—in an exercise familiar to lovers of *Molloy* and *The Castle*—as though his life,
both as an artist and as a man, depended on it. This popular
imagery of a shallow reality Philip imbued with such a weight
of personal sorrow and artistic urgency as to shape in painting
a new American landscape of terror.

Cut off from New York and living apart from Woodstock's
local artists, with whom he had little in common, Philip often
felt out of it: isolated, resentful, uninfluential, misplaced. It
wasn't the first time that his ruthless focus on his own imperatives had induced a black mood of alienation, nor was he the
first American artist embittered by the syndrome. It was as
common among the best as it was among the worst—only
with the best it was not necessarily a puerile self-drama concocted out of egomaniacal delusion. In many ways it was a
perfectly justified response for an artist like Guston, whose
brooding, brainy, hypercritical scrutiny of every last aesthetic
choice is routinely travestied by the misjudgments and simplifications that support a major reputation.

Philip and his gloom were not inseparable, however. In the
company of the few friends he enjoyed and was willing to see, he
could be a cordial, unharried host, exuding a captivating spiritual buoyancy unmarked by anguish. In his physical bearing,
too, there was a nimble grace touchingly at variance with the
bulky torso of the heavy-drinking, somewhat august-looking,
white-haired personage into whom darkly, Jewishly, Don Juan-
ishly handsome Guston had been transformed in his fifties. At
dinner, wearing those baggy-bottomed, low-slung khaki trou-
sers of his, with a white cotton shirt open over his burly chest
and the sleeves still turned up from working in the studio, he
looked like the Old Guard Israeli politicians in whom imperi-
ousness and informality spring from an unassailable core of

confidence. It was impossible around the Guston dining table, sharing the rich pasta that Philip had cooked up with a display of jovial expertise, to detect any sign of a self-flagellating component within his prodigious endowment of self-belief. Only in his eyes might you be able to gauge the toll of the wearing oscillation—from iron resolve through rapturous equilibrium to suicidal hopelessness—that underlay a day in the studio.

What caused our friendship to flourish was, to begin with, a similar intellectual outlook, a love for many of the same books as well as a shared delight in what Guston called "crapola," starting with billboards, garages, diners, burger joints, junk shops, auto body shops—all the roadside stuff that we occasionally set out to Kingston to enjoy—and extending from the flat-footed straight talk of the Catskill citizenry to the Uriah Heepisms of our perspiring president. What sealed the camaraderie was that we liked each other's new work. The dissimilarities in our personal lives and our professional fortunes did not obscure the coincidence of our having recently undertaken comparable self-critiques. Independently, impelled by very different dilemmas, each of us had begun to consider crapola not only as a curious subject with strong suggestive powers to which we had a native affinity but as potentially a tool in itself: a blunt aesthetic instrument providing access to a style of representation free of the complexity we were accustomed to valuing. What this self-subversion might be made to yield was anybody's guess, and premonitions of failure couldn't be entirely curbed by the liberating feeling that an artistic about-face usually inspires, at least in the early stages of not quite knowing what you are doing.

At just about the time that I began not quite to know what I was doing exulting in Nixon's lies, or traveling up to Cooperstown's Hall of Fame to immerse myself in baseball lore, or taking seriously the idea of turning a man like myself into a breast—and reading up on endocrinology and mammary glands—Philip was beginning not quite to know what he was doing hanging cartoon light bulbs over the pointed hoods of slit-eyed, cigar-smoking Klansmen painting self-portraits in hideaways cluttered with shoes and clocks and steam irons of the sort that Mutt and Jeff would have been at home with.

Philip's illustrations of incidents in *The Breast*, drawn on ordinary typing paper, were presented to me one evening at dinner shortly after the book's publication. A couple of years earlier, while I was writing *Our Gang*, Philip had responded to the chapters that I showed him in manuscript with a series of caricatures of Nixon, Kissinger, Agnew, and John Mitchell. He worked on these caricatures with more concentration than he did on the drawings for *The Breast*, and he even toyed with the thought of

publishing them as a collection under the title *Poor Richard*. The eight drawings inspired by *The Breast* were simply a spontaneous rejoinder to something he'd liked. The drawings were intended to do nothing other than please me—and did they!

For me his blubbery cartoon rendering of the breast into which Professor David Kepesh is inexplicably transformed—his vision of afflicted Kepesh as a beached mammary groping for contact through a nipple that is an unostentatious amalgam of lumpish, dumb penis and inquisitive nose—managed to encapsulate all the loneliness of Kepesh's humiliation while at the same time adhering to the mordantly comic perspective with which Kepesh tries to view his horrible metamorphosis. Though these drawings were no more than a pleasant diversion for Philip, his predilection for the self-satirization of personal misery (the strategy for effacing the romance of self-pity that stuns us in Gogol's "Diary of a Madman" and "The Nose") as strongly determines the images here as it does in those paintings where his own tiresome addictions and sad renunciations are represented by whiskey bottles and cigarette butts and forlorn insomniacs epically cartoonized. He may only have been playing around, but what he was playing with was the point of view with which he had set about in his studio to overturn his history as a painter and to depict, without rhetorical hedging, the facts of his anxiety as a man. Coincidentally, Philip, who died in 1980 at the age of sixty-six, represents himself in his last paintings as someone who also endured a grotesque transformation—not into a thinking, dismembered sexual gland but into a bloated, cyclopsian, brutish head that has itself been cut loose from the body of its sex.

Rereading Saul Bellow

[2000]

THE ADVENTURES OF AUGIE MARCH (1953)

THE TRANSFORMATION of the novelist who published *Dangling Man* in 1944 and *The Victim* in 1947 into the novelist who published *The Adventures of Augie March* in '53 is revolutionary. Bellow overthrows everything: compositional choices grounded in narrative principles of harmony and order, a novelistic ethos indebted to Kafka's *The Trial* and Dostoyevsky's *The Double* and *The Eternal Husband*, as well as a moral perspective that can hardly be said to derive from delight in the flash, color, and plenty of existence. In *Augie March*, a very grand, assertive, freewheeling conception of both the novel and the world the novel represents breaks loose from all sorts of self-imposed strictures, the beginner's principles of composition are subverted, and, like the character of five Properties in *Augie March*, the writer is himself "hipped on superabundance." The pervasive threat that organized the outlook of the hero and the action of the novel in *The Victim* and *Dangling Man* disappears, and the bottled-up aggression that was *The Victim*'s Asa Leventhal and the obstructed will that was Joseph in *Dangling Man* emerge as voracious appetite. There is the narcissistic enthusiasm for life in all its hybrid forms propelling Augie March, and there is an inexhaustible passion for a teemingness of dazzling specifics driving Saul Bellow.

The scale dramatically enlarges: the world inflates, and those inhabiting it, monumental, overwhelming, ambitious, energetic people, do not easily, in Augie's words, get "stamped out in the life struggle." The intricate landscape of physical being and the power-seeking of influential personalities make "character" in all its manifestations—particularly its ability indelibly to imprint its presence—less an aspect of the novel than its preoccupation.

Think of Einhorn at the whorehouse, Thea with the eagle, Dingbat and his fighter, Simon coarsely splendid at the Magnuses and violent at the lumberyard. From Chicago to Mexico and the mid-Atlantic and back, it's all Brobdingnag to Augie, observed, however, not by a caustic, angry Swift but by a word-painting Hieronymus Bosch, an American Bosch, an unsermonizing and optimistic Bosch, who detects even in the eeliest slipperiness of his creatures, in their most colossal finagling and conspiring and deceit, what is humanly enrapturing. The intrigues of mankind no longer incite paranoid fear in the Bellow hero but light him up. That the richly rendered surface is manifold with contradiction and ambiguity ceases to be a source of consternation; instead, the "mixed character" of everything is bracing. Manifoldness is fun.

Engorged sentences had existed before in American fiction—notably in Melville and Faulkner—but not quite like those in *Augie March*, which strike me as more than liberty-taking; when mere liberty-taking is driving a writer, it can easily lead to the empty flamboyance of some of *Augie March*'s imitators. I read Bellow's liberty-taking prose as the syntactical demonstration of Augie's large, robust ego, that attentive ego roving and evolving, always in motion, alternately mastered by the force of others and escaping from it. There are sentences in the book whose effervescence, whose undercurrent of buoyancy leave one with the sense of so much going on, a theatrical, exhibitionistic, ardent prose tangle that lets in the dynamism of living without driving mentalness out. This voice no longer encountering resistance is permeated by mind while connected also to the mysteries of feeling. It's a voice unbridled and intelligent both, going at full force and yet always sharp enough to cagily size things up.

Chapter XVI of *Augie March* is about the attempt, by Thea Fenchel, Augie's headstrong beloved, to train her eagle, Caligula, to attack and capture the large lizards crawling around the mountains outside Acatla, in central Mexico, to make that "menace falling fast from the sky" fit into her scheme of things. It's a chapter of prodigious strength, sixteen bold pages about a distinctly human happening whose mythic aura (and comedy too) is comparable to the great scenes in Faulkner—in *The Bear*, in *Spotted Horses*, in *As I Lay Dying*, throughout *The Wild Palms* —where human resolve pits itself against what is savage and untamed. The combat between Caligula and Thea (for the eagle's body and soul), the wonderfully precise passages describing the eagle soaring off to satisfy his beautiful fiendish trainer and miserably failing her, crystallize a notion about the will to power and dominance that is central to nearly every one of Augie's adventures. "To tell the truth," Augie says near the end of the book, "I'm good and tired of all these big personalities, destiny molders, and heavy-water brains, Machiavellis and wizard evildoers, big-wheels and imposers-upon, absolutists."

On the book's memorable first page, in the second sentence, Augie quotes Heraclitus: a man's character is his fate. But doesn't *The Adventures of Augie March* suggest exactly the opposite, that a man's fate (at least this man's, this Chicago-born Augie's) is the impinging character of others?

Bellow once told me that "somewhere in my Jewish and immigrant blood there were conspicuous traces of doubt as to whether I had the right to practice the writer's trade." He suggested that, at least in part, this doubt permeated his blood because "our own Wasp establishment, represented mainly by Harvard-trained professors," considered a son of immigrant Jews unfit to write books in English. These guys infuriated him.

It may well have been the precious gift of an appropriate fury that launched him into beginning his third book not with the words "I am a Jew, the son of immigrants" but, rather, by flatly decreeing, without apology or hyphenation, "I am an American, Chicago born."

Opening *Augie March* with those six words demonstrates the same sort of assertive gusto that the musical sons of immigrant Jews—Irving Berlin, Aaron Copland, George Gershwin, Ira Gershwin, Richard Rodgers, Lorenz Hart, Jerome Kern, Leonard Bernstein—brought to America's radios, theaters, and concert halls by staking their claim to America (as subject, as inspiration, as audience) in songs like "God Bless America," "This Is the Army, Mr. Jones," "Oh, How I Hate to Get Up in the Morning," "Manhattan," and "Ol' Man River"; in musical plays like *Oklahoma!*, *West Side Story*, *Porgy and Bess*, *On the Town*, *Show Boat*, *Annie Get Your Gun*, and *Of Thee I Sing*; in ballet music like *Appalachian Spring*, *Rodeo*, and *Billy the Kid*. Back in the teens, when immigration remained a vital phenomenon, back in the twenties, the thirties, the forties, even into the fifties, none of these American-raised boys whose parents or grandparents had spoken Yiddish had the slightest interest in writing shtetl kitsch such as came along in the sixties with *Fiddler on the Roof*. Having themselves been freed by their families' emigration from the pious orthodoxy and the social authoritarianism that were such a great source of shtetl entrapment, why would they want to? In secular, democratic, unclaustrophobic America, Augie will, as he says, "go at things as I have taught myself, free-style."

This assertion of unequivocal, unquellable citizenship in free-style America (and the five-hundred-odd-page book that followed) was precisely the bold stroke required to abolish anyone's doubts about the American writing credentials of an immigrant son like Saul Bellow. Augie, at the very end of his book, exuberantly cries out, "Look at me, going everywhere! Why, I am a sort of Columbus of those near-at-hand." Going where his pedigreed betters wouldn't have believed he had any right to go with the American language, Bellow was indeed Columbus for people like me, the grandchildren of immigrants, who set out as American writers after him.

SEIZE THE DAY (1956)

Three years after *The Adventures of Augie March* appeared, Bellow published *Seize the Day*, a short novel that is the fictional antithesis of *Augie March*. In form spare and compact and tightly organized, it is a sorrow-filled book, set in a hotel for the aged on the Upper West Side of Manhattan, a book populated largely by people old, sick, and dying, while *Augie March* is a vast, sprawling, loquacious book, spilling over with everything, including authorial high spirits, and set wherever life's fullness can be rapturously perceived. *Seize the Day* depicts the culmination, in a single day, of the breakdown of a man who is the opposite of Augie March in every important way. Where Augie is the opportunity seizer, a fatherless slum kid eminently adoptable, Tommy Wilhelm is the mistake maker with a prosperous old father who is very much present but who wants nothing to do with him and his problems. Inasmuch as Tommy's father is characterized in the book, it is through his relentless distaste for his son. Tommy is brutally disowned, eminently unadoptable, largely because he is bereft of the lavish endowment of self-belief, verve, and vibrant adventurousness that is Augie's charm. Where Augie's is an ego triumphantly buoyed up and swept along by the strong currents of life, Tommy's is an ego quashed beneath its burden— Tommy is "assigned to be the carrier of a load which was his own self, his characteristic self." The ego roar amplified by *Augie March*'s prose exuberance Augie joyously articulates on the book's final page: "Look at me, going everywhere!" *Look at me*—the vigorous, child's demand for attention, the cry of exhibitionistic confidence.

The cry resounding through *Seize the Day* is *Help me*. In vain Tommy utters, Help me, help me, I'm getting nowhere, and not only to his own father, Dr. Adler, but to all the false, rogue fathers who succeed Dr. Adler and to whom Tommy foolishly entrusts his hope, his money, or both. Augie is adopted left and right, people rush to support him and dress him, to educate and transform him. Augie's need is to accumulate vivid and flamboyant patron-admirers while Tommy's pathos is to amass mistakes: "Maybe the making of mistakes expressed the very purpose of his life and the essence of his being here." Tommy, at forty-four, searches desperately for a parent, any parent, to rescue him from imminent destruction, while Augie is already a larkily independent escape artist at twenty-two.

Speaking of his own past, Bellow once said, "It has been a lifelong pattern with me to come back to strength from a position of extreme weakness." Does his history of oscillation from the abyss to the peak and back again find a literary analogue in the dialectical relationship of these two consecutive books of the 1950s? Was the claustrophobic chronicle of failure that is *Seize the Day* undertaken as a grim corrective to the fervor informing its irrepressible predecessor, as the antidote to *Augie March*'s manic openness? By writing *Seize the Day*, Bellow seems to have been harking back to the ethos of *The Victim*, to a dour pre-Augie world where the hero under scrutiny is threatened by enemies, overwhelmed by uncertainty, stalled by confusion, held in check by grievance.

HENDERSON THE RAIN KING (1959)

Only six years after *Augie*, and there he is again, breaking loose. But whereas with *Augie* he jettisons the conventions of his first two, "proper" books, with *Henderson the Rain King* he delivers himself from *Augie*, a book in no way proper. The exotic locale, the volcanic hero, the comic calamity that is his life, the inner turmoil of perpetual yearning, the magical craving quest, the mythical (Reichian?) regeneration through the great wet gush of the blocked-up stuff—all brand-new.

To yoke together two mighty dissimilar endeavors: Bellow's Africa operates for Henderson as Kafka's castle village does for K., affording the perfect unknown testing ground for the alien hero to actualize the deepest, most ineradicable of his needs—to burst his "spirit's sleep," if he can, through the intensity of useful labor. "I want," that objectless, elemental cri de coeur, could as easily have been K.'s as Eugene Henderson's. There all similarity ends, to be sure. Unlike the Kafkean man endlessly obstructed from achieving his desire, Henderson is the undirected human force whose raging insistence miraculously *does* get through. K. is an initial, with the biographylessness—and the pathos—that that implies, while Henderson's biography weighs a ton. A boozer, a giant, a Gentile, a middle-aged multimillionaire in a state of continual emotional upheaval, Henderson is hemmed in by the disorderly chaos of "my parents, my wives, my girls, my children, my farm, my animals, my habits, my money, my music lessons, my drunkenness, my prejudices, my brutality, my teeth, my face, my soul!" Because of all his deformities and mistakes, Henderson, in his own thinking, is as much a disease as he is a man. He takes leave of home (rather like the author who is imagining him) for a continent peopled by tribal blacks who turn out to be his very cure. Africa as medicine. Henderson the Remedy Maker.

Brilliantly funny, all new, a second enormous emancipation, a book that wants to be serious and unserious at the same time (and is), a book that invites an academic reading while ridiculing such a reading and sending it up, a stunt of a book, but a sincere stunt—a screwball book, but not without great screwball authority.

HERZOG (1964)

The character of Moses Herzog, that labyrinth of contradiction and self-division—the wild man and the earnest person with a "Biblical sense of personal experience" and an innocence as phenomenal as his sophistication, intense yet passive, reflective yet impulsive, sane yet insane, emotional, complicated, an expert on pain vibrant with feeling and yet disarmingly simple, a clown in his vengeance and rage, a fool in whom hatred breeds comedy, a sage and knowing scholar in a treacherous world, yet still adrift in the great pool of childhood love, trust, and excitement in things (and hopelessly attached to this condition), an aging lover of enormous vanity and narcissism with a lovingly harsh attitude toward himself, whirling in the wash cycle of a rather generous self-awareness while at the same time aesthetically attracted to anyone vivid, overpoweringly drawn to bullies and bosses, to theatrical know-it-alls, lured by their seeming certainty and by the raw authority of their unambiguity, feeding on their intensity until he's all but crushed by it—this Herzog is Bellow's grandest creation, American literature's Leopold Bloom, except with a difference: in *Ulysses*, the encyclopedic mind of the author is transmuted into the linguistic flesh of the novel, and Joyce never cedes to Bloom his own great erudition, intellect, and breadth of rhetoric, whereas in *Herzog* Bellow endows his hero with all of that, not only with a state of mind and a cast of mind but with a mind that *is* a mind.

It's a mind rich and wide-ranging but turbulent with troubles, bursting, swarming with grievance and indignation, a bewildered mind that, in the first sentence of the book, openly, with good reason, questions its equilibrium, and not in highbrowese but in the classic vernacular formulation: "If I am out of my mind . . ." This mind, so forceful, so tenacious, overstocked with the best that has been thought and said, a mind elegantly turning out the most informed generalizations about a lot of

the world and its history, happens also to suspect its most fundamental power, the very capacity for comprehension.

The axis on which the book's adulterous drama turns, the
scene that sends Herzog racing off to Chicago to pick up a
loaded pistol to kill Madeleine and Gersbach and instead initi-
ates his final undoing, takes place in a New York courtroom,
where Herzog, loitering while waiting for his lawyer to show
up, comes upon the nightmare-parody version of his own suffering. It is the trial of a hapless, degraded mother who, with
her degenerate lover, has murdered her own little child. So
overcome with horror is Herzog at what he sees and hears
that he is prompted to cry out to himself, "I fail to understand!"—familiar-enough everyday words, but for Herzog a
humbling, pain-ridden, reverberating admission that dramatically connects the intricate wickerwork of his mental existence
to the tormenting grid of error and disappointment that is his
personal life. Since for Herzog understanding is an impediment to instinctive force, it is when understanding fails him
that he reaches for a gun (the very one with which his own
father once clumsily threatened to kill *him*)—though, in the
end, being Herzog, he cannot fire it. Being Herzog (and his
angry father's angry son), he finds firing the pistol "nothing
but a thought."

But if Herzog fails to understand, who *does* understand, and
what is all this thinking *for*? Why all this uninhibited reflection
in Bellow's books in the first place? I don't mean the run-on
blarney of characters like Tamkin in *Seize the Day*, or even King
Dahfu in *Henderson*, who seem to dish out their spoof wisdom
as much for Bellow to have the fun of inventing it as to create
a second realm of confusion in the minds of heroes already
plenty confused on their own. I'm referring to the nearly impossible undertaking that marks Bellow's work as strongly as it
does the novels of Robert Musil and Thomas Mann: the
struggle not only to infuse fiction with mind but to make
mentalness itself central to the hero's dilemma—to think, in
books like *Herzog*, about the *problem* of thinking.

Now, Bellow's special appeal, and not just to me, is that in his
characteristically American way he has managed brilliantly to
close the gap between Thomas Mann and Damon Runyon, but
that doesn't minimize the scope of what, beginning with *Augie*

March, he so ambitiously set out to do: to bring into play (into *free* play) the intellectual faculties that, in writers like Mann, Musil, and him, are no less engaged by the spectacle of life than by the mind's imaginative component, to make rumination congruent with what is represented, to hoist the author's thinking up from the depths to the narrative's surface without sinking the narrative's mimetic power, without the book's superficially meditating on itself, without making a transparently ideological claim on the reader, and without imparting wisdom, as do Tamkin and King Dahfu, flatly unproblematized.

Herzog is Bellow's first protracted expedition as a writer into the immense domain of sex. Herzog's women are of the greatest importance to him, enthralling and enchanting him—exciting his vanity, arousing his carnality, enlivening his emotions, channeling his love, drawing his curiosity, and, by registering his cleverness, charm, and good looks, feeding in the man the joys of a boy—in their adoration is his validation. And in their enmity is his misery. With every insult they hurl and every epithet they coin, with each fetching turn of the head, comforting touch of the hand, angry twist of the mouth, his women fascinate Herzog with that human otherness that so overpowers him in *both* sexes. But it is the women especially—until the final pages, that is, when Herzog turns away from his Berkshires retreat even well-meaning Ramona and the generous pleasures of the seraglio that are her specialty, when he at long last emancipates himself from the care of another woman, even this most gentle fondler of them all, and, so as to repair himself, undertakes what is for him the heroic project of living alone, shedding the women and, shedding with them, of all things, the explaining, the justifying, the thinking, divesting himself, if only temporarily, of the all-encompassing and habitual sources of his pleasure and anguish—it is the women especially who bring out the portraitist in Herzog, a multitalented painter who can be as lavish in describing the generous mistress as Renoir; as tender in presenting the adorable daughter as Degas; as compassionate, as respectful of age, as knowledgeable of hardship in picturing the ancient stepmother—or his own dear mother in her slavish immigrant suffering—as Rembrandt; as devilish, finally, as Daumier in depicting the adulterous wife who discerns, in Herzog's loving and scheming best friend, Valentine Gersbach, her vivid theatrical equal.

In all of literature, I know of no more susceptible male, of no man who brings a greater focus or intensity to his engagement with women than this Herzog, who collects them both as an adoring suitor and as a husband—a cuckolded husband getting a royal screwing who, in the grandeur of his jealous rage and in the naiveté of his blind uxoriousness, is a kind of comic-strip amalgam of General Othello and Charles Bovary. Anyone wishing to have some fun in retelling *Madame Bovary* from Charles's perspective, or *Anna Karenina* from Karenin's, will find in *Herzog* the perfect how-to book. (Not that one easily envisions Karenin, à la Herzog with Gersbach, handing over to Vronsky Anna's diaphragm.)

Herzog lays claim to being a richer novel even than *Augie March* because Bellow's taking on board, for the first time, the full sexual cargo allows for a brand of suffering to penetrate his fictional world that was largely precluded from *Augie* and *Henderson*. It turns out that even more is unlocked in the Bellow hero by suffering than by euphoria. How much more credible, how much more important he becomes when the male wound, in its festering enormity, ravages the euphoric appetite for "the rich life-cake," and the vulnerability to humiliation, betrayal, melancholy, fatigue, loss, paranoia, obsession, and despair is revealed to be so sweeping that neither an Augie's relentless optimism nor a Henderson's mythical giantism can stave off any longer the truth about pain. Once Bellow grafts onto Henderson's intensity—and onto Augie March's taste for grandiose types and dramatic encounters—Tommy Wilhelm's condition of helplessness, he puts the whole Bellovian symphony in play, with its lushly comical orchestration of misery.

In *Herzog*, there is no sustained chronological action—there's barely *any* action—that takes place outside Herzog's brain. It isn't that, as a storyteller, Bellow apes Faulkner in *The Sound and the Fury* or Virginia Woolf in *The Waves*. The long, shifting, fragmented interior monologue of *Herzog* seems to have more in common with Gogol's "Diary of a Madman," where the disjointed perception is dictated by the mental state of the central character rather than by an author's impatience with traditional means of narration. What makes Gogol's madman mad, however, and Bellow's sane, is that Gogol's madman, incapable of overhearing himself, is unfortified by the spontaneous current of irony and self-parody that ripples through Herzog's every other thought—even when he is most bewildered—and that is inseparable from his take on himself and his disaster, however excruciating his pain.

In the Gogol story, the madman obtains a bundle of letters written by a dog, the pet belonging to the young woman of whom he is hopelessly (insanely) enamored. Feverishly, he sits down to read every word the brilliant dog has written, searching for any reference to himself. In *Herzog*, Bellow goes Gogol one better: the brilliant dog who writes the letters is Herzog. Letters to his dead mother, to his living mistress, to his first wife, to President Eisenhower, to Chicago's police commissioner, to Adlai Stevenson, to Nietzsche ("My dear sir, May I ask a question from the floor?"), to Teilhard de Chardin ("Dear Father . . . Is the carbon molecule lined with thought?"), to Heidegger ("Dear Doktor Professor . . . I should like to know what you mean by the expression 'the fall into the quotidian.' When did this fall occur? Where were we standing when it happened?"), to the credit department of Marshall Field & Co. ("I am no longer responsible for the debts of Madeleine P. Herzog"), even, in the end, a letter to God ("How my mind has struggled to make coherent sense. I have not been too good at it. But have desired to do your unknowable will, taking it, and you, without symbols. Everything of intensest significance. Especially if divested of me").

This book of a thousand delights offers no greater delight than those letters, and no better key with which to both unlock Herzog's remarkable intelligence and enter into the depths of his turmoil over the wreckage of his life. The letters are his intensity demonstrated; they provide the stage for his intellectual theater, the one-man show where he is least likely to act the role of the fool.

MR. SAMMLER'S PLANET (1970)

"Is our species crazy?" A Swiftian question. A Swiftian note as well in the laconic Sammlerian reply: "Plenty of evidence."

Reading *Mr. Sammler's Planet*, I am reminded of *Gulliver's Travels*: by the overwhelming estrangement of the hero from the New York of the 1960s; by the rebuke he, with his history, embodies to the human status of those whose "sexual madness" he must witness; by his Gulliverian obsession with human physicality, human biology, the almost mythic distaste evoked in him by the body, its appearance, its functions, its urges, its pleasures, its secretions and smells. Then there's the preoccupation with the radical vincibility of one's physical being. As a frail, displaced refugee of the Holocaust horror, as one who escaped miraculously from the Nazi slaughter, who rose, with but one eye, from a pile of Jewish bodies left for dead by a German extermination squad, Mr. Sammler registers that most disorienting of blows to civic confidence—the disappearance, in a great city, of security, of safety, and, with that, the burgeoning among the vulnerable of fear-ridden, alienating paranoia.

For it is fear as well as disgust that vitiates Sammler's faith in the species and threatens his tolerance even for those closest to him—fear of "the soul . . . in this vehemence . . . the extremism and fanaticism of human nature." Having moved beyond the Crusoe-adventurousness of ebullient Augie and Henderson to delineate, as dark farce, the marital betrayal of the uncomprehending genius Herzog, Bellow next opens out his contemplative imagination to one of the greatest betrayals of all, at least as perceived by the refugee-victim Sammler in his Swiftian revulsion with the sixties: the betrayal by the crazed species of the civilized ideal.

Herzog, during his most searing moment of suffering, admits to himself, "I fail to understand!" But, despite old Sammler's Oxonian reserve and cultivated detachment, at the climax of *his* adventure—with license, disorder, and lawlessness within the network of his vividly eccentric family and beyond them, in New York's streets, subways, buses, shops, and college classrooms—the admission that is wrung from him (and that, for me, stands as the motto of this book) is far more shattering: "I am horrified!"

The triumph of *Mr. Sammler's Planet* is the invention of Sammler, with the credentials that accrue to him through his European education—his history of suffering history, and his Nazi-blinded eye—as "the registrar of madness." The juxtaposition of the personal plight of the protagonist with the particulars of the social forces he encounters, the resounding, ironic rightness of that juxtaposition, accounts for the impact here, as it does in every memorable fiction. Sammler, sharply set apart by his condition of defenseless dignity, strikes me as the perfect instrument to receive anything in society at all bizarre or menacing, the historical victim abundantly qualified by experience to tellingly provide a harsh, hardened twentieth-century perspective on "mankind in a revolutionary condition."

I wonder which came first in the book's development, the madness or the registrar, Sammler or the sixties.

HUMBOLDT'S GIFT (1975)

Humboldt's Gift is far and away the screwiest of the euphoric going-every-which-way out-and-out comic novels, the books that materialize at the very tip-top of the Bellovian mood swing, the merry music of the egosphere that is *Augie March*, *Henderson*, and *Humboldt* and that Bellow emits more or less periodically, between his burrowings through the dark down-in-the-dumps novels, such as *The Victim*, *Seize the Day*, *Mr. Sammler's Planet*, and *The Dean's December*, where the bewildering pain issuing from the heroes' wounds is not taken lightly either by them or by Bellow. *Herzog* strikes me as supreme among Bellow's novels for its magical integration of this characteristic divergence.

Humboldt is the screwiest, by which I also mean the most brazen of the comedies, loopier and more carnivalesque than the others, Bellow's only joyously open libidinous book and, rightly, the most recklessly crossbred fusion of disparate strains, and for a paradoxically compelling reason: Citrine's terror. Of what? Of mortality, of having to meet (regardless of his success and his great eminence) Humboldt's fate. Underlying the book's buoyant engagement with the scrambling, gorging, thieving, hating, and destroying of Charlie Citrine's on-the-make world, underlying everything, including the centrifugal manner of the book's telling—and exposed directly enough in Citrine's eagerness to metabolize the extinction-defying challenge of Rudolf Steiner's anthroposophy—is his terror of dying. What's disorienting Citrine happens also to be what's blowing narrative decorum to kingdom come: the panicky dread of oblivion, the old-fashioned garden-variety Everyman horror of death.

"How sad," says Citrine, "about all this human nonsense which keeps us from the large truth." But the human nonsense is what he loves and loves to recount and what delights him most about being alive. Again: "When . . . would I rise . . . above all . . . the wastefully and randomly human . . . to enter higher worlds?" Higher worlds? Where would Citrine be—where would *Bellow* be—without the randomly human driving the superdrama of the *lower* world, the elemental superdrama that is the worldly desire for fame (as exhibited by Von Humboldt Fleisher, the luckless, mentally unsound counterpart of fortunate, sane Citrine—Humboldt, who wishes both to be spiritual and to make it big, and whose nightmare failure is the flip-side travesty of Citrine's success), for money (Humboldt, Thaxter, Denise, plus Renata's mother the Señora, plus Citrine's brother Julius, plus more or less everyone else), for revenge (Denise, Cantabile), for esteem (Humboldt, Cantabile, Thaxter, Citrine), for the hottest of hot sex (Citrine, Renata, et al.), not to mention that worldliest of worldly desires, Citrine's own, the hellbent lusting after life eternal?

Why does Citrine wish so feverishly never to leave here if not for this laugh-a-minute immersion in the violence and the turbulence of the clownish greediness that he disparagingly calls "the moronic inferno"? "Some people," he says, "are so actual that they beat down my critical powers." And beat down any desire to exchange even the connection to their viciousness for the serenity of the everlasting. Where but the moronic inferno could his "complicated subjectivity" have so much to gorge upon?

And isn't it something like the same moronic inferno that Charlie Citrine excitedly memorializes as it rages in the streets, courtrooms, bedrooms, restaurants, sweat baths, and office buildings of Chicago that so sickens Artur Sammler in its diabolic 1960s-Manhattan incarnation? *Humboldt's Gift* seems like the enlivening tonic Bellow brewed to recover from the sorrowful grieving and moral suffering of *Mr. Sammler's Planet*. It's Bellow's cheerful version of Ecclesiastes: all is vanity and isn't it something!

WHAT'S HE IN CHICAGO FOR?

Humboldt on Citrine (my edition page 2): "After making this dough why does he bury himself in the sticks? What's he in Chicago for?"

Citrine on himself (page 63): "My mind was in one of its Chicago states. How should I describe this phenomenon?"

Citrine on being a Chicagoan (page 95): "I could feel the need to laugh rising, mounting, always a sign that my weakness for the sensational, my American, Chicagoan (as well as personal) craving for high stimuli, for incongruities and extremes, was aroused."

And (further along on page 95): "Such information about corruption, if you had grown up in Chicago, was easy to accept. It even satisfied a certain need. It harmonized with one's Chicago view of society."

On the other hand, there's Citrine's being out of place in Chicago (page 225): "In Chicago my personal aims were bunk, my outlook a foreign ideology." And (page 251): "It was now apparent to me that I was neither of Chicago nor sufficiently beyond it, and that Chicago's material and daily interests and phenomena were neither actual and vivid enough nor symbolically clear enough to me."

Keeping in mind these remarks—and there are many more like them throughout *Humboldt's Gift*—look back to the 1940s and observe that Bellow started off as a writer *without* Chicago's organizing his idea of himself the way it does Charlie Citrine's. Yes, a few Chicago streets are occasionally sketched in as the backdrop to *Dangling Man*, but, aside from darkening the pervasive atmosphere of gloom, Chicago seems a place that is almost foreign to the hero; certainly it is alien to him. *Dangling Man* is not a book about a man in a city; it's about a mind in a room. Not until the third book, *Augie March*, did Bellow fully apprehend Chicago as that valuable hunk of literary property, that tangible, engrossing American place that was his to claim as commandingly as Sicily was monopolized by Verga,

London by Dickens, and the Mississippi River by Mark Twain. It's with a comparable tentativeness or wariness that Faulkner (the other of America's two greatest twentieth-century novelist-regionalists) came to imaginative ownership of Lafayette County, Mississippi. Faulkner situated his first book, *Soldier's Pay* (1926), in Georgia, his second, *Mosquitoes* (1927), in New Orleans, and it was only with the masterly burst of *Sartoris*, *The Sound and the Fury*, and *As I Lay Dying*, in 1929–30, that he found—as did Bellow after taking *his* first, impromptu geographical steps—the location to engender those human struggles which, in turn, would fire up his intensity and provoke that impassioned response to a place and its history which at times propels Faulkner's sentences to the brink of unintelligibility and even beyond.

I wonder if at the outset Bellow shied away from seizing Chicago as his because he didn't want to be known as a Chicago writer, any more, perhaps, than he wanted to be known as a Jewish writer. Yes, you're from Chicago, and of course you're a Jew—but how these things are going to figure in your work, or if they should figure at all, isn't easy to puzzle out right off. Besides, you have other ambitions, inspired by your European masters, by Dostoyevsky, Gogol, Proust, Kafka, and such ambitions don't include writing about the neighbors gabbing on the back porch . . . Does this line of thought in any way resemble Bellow's before he finally laid claim to the immediate locale?

Of course, after *Augie* it was some ten years before, in *Herzog*, Bellow took on Chicago in a big way again. Ever since then, the distinctly "Chicago view" has been of recurring interest to him, especially when the city provides, as in *Humboldt*, a contrast of comically illuminating proportions between "the open life which is elementary, easy for everyone to read, and characteristic of this place, Chicago, Illinois" and the reflective bent of the preoccupied hero. This combat, vigorously explored, is at the heart of *Humboldt*, as it is of Bellow's next novel, *The Dean's December* (1982). Here, however, the exploration is not comic but rancorous. The mood darkens, the depravity deepens, and under the pressure of violent racial antagonisms, Chicago, Illinois, becomes demoniacal: "On his own turf . . . he found a wilderness wilder than the Guiana bush . . . desolation . . . endless square miles of ruin . . . wounds, lesions, cancers, destructive fury, death . . . the terrible wildness and dread in this huge place."

The book's very point is that this huge place is Bellow's no longer. Nor is it Augie's, Herzog's, or Citrine's. By the time he comes to write *The Dean's December*, some thirty years after *Augie March*, his hero, Dean Corde, has become the city's Sammler.

What is he in Chicago for? This Chicagoan in pain no longer knows. Bellow is banished.

THREE

EXPLANATIONS

Juice or Gravy?

ADULT LIFE—by which I mean the unpredictable, irrational unknown to which someone raised and educated like me brings the naive project of self-assertion once preparations have been completed to enter a world that is known, rational, and predictable—adult life began for me, as it often has begun for American young men during these last forty years, when I was discharged from the army.

The national news in the middle of August 1956 was not, of course, my return to civilian life but the nomination for the second time of Governor Adlai Stevenson of Illinois as the Democratic presidential candidate in Chicago and the nomination, the next day, of Senator Estes Kefauver of Tennessee as the vice-presidential candidate. Later that month the news wasn't that I had accepted an invitation to return to the University of Chicago—where I had received an M.A. in literature the year before—as a freshman composition instructor at an annual salary of $2800 but that President Eisenhower and Vice-President Richard Nixon were unanimously renamed their party's nominees at the Republicans' San Francisco convention. The big names in international news that summer were Faisal, Gomulka, Hammarskjöld, Makarios, Shepilov, Nehru, and Wilson. But I was twenty-three and the big name in the news for me was mine. And the big story about me was that I was about to make something far more exciting than a DeSoto hardtop or a Westinghouse washer-dryer or even an atomic bomb. I was about to manufacture a future, *my* future, though without the least idea that it might well be the future that would be manufacturing me.

But as the aggressively independent son of energetic, law-abiding, hyper-responsible, impeccably organized parents, as someone whose college years, like his childhood and adolescence, had gone off happily without a hitch, as a fortunate youngster whose life to date looked in every way to be blessed,

---

A talk delivered to the Lotos Club in New York, 1994.

I was as yet without any experience of that wholly impersonal antagonist to individual will who was waiting just around the corner to catch me by the tail, the great pervasive Anti-You.

And I was largely innocent, in those buoyant years before I was out on my own, of the Law of 26 (known also as TFHC, the theory of the frequency of hidden consequences), which postulates that the minimum number of repercussions, not only of every last thing one does or says but of everything one fails to do or to say, is twenty-six; that these twenty-six repercussions occur in addition to whatever repercussions one elects to foresee; and that these repercussions are of necessity opposed diametrically to the repercussions one was hoping to effectuate.

Coming out of the army at twenty-three, I didn't know any of this.

To be sure, the circumstances of my army discharge might well have begun to alert me to just how little one has to do with calling the shots that determine the ways in which an adult life develops. Though I'd gone into the army, under the post–Korean War draft, assuming that I would be serving a two-year stint, I was released halfway through because of an injury incurred in infantry basic training at Fort Dix, New Jersey, that had increasingly disabled me over the ensuing months. When I was in too much pain even to perform the Washington desk job to which I'd been assigned, I was sent to the army's gloomy rehabilitation center nearby, a spooky, lonely, wooded retreat in Forest Glen, Maryland, where the other patients in my ward were mostly amputees and paraplegics. Their miseries drastically dwarfed my own, and many nights I would listen in the dark to someone my age or younger crying aloud from his bed that this wasn't supposed to have happened. Eventually I was discharged for medical reasons, but still without having figured out, even after having lived and slept for over a month among the youthful victims of the most unlikely misfortunes, that invigorating expectations and an upbeat outlook are as much a fantasy as anything cooked up in the roiling brain of a paranoid schizophrenic.

I returned to Chicago suspecting that now, out from under the authority of the army, the true life foreordained for such as me would begin to unfold. But the medical discharge did not

magically obliterate the medical problem or the physical limitations it imposed. I discovered that I was no longer in charge
of my body the way I had been when I'd left Chicago in perfect
health only the year before, even though, throughout the day
and the evening, I forced myself to do everything expected of
me and everything I wanted to do. But the effort required was
sometimes daunting, and that's when the disequilibrium set in:
I couldn't believe what had happened to me. This was not the
future that I intended to manufacture. I thought, "Something is
going wrong." But nothing was going wrong. I was merely learning what most people learn, often through the medium of their
backside, by the age of two. As a brand-new adult from a secure
upbringing in a modest home—his childhood days and nights
grounded in predictability and pleasurable routine; through emu-
lation of the family elders, a regular way of doing things embedded benignly in his brain—I was learning how things happen
independently of one's exertions, schedules, or plans, how one's
tenacity, ingenuity, and forcefulness, how even all one's achieving,
can mean nothing and come to nothing.

A young woman I met a few months after my return to
Chicago amplified this education with a vengeance. Indeed, I
believe I originally fell for the enigma that she was to me and
became entranced by all the adventures in failure that she had
already fashioned into a vivid legend of her survivorship in
order to further my education by sitting at the feet of this jailbird's daughter who, still only in her twenties, but wholly unlike me, claimed to have known from earliest childhood on
everything there was to know about the fiendish power of the
Anti-You.

Yes, her father was in jail. Her father was in jail while mine,
predictably, reassuringly, altogether conventionally, was either
at work or at home. I didn't even know where the jail was in
Newark. I would guess now that it was in back of the Essex
County Courthouse on Market Street. I'd never even thought
while growing up to go out looking for it. Why would I? I
knew where Ruppert Stadium was, the home of the Triple-A
Newark Bears. I knew where the Empire burlesque house was,
the showcase for "Evelyn West and Her Treasure Chest." I
could find the airport, the public library, the "Y," the Beth Israel Hospital where I'd been born. I could direct you to

Bamberger's department store, to Military Park, to City Hall, to Penn Station, to Father Divine's Riviera Hotel, and to every movie theater downtown. But to where the jail was? Couldn't help you.

But she could. She knew where it was all right. It was in the embittered heart of the jailbird's daughter—the jail was *being* a jailbird's daughter. Yes, I had a lot to learn about jail, and she had a lot to teach about jail, and about all the good an individual's will can do when it is up against the humiliations of an unbidden grinding-down, a history of past privations that she hated just as viscerally as, over the next few years, we came to hate each other.

In the hours I had to myself at the end of the academic day— before I regularly hurried off to an evening class at L'Ecole de Hard Knocks with my aggrieved inamorata—I would sit alone in my tiny one-room apartment with my Olivetti portable trying to write dazzling short stories. A couple of stories I had written at night in the army had already appeared in literary quarterlies and one had even garnered some attention, but these stories were not dazzling, they were derivative, and I planned to dazzle in my very own way.

Why not? There was nobody in my apartment to stop me— nobody else could have fit in. Nor was there anything I saw to impede me when I looked in the mirror over the bathroom sink each morning and said aloud to my reflection, "All you have to do is work!" and so I set forth, using every free minute I had, working to become a writer who was dazzling and believing that where my ambition was altogether clear and focused, where my fortitude was limitless, my dedication total, and mine was the imagination wholly in charge, I could not but achieve what I wanted. I instructed the unyielding young face in the mirror, "Attack! Attack!" certain that I would prevail, if only by sheer perseverance.

Usually in those days I ate dinner for under $2 at the student commons, a block away from where I lived. But once a week or so, for another buck, I had a thick pink slice of the house specialty, roast beef, at Valois, a plain neighborly cafeteria back in the 1950s, up on 53rd Street not far from the lake, where about as many working people as university people were dinnertime regulars. I always tried to find a vacant seat at a table from which one could see the face and hear the voice of the small Sicilian counterman who back then stood to the side of the guy who sliced up and served the roast beef and whose job was to inquire of each and every roast beef customer, "Juice or gravy?" and then to generously ladle onto the plate whichever was requested. By "juice" he meant the blood the meat secreted while being cooked.

In a singsong, accented delivery that gave a light musical emphasis to the first word, he must have asked, "Juice or gravy?" as many as fifty times while I leisurely enjoyed my dinner right along with the intriguing monotony of his three little words. Time after time the same interrogation. One unit of two syllables following two of one. That was the whole verbal task.

One evening at the cafeteria, after proceeding in the line along the serving counter to assemble my customary meal— my preference was always for the juice, though I was never unceremonious enough to order it without first being asked— I carried the tray to the table where I liked to sit and found there four empty chairs; unusual at that hour, but then it had been storming all day and I myself had almost decided to stay home and begin grading the week's hundred freshman compositions while I ate baked beans heated up out of a can. It could be that I had gone out in that weather only so as to hear—before I settled in for a long evening of correcting comma faults and unsnarling sentences—the four-syllable haiku chanted by the intrepid ladler that always managed to cheer me up. It may well have been nothing more than that then, nothing more than practically nothing, that goaded me out in the heavy rain not merely to discover four empty chairs at my favorite table but to come upon an 8½-by-11 sheet of white typing paper that a previous diner had forgotten or abandoned on the table at my preferred place—a sheet of paper, as it would turn out, that would ensnare me for decades.

Typewritten on the paper, in the form of a long single-spaced unindented paragraph, were nineteen sentences that taken together made no sense at all. Though no author's name appeared anywhere on either the front or the back of the page, I figured that the nineteen sentences, amounting to some four hundred or so words, were more than likely the work of a neighborhood savant with an interest in experimental or automatic writing, and that this page must be a sample of one or the other. Here is what was written on that single sheet of paper:

The first time I saw Brenda she asked me to hold her glasses. Dear Gabe, The drugs help me bend my fingers around a pen. Not to be rich, not to be famous, not to be mighty, not even to be happy, but to be civilized—that was the dream of his life. She was so deeply imbedded in my consciousnesss that for the first year of school I seem to have believed that each of my teachers was my mother in disguise. Sir, I want to congratulate you for coming out on April 3 for the sanctity of human life, including the life of the yet unborn. It began oddly. Call me Smitty. Far from being the classic period of explosion and tempestuous growth, my adolescence was more or less a period of suspended animation. Temptation comes to me first in the conspicuous personage of Herbie Bratasky, social director, bandleader, crooner, comic, and m.c. of my family's mountainside resort hotel. First, foremost, the puppyish, protected upbringing above his father's shoe store in Camden. It was the last daylight hour of a December afternoon more than 20 years ago—I was 23, writing and publishing my first short stories, and like many a *Bildungsroman* hero before me, already contemplating my own massive *Bildungsroman*—when I arrived at his hideaway to meet the great man. "What the hell are you doing on a bus, with your dough?" When he is sick, every man wants his mother; if she's not around, other women must do. "Your novel," he says, "is absolutely one of the five or six books of my life." Ever since the family doctor, during a routine checkup, discovered an abnormality on his EKG and he went in overnight for the coronary catheterization that revealed the dimensions of the disease, Henry's condition had been successfully treated with drugs, enabling him to work and carry on his life at home exactly as before. Dear Zuckerman, In the past, as you know, the facts have always been notebook jottings, my way of springing into fiction. "I'll write them down. You begin." My father had lost most of the sight in his right eye by the time he'd reached 86, but otherwise he seemed in phenomenal health for a man his age when he came down with what the Florida doctor diagnosed, incorrectly, as Bell's palsy, a viral infection that causes paralysis, usually temporary, to one side of his face. For legal reasons, I have had to alter a number of facts in this book.

Now this document—this prank—this gift—this incomprehensible whatever-it-was—this *nothing*—came my way some dozen years before the words "coronary catheterization" referred to anything real in the medical world and some thirty years before my own eighty-six-year-old father developed a fatal brain tumor that was indeed initially misdiagnosed by a Florida physician as Bell's palsy. The extraordinary prescience manifest in sentences fifteen and eighteen would seem at first glance inexplicable, until one remembers that it's not entirely unusual for something to come to pass in the real world that one had previously laid out only imaginatively on paper. The phenomenon is, in fact, far from unknown to anyone whose work day in and out over the decades is to fashion from words a likeness to life. It's happened at times to me, it's happened to others, and so it's not impossible that it happened to whoever came up with sentences fifteen and eighteen. Or should I say whoever came up with sentence fifteen and whoever then came up with sentence eighteen? For how can I know, even today, if a single whimsical author was the compositor of this fanciful document or if there was a different whimsical author for each sentence, a theory which might provide an explanation for the paragraph's radical randomness and for how it came to be lacking any discernible logic or order.

That I didn't lose this single page over the next year is no less of a miracle than that it should have turned up as it did in the first place. Though I could never bring myself to discard it, I also did nothing at first not to misplace it. After forgetting about it for months on end, I'd find it on the floor beside the waste basket next to my desk, or tucked in among my students' weekly themes, or beside the telephone with the yellow tablet of lined paper that served as a scratch pad for messages and for the lists that I, like my orderly mother before me, always drew up on Sundays of the chores to be undertaken that week.

It only occurred to me that it too was a list of things to be done when, instead of scanning it in vain—as I did each time it made an appearance—like some literary hound looking for an inherent stratagem that would disclose an overall unified meaning, I came to realize what would surely have been obvious at the outset to anyone less well trained—or perhaps less poorly trained—in the art of exegesis than I was back then. I saw that these sentences, as written, had *nothing* to do with one another. I saw that if a meaningful design were to be discernible in the paragraph, it would have to be applied from without rather than ingeniously unearthed from decipherable allusions within.

What I eventually realized was that these were the first lines of the books that it had fallen to me to write.

Don't ask how I understood that these were the first rather than the last or fiftieth or five hundredth lines. Don't ask why I assumed that the books that were to be written by me had to be written in exactly the sequence in which the sentences were laid out in that inchoate paragraph. Why not in the reverse sequence? Or scattershot, in no sequence at all? Don't ask me to justify the scheme that I carried away from that mysterious piece of paper at the age of twenty-three since at sixty-one I am no longer so eager as I once was to rationalize the irrational or to assign myself blindly to a monumental task for some illusory purpose—I would like to think that I have lived long enough to no longer be such a slave of the why or such a driven captive of a fixated will. I am even willing to concede that the conclusion I drew was utterly groundless and that my entire career up until today has been founded in an imbecilic premise. It stuns, it even shames me now, to think that, at twenty-three, I took upon myself the absurd and seemingly undoable task of ascertaining, with all the precision I could muster, the tens of thousands of words that should follow ineluctably from each one of these nineteen introductory sentences. Suppose I had found another sheet of paper filled with other words or had found a blank sheet of paper or no paper at all there at my usual place at the cafeteria. Suppose the busboy had beat me to the punch and crumpled it in among the dirty dishes. Suppose I'd come to my senses and tossed the paper into the garbage once I had gotten home. What books would I have written then? Might I have written no books at all? Suppose I had stayed indoors that evening in Chicago and eaten beans instead of coming to believe, over my slice of roast beef, that I had been charged to make a life's work out of what may only have been some student wag's idea of a Dada-esque stunt. Fair or unfair? Lucky or unlucky? Meaningful or meaningless? Accidental or foreordained? Juice or gravy?

Well, whether it was or wasn't mine to do, the job is now completed. The books that, by my lights, over the years, had to unspool syllable by syllable from each of these sentences are finished and done with. As of 1994, there is now a little red check mark beside every single sentence on that piece of paper whose existence has been a secret that I have never before re-vealed to anyone. "For legal reasons, I have had to alter a number of facts in this book." So begins the preface to *Opera-tion Shylock*, published in 1993, and so has ended what began on a stormy night in Chicago thirty-seven years ago. At long last divested of what may well appear to others—as certainly it has too often appeared to me—to have been a bizarre if not impossible self-imposed burden; shed of an imperviousness to the claims of virtually everything but an ironclad responsibility to a spate of gibberish that I found on a scrap of paper in a Chicago cafeteria; released finally from an obsessive, solitary struggle, resembling a lunatic's pointless pursuits in a padded cell, where do I go from here? After such madness, wherein lies sanity for one like me?

Patrimony

T HE PERSON who should be standing here today to receive an award of honor from the New Jersey Historical Society is not the author of *Patrimony* but the subject of *Patrimony*, my father, Herman Roth, whose tenure as a resident New Jerseyan did not end like mine after less than two decades but extended without interruption from his birth in Newark's Central Ward in 1901 to his death in an Elizabeth hospital eighty-eight years later and who, for nearly half his life, sold life insurance here, beginning in the 1930s as an agent in Newark and continuing in the '40s, '50s, and '60s as a manager in Union City, Belleville, and finally just outside of Camden, down in Maple Shade, where he retired from the Metropolitan Life at the age of sixty-three. Working—as a life insurance salesman did back then—as intimately as a family doctor or a social worker with every class and ethnic category in North and South Jersey, talking for nearly forty years to thousands of families here about life-and-death matters in the toughest human terms ("They can't win," my father told me, "unless they die"), he came to possess a rich familiarity with the workaday lives of the citizens of this state that far exceeds my own and one for which a realistic novelist native to this region could only envy him. I would not hesitate to place his encyclopedic knowledge of prewar Newark alongside James Joyce's overbrimming sense of the Dublin that he renders with such lavish precision in his fiction.

It's the insurance man and not the novelist who came to know, from a vast personal experience, with his own brand of awareness and practical intelligence, the social history of Newark, New Jersey's largest and, during the decades my father was employed there, its liveliest and most productive city, to know it not just neighborhood by neighborhood, not even just block by block and house by house and flat by flat but door by door, hallway by hallway, stairwell by stairwell, furnace

New Jersey Historical Society Award acceptance speech, October 5, 1992.

room by furnace room, kitchen by kitchen. It's he and not I who knew palpably the ongoing story of its population, if not in every last particular, then—in the years when he was out all day and most evenings collecting premiums on the policies he sold, as little sometimes as a quarter a week from the poor—birth by birth, death by death, illness by illness, catastrophe by catastrophe. It was he and not I who, by virtue of an occupation that took him daily among the people and into their homes however lowly, became something of an amateur urbanologist in the city of Newark, an anthropologist-without-portfolio from one end of the state to the other, and it is for the prodigious substantiality of this achievement, his far-from-ordinary entanglement with the breadth and depth of the everyday existence of a hard-bitten city's seemingly insignificant lives, that I'd like to accept this award in his name.

Between 1870 and 1910, into a prospering manufacturing city of 100,000—a population largely of English-speaking ancestry—a quarter of a million foreign immigrants came to settle in Newark, Italians, Irish, Germans, Slavs, Greeks, and Jews, some forty thousand Jews from Eastern Europe. Among them were my penniless young grandparents, Sender and Bertha Roth. My father, born in 1901, was their firstborn American child, the middle child of seven, six boys and a girl, and very much the man in the middle for most of his life. To negotiate from the middle, between the impositions of the past, as embodied in the customs and values of his Yiddish-speaking parents, and the claims of the future, as articulated in their very bearing by his American children, became not only his task but the endeavor of his entire generation of immigrant offspring born more or less with the new century in a new world, a generation of which only a handful survive.

In a sense every American generation is a middle generation maneuvering between allegiances that are bestowed at birth and the requirements of a drastically transforming society. The struggle to contend from the middle, to be responsible to the bond of one's earliest loyalties and to defend the old way of life from being wiped away—particularly in the domain of morality—while at the same time releasing one's children into a society demanding, promising, even menacing in a wholly new and uncertain way, is perhaps the quintessential American cultural battle that produces the classic family collisions. I don't think that many generations could have experienced any more pointedly the conflicts inherent to this struggle—and the arsenal of humiliations and reversals ignited by intimidating antagonists—than did the generation born to those newly arrived immigrant parents in the decades before the First World War.

Assimilation is too weak a word, conveying too many negative connotations of deference and submissiveness and muzzling and proposing a story insufficiently gritty to describe this process of negotiation as it was conducted by my father and his like. Their integration with the American actuality was more robust than that and more complicated; it was a two-way convergence, something like the extraction and exchange of energy that is metabolism, a vigorous interchange in which Jews discovered America and America discovered Jews, a valuable cross-fertilization that produced an amalgam of characteristics and traits that constituted nothing less than the fruitful invention of a new American type: the citizen formed by a fusion of allegiances and customs, not entirely flawless in design, not without painful points of friction, but one that yielded, at its best (and clearly so in my father), a constructive mindset radiating vitality and intensity—a dense and lively matrix of feeling and response.

The generation I'm talking about was largely unschooled and undereducated. During these years at the turn of the century when, living in Newark, there were two and a half times as many new immigrants as there were native Newarkers, 70 percent of Newark's schoolchildren—and two-thirds of all Newark schoolchildren were then the offspring of immigrants—didn't make it past the fifth grade. My father was one of the elite who got as far as the eighth grade before leaving school to go to work for the rest of their lives. In contrast to the experience of *their* offspring—my generation—their education took place not predominantly in the classroom but in the workplace. On the job is where their outlook was molded and where they derived their primary knowledge of the American world.

The place of employment—the brewery, the tannery, the docks, the factory floor, the produce market, the building site, the dry-goods stall, the pushcart stand—was not necessarily the ideal ambience to disabuse one of one's prejudices, to enlarge one's sympathies, or to foster new habits, practices, and modes of deportment to replace those that seemed, jarringly and all at once, to be purposeless or restrictive or, over time, just plain odd. But this nonetheless is where the accretion began, unheard-of new American identities engendered not by schools, teachers, and civics textbooks, not, most certainly, by educational programs in ethnic studies, but shaped spontaneously, extemporaneously—though not without pathos and blundering, anger and bruising, defiance, resistance, tears, and affronts—by the tangible churned-up mutability of a thriving city.

The man or woman in the middle takes blows from both sides. First these children of the immigrant generation were made to feel inferior to the natives, ignorant in all sorts of social matters, graceless, crude, and worse, then they were made to feel obtuse and intellectually inferior to the children for whom they'd undergone their hardships. Yet how else to erase this gap but through the university? By virtue of the elixir known as "a good education," provided with and protected by our diplomas and degrees, we would carry through to completion the manifold processes of Americanization. What began when my rabbinically trained grandfather went to work at the tail end of the nineteenth century in a Newark hat factory concluded when I received a master's degree in English literature at the University of Chicago virtually smack in the middle of the twentieth. In three generations, in about sixty years, in really no time at all, we had done it—we were hardly anything like what we were when we got here. From the historical perspective, we had become, owing to some primal American driving force, unrecognizable new beings reconstructed almost overnight. Thus proceeds, at the most commonplace level, the rapidly unfolding drama of our history, which changes what is into what it is not and elucidates the mystery of how we turn up as ourselves.

I hope these few words explain to you why I'd like to receive this award in behalf of my father, who died just three years ago. During a lifetime as the embattled man in the middle here in New Jersey, he enacted the consolidating struggle that defined the lives of that all-but-vanished generation whose family tenure in America is just about coming up to one hundred years. He is far more deserving than I. As a chronicler of Newark, I have only stood on his shoulders.

Yiddish/English

RECENTLY, WHILE visiting Cambridge, Massachusetts, I enjoyed an extraordinary dinner with three friends, two of them writers—the American novelist Saul Bellow and the Israeli novelist Aharon Appelfeld—the third a literature professor at Boston University, Janis Freedman Bellow, Saul's wife. I arranged for us all to get together at a Cambridge restaurant after Saul and Aharon expressed to me an interest in meeting each other.

I first met Saul Bellow in 1957, when I was a young instructor at the University of Chicago, and the author of *The Adventures of Augie March* visited the university. I first met Aharon Appelfeld in 1980, when I was living in London, and the author of *Badenheim 1939* came there to deliver a lecture. I had been separately in the company of each of these remarkable men on numerous occasions since then, and so I did not anticipate that when I brought them together they would be rather different social creatures from the Saul and the Aharon I had previously come to know, or that they would become remarkable to me in a radiantly new way.

That was because I had never before heard them—or seen them—speaking Yiddish. And it was Yiddish that they spoke to each other for most of that evening. Saul learned his Yiddish as a boy growing up among immigrant Jews in Montreal and Chicago in the teens and twenties of this century. Aharon, whose first language was the German that he learned as a child in Bukovina—and whose fiction is written in Hebrew—learned his Yiddish in Israel in the 1940s and '50s, at the university as a student of the language and, on the streets of Tel Aviv and Jerusalem, from Holocaust survivors like himself.

What changed about the two of them when they conversed at length in Yiddish? Everything. The entire way they animated themselves changed. Their relationship to their sobriety changed. Their relationship to their excitement changed. Their relationship to their urbanity changed. Their relationship to their very faces

---

YIVO Institute for Jewish Research Lifetime Achievement Award acceptance speech, December 4, 1997.

changed. Each seemed a magical new commingling of himself, in possession of a previously inactive dimension of himself.

It wasn't that Aharon and Saul appeared to be working themselves more deeply, through Yiddish, into their conversation. It wasn't as if in Yiddish they found some deeper meaning to existence. It was, rather, as if they had found there *another* meaning, a different picture of life that, in turn, put them into an altogether different state of mind and of psychic awareness. I had, for instance, never observed Aharon being so theatrical or seen so nakedly his instinct for play, nor had I ever before seen Saul so boyishly heedless of his social aplomb. Forget that they were Saul Bellow and Aharon Appelfeld. It seemed at that moment as though there was nothing these two literary geniuses had more talent for than speaking Yiddish. Something about their vibrant interplay seemed to provide access to the most subjective substrata of their being, as though with Yiddish they could bring to the surface the words to give vent to everything, big and small, that had previously been unutterable. They had shed in a flash those impediments that can cramp conversation on a first meeting and floated into the rarest kind of affinity. It was as if in the whole wide world each had found a long-lost brother and consequently everything they said assumed a fresh significance, a meaning such as it could not possibly have for two men who shared a less unique link.

I believe it was as beguiling to Janis as it was to me just to sit quietly by and watch the great master of American English and the great master of modern Hebrew speaking, with undisguised delight, so effortlessly and yet with such eagerness, this language of a radically other place and time, to observe them under the enchantment of that annihilated verbal elsewhere, so happily and linguistically interlinked, like two frolicking dogs shamelessly scenting each other. The words and their meanings seemed so rooted in them, so humanly a part of them, at the same time, poignantly enough, that they were lodged in something and somewhere the loss of which is too enormous to contemplate, something that once had flourished and has all but disappeared—every word spoken, every inflection, was permeated by that colossal vanished world. No wonder they seemed so gleefully effervescent and brought almost to the point of mania, these two admirable artists of here and now: they were rewinding the clock of history right before our eyes. It almost seemed, when they were at their highest pitch, that they might never be able to revert to their recognizable other selves again. What a sensational flight they were on! We were astounded, enthralled participants and onlookers alike. We were all in the hands of Yiddish.

Aharon and Saul had only each other to speak to in Yiddish at dinner that night because neither Janis nor I is Yiddish-speaking, which is not to say that we two weren't under the stimulating spell of the situation and the mellifluous vibrations of the rapport we were witnessing. Aharon Appelfeld was born in 1932 in Bukovina, Romania, while I was born the following year in Newark, New Jersey. Saul's parents were Jews born in Russia in the nineteenth century while mine were Jews born in New Jersey in the twentieth. Herman Roth and Bess Finkel were Americans from day one and so my native tongue is English. And it is under *its* enchantment that I have lived now for sixty-four years. For someone with my biography, English has, of course, long since ceased to be yet another unforeseen accident that has befallen the Jews. It is English, and English alone, that holds my world together. I am mute except for English. Robbed of it I would be plunged into complete mental darkness.

I have worked to escape from any number of life's traps, but never from the captivity of English. English not only points to and represents reality for me, it is in itself a real thing: the most real of real things. Nothing is more tangible. Life *is* English. I am a man of English made. Writing in English is the greatest ordeal my life has presented me. There are the times when I've had what suffices for consummation, enjoyed the slugfest for what it is, and emerged in one piece; but, in spite of my determination, writing in English has also been an affliction and the cause of the most serious dismay. Conversely, without it my life might have come to nothing—for all I know, wrestling with another fate I might well have fallen prey to far worse travails and have known futility unimaginable to me now. My aesthetic responsibility—the Mosaic imperative of the American novelist— is to the English language, the native tongue with which I for one seek to press my fantasies of actuality, those unbridled hallucinations disguised as realistic novels, onto the world.

That YIVO should honor me for a lifetime's achievement in English—that you who have assiduously preserved the Eastern European Jewish record in Yiddish, Polish, Russian, German, and Hebrew, should wish to recognize any Jew for his achievement in English . . . well, that, if I may say so, is *your* achievement, and, for that, I would like to recognize *you*.

You have been most generous to me. Thank you.

"I Have Fallen in Love with American Names"

THE WRITERS who shaped my sense of my country were mostly born in America some thirty to sixty years before me, around the time that millions of the impoverished were leaving the Old World for the New and the tenement slums of our cities were filling up with, among others, Yiddish-speaking immigrants from Russia and Eastern Europe. These writers knew little about the families of a youngster like myself, a rather typical American grandchild of four of these poor nineteenth-century Jewish immigrants, whose own children, my parents, grew up in a country which they felt entirely a part of and toward which they harbored a deep devotion—a replica of the Declaration of Independence hung framed in our hallway—and this despite there being others who thought of them as alien outsiders. Born in New Jersey at the start of the twentieth century, my mother and father were happily at home in America, even though they had no delusions and knew themselves to be socially stigmatized and regarded as repellent by any number of their anointed betters, and even though they came to maturity in an America that, until the decades following World War II, systematically excluded Jews from much of the country's institutional and corporate life.

The writers who shaped and expanded my sense of America were mainly small-town midwesterners and southerners. None were Jews. What shaped them was not the mass immigration of 1880–1910 that had severed my family from the old country constraints of a ghetto existence and the surveillance of religious orthodoxy and the threat of anti-Semitic violence but the overtaking of the farm and the farmer's indigenous village values by the pervasive business civilization and its profit-oriented pursuits. These were writers shaped by the industrialization of agrarian America that caught fire in the 1870s and that, by providing jobs for that horde of cheap labor who were the unskilled immigrants, expedited the immigrant absorption

———
Acceptance speech, on being awarded the National Book Foundation's Medal for Distinguished Contribution to American Letters, November 20, 2002.

into society and the Americanization, largely by way of the public school system, of the immigrant offspring. They were shaped by the transforming power of the industrialized cities— by the hardships of the urban working poor that were inspiring the union movement as much as by the acquisitive energy of the omnivorous capitalists and their trusts and monopolies and their union busting. They were made, in short, by the force that, since the country's inception, has been at the heart of the national experience and that drives the national legend still: relentless, destabilizing change and the bewildering conditions that come in its wake—change on the American scale and at the American speed: radical impermanence as an enduring tradition.

What attracted me to these writers when I was a raw reader of sixteen, seventeen, and eighteen—I am thinking, among others, of Theodore Dreiser, born in Indiana in 1871, Sherwood Anderson, born in Ohio in 1876, Ring Lardner, born in Michigan in 1885, Sinclair Lewis, born in Minnesota in 1885, Thomas Wolfe, born in North Carolina in 1900, Erskine Caldwell, born in Georgia in 1903—what drew me to them was my great ignorance of the thousands of miles of America that extended north, south, and west of Newark, New Jersey, where I was raised. Yes, I had been born to these parents, in this time, with their struggles, but I would volunteer to become the child of these writers as well and through my immersion in their fiction try to apprehend their American places as a second reality that was, to an American kid in a Jewish neighborhood in industrial Newark, a vivifying expansion of his own. Through my reading, the mythohistorical conception I had of my country in grade school—from 1938 to 1946—began to be divested of its grandiosity by its unraveling into the individual threads of American reality the wartime tapestry that paid moving homage to the country's idealized self-image.

Fascination with the country's uniqueness was especially strong in the years after World War II, when, as a high school student, I began to turn to the open stacks of the Newark Public Library to enlarge the sense of where I lived. Despite the tension, even the ferocity, of antagonisms of class, race, region, and religion that underlay the national life, despite the conflict between labor and capital that accompanied industrial development—the battle over wages and hours that was ongoing and at times violent, even during the war—America from 1941 to 1945 had been unified in purpose as never before. Later, a collective sense of America as the center of the most spectacular of the postwar world's unfolding dramas had been born not just of chauvinistic triumphalism but out of a realistic appraisal of the undertaking behind the victory of 1945, a feat of human sacrifice, physical effort, industrial planning, managerial genius, labor and military mobilization—a marshaling of communal morale that would have seemed unattainable during the Great Depression of the previous decade.

That this was so highly charged a historical moment in America was not without its impact on what I was reading and why, and it accounted for a good deal of the authority these formative writers had over me. Reading them served to confirm what the gigantic enterprise of a brutal war against two formidable enemies had dramatized daily for almost four years to virtually every Jewish family ours knew and every Jewish friend I had: one's American connection overrode everything, one's American claim was beyond question. Everything had repositioned itself. There had been a great disturbance to the old rules. One was ready now as never before to stand up to intimidation and the remains of intolerance, and instead of just bearing what one formerly put up with, one was equipped to set foot wherever one chose. The American adventure was one's engulfing fate.

The country's biggest, best-known city lay only twelve miles east of my street in Newark. You had only to cross two rivers and an expansive salt marsh by bridge, then a third broad river, the Hudson, via a tunnel, to leave New Jersey and reach by train the then most populous city on earth. But because of its magnitude—and perhaps because of its proximity—New York City was not the focus of my youthful brand of postwar nativist romanticism.

In the 1927 poem whose famous final six words are "Bury My Heart at Wounded Knee," Stephen Vincent Benét had spoken as much for a Roosevelt-reared Jewish boy like me as for a wellborn Yale graduate like himself with the poem's guilelessly Whitmanesque opening line: "I have fallen in love with American names." It was precisely in the sounding of the names of its distant places, in the country's spaciousness, in the dialects and the landscapes that were at once so American yet so unlike my own that a youngster with my susceptibilities found the most potent lyrical appeal. That was the heart of the fascination: one, everyone, was a wisecracking, slang-speaking, in-the-know street kid of an unknowable colossus. Only locally could I be a savvy cosmopolite; out in the vastness of the country, adrift and at large there, every American was a hick, with the undisguisable emotions of a hick, defenseless as even a sophisticated littérateur like Stephen Vincent Benét against the pleasurable sort of sentiment aroused by the mere mention of Spartanburg, Santa Cruz, the Nantucket Light, as well as unassuming Skunktown Plain, Lost Mule Flat, and titillatingly named Little French Lick. There was the shaping paradox: our innate provincialism *made* us Americans, unhyphenated at that, in no need of an adjective, suspicious of any adjective that would narrow the implications of the imposingly all-inclusive noun that was—if only because of the galvanizing magnum opus called World War II—our birthright.

A Newark Jew? Call me that and I wouldn't object. A product of the lower-middle-class Jewish section of industrial Newark with its mix of self-characterizing energies and social uncertainties, with its determined, optimistic assessment of its children's chances, with its wary take on its non-Jewish neighbors, the progeny of this contiguous prewar Jewish community rather than of Newark's prewar Irish, Slavic, Italian, or black sections . . . sure, "Newark Jew" described well enough someone who had grown up as I had at the city's southwest corner, the Weequahic neighborhood, in the 1930s and '40s. Being a Newark Jew in a largely working-class city where political leverage accrued through ethnic pressure, where both historical fact and folkloric superstition sustained a steady undercurrent of xenophobic antipathy in each ethnic precinct, where the apportionment of jobs and vocations often divided along religious and racial lines—all this contributed enormously to a child's self-definition, his sense of specialness, and his way of thinking about his discrete community in the local scheme of things. What's more, attuning one's senses to the customs peculiar to each city neighborhood had to have alerted one early on to the perpetual clash of interests that propels a society and that sooner or later will provoke in the incipient novelist the mimetic urge. Newark was my sensory key to all the rest.

A Newark Jew—why not? But an *American Jew*? A *Jewish American*? For my generation of native born—whose omnipresent childhood spectacle was the U.S.A.'s shifting fortunes in a prolonged global war against totalitarian evil and who came of age and matured, as high school and college students, during the remarkable makeover of the postwar decade and the alarming onset of the Cold War—for us no such self-limiting label could ever seem commensurate with our experience growing up altogether consciously *as* Americans, with all that means, for good and ill. After all, one is not always in raptures over this country and its prowess at nurturing, in its own distinctive manner, unsurpassable callousness, matchless greed, small-minded sectarianism, and a gruesome infatuation with firearms. The list could go on of the country at its most malign, but my point is this: I have never conceived of myself for the length of a single sentence as an American Jewish or Jewish American writer, anymore than I imagine Dreiser or Hemingway or Cheever thought of themselves while at work as American Christian or Christian American or just plain Christian writers. As a novelist I think of myself, and have from the beginning, as a free American and—though hardly unaware of the general prejudice that persisted here against my kind till not that long ago—as irrefutably American, fastened throughout my life to the American moment, under the spell of the country's past, partaking of its drama and destiny, and writing in the rich native tongue by which I am possessed.

My Uchronia

IN DECEMBER of 2000, I was reading the bound proofs of Arthur Schlesinger's autobiography and found myself especially interested in his description of the events of the late 1930s and 1940s as they impinged on his life as a young man traveling in Europe and then back home in Cambridge, Massachusetts. They had impinged on my life, too, though I was only a small child at the time. The great world came into our house every day through the news reports on the radio that my father listened to regularly and the newspapers that he brought home with him at the end of the day and through his conversations with friends and family and their discernible anxiety over what was going on in Europe and here in America. Even before I started school, I already knew something about Nazi anti-Semitism and about the American anti-Semitism that was being stoked by eminent figures like Henry Ford and Charles Lindbergh, who, in those years, along with movie stars like Chaplin and Valentino, were among the most famous international celebrities of the century. The combustion-engine genius Ford and the aeronautical ace Lindbergh—and our nation's anti-Semitic propaganda minister, the radio priest Father Charles Coughlin—were anathema to my father and his circle of friends. By choice, virtually nobody from our Newark Jewish neighborhood owned a Ford automobile despite its being the most popular car in the country.

In his autobiography, I came upon a sentence in which Schlesinger remarks that there were some Republican isolationists who wanted to run Lindbergh for president in 1940. That's all there was, that one sentence with its reference to Lindbergh and a single fact about his political prominence that I'd not known. It made me think, "What if they had?" and with a pen I noted the question in the margin. Between writing down that question and finishing the book there were three years of work, but that's how the idea came to me for *The Plot Against America*.

Written in 2004.

To tell the story of Lindbergh's presidency from the point of view of my own family was a spontaneous and immediate choice, the structural given; to alter the history by making Lindbergh America's thirty-third president while keeping everything else autobiographically close to the factual truth—that was the contour of the job as I saw it. I wanted to make as authentic as I could the atmosphere of the moment, to contrive a reality as believably American as the reality in Schlesinger's autobiography, even if, unlike him, I was giving our twentieth century a twist that it had not taken.

My book also gave me an opportunity to bring back into life my dead parents and restore to them the robust coupledom they shared at the height of their powers in their late thirties— my father, with the vast energy he was able to summon forth to serve what I refer to as his "reforming instincts," and my tireless, spirited mother, "performing each day in methodical opposition to life's unruly flux"—the most unfaltering of loving mothers and fathers living their hard-won lower-middle-class family life with a steady, levelheaded persistence, and, luckily enough, without an Aryan white supremacist in the White House. I've tried to portray them here as faithfully as I could—as though I were, in fact, writing nonfiction. My brother, Sandy, I've portrayed with more latitude, manipulating his disposition and his appetites so as to be able to stretch the dimensions of the story and enlarge his participation in it. After Sandy had read the finished manuscript I'd sent him, he slyly told me, "You've made me more interesting than I was." Maybe, maybe not, but as a brother five years my senior who could draw wonderfully, who could jitterbug, who was very handsome and seemed, at least to a kid brother, to have a way with girls, he did indeed loom over me in the awe-inspiring way I describe, even if he did not conform to his novelistically enhanced character in every last singularity.

The writing, then, put me imaginatively in touch with my late parents decades after their deaths, in touch too with that long bygone era, and in touch as well with the kind of child I once was or remember myself to have been, because I've tried to portray him faithfully too. But for me the greatest bonanza —because it's what lends the story a depth of pathos beyond ours, I think—wasn't the deliberate replication of the family

Roth and their environs circa 1940 but the invention of that most unfortunate family living directly downstairs from them, the Wishnows, as I named them, upon whom falls the full brunt of Lindberghian anti-Semitism, and in particular the begetting of their son, Seldon Wishnow, my other self, my needful, nightmare self, that nice, lonely little kid in your class whom you run away from when you're yourself a kid because he demands to be befriended by you in ways that another child cannot stand. He's the responsibility that you can't get rid of. The more you want to get rid of him, the less you can, and the less you can, the more you want to get rid of him. And that the immature little Roth boy wants to get rid of him is what leads to the book's most harrowing cataclysm.

I had no literary models for disarranging the historical past. I was familiar with books that imagined a historical future, notably *1984*. But much as I admire *1984*, I didn't bother rereading it to study its method. In *1984*—written in 1948 and published a year later—Orwell presupposes a gigantic historical catastrophe that renders his world unrecognizable. There were, to be sure, twentieth-century political models for similar catastrophes in both Hitler's Germany and Stalin's Russia. But since my talent isn't for staging events on an Orwellian scale, I imagined instead something much reduced in size, small and straightforward enough, I hoped, to be credible, something, moreover, that might well have happened in the American presidential election of 1940, at a time when the country was angrily divided between Republican isolationists, who, not without reason, wanted no part in an atrocious second European war a mere twenty-odd years after the conclusion of the first one—and who probably comprised a slight majority of the populace—and Democratic interventionists, who didn't necessarily want to go back to war either but who believed that Hitler had to be stopped before he invaded and conquered England and Europe was entirely his.

As I figured it, Wendell Willkie, the historical 1940 Republican nominee, wasn't the Republican to defeat the highly regarded interventionist Roosevelt, simply because Willkie was an interventionist himself. But what if, instead of Willkie, it was Lindbergh who had run in 1940, with that boyish manly aura and heroic glamour of his, with the enormous worldwide celebrity he had achieved from his 1927 solo flight across the Atlantic, and, especially, with his unshakeable isolationist convictions that committed him to keeping the country from participating in yet another slaughter on foreign soil. I don't think it's at all far-fetched to imagine the election outcome as I do in the book, with Lindbergh's depriving Roosevelt of an unprecedented third presidential term. For Orwell to imagine a world as monstrously transformed as that of *1984* was indeed far-fetched, and knowingly so—his book wasn't conceived as an imminent prophecy but as a futuristic horror story embodying a political warning. Orwell imagined a huge change in the future with horrendous consequences for everyone; I imagined a change in the past on a much reduced scale, one eliciting horror for a relative few. He imagined a dystopia, I imagined a uchronia.

Why did I choose Lindbergh? As I said, first off because it wasn't at all outlandish to me to conceive of his running and winning as he does in my book. However, Lindbergh also chose himself as the leading political figure in a novel where I wanted America's Jews to feel the pressure of a genuine widespread anti-Semitic threat not merely at the personal level but as a pervasive, insidious, native menace capable of emerging anywhere. Lindbergh as a socio-political force in the 1930s and '40s was distinguished not solely by his isolationism but by his racist attitude toward Jews—shallow, bigoted views that are reflected unambiguously and poisonously in his speeches, diaries, and letters. Lindbergh was, at his core, a white supremacist, an ideological racist in the eugenics mode, and, leaving aside his friendship with individual Jews like Harry Guggenheim, he couldn't and didn't perceive Jews, taken as a group, as the genetic, moral, or cultural equals of Nordic white men like himself and did not consider them desirable American citizens other than in small numbers. None of this means that as president he might necessarily have turned on the Jews and persecuted them as openly and savagely as Hitler did in Germany when he came to power, but then he doesn't do that in my book either. What matters most in my book isn't what hardships he inflicts on the Jews (which, by Nazi standards, are decidedly minor, once he's signed a nonaggression pact with Hitler and allowed for a Nazi embassy in Washington) but what Jews suspect he might be capable of doing given his public utterances, most specifically his vilification of the country's Jewish citizens, in a nationwide radio address, as alien warmongers indifferent to America's vital interests. The real Lindbergh did, in fact, give just such an inflammatory speech on September 11, 1941, at a Des Moines America First rally; in my book, to suit the fictional time-scheme, I move the speech back to the previous year, but I don't alter either its content or its impact.

At the center of this story is a child, myself at seven, eight, and nine years of age. The story is narrated by me as an adult looking back some sixty years at the experience of that child's family during the Lindbergh presidency—the book begins with the adult explaining, "Fear presides over these memories" —but nonetheless a child plays a role in this book comparable in importance to the role generally played by adults in my other books.

During the early months of writing, I found it constraining to be looking at this calamity over the shoulder of a child. It took a certain amount of trial and error before I figured out how to let the boy be a boy while at the same time introducing through the adult's voice a mediating intelligence. I had somehow to make the two one, the mediating intelligence that discerns the general and the child's brain that degeneralizes the general, that cannot see outside the child's own life and that reality never impresses in general terms. I had to present a narrative in which things are described both as they happened and as they are considered through hindsight, joining the authenticity of the child's experience to the maturity of the adult's observations. Whereas his father struggles with his America falling apart and the terrible invasion of history, the boy is still living in the micro-heroic America of his stamp collection and, indeed, tries at one point to escape history (beginning with his own) by running away from home to a nearby Catholic orphanage. He is an imaginative child in a turbulent time, his familiar, protective neighborhood and his own cozy household overtaken by perpetual fear.

Four boys figure prominently in the action of this book, one of whom—the boy downstairs, Seldon Wishnow—isn't merely, like the younger Roth child, a nine-year-old confronted by too many problems but the book's most tragic figure, a trusting American Jewish kid who suffers something like the European

Jewish experience. He is not the child who survives the ordeal to tell the tale many years later but the one whose childhood is destroyed by it. It's these children in the book who join the trivial to the tragic.

I chose the famous gossip columnist and radio journalist Walter Winchell as the chief antagonist to Lindbergh because, to begin with, the real Walter Winchell detested Lindbergh for his politics and along with people like the renowned columnist Dorothy Thompson and Roosevelt's interior secretary, Harold Ickes, attacked him as pro-Nazi from the moment that the famed aviator became the preeminent voice of the America First version of nonintervention. Needless to say, Winchell was never a candidate for president, as I have him being in my book, or a prominent member of any political party. I chose Winchell to lead the political opposition because Winchell was the outsize social creature that he was. As Mayor LaGuardia says of him in his eulogy over Winchell's body after Winchell has been gunned down while campaigning as a Democratic presidential candidate against a Lindbergh second term—the next presidential candidate to be assassinated would be Robert Kennedy—"Walter is too loud, Walter talks too fast, Walter says too much, and yet, by comparison, Walter's vulgarity is something great, and Lindbergh's decorum is hideous." In short, I wanted Lindbergh to be opposed not by a crusading saint who is the incarnation of all that is best in America but by the most famous gossip columnist the country has ever known, gross, brazen, and vituperative both by instinct and design, whose enemies considered him to be, among his many other repellent attributes, the loudest of the loudmouth Jews. Winchell was to gossip what Lindbergh was to flight: the record-breaking pioneer.

The book began inadvertently, as a thought experiment. Before reading the Schlesinger autobiography, I had no such novel in mind nor was it a novel of a kind I was looking to write. The subject, let alone the approach, would never have occurred to me on its own. I frequently write about things that don't happen, but never before about history that didn't happen. The American triumph is that despite the institution-alized anti-Semitic bias of the Protestant hierarchy at the time, despite the virulent Jew hatred of the German-American Bund and the Christian Front, despite the Christian supremacy preached by Henry Ford and Father Coughlin and the Rev. Gerald L. K. Smith, despite the distaste for Jews unashamedly expressed by well-known journalists like Westbrook Pegler and Fulton Lewis, despite the blindly self-loving Aryan anti-Semitism of Lindbergh himself, it *didn't* happen here.

At the moment when it should have happened, when there were many of the seeds for its happening, when it well might have happened, it did not happen. And the Jews here have become all they became *because* it did not happen. All that tormented them in Europe never approached European proportions in America. The "what if" in America was somebody else's reality. All I do in my novel is to defatalize the past—if such a word exists—showing how it might have been different and might have happened here. Nor is it my intention to insinuate that this can and one day *will* happen. *The Plot Against America* is an exercise not in historical prediction but in historical speculation, sheer conjecture. History has the final say, and history did it otherwise.

Why it didn't happen here is another book, one about how lucky we Americans are. There was exclusion enough in America, to be sure. Jews were deliberately and systematically excluded from partaking of certain advantages and making certain affiliations and entering important portals at every level of American society, and exclusion is a primary form of humiliation, and humiliation is crippling—it does terrible injury to people, it distorts them, it deforms them, it enrages them, as every American minority can attest. In this book it's the humiliation of exclusion that helps to tear apart and nearly disable the Roth family. What is it to be a man, a woman, a child in such circumstances, and *not* be humiliated? How do you remain strong when you are not welcome? How do you escape the disfigurement? That is the topic under investigation.

Some readers are going to want to take this book as a roman à clef to the present moment in America. That would be a mistake. It is not my objective to be metaphoric or allegorical. I set out to do exactly what I've done: reconstruct the years 1940–42 as they might have been if Lindbergh and not Willkie had been the Republican nominee and Lindbergh instead of Roosevelt had been elected president in the 1940 election. My imaginative effort was directed not toward illuminating the present through the past but illuminating the past through the past. I wanted my family to be up against it precisely as they would have been had history turned out as I've skewed it in this book and they were overpowered by the forces arrayed here against them. Forces arrayed against them then, not now.

Kafka's fiction played a significant role in the strategy of the Czech writers who were opposing the Russians' puppet government in Communist Czechoslovakia in the 1960s, '70s, and '80s, a phenomenon that alarmed those in power and caused them to prohibit the sale of his books and to remove them from library shelves throughout the country. But, clearly, it wasn't to rally those future writers or to intimidate their future rulers that Kafka wrote *The Trial* and *The Castle* in the early years of the twentieth century. Those writers in Prague in the late twentieth century were well aware that they were willfully violating the integrity of Kafka's implacable imagination, though they went ahead nonetheless, with all their canniness and fervor, to exploit his books as a political weapon during a horrible national crisis. Literature is manipulated to serve all sorts of purposes, objectives public and private, but one oughtn't to confuse such arbitrary applications with the arduously attained reality that an author has succeeded in actualizing in a work of art. There is fiction, after all, in no way approaching the quality of Kafka's, that can come to be canonized as art not for its aesthetic value but, however uninspired it may be as literature—witness Soviet socialist realism—because of its usefulness as propaganda and its value, to a political cause or movement, as a placard in disguise.

The Plot Against America has appended to it a postscript of twenty-seven closely printed pages of historical and biographical information—what I call the "true chronology" of those years. No other book of mine carries anything resembling such a caboose, but I felt obliged here to recognize exactly when and how historically verifiable lives and events are bent to my fictional goals. Since I'd prefer that there is no confusion in the mind of the reader about where historical fact ends and historical imagining begins, I chose to present, at the conclusion, this brief survey of the era as it actually transpired. I want thus to make clear that I haven't dragged real historical figures bearing their own names into my story and attributed points of view to them gratuitously and recklessly or forced them to behave implausibly—unexpectedly, surprisingly, shockingly, but not implausibly. Charles Lindbergh, Anne Morrow Lindbergh, Henry Ford, Fiorello LaGuardia, Walter Winchell, F.D.R., Montana Senator Burton Wheeler, Interior Secretary Harold Ickes, Newark gangster Longy Zwillman, Newark rabbi Joachim Prinz—I for one had to believe that each might well have done or said something very like what I have him or her doing or saying in the circumstances I imagine. I present twenty-seven pages of the documentary evidence that underpins a historical unreality of 362 pages in the hope of establishing the book as something other than heedlessly or indiscriminately fabulous.

History claims everybody, whether they know it or like it. In recent books, including this one, I take that central fact of life and magnify it through the lens of critical events I've lived through as a twentieth-century American. I was born in 1933, the year that Hitler came to power and F.D.R. was inaugurated for the first of four times as president and Fiorello LaGuardia was elected mayor of New York and Meyer Ellenstein became the mayor of Newark, my city's first and only Jewish mayor. As a small child I heard on our living room radio the voices of Nazi Germany's Führer and America's Father Coughlin deliver their anti-Semitic rants. Fighting and winning the Second World War was the great national preoccupation, its do-or-die mission, from December 1941 to August 1945, the heart of my grade school years. The Cold War and the domestic anti-Communist crusade overshadowed my high school and college years as did the uncovering of the monstrous truth of the Holocaust and the beginning of the terror of the atomic era. The Korean War ended shortly before I was drafted into the army, and the Vietnam War and the upheaval it fomented at home—along with the assassination of key American political leaders—clamored for attention every day throughout my thirties.

And now Aristophanes, the clown who surely must be God, has given us George W. Bush, a man unfit to run a hardware store let alone a nation like this one, a man who has merely reaffirmed for me the maxim that informed the writing of all these books and that makes our lives as Americans as precarious as anyone else's: *all the assurances are provisional*, even here in a two-hundred-year-old democracy. We are ambushed, even as free Americans in a powerful republic armed to the teeth, by the unpredictability that is history. "Turned wrong way round," I write in my uchronia, "the relentless unforeseen was what we schoolchildren studied as 'History,' harmless history, where everything unexpected in its own time is chronicled on the page as inevitable. The terror of the unforeseen is what the science of history hides, turning a disaster into an epic."

In writing these books grounded in historical premises, I've tried to turn the epic back into the disaster as it was suffered without foreknowledge, without preparation, by people whose American expectations, though not necessarily either innocent or delusional, were for something very different from what they got.

Eric Duncan

SEVENTY-FIVE. How sudden! It may be a commonplace to note that our time here steals away at a terrifying speed, but it nonetheless remains astonishing that it was just 1943—it was 1943, the war was on, I was ten, and at the kitchen table, my mother was teaching me to type on her big Underwood typewriter, its four upward-sloping rows of round white keys differentiated by black letters, numerals, and symbols that, taken together, constituted all the apparatus necessary to write in English.

I was at the time reading the sea stories of Howard Pease, the Joseph Conrad of boys' books, whose titles included *Wind in the Rigging*, *The Black Tanker*, *Secret Cargo*, and *Shanghai Passage*. As soon as I'd mastered the Underwood's keyboard and the digital gymnastics of the touch system of typing, I inserted a clean sheet of white paper into the typewriter and tapped out in caps at its exact center a first title of my own: *Storm Off Hatteras*. Beneath the title I didn't type my name, however. I was well aware that Philip Roth wasn't a writer's name. I typed instead "by Eric Duncan." That was the name I chose as befitting the seafaring author of *Storm Off Hatteras*, a tale of wild weather and a tyrannical captain and mutinous intrigue in the treacherous waters of the Atlantic. There's little that can bestow more confidence and lend more authority than a name with two hard Cs in it.

In January 1946, three years later, I graduated from a public elementary school in Newark, New Jersey—ours was the first postwar class to enter high school. That a brand-new historical moment was upon us was not lost on the brightest students in the class, who had been eight and nine when the war began and were twelve and thirteen when it concluded. As a result of the wartime propaganda to which we'd been regularly exposed for close to five years—and because of our almost all being knowledgeable, as Jewish children, about anti-Semitism—we

---

Remarks at Roth's seventy-fifth birthday celebration at Columbia University, April 11, 2008.

had come to be precociously alert to the inequalities in American society.

The heady idealistic patriotism we were inculcated with during the war spilled over in the war's immediate aftermath into a burgeoning concern with contemporary social injustice. For me this led to my being teamed up by our eighth-grade teacher with a clever female classmate to write—in part on my mother's Underwood—the script for a graduation play we called "Let Freedom Ring."

Our one-act play, a quasi-allegory with a strong admonitory bent, pitted a protagonist named Tolerance (virtuously performed by my coauthor) against an antagonist named Prejudice (sinisterly played by me). It included a supporting cast of class members who, in a series of vignettes in which they were shown attending to their harmlessly healthy-minded pursuits —and intended to advertise how wonderful all these people were—played representatives of ethnic and religious minorities unjustly suffering the injurious inequities of discrimination. Tolerance and Prejudice, invisible to the others on stage, stood just to the side of each uplifting scene arguing over the human status of these various and sundry non-Anglo-Saxon Americans, Tolerance quoting exemplary passages from the Declaration of Independence, the Constitution of the United States, and the newspaper columns of Eleanor Roosevelt, while Prejudice, appraising her from head to foot with as much pity as disgust, and in a tone of voice he wouldn't have dared to use at home, said the nastiest things about these worthy minorities' inferiority that he could get away with in a school play. Afterward, in the corridor outside the auditorium, giving me a fervent hug to express her delight in my achievement, my proud, admiring mother told me, while I was still in my costume of head-to-foot black, that sitting at the edge of her seat in the audience she, who had never struck anyone in all her life, had wanted to slap my face. "How ever did you learn to be so contemptible!" she laughed. "You were thoroughly despicable!" In truth, I didn't know—it just seemed to have come to me out of nowhere. Secretly it thrilled me to think I had a natural talent for it.

"Let Freedom Ring" ended with the full cast of miscellaneous minorities hand in hand at the footlights joining Tolerance with everything they had as she rousingly sang "The

House I Live In," a 1942 pop oratorio in praise of the American melting pot famously recorded back then by Frank Sinatra. Meanwhile, exiting stage right, bound alone for his evil abode, loathsome Prejudice stalked off in bitter defeat, shouting angrily at the top of his voice, in a sentence I'd stolen from somewhere, "This great experiment cannot last!"

That was the beginning, the hometown launching of a literary career leading right up to today. It isn't entirely far-fetched to suggest that the twelve-year-old who coauthored "Let Freedom Ring!" was father to the man who wrote *The Plot Against America*. As for Eric Duncan, that estimable Scotsman, years after crediting him with the authorship of *Storm Off Hatteras*, I sometimes had reason to wish that I had donned that pseudonym before *Portnoy's Complaint* went forth into the world. How different life would have been!

Errata

I. THE HUMAN STAIN

Dear Wikipedia,

I am Philip Roth. I had reason recently to read for the first time the Wikipedia entry discussing my novel *The Human Stain*. The entry contains a serious misstatement that I would like to ask to have removed. This item entered Wikipedia, which is, of course, everyone's handiest encyclopedia, not from the world of fact but from the babble of literary gossip—there is no truth in it at all.

Yet when, through an official interlocutor, I recently petitioned Wikipedia to delete this misstatement, along with several others, my interlocutor was told by the "English Wikipedia Administrator"—in a letter dated August 25th and addressed to my interlocutor—that I, Roth, was not a credible source: "I understand your point that the author is the greatest authority on their own work," writes the Wikipedia Administrator—"but we require secondary sources."

Thus was created the occasion for this open letter. After failing to get a change of importance made through the usual channels, I don't know how else to proceed.

My novel *The Human Stain* was described in the entry as "allegedly inspired by the life of the writer Anatole Broyard." (The precise language has since been altered by Wikipedia's collaborative editing, but this falsity still stands.)

This allegation is in no way substantiated by fact. *The Human Stain* was inspired by an unhappy event in the life of my late friend Melvin Tumin, professor of sociology at Princeton for some thirty years. One day in the fall of 1985, while Mel, who was veracious in all things large and small, was taking the roll in a sociology class, he noted that two of his students had as yet not attended a single class session or attempted to

---

The first section of this open letter to Wikipedia appeared on *The New Yorker* blog, September 6, 2012. Subsequently Wikipedia either expunged or corrected the errors cited in the full text of the letter.

meet with him to explain their failure to appear, though it was by then the middle of the semester.

Having finished taking the roll, Mel queried the class about these two students whom he had never met. "Does anyone know these people? Do they exist or are they spooks?"—the very questions that Coleman Silk, the protagonist of *The Human Stain*, asks of his classics class at Athena College in Massachusetts.

Almost immediately Mel was summoned by university authorities to justify his use of the word "spooks," since the two missing students, as it happened, were both African-American, and "spooks" at one time in America was a pejorative designation for blacks, spoken venom milder than "nigger" but intentionally degrading nonetheless. A witch hunt ensued during the following months from which Professor Tumin emerged blameless but only after he had to provide a number of lengthy depositions proving himself innocent of the charge of hate speech.

A myriad of ironies, comical and grave, abounded, as Mel Tumin had first come to nationwide prominence among sociologists, urban organizers, civil-rights activists, and liberal politicians with the 1959 publication of his groundbreaking sociological study "Desegregation: Resistance and Readiness," and then, in 1967, with "Social Stratification: The Forms and Functions of Inequality," which soon became a standard sociological text. Moreover, before coming to Princeton, he had been director of the Mayor's Commission on Race Relations, in Detroit. Upon his death, in 1995, the headline above his *New York Times* obituary read "MELVIN M. TUMIN, 75, SPECIALIST IN RACE RELATIONS."

But none of these credentials counted for much when the powers of the moment contrived to take down Professor Tumin from his high academic post for no reason at all, much as Professor Silk is disgraced and taken down in *The Human Stain*.

And it is *this* circumstance that inspired me to write *The Human Stain*: not something that may or may not have happened in the Manhattan life of the cosmopolitan literary figure Anatole Broyard but what actually did happen in the life of Professor Melvin Tumin, sixty miles south of Manhattan in the college town of Princeton, New Jersey, where I had met

Mel, his wife, Sylvia, and their two sons when I was Princeton's writer-in-residence in the early nineteen-sixties.

As with the distinguished academic career of the main character of *The Human Stain*, Mel's career, having extended for over forty years as a scholar and a teacher, was besmirched overnight because of his having purportedly debased two black students he'd never laid eyes on by calling them "spooks." To the best of my knowledge, no event even remotely like this one marred Broyard's reputation or his long, successful career at the highest reaches of the world of literary journalism.

The "spooks" altercation is the initiating incident of *The Human Stain*. It is the core of the book. There is no novel without it. There is no Coleman Silk without it. Every last thing we learn about Coleman Silk over the course of three hundred and sixty-one pages begins with his being fingered for having uttered "spooks" aloud in a college classroom. In that one word, spoken by him altogether innocently, lies the source of Silk's anger, his anguish, and his downfall. His heinous, needless persecution stems from that alone, as does his futile and ultimately fatal attempt at renewal and regeneration.

All too ironically, that and *not* his enormous lifelong secret —he is the light-skinned offspring of a respectable black family from East Orange, New Jersey, one of the three children of an optician-cum-railroad-dining-car porter and a registered nurse, who successfully presents himself as white from the moment he enters the U.S. Navy at nineteen—is the cause of his humiliating demise.

As for Anatole Broyard, was he ever even in the Navy? The Army? Prison? Graduate school? The Communist Party? Had he ever otherwise been the innocent victim of institutional harassment? I had no idea. He and I barely knew each other. Over more than three decades, I ran into him, casually and inadvertently, maybe three or four times before a protracted battle with prostate cancer ended his life, in 1990.

Coleman Silk, on the other hand, is killed malevolently, murdered in an intentional car crash while driving with his unlikely mistress, Faunia Farley, a local farmhand and lowly janitor in the very college where he has been a highly esteemed dean. The revelations that flow from the specific circumstances of Silk's murder stun his survivors and lead to the novel's ominous conclusion on a desolate, iced-over lake where a showdown of sorts occurs between the author Nathan Zuckerman and Faunia and Coleman's executioner, Faunia's ex-husband, the deranged Vietnam vet Les Farley. Neither Silk's survivors nor his murderer nor his janitor mistress found their source anywhere other than in my imagination. In Anatole Broyard's biography there were no comparable people or events as far as I knew.

I knew nothing of Anatole Broyard's mistresses or, if he ever had any, who they were or if a woman like Faunia Farley, injured and harassed by men from the age of four, had ever come along to help savagely seal his ghastly fate as she does Coleman Silk's and her own. I knew nothing at all of Broyard's private life—of his family, parents, siblings, relatives, education, friendships, marriage, love affairs—and yet these most intimate aspects of Coleman Silk's private life constitute practically all of the story narrated in *The Human Stain*.

I've never known, spoken to, or, to my knowledge, been in the company of a single member of Broyard's family. I did not even know whether he had any children. The decision to have children with a white woman and possibly be exposed as a black man by the pigmentation of his offspring causes much disquietude in Coleman Silk. Whether Broyard suffered such feelings I had no way of knowing, and I still have none.

I never took a meal with Broyard, never went with him to a bar or accompanied him to a ballgame or a dinner party or a restaurant, never saw him in the sixties when I was living in Manhattan and on occasion socialized at a party. I never watched a movie or played cards with him or showed up at a single literary event with him as either a participant or a spectator. As far as I know, we did not live anywhere in the vicinity of each other during the ten or so years in the late '50s and the '60s when I was living and writing in New York and he was a book reviewer and cultural critic for the *New York Times*. I never ran into him accidentally in the street, though once—as best I can remember, in the 1980s—we did come upon each other in the Madison Avenue men's store Paul Stuart, where I was purchasing shoes for myself. Since Broyard was by then the *Times*'s most intellectually stylish book reviewer, I told him that I would like to have him sit down in the chair beside me and allow me to buy him a pair of shoes as well, hoping thereby, I forthrightly admitted, to deepen his appreciation for my next book. It was a playful, amusing encounter, it lasted ten minutes at most, and it was the only such encounter we ever had.

As best I remember, we never bothered to have a serious conversation but once, after I'd published *Portnoy's Complaint*, when we sat and talked about writing for an hour. Badinage was our specialty, with the result that I never learned from Broyard who were his friends or his enemies, did not know where or when he had been born and raised, knew nothing about his economic status in childhood or as an adult, knew nothing of his politics or his favorite sports teams or if he had any interest in sports at all. I did not even know where he was presently living on that day when I offered to buy him that expensive pair of Paul Stuart shoes. I knew nothing about his mental health or his physical well-being, and I only learned he was dying of cancer months after he'd been diagnosed, when he wrote about his struggle with the disease in the *New York Times Magazine*.

I knew him only as—unlike Coleman Silk, a revolutionary dean at Athena College in western Massachusetts, where he is the center of controversy over standard college matters like the curriculum and requirements for tenure—a generally generous reviewer of my books. Yet after admiring the candor and bravery of the article about his imminent death, I got Broyard's home number from a mutual acquaintance and called him. That was the first and last time I ever spoke to him on the phone. He was charmingly ebullient, astonishingly exuberant, and laughed heartily when I reminded him of us in our prime on the lifeguard's beach in Amagansett in 1958, which was where and when we first met. I was twenty-five then, he thirty-eight. It was a beautiful midsummer day, and I remember that I went up to him on the beach to introduce myself and tell him how much I had enjoyed his brilliant "What the Cystoscope Said." The story had appeared in my last year of college, 1954, in the fourth number of the most sterling literary magazine of the era, the mass-market paperback *Discovery*.

Soon there were four of us—newly published writers of about the same age—bantering together while tossing a football around on the beach. Those twenty minutes or so constituted the most intimate involvement Broyard and I ever had and brought to an eventual total of about ninety the number of minutes we would ever spend in each other's company. Before I left the beach that day, someone told me that Broyard was rumored to be an "octoroon." I didn't pay much attention or, back in 1958, lend much credence to the news. In my experience, octoroon was a word rarely heard beyond the American South. It's not impossible that I had to look it up in the dictionary later to be sure of its precise meaning.

Broyard was actually the offspring of two black parents. I didn't know this then, however, or when I began writing *The Human Stain*. Yes, someone had once idly remarked in my presence that the man was the offspring of a quadroon and a black, but that unprovable bit of unlikely hearsay was all of any substance that I ever knew about Broyard—that and what he wrote in his books and articles about literature and the literary temper of his time. In the two excellent short stories Broyard published in *Discovery*—the other, "Sunday Dinner in Brooklyn," appeared in 1953—there was no reason not to believe that the central character and his Brooklyn family were, like the author, a hundred per cent white.

My protagonist, the academic Coleman Silk, and the real writer Anatole Broyard first passed themselves off as white men in the years before the civil-rights movement began to change the nature of being black in America. Those who chose back then to pass (this word, by the way, doesn't appear in *The Human Stain*) imagined that they would not have to share in the deprivations, humiliations, injuries, and injustices more than likely to come their way should they leave their identities as they'd found them. During the first half of the twentieth century, there wasn't just Anatole Broyard alone—there were thousands, maybe tens of thousands, of light-skinned men and women who decided to escape the rigors of institutionalized segregation and the ugliness of Jim Crow and race hatred by burying for good their original black lives.

I had no idea what it was like for Anatole Broyard to flee from his blackness because I knew nothing about Anatole Broyard's undisclosed blackness, or, for that matter, his proclaimed whiteness. But I knew everything about Coleman Silk because I had invented him as a full-blown character from scratch, just as in the five-year period before the 2000 publication of *The Human Stain* I had invented the puppeteer Mickey Sabbath of *Sabbath's Theater* (1995), the glove manufacturer Swede Levov of *American Pastoral* (1997), and the politically compromised brothers Ringold in *I Married a Communist* (1998), one a high-school English teacher and the other a star of radio during the McCarthy era.

Finally, to be inspired to write an entire book about a man's life, you must of necessity have considerable interest in the man's life, and frankly, though I particularly admired the story "What the Cystoscope Said" when it appeared in 1954 and told the author as much, over the years I otherwise had no interest in the adventures of Anatole Broyard. Neither Broyard nor anyone associated with Broyard had anything to do with my imagining anything in *The Human Stain*.

Novel writing is a game of let's pretend. Like most every other novelist I know, once I had what Henry James called "the germ"—in this case, Mel Tumin's story of p.c. muddle-headedness wildly out of hand at Princeton—I proceeded to pretend and to invent the doomed Faunia Farley, the damaged Les Farley, and the disgraced Coleman Silk: his American family lineage; his grave and domineering father; his suffering mother; his angry, disapproving brother; his sister, the schoolteacher, who is his strongest judge at the conclusion of the book; the girlfriends of his youth, both white and black; his brief professional career as a rising young boxer; the New England college where he rises to be dean; his professional colleagues both hostile and sympathetic; his chosen field of study; his overwrought, bedeviled wife; his children both hostile and sympathetic; and the thousands more biographical granules whose profusion and mass taken together constitute the major fictional character at the center of the elaborate prose artifact that is a realistic novel.

2. NATHAN ZUCKERMAN

Under the section "Influences and themes," Wikipedia writes, "Jewish sons such as most infamously Alexander Portnoy and later Nathan Zuckerman rebel by denouncing Judaism."

No. My fictional character Nathan Zuckerman does not have a denunciatory quarrel with being Jewish, and rebellion against Judaism is hardly what drives him in any of the nine Zuckerman books, beginning with *The Ghost Writer* (1979) and ending with *The Human Stain* (2000) and *Exit Ghost* (2007). Far from his denouncing Jews, in *The Ghost Writer*, as a neophyte writer, Zuckerman is denounced *by* Jews for a short story he has published—his first—which some of his Jewish readers take to be fuel for anti-Semitism. But the point of *The Ghost Writer* is that their accusation—that the author Zuckerman himself is dangerously anti-Semitic—is false, even though the making of it happens to unhinge Zuckerman's father, especially as it emanates most tellingly from their hometown's eminent Jewish jurist, Newark's Judge Leopold Wapter. Seeking solace because of the rift his writing has caused in his family, Zuckerman accepts an invitation from the celebrated Jewish writer E. I. Lonoff to meet him and visit overnight with him and his wife in their Berkshire home. Zuckerman wouldn't, of course, last five minutes as Lonoff's guest were he a programmatic or even occasional denouncer of Jews—to label young Zuckerman as such is, in fact, to appropriate the judge's righteous philistinism rather than the wisdom and judgment of Lonoff. There's not a passage in *The Ghost Writer*, particularly where Zuckerman, in a sustained reverie, reimagines Anne Frank, that does not render presumptuous, indeed worse, his excoriation by the judge.

In *The Counterlife* (1986), when Zuckerman, now living in London, is rudely confronted about his Jewish background by his Christian sister-in-law-to-be, who has a decided distaste for Jews, he is appalled by the nastiness of her upper-class English strain of anti-Semitism and tells her as much. Still earlier in *The Counterlife*, a woman in the swank hotel restaurant where he is having dinner with his non-Jewish wife, Maria, crudely lets it be known that she finds his Jewish presence repellent. Rising to stand before her table, his face "boiling hot," Zuckerman says, "You are most objectionable, madam, grotesquely objectionable, and if you continue shouting about the stink [the stink of his Jewishness wafting over to her from where he is seated with Maria on a nearby banquette], I am going to request that the management have you expelled."

Once again the denunciation by Zuckerman is not of the Jews but of those who would publicly defame and humiliate Jews.

The final pages of *The Counterlife* consist of Zuckerman's plea to his pregnant wife to allow him to observe Jewish tradition and have their child circumcised should it be a boy. "Circumcision," he writes to her, "confirms that there is an us, and an us that isn't solely him and me." In the wake of the anti-Semitic outburst his mere presence aroused in Maria's sister and in the bigoted woman at the restaurant, he concludes, "England's made a Jew of me in only eight weeks, which, on reflection, might be the least painful method. A Jew without Jews, without Judaism, without Zionism, without Jewishness, without a temple or an army or even a pistol, a Jew clearly without a home, just the object itself, like a glass or an apple."

This is not a denunciation of Jews. It is a description of a Jew of the kind that Zuckerman is. There is no animus in it.

3. OPERATION SHYLOCK

"According to his pseudo-confessional novel *Operation Shylock* (1993)," Wikipedia writes, "Roth suffered a nervous breakdown in the late 1980s."

To begin with, there is no way to conclude anything with certainty about the flesh-and-blood author from something that is said about a character in a novel, obviously not from a "pseudo" (meaning concocted or unreal) confessional one, and not from this particular concoction where I and, simultaneously and vigorously, someone else appear under my own name as yoked characters, or what in literature courses are called "doubles."

In *Operation Shylock*, I propose sides to "my" character that are not mine, motives that are not mine, and describe bizarre encounters that never occurred where I sometimes act in ways that I have not yet had the opportunity to perform outside the sanctuary of my imagination. Even in a fiction that may have decidedly autobiographical roots, one is always at a distance from one's sources anyway, and that distance is always in flux. One's position vis-à-vis one's sources is not static but sliding. The final words of *Operation Shylock* couldn't be more bluntly pertinent: "This confession is false."

In the book, I travel to Israel, a place where life is a vicious debate and struggle is everywhere. I survey the emergency that has been the Jewish twentieth century and behold its contemporary apogee, all these Jews and their horrible scars alongside all these Palestinians and their horrible scars, everyone held accountable by his genealogy and fearfully wondering, "How much more history can we take?" Every Jewish claim makes its clamorous appearance, every Jewish conflict, urge, anomaly, predisposition, ambition, terror, wound, all the Jewish polarities. And shadowing everything is the Holocaust. I tried in this book to delineate the drama of being a Jew at the current moment by imagining what feeds a Jewish conscience and by examining Jewish divisiveness and the reaches of Jewish memory. Here Comes Everybody Jewish. Leon Klinghoffer. Jonathan Pollard. Menachem Begin. Meir Kahane. Eliot's Bleistein. Shakespeare's Shylock. Irving Berlin. And dozens more. It has been said that inside every Jew there is a mob of Jews, or, as Elias Canetti (also a Jew) put it, "the Jews are most different from other people, but, in reality, they are different from each other." This diverse mob of Jews is the mob that verbosely commandeers my book all the while that Wikipedia finds nothing to note about my four hundred eventful pages of often dreamlike happenings other than that "according to his pseudo-confessional novel *Operation Shylock* (1993), Roth suffered a nervous breakdown in the late 1980s."

Well, though there are certainly two characters in *Operation Shylock* called by my name, neither one suffers a nervous breakdown. *Operation Shylock*'s "real" Philip Roth undergoes instead an adverse drug reaction to the sleeping pill Halcion, as I did in 1987, when I was 54.

Recently in the *Atlantic*, in an article titled "Roth v. Roth v. Roth," Joseph O'Neill wrote that I suffered "a crack-up" in my fifties. I corrected O'Neill in a letter to the *Atlantic* of June 2012. What I wrote there bears repeating since the Wikipedia entry about me could well have been O'Neill's source.

"After knee surgery in March 1987," I wrote to the *Atlantic*, "I was prescribed the sleeping pill Halcion, a sedative hypnotic in the benzodiazepine class of medications that can induce a debilitating cluster of adverse effects, sometimes called 'Halcion madness.' At the time it was prescribed post-operatively for me by the orthopedic surgeon, Halcion had already been taken off the market in Holland, Germany, and elsewhere because of extreme psychological side effects leading even to suicide. . . . Among the symptoms it can cause are amnesia, paranoia, and hallucinations.

"My own adverse reaction to Halcion, which corresponded to a clinically well-defined adverse reaction, one that has been exhaustively documented in the medical literature, started when I began taking the drug and resolved promptly when, with the helpful intervention of my family doctor, I stopped."

I stopped in life, *Operation Shylock*'s P. R. stops on page 26. However, in the aftermath of the hellish experience, while seemingly back on track again "ordering daily life as completely as [he] ever had before," my character "privately remained half-convinced" that it was some interior disablement of his and not a side-effect of "Upjohn's magic little sleeping pill [that] had made the [collapse] happen." In the light of all the unlikely and taxing events that, in Israel, swamp him on just about every page of the book's remaining 371 pages, he persists for a time in being susceptible to the insidious idea that it is he and not Halcion that is somehow undermining him and generating his highly implausible Holy Land adventures.

None of this has anything to do with anyone "in the late 1980s" having a nervous breakdown either in the written or the unwritten world.

4. AMERICAN PASTORAL

The Wikipedia entry for my 1997 novel *American Pastoral*, on the basis of the most superficial evidence of affinity, mistakenly identifies yet another real-life model for another of my protagonists. "The inspiration for the Levov character was a real person: Seymour 'Swede' Masin, a phenomenal, legendary all-around Jewish athlete who, like the Levov character, attended Newark's Weequahic High School. Like the book's protagonist, Swede Masin was revered and idolized by many local middle-class Jews." The entry concludes by noting that "Both 'Swedes' were tall and had distinctively blond hair and blue eyes . . . Both attended a teachers' college in nearby East Orange, both married out of their faith, both served in the military and, upon their return, both moved to the suburbs of Newark."

Seymour Masin, in the 1930s, and my "Levov character," in the early 1940s, did both attend Newark's Weequahic High School—as did I in the late 1940s. Masin graduated only a few years after the school's 1933 founding, five years before Pearl Harbor and fourteen years before my own graduation in 1950. Consequently, I had never seen him in action as an athlete, I had never seen him in the flesh anywhere else, nor had I even seen a picture of him. I knew nothing about him when I was writing *American Pastoral* other than that he had been an outstanding all-around athlete well before my time and that his nickname was "Swede." Those were the two facts that I appropriated from Seymour Masin's life and the only tenable points of connection. I knew nothing of his biography otherwise—he was indeed "legendary," a remote unparticularized archetype and no more. I did not even know his given name, for if I had, so as to remove any possibility of libel, I would certainly not have called my character Seymour. After considering some half dozen or so names I settled on Seymour because it was one of the more common names for Jewish boys of his generation and mine and for euphonious reasons. Two-syllable Seymour alliterated with monosyllabic Swede, fit phonetically neatly, and (radically unlike the ironic cognomen Swede) remained harmonious ethnically with Levov.

Of course both Swedes "were tall and had distinctively blond hair and blue eyes." Why else would each of these anomalous-looking Jewish kids have been nicknamed Swede? Both attended a teacher's college in nearby East Orange? Not true. My fictitious Swede and his fictitious wife Dawn attended now-defunct Upsala, an excellent coeducational liberal arts college in East Orange, while the real Swede Masin attended East Orange's Panzer College of Physical Science and Hygiene (later merged with Montclair State Teachers College), a school then mainly serving to train phys ed instructors, with a student population of about two hundred. (Incidentally, like Swede Masin—though proving nothing—Bucky Cantor, the gym teacher hero of *Nemesis*, published twenty-three years after

American Pastoral, is also a graduate of Panzer.) Both Swedes married out of their faith? Beginning with that generation of American Jews and increasingly in subsequent generations, more than a few young men dared to do exactly that, often, as in *American Pastoral*, contrary to their parents' wishes. That both Swedes "served in the military" simply follows from when they were born—only a handful of their generation *didn't* serve. Swede Masin may well have moved to a Newark suburb. Wikipedia contends as much and I just don't know. But Swede Levov did not. Where he set up house with his young wife after coming out of the service was, in fact, a bitter point of contention with his strongly opinionated father, who instead wanted his son and business partner to be living nearby in the wealthy, fast-growing suburban development of New-stead in South Orange, sometimes mockingly invoked among self-satirizing Jews in those days as "Jewstead." My Swede chose to make his home well beyond the Newark suburbs near the village I named Old Rimrock out past Morristown in Morris County—and, altogether deliberately, out past the Jews—with the result that the argument between father and son about where the Swede should live, as well as in what faith he should marry and raise his children, is not quietly passed over in my book.

There was, in short, a rudimentary logic to my invention of Swede Levov that not surprisingly mirrored a few far from exceptional or singular details in Swede Masin's biography that was otherwise as remote from the events and circumstances of the horrific downfall of the fictional Swede Levov narrated in *American Pastoral*—and his deeds and torments as a father, husband, and son—as it could be. So too with Swede Levov's significant life as a hands-on employer: the all-embracing world of the prosperous family manufacturing business—Newark Maid Gloves, on Newark's Central Avenue, the three-story factory where much of the novel's most dramatic action occurs, including battlefield scenes from the Newark riots of 1967—was completely unknown to Swede Masin, who, after a brief stint as a professional basketball player, spent his entire working life as a salesman.

A few years after the publication of *American Pastoral* I attended an evening honoring my work at the New Jersey

Performing Arts Center in Newark. Unknown to me, an elderly though fit-looking Swede Masin was in the audience that night, and when the program was over he introduced himself and his daughter to me at a reception in the lobby. Masin's daughter (two Masin sons were not present), then probably in her thirties or forties, couldn't wait to make clear to me, albeit in a charmingly amusing way, that she had nothing in common with the antiwar terrorist Merry, Swede Levov's daughter and only child, whose destruction of herself and her family—by clandestinely planting a bomb at the tiny Old Rimrock postal station to protest the Vietnam War—is the action on which the entire novel pivots and its repercussions dominate (and poison) the lives of the book's major characters throughout. Merry Levov's bomb kills a beloved doctor who happens to be stopping by to mail a letter on his way to the local community hospital where he is chief of staff. Later, continuing to challenge the legality of the war in her lurid wanderings through the American antiwar underground (twice she is the victim of rapists), Merry Levov kills three more people with her bombs. Indeed, if any family could have monopolized my imagination by serving as an authentic rather than a negligible "inspiration" for the tortured Levovs it was the family of the distinguished civil-rights lawyer and counsel to eminent left-wing clients the late Leonard Boudin, an acquaintance of mine whose own young daughter's career as a notorious antiwar terrorist and member of the violent Weather Underground during and after the Vietnam War had the most terrible consequences for all of them.

Just as Merry's predilection for political violence—and everything else about her rebellious life—had nothing whatsoever to do with the robust, nonviolent Ms. Masin so too, her father good-humoredly and gratefully acknowledged, nothing in the tragic story of Swede Levov, other than his nickname and his athletic prowess at Weequahic, had anything of substance to do with him. Swede Masin understood that I had merely lifted a few facts from a total stranger's biography, fewer even than you'd find on his driver's license, though he did find it uncanny, he told me before we parted that night, that Swede Levov's wife—whose daughter's disappearance and criminality shatter her—is portrayed in an early section of *American*

Pastoral as a 1949 Miss America contestant, since his own wife, from whom he was divorced, had once been a beauty queen in an Essex County beauty contest. I replied that the coincidence wasn't as strange as he thought and repeated to him what the most impeccable of narrative artists, Gustave Flaubert, once said on this very subject: "Everything one invents is true, you may be perfectly sure of that. Poetry is as precise as geometry."

This quotation of Flaubert's comes from a famous letter of his dated August 1853, when he was midway through the triumphant five-year ordeal of writing *Madame Bovary*. "After a certain point in one's calculations," Flaubert continues, "one never is wrong about matters of the soul. My poor Bovary, without a doubt, is suffering and weeping in twenty villages in France at this very moment."

Sincerely,

Philip Roth

"Tyranny Is Better Organized than Freedom"

I WAS twelve years old when I entered Weequahic's Hawthorne Avenue Annex in February 1946. The Annex, a fifteen-minute bus ride for me from the main high school, was where you went as a Weequahic High School freshman in those days. The first teacher I had to face on the first hour of my first day at the Annex was Bob Lowenstein. Dr. Lowenstein. Doc Lowenstein. He was fresh from serving overseas in World War II, unlike most high school teachers he was (unassumingly) in possession of a PhD, and what was apparent even to a twelve-year-old was that this was a formidable ex-G.I. who did not suffer fools gladly.

Bob was my homeroom teacher. This meant that I saw him first thing in the morning, every single day of the school year. I was never to take a course with him—I had Mademoiselle Glucksman for French and Señorita Baleroso for Spanish—but I didn't forget him. Who at Weequahic did? Consequently, when it came his turn to be besieged by the anti-Communist crusade of the 1940s and '50s, I followed his fate as best I could in the stories that I had my parents clip from the Newark newspapers and mail to me.

I don't remember how we came together again in the 1990s, more than forty years after I'd graduated from Weequahic High. I was back in America from having lived largely abroad for some twelve years and either I wrote to him about something or he wrote to me about something and we met for lunch at Zelda and his house in West Orange. In the spirit of Bob Lowenstein, I put the matter before you in the plainest language, as directly as I can: I believe we fell in love with each other.

He sent me his poems in the mail, sometimes as soon as he'd finished writing them, and I sent him my books when they were published. I even sent him the final draft of one book—*American Pastoral*—to read in manuscript. There was lots in the book about early-twentieth-century Newark and, as Bob was born in Newark in 1908, I wanted to pass it before him to make sure I'd got everything right.

Memorial tribute to Dr. Robert Lowenstein, April 20, 2013.

I sent a driver down to West Orange to drive him the two and a half hours to my house in northwest Connecticut and together the two of us had lunch and I asked him to tell me what he'd made of what I'd written. We talked over lunch—we talked all afternoon long. He had, as usual, a lot to say, and I believe I listened no less attentively than I had in that 8:30 homeroom at the Hawthorne Avenue Annex when he read out the announcements for the school day.

In my novel *I Married a Communist*, the narrator, Nathan Zuckerman, says, "I think of my life as one long speech that I've been listening to." Bob's is one of those persuasive voices I can still hear speaking to me. The tang of the real permeated his talk. Like all great teachers, he personified the pedagogical drama of transformation through talk.

I should mention that when he arrived at my Connecticut house from West Orange, he got out of the car with a book in his hand. What he'd been reading on the drive up were the poems, in French, written by the French Catholic poet Charles Péguy during the course of a brief life that ended a hundred years ago. I knew, of course, that Bob was a serious man, but only when I saw that he took Péguy for company on the road did I realize just how serious.

In 1993, when I turned sixty, I gave a reading at South Orange's Seton Hall University and the reading's sponsors threw a birthday party for me afterward. Bob and Zelda were there. In fact, my reading that night was introduced by Bob, who lived a mile from Seton Hall and never missed one of their poetry readings. He was then eighty-five. That he had twenty more years of sparkling life left in him—well, who could have known that, except perhaps Bob himself?

I had written to ask him to introduce me, and seeing him up at the Seton Hall lectern that night recounting with great wit and sharpness and charm our first acquaintance as pupil and teacher made me inordinately happy. He looked to be pretty happy too.

Bob was the model for a major figure in my novel *I Married a Communist*, a book I published in 1998 recalling the anti-Communist period and that savage, malicious mauling that people unjustly persecuted like Bob suffered in those years from the teeth and the claws of the scum then in power.

The character is a retired high school teacher named Murray Ringold, and, like Bob, he teaches at Weequahic High, though not, like Bob, Romance languages but English. I also altered Bob's appearance, his war record, and certain details of his personal life—Bob didn't, for example, have a hotheaded murderer for a brother or a wife who was the victim of a fatal crime in Newark—but otherwise I tried to remain true to the force of his virtues, as I perceived them.

I also included in passing his singular pleasure of hurling a blackboard eraser when what was said by the pupil at whom the eraser was thrown seemed to him radically knuckleheaded and the oafish embodiment of inattentiveness, the crime of crimes.

The subject of *I Married a Communist* is, at bottom, tutelage, guidance, education, in particular the education of an eager, earnest, and impressionable adolescent in how to become—as well as how not to become—a bold and honorable and effective man. This honorable becoming is no easy task, for there are always two large stumbling blocks: the impurity of the world and the impurity of oneself, not to mention one's imperfections of intelligence, emotion, foresight, and judgment.

Those shepherding the growth of the adolescent in question —Nathan Zuckerman of Newark's Weequahic section—are mainly the American patriot Tom Paine, the era's renowned radio writer Norman Corwin, the historical novelist Howard Fast, the English teacher Murray Ringold, and Murray's brother, the angry Communist zealot Ira Ringold, whose murderous rage, whose own destructive core, the man himself is vainly in flight from. There is also his goodhearted father. "The men who schooled me," Nathan calls them. "The men I came from."

This book about a boy and his men opens with a brief portrait of Murray Ringold, the Ringold brother who is not violent and whose rage is tempered and specifically reserved for unwarrantable injustice. Murray Ringold, by the way, undergoes an education of his own, as did Bob, of course, when, caught in the trap set to ruin so many promising careers of that American moment—a casualty like thousands of others of the first shameful decade in his country's postwar history—this splendid teacher was forced for six years out of the Newark school system and his chosen profession, banished as a political deviant and a dangerous man to let loose on the young.

I refer now not to a boy's but to an adult's education: in loss, grief, and that inescapable component of living, betrayal. Bob had iron in him and he resisted the outrage of the injustice with extraordinary courage, optimism, and bravery, but he was a man, and he felt it as a man, and so he suffered too.

I hope that in my novel I have given ample recognition to the qualities of our late, legendary, and noble friend, who understood, as did the poet Charles Péguy, that "tyranny is always better organized than freedom." I don't know how Péguy found this out but Bob learned it the hard way.

I conclude with a few lines from the opening of *I Married a Communist*. I am describing the fictional high school teacher Murray Ringold, better known to those of us in the unwritten world as Doc Lowenstein:

> He was altogether natural in his manner and posture while in his speech verbally copious and intellectually almost menacing. His passion was to explain, to clarify, to make us understand, with the result that every last subject we talked about he broke down into its principal elements no less meticulously than he diagrammed sentences on the blackboard. . . . Mr. Ringold brought with him into the classroom a charge of visceral spontaneity that was a revelation to tamed, respectabilized kids who were yet to comprehend that obeying a teacher's rules of decorum had nothing to do with mental development. There was more importance than perhaps even he imagined in his winning predilection for heaving a blackboard eraser in your direction when the answer you gave didn't hit the mark. . . . You felt, in the sexual sense, the power of a male high school teacher like Murray Ringold—masculine authority uncorrected by piety—and you felt, in the priestly sense, the vocation of a male high school teacher like Murray Ringold, who wasn't lost in the amorphous American aspiration to make it big, who—unlike the school's women teachers at that time—could have chosen to be almost anything else and chose instead, for his life's work, to be ours. All he wanted all day long was to deal with young people he could influence, and his biggest kick in life he got from their response.

Farewell, esteemed mentor.

A Czech Education

From 1972 through 1977, I traveled to Prague every spring for a week or ten days to see a group of writers, journalists, historians, and professors there who were being persecuted by the Soviet-backed totalitarian Czech regime.

I was followed by a plainclothesman most of the time I was there and my hotel room was bugged, as was the room's telephone. However, it was not until 1977, when I was leaving an art museum where I'd gone to see a ludicrous exhibition of Soviet socialist realism painting, that I was detained by the police. The incident was unsettling and the next day, heeding their suggestion, I left the country.

Though I kept in touch by mail—sometimes coded mail—with some of the dissident writers I'd met and befriended in Prague, I was not able to get a visa to return to Czechoslovakia again for twelve years, until 1989. In that year the Communists were driven out and Václav Havel's democratic government came to power, wholly legitimately, not unlike General Washington and his government in 1788, through a unanimous vote of the Federal Assembly and with the overwhelming support of the Czech people.

Many of my hours in Prague were spent with the novelist Ivan Klíma and his wife, Helena, who is a psychotherapist. Ivan and Helena both spoke English and, along with a number of others—among them the novelists Ludvík Vaculík and Milan Kundera, the poet Miroslav Holub, the literature professor Zdenek Strybyrny, the translator Rita Budínová-Mlynarová, whom Havel later appointed his first ambassador to the U.S., and the writer Karol Sidon, after the Velvet Revolution the chief rabbi of Prague and eventually of the Czech Republic—these friends gave me a thoroughgoing education in what unstinting government repression was like in Czechoslovakia.

This education included visits with Ivan to the places where his colleagues, like Ivan stripped of their rights by the

Speech accepting the PEN Literary Service Award, 2013 PEN Literary Gala, April 30, 2013.

authorities, were working at the menial jobs to which the omnipresent regime had maliciously assigned them. Once they
had been thrown out of the Writers' Union, they were forbidden to publish or to teach or to travel or to drive a car or to
earn a proper livelihood each at his or her preferred calling.
For good measure, their children, the children of the thinking
segment of the population, were forbidden to attend academic
high schools rather as their parents who were writers were officially ousted from literature.

Some among the repudiated whom I met and spoke with
were selling cigarettes at a streetcorner kiosk, others were
wielding a wrench at the public water works, others spent their
days on bicycles delivering buns to bakeries, still others were
washing windows or pushing brooms as a janitor's assistant at
some out-of-the-way Prague museum. These people, as I've
indicated, were the cream of the nation's intelligentsia.

So it was, so it is, in the clutches of totalitarianism. Every
day brings a new heartache, a new tremor, more helplessness,
more hopelessness, and yet another unthinkable forfeiture of
freedom and free thought in a censored society already bound
and gagged. The usual rites of degradation prevail: the ongoing unmooring of one's personal identity, the suppression of
one's personal authority, the elimination of one's security—a
craving for solidity and equanimity in the face of ever-present
uncertainty and the seeming unreality of it all. Unforeseeable-
ness is the new norm and perpetual anxiety the injurious
result.

And to enhance the disgrace, anger appears in all its scorch-
ing monotony. Beset by the torture of anger. The maniacal
raving of a manacled being. Frenzies of futile rage ravaging
only oneself. Alongside your spouse and your children, imbib-
ing the tyranny with your morning coffee. Totalitarianism's
remorseless trauma-inducing machine cranking out the worst
of everything and, over time, over the desperate days and
months and years of waiting for the disaster to end, everything
becoming more than one's endurance can withstand.

One diverting anecdote from a grim and unamusing epoch
and then I'll be done.

On the evening of the day following my escapade with the
police, when in haste I wisely left Prague for home, Ivan was

picked up from his house by the police and, not for the first time, questioned by them for hours. Only this time they did not hector him all night about the clandestine seditious activities of Helena and himself and their cohort of troublesome dissidents and disturbers of the unlawful peace. Instead—in a refreshing change for Ivan—they inquired about my annual visits to Prague.

As Ivan later told me in a letter, he had only one answer to give them throughout their dogged nightlong inquisition about why I was hanging around the city every spring.

"Don't you read his books?" Ivan asked the police.

As might be expected, they were stymied by the question, but Ivan quickly enlightened them.

"He comes for the girls," Ivan said.

The Primacy of Ludus

WHEN EMERSON famously wrote, "There can be no excess to love, none to knowledge, none to beauty," he clearly did not have in mind the profuse and none too pure-minded excesses of the likes of *Portnoy's Complaint* or *Sabbath's Theater* or *The Dying Animal*.

The moral aspect of these books of mine, not to mention the moral progress of protagonists emanating the brackish odor of licentious conduct, would surely not have garnered his esteem or furnished him with his chief spiritual pleasures and—were he still to be seen aloofly walking the streets of Boston and Concord—might well have disinclined him to judge this seemingly benign ceremony as anything but an affront to Transcendental belief and to the divine potentialities of Man.

And yet, correct as he would have been to reprove me, at the very least, with condescension, here I am! I have been summoned to appear tonight before this academy and have arrived as I was instructed to, not in my tattered carnival motley but in a decent suit and a proper tie and a tamed state.

I thank you and so too do the protagonists of the novels I mentioned at the outset, a decidedly untranscendental club utterly deficient in an exalted conception of being or an urgent concern with the education of humanity or the essence of religion or the genius of Goethe. It is not a club concerned with man as he should be and the ideal right.

Rather, it is a circle of men tending toward mischievous provocation, satiric improvisation, spirited impersonation, farcical abandon, ironic irreverence, immoderate monologue, clamoring corporeality, mock raving, plain mockery, ceaseless craving, and besmirchment by the unseemly instincts. The primacy of *ludus*, of play unabashed, is ubiquitous, and so too is the subversive voice, fired as it is by a scrutinizing mistrust of the values venerated by others and all their splendid ideas.

Speech accepting the Emerson–Thoreau Medal, American Academy of Arts and Sciences, October 11, 2013.

Here is where the excess lies: in the unidyllic messiness and impurity of living all the intrusive improbabilities that throw certainty on its head.

It is a circle—better perhaps, a circus, an antic troupe of profane performers—whose membership includes the erotically seared figure of fun Alexander Portnoy, the pagan puppeteer of his own indecent theater Mickey Sabbath, and the dangerous faculty mentor to the sexually effervescent of the American sixties and academic champion of the gratification of soul and body both Professor David Kepesh. Each is menaced by the sirenlike lure of the enticing comely—reeling partakers of that species of unflagging carnality that Stephen Dedalus in *Ulysses* calls "dongiovannism." Invariably there is a humorous absurdity to their misery whenever they put themselves at the mercy of this wanton enterprise whose barbarity they can never properly assess. No wonder that in dealing with the dynamo of the libidinous, there is more than a tinge of the demented about them.

When Thoreau speaks in "Walking" of "the awful ferity"—the savagery—"with which . . . lovers meet," I am afraid he describes the font and the pinnacle of David Kepesh's happiness. The clownish members of this troupe have indisputably established—to borrow a locution characteristic of Emerson—"an original relation to the universe."

"Build . . . your own world," Emerson urged each individual, and no one can say that isn't what these refractory fellows perpetrate, even while they secure, unavoidably, the angry antipathy of the ideologically anointed and of those wholeheartedly invested in the elevated mores of their locale. The inescapable clash of values and the harangue that comes of it is both their contrarian fate and their innermost delight. It is the catalyst, in these books, for a comic drama from which, even in the midst of all the mirth emanating from the carnivorous prowling around, moral struggle is rarely absent. None of the three exists in a state of righteous repose and there is no dearth of emotional woe. Before the drama is over, everyone adhering to the dongiovannist worldview—whose devotion is to the opposite of what is ordained and whose ability to inspire animosity is boundless—will most assuredly meet his match.

I am deeply honored to be the recipient of so prestigious an award and especially pleased to have been elected to the company of such notable predecessors, among them twentieth-century literary masters whom I most admire.

My ludic libertines and I thank you again.

Interview on The Ghost Writer

Cynthia Haven: "There is no life without patience." This thought is expressed at least twice in *The Ghost Writer*. Could you expand on it a little?

Philip Roth: I can expand on it only by reminding you that these words are spoken not by me but by a character in a book, the eminent short-story writer E. I. Lonoff. It is a maxim Lonoff has derived from a lifetime of agonizing over sentences and does a little something, I hope, to portray him as writer, husband, recluse, and mentor.

One of the means of bringing characters to life in fiction is through what they say. The dialogue is an expression of their thoughts, beliefs, defenses, wit, repartee, etc., a depiction of their responsive manner in general. I am trying to depict Lonoff's verbal air of simultaneous aloofness and engagement, and too his pedagogical turn of mind, particularly in this case when he is talking to his students. What a character says is determined by who is being spoken to, what effect is desired, by who he or she is and what he or she wants at the moment of speaking. Whatever signal is being flashed by the words you quote derives from the specificity of the encounter that elicits them.

Haven: You've said of your two dozen or so novels, "Each book starts from ashes." How did *The Ghost Writer*, in particular, rise from the ashes? Could you describe how it came about, and your labor pains bringing it into being?

Roth: How I began *The Ghost Writer* almost forty years ago? I can't remember. The big difficulty came with deciding on the role Anne Frank was to have in the story.

Haven: It must have been a controversial choice, since she has held a somewhat sacrosanct space in our collective psychic life—even more so in 1979, when the book was published, and

---

February 3, 2014, for Stanford University's "Another Look" event.

even more than that in 1956, when the action of your book takes place, a little over a decade after the war's end. Were you criticized for this portrayal? How has the perception of her changed in the years since the book was published, especially given Cynthia Ozick's landmark 1997 essay, "Who Owns Anne Frank?" which decried the kitschification of Frank?

Roth: I could have had Amy Bellette *be* Anne Frank, and don't think I didn't put in time trying to pull that off. The attempt wasn't fruitful because, in Cynthia Ozick's words, I did not want to "own" Anne Frank and assume a responsibility so grand, however much I had been thinking about bringing her story, which had so much power over people, particularly Jews of my generation—*her* generation—into my fiction as early as ten and fifteen years earlier. I did want to imagine, if not the girl herself—I wanted to imagine that too, though in ways others had ignored—the function the girl had come to perform in the minds of her vast following of receptive readers. One of them is my protagonist, young Nathan Zuckerman, trying here to get used to the idea that he was not born to be nice and for the first time in his life being called to battle. Another is Newark's Jewish sage, Judge Wapter, community watchdog over the conscience of others. Another is Zuckerman's poor baffled mother, anxiously wondering if her beloved son is an anti-Semite dedicated to wiping out all that is good.

I portrayed some who, as you suggest, had sanctified Anne Frank, but mainly I decided to let the budding, brooding writer (for pressing reasons having to do with the wound of remorse and the salve of self-justification) do the imagining. Through a close reading of her diary, young Zuckerman endeavors to rehabilitate her as something other than a saint to be idolized. For him confronting Anne Frank is momentous not because he is meeting her face-to-face but because he is engaged in a sympathetic attempt to fully imagine her—to wipe away Broadway's version of her and the popular canonization of her, to think independently of all that and to start from scratch again with just her words—which is perhaps an even more exacting assignment. At any rate, that is how I solved the "owning" problem that befuddled me at the outset.

Was I criticized for this portrayal? Of course there were

flurries. There are always flurries. There are those among us always poised to be affronted and to deplore a book as the work of the devil should the book happen to undertake investigating an object of idealized veneration—or even just of routine piety—whether it is a historical event placed under fictional scrutiny, a political movement, a stirring ideology, or a sect, people, clan, nation, church that regards itself in ways that are not always shored up by reality. Where everything is requisitioned for the cause, there is no room for fiction (or history or science) that is undertaken as something other than propaganda.

Haven: Many consider you the preeminent Jewish American writer. You told one interviewer, however, "The epithet 'American Jewish writer' has no meaning for me. If I'm not an American, I'm nothing." You seem to be so much both. Can you say a little more about your rejection of that description?

Roth: "An American-Jewish writer" is an inaccurate description and misses the point. The novelist's foremost preoccupation is with his or her language: many a writer will die finding the right next word. And for me, as for DeLillo, Erdrich, Oates, Stone, Styron, and Updike, the right next word is an American-English word. Even if I wrote in Hebrew or Yiddish I would not be a Jewish writer. I would be a Hebrew writer or a Yiddish writer. The American republic is 238 years old. My family has been here for 120 years or more than half of America's existence. They arrived during the second term of President Grover Cleveland, only seventeen years after the end of Reconstruction. Civil War veterans were in their fifties. Mark Twain was alive. Henry Adams was alive. Henry James was alive. All were in their prime. Walt Whitman was dead just two years. Babe Ruth hadn't been born. If I don't measure up as an American writer, at least leave me to my delusion.

Haven: At one point in *Exit Ghost*, your 2007 coda to *The Ghost Writer*, Amy Bellette says to Nathan Zuckerman that she thinks Lonoff has been talking to her from beyond the grave, telling her, "Reading/writing people, we are finished, we are ghosts witnessing the end of a literary era." Are we? At times you have thought so—I refer to your conversation with Tina

Brown in 2009, when you said you thought the audience for novels two decades from now would be about the size of the group that reads Latin poetry. This is about more than just Kindle, isn't it?

Your comments were even broader in 2001, when you told the *Observer*, "I'm not good at finding 'encouraging' features in American culture. I doubt that aesthetic literacy has much of a future here." Is there a remedy?

Roth: I can only repeat myself. I doubt that aesthetic literacy —an acute sensitivity or receptivity to the devices through which fiction imposes its unique hold on the reading mind—has much of a future here. Two decades on, the size of a discerning audience of adroit amateur readers for the literary novel will be about the size of the group who read Latin poetry—read Latin poetry now, that is, and not who read it during the Renaissance.

Haven: You won't be attending the February 25 "Another Look" event for *The Ghost Writer*, which is a shame, because it's Stanford's effort to discuss great short works of fiction with a wider community, bringing in guest authors as well as Stanford scholars. Book clubs have proliferated across the country. Do they offer the possibility of extending and deepening interest in the novel? Or are we kidding ourselves?

Roth: I've never attended a meeting of one. I know nothing about book clubs. From my many years as a university literature teacher I do know that it takes all the patient ingenuity one can muster over the course of a semester to get even the best undergraduates to read precisely the fiction at hand with all their intelligence, without habitual moralizing, ingenious interpretation, biographical speculation, or their falling victim to the steamrolling generalization. Is such protracted rigor the hallmark of book clubs?

Haven: You told Tina Brown in 2009, "I wouldn't mind writing a long book which is going to occupy me for the rest of my life." Yet, in 2012, you said emphatically that you were done with fiction. We can't bring ourselves to believe you've completely stopped writing. Do you really think your talent will let you quit?

Roth: Well, you should believe me, because I haven't written a word of fiction since 2009. I have no desire any longer to write fiction. I did what I did and it's done.

Haven: Each of your books seems to have explored various questions you had about life, about sex, about aging, about writing, about death. What questions preoccupy you now?

Roth: Currently, I am studying nineteenth-century American history. The questions that preoccupy me at the moment have to do with Bleeding Kansas, Judge Taney and Dred Scott, the Confederacy, the 13th, 14th, and 15th amendments, Presidents Johnson and Grant and Reconstruction, the Ku Klux Klan, the Freedmen's Bureau, the rise and fall of the Republicans as a moral force and the resurrection of the Democrats, the over-capitalized railroads and the land swindles, the consequences of the depressions of 1873 and 1893, the final driving out of the Indians, American expansionism, land speculation, white Anglo-Saxon racism, Armour and Swift, the Haymarket riot and the making of Chicago, the no-holds-barred triumph of capital, the burgeoning defiance of labor, the great strikes and the violent strikebreakers, the implementation of Jim Crow, the Tilden-Hayes election and the Compromise of 1877, the immigrations from southern and eastern Europe, 320,000 Chinese entering America through San Francisco, women's suffrage, the temperance movement, the Populists, the Progressive reformers, figures like Charles Sumner, Thaddeus Stevens, William Lloyd Garrison, Frederick Douglass, President Lincoln, Jane Addams, Elizabeth Cady Stanton, Henry Clay Frick, Andrew Carnegie, J. P. Morgan, John D. Rockefeller, etc. My mind is full of *then*.

Interview with Svenska Dagbladet

I know that you have reread all of your books recently. What was your verdict?

When I decided to stop writing five years ago I did, as you say, sit down to reread the thirty-one books I'd published between 1959 and 2010. I wanted to see whether I'd wasted my time. You never can be sure, you know.

My conclusion, after I'd finished, echoes the words spoken by an American boxing hero of mine, Joe Louis. He was world heavyweight champion from the time I was four until I was sixteen. He had been born in the Deep South, an impoverished black kid with no education to speak of, and even during the glory of the undefeated twelve years, when he defended his championship an astonishing twenty-six times, he stood aloof from language. So when he was asked upon his retirement about his long career, Joe sweetly summed it up in just ten words. "I did the best I could with what I had."

In some quarters it is almost a cliché to mention the word "misogyny" in relation to your books. What, do you think, prompted this reaction initially, and what is your response to those who still try to label your work in that way?

Misogyny, a hatred of women, provides my work with neither a structure, a meaning, a motive, a message, a conviction, a perspective, or a guiding principle. This is contrary, say, to how another noxious form of psychopathic abhorrence—and misogyny's equivalent in the sweeping inclusiveness of its pervasive malice—anti-Semitism, a hatred of Jews, provides all those essentials to *Mein Kampf*. My traducers propound my alleged malefaction as though I have spewed venom on women for half a century. But only a madman would go to the trouble of writing thirty-one books in order to affirm his hatred.

March 16, 2014, with Daniel Sandstrom of Stockholm's *Svenska Dagbladet*.

In some quarters, "misogynist" has evolved into a glibly stig-matizing denunciation used almost as laxly as was "Communist" by the McCarthyite right in the 1950s or the catchall words "bourgeois" and "reactionary" that peppered the routine excori-ation of their enemies by the old Communist propaganda ma-chine—and for very like the same purpose. For some devotees it's even been turned by promiscuous use into little more than a swearword when, in fact, employed responsibly, with precision, it designates a wicked social pathology, one that may even be the prelude to violence.

In fifty-odd years of publishing fiction, I have only twice been seriously told that certain things must not be put into words—in the beginning by those Jews who labeled me a Jew-hater and assigned to my work an entirely alien and vicious signifi-cance, and later by those who labeled me a woman-hater, whose reflexive moralizing brands as heresy any many-sided investigation, such as fiction undertakes without censorship or circumvention, of the workings of desire and the libidinous passions; those to whom art is suspect that does not enforce the moment's dogma about the vast realm of the erotic and the adventures of the body in its protracted slide from exuber-ant vitality to decrepitude.

The men in your books are often misinterpreted. Some reviewers make the, I believe, misleading assumption that your male char-acters are some kind of heroes or role models; if you look at the male characters in your books, what traits do they share—what is their condition?

My focus has never been on masculine power rampant and tri-umphant but rather on the antithesis: masculine power impaired. I have hardly been singing a paean to male superiority but rather representing manhood stumbling, constricted, humbled, devas-tated, and brought down. Vulnerability is paramount. I'm not a mythmaker. My intention is to present my fictional men not as they should be but vexed as men are.

The drama issues from the assailability of vital, tenacious men with their share of peculiarities who are neither mired in weakness nor made of stone and who, almost inevitably, are bowed by blurred moral vision, real and imaginary culpability, conflicting allegiances, urgent desires, uncontrollable longings, unworkable love, the culprit passion, the erotic trance, rage, self-division, betrayal, drastic loss, vestiges of innocence, fits of bitterness, lunatic entanglements, consequential misjudgment, understanding overwhelmed, protracted pain, false accusation, unremitting strife, illness, exhaustion, estrangement, derangement, aging, dying, and, repeatedly, inescapable harm, the rude touch of the terrible surprise—unshrinking men stunned nevertheless by the life one is defenseless against, including especially history: the unforeseen that is constantly recurring as the current moment.

It is the social struggle of the current moment on which a number of these men find themselves impaled. It isn't sufficient, of course, to speak of "rage" or "betrayal"—rage and betrayal have a history, like everything else. The novel maps the ordeal of that history.

"The struggle with writing is over" is a recent quote. Could you describe that struggle, and also, tell us something about your life now when you are not writing?

Everybody has a hard job. All real work is hard. My work happened also to be undoable, or so I found it to be. Morning after morning for fifty years, I faced the next page defenseless and unprepared. Writing for me was a feat of self-preservation. Obstinacy, not talent, saved my life. It was also my good luck that happiness didn't matter to me and I had no compassion for myself. Though why such a task should have fallen to me I have no idea. Maybe writing protected me against even worse menace.

Now? Now I am a bird sprung from a cage instead of (to reverse Kafka's famous conundrum) a bird in search of a cage. The horror of being caged has lost its thrill. It is now truly a great relief, something close to a sublime experience, to have nothing more to worry about than death.

You belong to an exceptional generation of postwar writers, who defined American literature for almost half a century: Bellow, Styron, Updike, Doctorow, DeLillo. What made this golden age happen and what made it great? Did you feel, in your active years, that these writers were competition or did you feel kinship—or both? And why were there so few female writers with equal success in that same period? Finally: What is your opinion of the state of contemporary American fiction now?

I agree that it's been a good time for the novel in America, but I can't say why. Maybe it is the absence of certain things that somewhat accounts for it. The American novelist's indifference to, if not contempt for, "critical" theory. Aesthetic freedom unhampered by all the high-and-mighty isms and their humorlessness. Writing that is uncontaminated by political propaganda —or even political responsibility. The absence of any "school" of writing. In a place so vast, no single geographic center from which the writing originates. Anything but a homogeneous population, no basic national unity, no single national character, social calm utterly unknown, even the general obtuseness about literature, the inability of the preponderance of citizens to read any of it with even minimal comprehension, confers a certain freedom. It's somehow inebriating that writers really don't mean a goddamn thing to nine-tenths of the population.

Very little truthfulness anywhere, antagonism everywhere, so much calculated to disgust, the gigantic hypocrisies, no holding fierce passions at bay, the ordinary viciousness you can see just by pressing the remote, explosive weapons in the hands of creeps, the gloomy tabulation of unspeakable violent events, the unceasing despoliation of the biosphere for profit, surveillance overkill that will only grow worse, great concentrations of wealth financing the most undemocratic malevolents around, science illiterates still fighting the Scopes trial eighty-nine years on, economic inequities the size of the Ritz, indebtedness on everyone's tail, families not knowing how bad things can get, money being squeezed out of every last thing—*that* frenzy— and (by no means new) government hardly by the people through representative democracy but rather by the great financial interests, the old American plutocracy worse than ever.

You have three hundred million people on a continent three thousand miles wide doing the best they can with their inexhaustible troubles. We are witnessing a new and benign admixture of races on a scale unknown since the malignancy of slavery. I could go on and on. It's hard not to feel close to existence here. This is not some quiet little corner of the world.

Do you feel that there is a preoccupation in Europe with Ameri-can popular culture? And, if so, that this preoccupation has clouded the reception of serious American literary fiction in Europe?

The power in any society is with those who get to impose the fantasy. It is no longer, as it was for centuries throughout Europe, the church that imposes its fantasy on the populace, nor is it the totalitarian superstate that imposes the fantasy, as it did for twelve years in Nazi Germany and for sixty-nine years in the Soviet Union. Now the fantasy that prevails is the all-consuming, voraciously consumed popular culture, seemingly spawned by, of all things, freedom. The young especially live according to beliefs that are thought up for them by the society's most unthinking members and by the businesses least impeded by innocent ends. Ingeniously as their parents and teachers may attempt to protect the young from being drawn, to their detriment, into the idiotic amusement park that is now universal, the preponderance of the power is not with them.

I cannot see, however, what any of this has to do with American literary fiction, even if, as you suggest, "this preoccupation has [or may have] clouded the reception of serious American fiction in Europe." You know, in Eastern Europe, the dissident writers used to say that "socialist realism," the reigning Soviet aesthetic, consisted of praising the Party so that even *they* understood it. There is no such aesthetic for serious literary writers to conform to in America, certainly not the aesthetic of popular culture.

What has the aesthetic of popular culture to do with formidable postwar writers of such enormous variety as Saul Bellow, Ralph Ellison, William Styron, Don DeLillo, E. L. Doctorow, James Baldwin, Wallace Stegner, Thomas Pynchon, Robert Penn Warren, John Updike, John Cheever, Bernard Malamud, Robert Stone, Evan Connell, Louis Auchincloss, Walker Percy, Cormac McCarthy, Russell Banks, William Kennedy, John Barth, Louis Begley, William Gaddis, Norman Rush, John Edgar Wideman, David Plante, Richard Ford, William Gass, Joseph Heller, Raymond Carver, Edmund White, Oscar Hijuelos, Peter Matthiessen, Paul Theroux, John Irving, Norman

Mailer, Reynolds Price, James Salter, Denis Johnson, J. F. Powers, Paul Auster, William Vollmann, Richard Stern, Alison Lurie, Flannery O'Connor, Paula Fox, Marilynne Robinson, Joyce Carol Oates, Joan Didion, Hortense Calisher, Jane Smiley, Anne Tyler, Jamaica Kincaid, Cynthia Ozick, Ann Beattie, Grace Paley, Lorrie Moore, Mary Gordon, Louise Erdrich, Toni Morrison, Eudora Welty (and I have by no means exhausted the list) or with serious younger writers as wonderfully gifted as Michael Chabon, Junot Díaz, Nicole Krauss, Maile Meloy, Jonathan Lethem, Nathan Englander, Claire Messud, Jeffrey Eugenides, Jonathan Franzen, Jonathan Safran Foer (to name but a handful)?

You have been awarded almost every literary prize, except one. And it is no secret that your name is always mentioned when there is talk of the Nobel Prize in Literature—how does it feel to be an eternal candidate? Does it bother you, or do you laugh about it?

I wonder if I had called *Portnoy's Complaint* "The Orgasm Under Rapacious Capitalism," if I would thereby have earned the favor of the Swedish Academy.

In Claudia Roth Pierpont's Roth Unbound, *there is an interesting chapter on your clandestine work with persecuted writers in Czechoslovakia during the Cold War. If a young author—a Philip Roth born in, say, 1983—were to engage in the global conflicts of 2014, which ones would he pick?*

I don't know how to answer that. I for one didn't go to Prague with a mission. I wasn't looking to "pick" a trouble spot. I was on a vacation and had gone to Prague looking for Kafka.

But the morning after I arrived, I happened to drop by my publishing house to introduce myself. I was led into a conference room to share a glass of slivovitz with the editorial staff. Afterwards one of the editors asked me to lunch. At the restaurant, where her boss happened to be dining too, she told me quietly that all the people in that conference room were "swine," beginning with the boss—party hacks hired to replace those editors who, four years earlier, had been fired because of their support for the reforms of the Prague Spring. I asked her about my translators, a husband-and-wife team, and that evening I had dinner with them. They too were now prevented from working, for the same reasons, and were living in political disgrace.

When I returned home, I found in New York a small group of Czech intellectuals who had fled Prague when the Russian tanks rolled in to put down the Prague Spring. By the time I returned to Russian-occupied Prague the following spring, I wasn't vacationing. I was carrying with me a long list of people to see, the most endangered constituents of an enslaved nation, the proscribed writers for whom sadism, not socialism, was the state religion. The rest developed from that.

Yes, character is destiny, and yet everything is chance.

Can you say something about your last four books, the short novels collected by Library of America in the single volume Nemeses? *How do you account for your shift to this shorter fictional form at the conclusion of your career?*

An irrational catastrophe informs each of these four books. A personal calamity occurs and the punishment machine runs amok. There's a precipitate alteration of the moral landscape: punishment without crime, punishment disproportionate to the crime. The subject is disproportion. Where and what is the cause initiating such horrific results? Absurdity is improbably the order of the day, being in the wrong is a capital crime, and escape is bungled and leads nowhere.

Fiction frequently defines human nature by extreme situations. These four short books do just that. Their pathos is grounded in the innocence of people when they are truly up against it, when the greatest emergency imaginable arises and existence becomes an inexplicable problem they cannot solve. All accustomed safeguards vanish, abruptly nothing is on one's side, and, however impregnable one may once have seemed, however gifted, determined, decisive, however rectitudinous, disaster ensues—and nothing is more real. I was tempted to take a maxim of Kafka's as an epigraph for the four books together: "In the struggle between you and the world, bet on the world."

Although I'm accustomed to the novelistic pleasures of amplification, these are books in which the storytelling scale shrinks and the task is to chart the movement of a life in a relatively few pages. One resorts to one's summary powers and answers a need to narrow the perspective and sharpen the conflict.

How account for the change to a shorter fictional form? Fortitude running down in the face of the daily frustration, fascination dwindling with my allotment of stories, stamina insufficiently copious for the long haul—none of that's impossible. But if that is so, I would hope that I nonetheless located the depths of the story and maintained a high measure of intensity—sometimes limitations or impediments may provoke new prospects and squeezed out of shape you Ovidianly evolve into something else.

Inasmuch as writing these books directly preceded my deciding in 2010 to retire as a novelist at the age of seventy-seven, my progression looks to have moved, in its final decades, from the long form to the shorter form to nothing—from amplification to compression to silence, a silence born of a strong suspicion that I'd done my best work and anything more would be inferior. I was by this time no longer in possession of the mental vitality or the verbal energy or the physical fitness needed to mount and sustain a large creative attack of any duration on a complex structure as demanding as the novel—and as virtually every serious novelist can attest, even at the very top of one's form, the quotient of self-torture in this occupation is rarely small. Every talent has its terms—its nature, its scope, its force; also its term, a tenure, a lifespan. For a slew of implacable reasons, the wild venture was over. The groaning and the exhilaration were over. Not everyone can be fruitful forever.

I know now what it takes a lifetime to discover. I know how it all turned out.

If you would interview yourself at this point in your life—there must be a question that you haven't been asked, that would be obvious and important, but has been ignored by the journalists? What would that be?

Perversely enough, when you ask about a question that has been ignored by journalists, I think of the question that any number of them cannot seem to ignore. The question goes something like this: "Do you still think such-and-such? Do you still believe so-and-so?" and then they quote something spoken not by me but by a character in a book of mine. If you won't mind, may I use the occasion of your final question to say what is probably already clear to the readers of the literary pages of *Svenska Dagbladet*, if not to the ghosts of the journalists I am summoning up?

Whoever looks for the writer's thinking in the words and thoughts of his characters is looking in the wrong direction. Seeking out a writer's "thoughts" violates the richness of the mixture that is the very hallmark of the novel.

The thought of the novelist lies not in the remarks of his characters or even in their introspection but in the plight he has invented for his characters, in the juxtaposition of those characters and in the lifelike ramifications of the ensemble they make. Their density, their substantiality, their lived existence actualized in all its nuanced particulars is his thought metabolized.

The thought of the writer lies in the choice of an aspect of reality previously unexamined in the way that a writer conducts an examination. The thought of the writer is embedded everywhere in the course of the novel's action. The thought of the writer is figured invisibly in the elaborate pattern—in the constellation of imagined things—that is the architecture of the book: what Aristotle called simply "the arrangement of the parts," the "matter of size and order." The thought of the novel is embodied in the moral focus of the novel. The tool with which the novelist thinks is the scrupulosity of his style. Here, in all this, lies whatever cogency his thought may have.

The novel is in *itself* his mental world. A novelist is not a tiny cog in the great wheel of human thought. He is a tiny cog in the great wheel of imaginative literature. Finis.

Forty-Five Years On

REREADING *Portnoy's Complaint* forty-five years on, I am shocked and pleased: shocked that I could have been so reckless, pleased to be reminded that I was once so reckless. I certainly didn't understand while at work back then that henceforth I was never to be free of this psychoanalytic patient I was calling Alexander Portnoy—indeed, that I was on the brink of swapping my identity for his and that, subsequently, in many minds, his persona and all its paraphernalia would be understood to be mine and that my relations with people known and unknown would shift accordingly.

Portnoy's Complaint was the fourth of thirty-one books. In writing it, I wasn't looking for my freedom from anything other than the writer I had started out to be. I was looking not for my catharsis as a neurotic or my revenge as a son, as some suggested, but rather for an enlivening liberation from traditional approaches to storytelling. While the protagonist may be straining to elude the bonds of moral conscience, I was attempting to break loose from a no less pervasive literary conscience that had been shaped by my reading, my schooling, and an ingrained sense of prose decorum and compositional propriety that I'd earnestly gravitated to as a graduate student and a young English instructor. Impatient with the virtues of logical progression, I wanted now to eschew the orderly, coherent development of an imagined world—the course I had followed in my first three books—and to advance helter-skelter, in a frenzy, as the classic analytic patient prescriptively proceeds in the throes of associative freedom.

To help this emancipating fit of frenzy along, I portrayed a man who is the repository of every unacceptable thought, a respected and upstanding thirty-three-year-old lawyer privately possessed by dangerous sensations, savage grievances, sinister feelings, and stalked unrelentingly by lust. I wrote about the quotient of the unsocialized that is rooted in almost everyone and suppressed by each with varying degrees of success. Here

---

Written in 2014.

we get to overhear attorney Portnoy at the analytic patient's extemporizing task of managing (or mismanaging) his disorder.

Portnoy is as rich with ire as with erotic desire. But who isn't? Look at Robert Fagles's translation of *The Iliad*. What's the first word? "Rage." That is how the whole of European literature begins: singing the virile rage of Achilles, who wants his girlfriend back.

One writes a repellent book (and *Portnoy's Complaint* was taken by many to be solely that) not to be repellent but to represent the repellent, to expose the repellent with all one's finesse, to reveal how it looks and what precisely it is. Chekhov wisely advised both readers and writers that the task of the literary artist lies not in solving problems but in properly presenting the problem.

Inasmuch as the Freudian ground rule is that nothing in a personal history is too petty or vulgar to speak about and nothing, likewise, too monstrous or grand, the psychoanalytic session provided me with the appropriate setting to give frenzy its due. The analyst's office, the locale of the book, is that place where one need censor nothing. The rule is there is no rule, and that was the rule that I pledged myself to observe to depict a son's satiric mockery of his Jewish family, wherein the most comical object of mockery proves to be the ridiculing son himself, enveloped as he is by clamorous self-satire. The ugly aggression of satire combined with satire's hyperrealism—the portraiture verging on caricature, the zeal for the off-color and the outlandish—was not, of course, to everyone's taste nor was the coarseness of Portnoy's polemic, the rawness of his appetite, and the guilty gloating over the funhouse orgasms. I, on the other hand, was carried on the wings of mirth far from my initial emergence as a well-mannered writer.

The grotesque conception that Portnoy has of his life owed much to regulations, inhibitions, and taboos that no longer hold sway among our erotically unfettered youth, even in the remotest American hamlet. Yet during a postwar American adolescence in the 1940s—a long half-century before internet pornography was even dreamed of—these restraints prevailed in the constricted jurisdiction where Portnoy was so vexedly confronting the outlaw reality of a licentious nature: the maniacal obstinacy of tumescence, the despotic tyranny of testosterone. Because of the drastic alteration in moral perspective over the last forty-five years, news of a carnality seemingly so calamitous when Portnoy first trumpeted his phallic history to his analyst in 1969 has in our time been largely defused. As a result, my immoderate book born in the tumult of the sixties is now as dated as *The Scarlet Letter* or as *Portnoy*'s coeval stablemate, Updike's *Couples*, another genitalic novel then still shocking enough to challenge a generation's already flagging certainties about the boundaries of eros and the prerogatives of lust.

Alexander Portnoy, R.I.P.

The Ruthless Intimacy of Fiction

I

TEMPTING AS it is, I will not bury you tonight beneath a ton of stories about my happy childhood in the Weequahic section of this city or about my emotional affinity to nearly every commonplace, unpoetic thing that was the Newark of my day. There is no good reason for an eighty-year-old man to regret that things were once different or to bore people with a pathetic fondness for carrying on about how everything back then was otherwise.

The Weequahic section is a twenty-minute bus ride from this spot. I know because we made school trips by bus to the museum to look at the famous jewelry collection, many of the pieces Newark-made, when I was a pupil at Chancellor Avenue Elementary School from 1938 to 1946.

But I'll say no more about Chancellor Avenue School or about how, when I was a pupil there, there were only eight teams in the National League and eight in the American or about how we used to painstakingly pick the silver foil clean from the empty cigarette packs we found crumpled up in the gutter and roll them into a substantial ball of foil that we carried with our school books to school for the war effort.

Nor will I tell you about the most thrilling day of my young American life, August 14, 1945, when, after three and a half years of our living in a mobilized country at war on two enormous fronts at the opposite rims of the Eastern Hemisphere, Japan, our last enemy, surrendered. Or about the most thrilling night of my young American life when the Democrat Truman upset the Republican Dewey in 1948. Or about the longest, saddest day of my young American life, the spring day in April 1945, less than four weeks before the war against Nazi Germany ended in Europe, when Roosevelt, four times elected, president of the United States from the day I was born, died

Eightieth birthday address at the Newark Museum, March 19, 2013.

suddenly of a cerebral hemorrhage at the age of sixty-three. Our family seething in sadness. Our *country* seething in sadness.

Between December 1941 and August 1945, an American child didn't just live at home, in the neighborhood, and at school. If the child was at all attentive and curious, he or she also lived within the ethos of a tragic catastrophe that was global. The terrifying symbol of its tragic nature was the plain little gold-star flag, about half the size of our car's license plate, that hung in the front window where a son or a father or a husband of the household had been killed in action. The mother of that family became known as "a Gold Star Mother." There were two such flags in the windows of flats along our Newark street, and it was difficult for most kids to pass those windows on the way to school in their usual childish state of school-going levity.

I wondered back then what it could possibly be like for a child having to tiptoe into one of those houses as a member of the grieving family, sobbing with everyone over dinner, falling stricken into one's bed at night, awakening horrified every morning, mute with grief in the home that lay behind the drawn blackout shades and that gold-star flag, in rooms still harrowingly rich with the mementos and memories of the dear one only recently robbed of the rest of his life. How would the bereft creature who was oneself ever again be a child? I wondered what it would be like never again to know delight.

Some forty years later, when I came to write *Sabbath's Theater*, I found out for myself by imagining the anguish of the grieving Sabbaths of Bradley Beach, New Jersey.

I will not test your patience tonight with stories about the Osborne Terrace Library, a small branch of the main Newark library a mile or so from my house, and of how I bicycled there as a boy every two weeks to borrow books. I carried the books home, half a dozen at a time, in the basket of my bike. But I've told that story already and probably, you are thinking, in more than one book. Nobody needs to hear any more about my bicycle basket.

In my defense, however, I should insert here that remembering objects as mundane as a bicycle basket was a not insignificant part of my vocation. The deal worked out for me as a novelist was that I should continuously rummage around in memory for thousands and thousands of just such things. Unlikely as it may seem, a passion for local specificity—the expansive engagement, something close to fascination, with a seemingly familiar, even innocuous, object like a lady's kid glove or a butcher shop chicken or a gold-star flag or a Hamilton wristwatch, according to Poppa Everyman the Elizabeth, New Jersey, jeweler, "the best watch this country ever produced, the premier American-made watch, bar none."

I was saying that this passion for specificity, for the hypnotic materiality of the world one is in, is all but at the heart of the task to which every American novelist has been enjoined since Herman Melville and his whale and Mark Twain and his river: to discover the most arresting, evocative verbal depiction for every last American thing. Without strong representation of the thing—animate or inanimate—without the crucial representation of what is real, there is nothing. Its concreteness, its unabashed focus on all the mundanities, a fervor for the singular and a profound aversion to generalities is fiction's lifeblood. It is from a scrupulous fidelity to the blizzard of specific data that is a personal life, it is from the force of its uncompromising attentiveness, from its *physicalness*, that the realistic novel, the insatiable realistic novel with its multitude of realities, derives its ruthless intimacy. And its mission: to portray humanity in its particularity.

Enjoined to this verbal task, I must add, until about three years back, when I for one awoke one fine morning with a smile on my face, understanding that miraculously, seemingly in my sleep, I had at long last eluded my lifelong master: the stringent exigencies of literature.

I will not speak about the park, Olmsted's vast and beautiful Weequahic Park, our wooded, hilly countryside, our skating pond, our fishing hole, our necking parlor, our pick-up place, where Portnoy's uncle Hymie parked his car to pay cold cash to the Polish janitor's shiksa daughter Alice to stay away from his son Heshie.

Or about the dirt playing field, a hundred and fifty yards long, some sixty yards wide, a big field just down Summit Avenue from my house. Steam-shovels had gouged it out of the Chancellor Avenue hill in the 1930s. "The field" was what everyone called it, the field where, in *Nemesis*, Bucky Cantor throws the javelin. "Running with the javelin aloft, stretching his throwing arm back behind his body, bringing the throwing arm through to release the javelin high over his shoulder—and releasing it then like an explosion."

I am finished with that stuff too. I've described my last javelin throw and my last stamp album and my last glove factory and my last jewelry store and my last breast and my last butcher shop and my last family crisis and my last unconscionable betrayal and my last brain tumor of the kind that killed my father.

I don't want to describe the blade of the auger that you use for ice-fishing or a boy ecstatically bodysurfing at the Jersey Shore or Newark, this city, going up in flames or the U.S. under President Charles Lindbergh or Prague under the totalitarian boot of the Soviet Union or a Jewish superpatriot's diatribe in a West Bank settlement or a Christmas carol service seated beside an anti-Semitic sister-in-law in a London church or the moral unreadiness of the parents of a terrorist daughter or what Shakespeare called the "fangs of malice."

I don't want to describe, spadeful by spadeful, how a grave is dug or how it is filled back up to the brim. I don't want to describe another death or even just the simple drama of the daily pleasure of living the human comedy. I don't wish any longer to contemplate in fiction the destructive, the blighted, the bruised, the assailable, the accused, their accusers, or even those who are whole, sane, and beautifully intact and who accept life bravely and joyfully.

I won't tell you tonight about the prize fights at Laurel Garden. You saw a snippet of a championship fight, usually a penultimate knockdown followed by the crushing knockout, in the newsreels on Saturday afternoons at the Roosevelt Theater. But you only witnessed the damage being inflicted first-hand—the brute force up close—at Newark's Laurel Garden. The sporting arena was located on Springfield Avenue not that far from this museum.

The war. The school. The park. The field. The museum. The library. The fights. All of which over the years inspired in me, when I was working at my best, what I once described elsewhere as "that lubricious sensation that is fluency."

For a treat, my father took my older brother and me to the fights when we were kids. This wasn't New York and Madison

Square Garden in its heyday, it was Newark and Laurel Garden
during the war and so half the fighters were bums. My brother
and I would bet a nickel on each fight—one of us taking the
black guy and the other the white guy or if both fighters were
of the same race we bet the light trunks versus the dark trunks.
On a bad night I could blow my weekly twenty-five cent allowance at the fights.

But fight night at Laurel Garden provided a sublime experience for a ten-year-old boy. It was practically a spiritual phenomenon. For me it had the synagogue beat by a mile.
Mischievous, masculine joys! You could be asphyxiated by
merely one gulp of what passed for air inside Laurel Garden.
Grown men, in gruff, indignant voices that sounded comically
musical to my ears, would roar abusive encouragement at the
fighters. The coarse Newark libretto for an *opera buffa*.

And that, by the way, was how I found out half the fighters
were bums. I would never have known on my own. But the
wise guys, the tough guys, the roughnecks and hoodlums
seated upstairs in the gallery—collectively smoking themselves
to death—told the whole smelly arena as much. "You bum!
You bum you!" A boy's first encounter with the thrilling
profane.

I won't tell you about seeing Jackie Robinson in 1946, the
year before he broke into the lily-white big leagues, with the
Brooklyn Dodgers, as baseball's first black player. He was with
the Brooklyn farm club then, the Montreal Royals. They were
playing against our triple-A Yankee minor league farm club,
the Newark Bears, at Ruppert Stadium here in the Fifth Ward,
the working-class neighborhood more evocatively known both
as Down Neck and the Ironbound.

At a quarter a ticket on weekdays, it was just us kids, boys
still blessedly ignorant of eros whose greatest lust was no less
for the subtleties than for the individual heroism of the game
of baseball. It was just us boys and the drunks scattered thinly
about in the bleachers. Most of the drunks didn't bother anyone but slept the afternoon away whimpering and snoring in
the summer sun.

But there was one of them, I remember, an inspired one,
who would rouse himself every inning or so and, looking
groggily around, try to figure out where he was. And then, no

matter what was going on in the game—about which he had no idea—he would stand up and, swaying on wobbly legs, enigmatically holler from between his hands, "Walk eem, walk eem—he's a bad man!"

But you surely didn't come over to Newark to sit here all night listening to this stuff. Professor Finkielkraut tells me that the Greek rhetorical term for this stuff—for saying you are not going to talk about something and then, for a doubtful ironic effect, talking about it—is either "paralipsis" or "prolepsis." Best then to take a less classical approach from here on out, one easier for even a friendly audience to bear, even if it doesn't camouflage one's emotions quite so well.

2

Before I read from my 1995 novel, *Sabbath's Theater*, allow me to say something about the book and its protagonist.

Sabbath's Theater takes as its epigraph a line of the aged Prospero's in act five of *The Tempest*, Prospero's concession that as inexpungible a truth as there is—the irksome law of cessation—has come to permeate his brain.

"Every third thought," says Prospero, "shall be my grave."

I could have called the book *Death and the Art of Dying*. It is a book in which breakdown is rampant, suicide is rampant, hatred is rampant, lust is rampant. Where disobedience is rampant. Where death is rampant.

Mickey Sabbath doesn't live with his back turned to death the way that normal people like us do. No one could have concurred more heartily with the judgment of Franz Kafka than would Sabbath, when Kafka wrote, "The meaning of life is that it stops."

To meet the dead, to be reunited with them, is never far from Sabbath's mind. The closer he gets to the dead—to *his* dead—the stronger the geyser of tormented feeling and the further he moves from the wild and antagonistic performance that is his life. The book is a savage journey with the dead into his own raw wound.

His book is death-haunted—there is Sabbath's great grief about the death of others and a great gaiety about his own. There is leaping with delight, there is also leaping with despair.

Sabbath learns to mistrust life when his adored older brother is killed in World War II. It is Morty's death that determines how Sabbath will live. The death of Morty sets the gold standard for grief.

Through the blow of death Sabbath is edified way ahead of his time by the crises that are born of contingency. He is transformed utterly at the age of fifteen by the unimaginable made gruesomely real, when everything essential to life disappears in a blink.

In this novel, the corpses aren't hidden under the floor upon which the living dance through life. Here the corpses get to dance too. No death goes undescribed, and no loss either. Everybody who enters here, everybody, is wedded to death and nobody escapes grieving. There is loss, death, dying, decay, grief—and laughter! Ungovernable laughter! Pursued by death and followed everywhere by laughter.

This Sabbath is a jokester like Hamlet, who winks at the genre of tragedy by cracking jokes as Sabbath winks at the genre of comedy by planning suicide.

Yet where love is great and loss real—as with his brother, his mother, his father, and Drenka, the mistress he visits nightly while she pitilessly wastes away on her deathbed—there the guile disappears. Then even Sabbath, corpulent, cunning, imprudent, arthritic, defeated, unpardonable Mickey Sabbath, loathsome and clad like a freak though he is, hurled perpetually from levity to gravity, from repugnance to melancholia, from mania to buffoonery, out of sympathy with the august moral sentiments and the laudable ideologies of communal accord, a kiln of antagonism, and like so much of flawed humanity, unable ever to tear free of himself, this very same Sabbath is carried off by extremes of misery.

Such depths as Sabbath evinces lie in his polarities. What's clinically denoted by the word "bi-polarity" is something puny compared to what's brandished by Sabbath. Imagine, rather, a multitudinous intensity of polarities, polarities piled shamelessly upon polarities to comprise not a company of players but this single existence, this theater of one.

Unlike Swede Levov in my subsequent novel, *American Pastoral*, Sabbath is anything but the perfect external man. His is, rather, the instinctual turbulence of the man beneath the man: the unmanageable man, the unexonerated man—better, the refractory man: refractory meaning "resistant to treatment or cure," refractory meaning "capable of enduring high temperatures." Refractory not as a pathology but as a human position. The refractory man being the one who will not join.

His refractory way of living—unable and unwilling to hide anything and, with his raging, satirizing nature, mocking everything, living beyond the limits of discretion and taste and blaspheming against the decent—this refractory way of living is his uniquely Sabbathian response to a place where nothing keeps its promise and everything is perishable. A life of unalterable contention is the best preparation he knows of for death. In his incompatibility he finds his truth.

3

To commemorate my having been generously granted sufficient time and enough good health to have finished thirty-one books, I want to read to you some pages that I like as well as any pages I've ever written. And, after having recently concluded over half a century struggling with writing, I'm far from liking all of the pages I've written.

Here is Sabbath at a cemetery at the Jersey Shore searching alone for the graves of his grandparents, his parents, and Morty, the brother whose twin-engine B-25J was shot down as he piloted a routine bombing run over the Japanese-occupied Philippines on December 13, 1944. It is fifty years later yet Mickey Sabbath, now sixty-four, searches still for the irreplaceable brother. Loss governs his world.

From *Sabbath's Theater*, the bottom of page 363 to the middle of 370.

Getting to the old graves, to the burial ground established in the early days by the original seashore Jews, he gave the funeral in progress a wide berth and was careful to steer clear of the watchdogs when he passed the little prayer house. These dogs had not yet been made conversant with the common courtesies, let alone the ancient taboos that obtain in a Jewish cemetery. Jews guarded by dogs? Historically very, very wrong. His alternative was to be buried bucolically on Battle Mountain as close to his late mistress, Drenka, as he could get. This had

occurred to him long before today. But whom would he talk
to up there? He had never found a goy yet who could talk fast
enough for him. And there they'd be slower than usual. He
would have to swallow the insult of the dogs. No cemetery is
going to be perfect.

After ten minutes of rambling about in the drizzle, searching
for his grandparents' graves, he saw that only if he traveled
methodically up and down, reading every headstone from one
end of each row to the other, could he hope to locate Clara and
Mordecai Sabbath. Footstone inscriptions he could ignore—
they mostly said "At Rest"—but the hundreds upon hundreds
of headstones required his concentration, an immersion in
them so complete that there would be nothing inside him but
these names. He had to shrug off how these people would have
disliked him and how many of them he would have despised,
had to forget about the people they had been alive. Because
you are no longer insufferable if you are dead. He had to drink
in the dead, down to the dregs. They were buried, after all, not
that far under the crust of the earth.

Our beloved mother Minnie. Our beloved husband and father
Sidney. Beloved mother and grandmother Frieda. Beloved husband and father Jacob. Beloved husband, father, and grandfather
Samuel. Beloved husband and father Joseph. Beloved mother
Sarah. Beloved wife Rebecca. Beloved husband and father Benjamin. Beloved mother and grandmother Tessa. Beloved mother
and grandmother Sophie. Beloved mother Bertha. Beloved husband Hyman. Beloved husband Morris. Beloved wife and mother
Rebecca. Our beloved daughter and sister Hannah Sarah. Our
dear father Marcus. On and on and on.

Nobody beloved gets out alive. Our son and brother Nathan.
Our dear father Edward. In memory of my beloved husband
and our dear father Lewis. And on mine, beloved what? Just
that: Beloved What. David Schwartz, beloved son and brother,
died in service of his country 1894–1918. In memory of Ger-
tie, a true wife and loyal friend. Our son, nineteen years old,
1903–1922. No name, merely "Our son."

And here we are. Sabbath. Clara Sabbath 1872–1941. Mordecai Sabbath 1871–1923. There they are. Simple stone. And a pebble on top. Who'd come to visit? Mort, did you visit Grandma?
Dad? Who cares? Who's left? What's in there? The box isn't
even in there. You were said to be headstrong, Mordecai, bad
temper, big joker . . . though even you couldn't make a joke
like this. Nobody could. Better than this they don't come. And

Grandma. Your name, the name also of your occupation. A matter-of-fact person. Everything about you—your stature, those dresses, your silence—said, "I am not indispensable."

No contradictions, no temptations, though you were inordinately fond of corn on the cob. Mother hated having to watch you eat it. The worst of the summer for her. It made her "nauseous," she said. I loved to watch. Otherwise you two got along. Probably keeping quiet was the key, letting her run things her way. Openly partial to Morty, Grandpa Mordecai's namesake, but who could blame you? You didn't live to see everything shatter. Lucky. Nothing big about you, Grandma, but nothing small either. I'll take you just as you were. A kind and gentle soul who persevered. Life could have marked you up a lot worse. Born over there in the tiny town of Bilkamin, died here at Pitkin Memorial.

Have I left anything out? Yes. You used to love to clean the fish for us when Morty and I came home at night from surf casting. Mostly we came home with nothing, but the triumph of walking home from the beach with a couple of big blues in the bucket! You'd clean them in the kitchen. Fillet knife right at the opening, probably the anus, slit it straight up the center till you got behind the gills, and then (I liked watching this part best) you would just put your hand in and grab all the good stuff and throw it away. Then you scaled. Working against the scales and somehow without getting them all over the place. It used to take me fifteen minutes to clean it and half an hour to clean up after. The whole *thing* took you ten minutes. Mom even let you cook it. Never cut off the head and the tail. Baked it whole. Baked bluefish, fresh corn, fresh tomatoes, big Jersey tomatoes. Grandma's meal.

Yes, it was something down on the beach at dusk with Mort. Used to talk to the other men. Childhood and its terrific markers. From about eight to thirteen, the fundamental ballast that we have. It's either right or it's wrong. Mine was right. The original ballast, an attachment to those who were nearby when we were learning what feeling was all about. A good thing to be able to contemplate for a final time—certain high points, certain human high points.

Hanging out with the man next door and his sons. Meeting and talking in the yard. Down on the beach, fishing with Mort. Rich times. Morty used to talk to the other men, the fishermen. Did it so easily. To me everything he did was so authoritative. One guy in brown pants and a short-sleeve white shirt and with a cigar always in his mouth used to tell us he didn't give a shit about catching fish (which was lucky, since he rarely pulled in more than a sand shark)—he told us kids, "The chief pleasure of fishing is getting out of the house. Gettin' away from women."

We always laughed, but for Morty and me the bite was the thrill. With a blue you get a big hit. The rod jolts in your hand. Everything jolts. Morty was my teacher fishing. "When a striper takes the bait," he told me, "it'll head out. If you stop the line from paying out it'll snap. So you just have to let it out. With a blue, after the hit, you can just reel it in, but not with a striper. A blue is big and tough, but a striper will fight ya." Getting blowfish off the hook was a problem for everybody but Mort—spines and quills didn't bother him. The other thing that wasn't much fun to catch was rays. Do you remember when I was eight how I wound up in the hospital, Grandma? I was out on the jetty and I caught a huge ray and it bit me and I just passed out. Beautiful, undulating swimmers but predatory sons of bitches, very mean with their sharp teeth. Ominous. Looks like a flat shark. Morty had to holler for help, and a guy came and they carried me up to the guy's car and rushed me to Pitkin.

Whenever we went out fishing, you couldn't wait for us to get back so you could clean the catch. Used to catch shiners. Weighed less than a pound. You'd fry four or five of them in a pan. Very bony but great. Watching you eat a shiner was a lot of fun, too, for everyone but Mother. What else did we bring you to clean? Fluke, flounder, when we fished Shark River inlet. Weakfish. That's about it.

When Morty joined the Air Corps, the night before he left we went down to the beach with our rods for an hour. Never got into the gear as kids. Just fished. Rod, hooks, sinkers, line, sometimes lures, mostly bait, mostly squid. That was it. Heavy-duty tackle. Big barbed hook. Never cleaned the rod. Once a summer splashed some water on it. Keep the same rig on the whole time. Just change the sinkers and the bait if we wanted to fish on the bottom.

We went down to the beach to fish for an hour. Everybody in the house was crying because Morty was going to war the next day. You were already here, Grandma. You were gone. So I'll tell you what happened. October 10, 1942. He'd hung around through September because he wanted to see me bar mitzvahed, wanted to be there. The eleventh of October he went to Perth Amboy to enlist.

The last of the fishing off the jetties and the beach. By the middle, the end of October, the fish disappear. I'd ask Morty—when he was first teaching me off the jetties with a small rod and reel, one made for fresh water—"Where do the fish go to?" "Nobody knows," he said. "Nobody knows where the fish go. Once they go out to sea, who knows where they go to? What do you think, people follow them around? That's the mystery of fishing. Nobody knows where they are."

We went down to the end of the street that evening and down the stairs and onto the beach. It was just about dark. Morty could throw a rig a hundred and fifty feet even in the days before spin casting. Used the open-faced reels. Just a spool with a handle on it. Rods much stiffer then, much less adroit reel and a stiffer rod. Torture to cast for a kid. In the beginning I was always snarling the line. Spent most of the time getting it straightened out. But eventually I got it. Morty said he was going to miss going out fishing with me. He'd taken me down to the beach to say so long to me without the family carrying on around us.

"Standing out here," he told me, "the sea air, the quiet, the sound of the waves, your toes in the sand, the idea that there are all those things out there that are about to bite your bait. That thrill of something being out there. You don't know what it is, you don't know how big it is. You don't even know if you'll ever see it." And he never did see it, nor, of course, did he get what you get when you're older, which is something that mocks your opening yourself up to these simple things, something that is formless and overwhelming and that probably is dread. No, he got killed instead.

And that's the news, Grandma. The great generational kick of standing down on the beach in the dusk with your older brother. You sleep in the same room, you get very close. He took me with him everywhere. One summer when he was about twelve he got a job selling bananas door-to-door. There was a man in Belmar who sold only bananas, and he hired Morty and Morty hired me, age seven. The job was to go along the streets hollering, "Bananas, twenty-five cents a bunch!" What a great job. I still sometimes dream about that job. You got paid to shout "Bananas!"

On Thursdays and Fridays after school let out for the day, he went to pluck chickens for the kosher butcher, Feldman. A farmer from Lakewood used to call on Feldman and sell him chickens. Morty would take me along to help him. I liked the worst part best: spreading the Vaseline all the way up your arms to stymie the lice. The chickens were infested with lice. It made me feel like a little big shot at eight or nine not to be afraid of those horrible swarming lice, to be, like Mort, utterly contemptuous of them and just pluck Feldman's chickens.

And he used to protect me from the Syrian Jews. Kids used to dance on the sidewalk in the summertime outside Mike and Lou's. Jitterbug to the jukebox music. I doubt you ever saw that, Grandma. When Morty was working at Mike and Lou's one summer he'd bring home his apron and Mom would wash it for him for the next night. It would be stained yellow from the mustard and red from the relish. The mustard came right with him into our room when he came into our room at night. Smelled like mustard, sauerkraut, and hot dogs. Mike and Lou's had good hot dogs. Grilled.

The Syrian guys, the Syrian Jews, used to dance outside Mike and Lou's on the sidewalk, used to dance by themselves together like sailors. They had a little kind of Damascus mambo they did, very explosive steps. All related they were, clannish, and with very dark skin. The Syrian kids who joined our card games played a ferocious blackjack. Their fathers were in buttons, thread, fabrics then. Used to hear Dad's crony, the upholsterer from Neptune, talking about them when the men played poker in our kitchen on Friday nights. "Money is their god. Toughest people in the world to do business with. They'll cheat you as soon as you turn around."

Some of these Syrian kids made an impression. One of them, one of the Gindi brothers, would come up to you and take a swing at you for no reason, come up and kill you and just look at you and walk away. I used to be hypnotized by his sister. I was twelve. She and I were in the same class. A little, hairy fireplug. Huge eyebrows. I couldn't get over her dark skin. She told Gindi something that I said, so once he started to rough me up. I was deathly afraid of him. I'm still afraid of him. I should never have looked at her, let alone said anything to her. But the dark skin got me going. Always has.

He started to rough me up right in front of Mike and Lou's, and Morty came outside in his mustard-stained apron and told Gindi, "Stay away from him." And Gindi said, "You gonna make me?" And Morty said, "Yes." And Gindi took one shot at him and opened up Morty's whole nose. Isaac Gindi. His form of narcissism never enchanted me. Sixteen stitches. Those Syrians lived in another time zone. They were always whispering among themselves. But I was twelve, inside my pants things were beginning to reverberate, and I could not keep my eyes off his hairy sister. Sonia. Sonia was her name. Sonia had another brother, as I recall, Maurice, who was not human either.

But then came the war. I was thirteen, Morty was eighteen. Here's a kid who never went away in his life, except maybe for a track meet. Never out of Monmouth County. Every day of his life he returned home. Endlessness renewed every day. And the next morning he goes off to die. But then, death is endlessness par excellence, is it not? Wouldn't you agree? Well, for whatever it is worth, before I move on: I have never once eaten corn on the cob without pleasurably recalling the devouring frenzy of you and your dentures and the repugnance this ignited in my mother. It taught me about more than mother-in-laws and daughter-in-laws; it taught me everything. This model grandmother, and Mother had all she could do not to throw you out into the street. And my mother was not unkind—you know that. But what affords the one with happiness affords the other with disgust. The interplay, the ridiculous interplay, enough to kill all and everyone.

Beloved wife and mother Fannie. Beloved wife and mother Hannah. Beloved husband and father Jack. It goes on, the names as proximate to them as we can get. The names one never has to struggle to recall. Our beloved mother Rose. Our beloved father Harry. Our beloved husband, father, and grandfather Meyer. People. All people.

In the earth turned up where Leah Goldman, another devoted wife, mother, and grandmother, had just been united with one of her family, a beloved one as yet unidentified, Sabbath found pebbles to place on the stones of his mother, his father, and Morty.

Here I am.

Chronology

Born Philip Roth on March 19 in Newark, New Jersey, second child of Herman Roth and Bess Finkel. (Bess Finkel, the second child of five, was born in 1904 in Elizabeth, New Jersey, to Philip and Dora Finkel, Jewish immigrants from near Kiev. Herman Roth was born in 1901 in Newark, New Jersey, the middle child of seven born to Sender and Bertha Roth, Jewish immigrants from Polish Galicia. They were married in Newark on February 21, 1926, and shortly afterward opened a small family-run shoe store. Their son Sanford ["Sandy"] was born December 26, 1927. Following the bankruptcy of the shoe store and a briefly held position as city marshal, Herman Roth took a job as agent with the Newark district office of the Metropolitan Life Insurance Company, and would remain with the company until his retirement as district manager in 1966.) Family moves into second-floor flat of two-and-a-half-family house (with five-room apartments on each of the first two floors and a three-room apartment on the top floor) at 81 Summit Avenue in Newark. Summit Avenue was a lower-middle-class residential street in the Weequahic section, a twenty-minute bus ride from commercial downtown Newark and less than a block from Chancellor Avenue School and from Weequahic High School, then considered the state's best academic public high school. These were the two schools that Sandy and Philip attended. Between 1910 and 1920, Weequahic had been developed as a new city neighborhood at the southwest corner of Newark, some three miles from the edge of industrial Newark and from the international shipping facilities at Port Newark on Newark Bay. In the first half of the twentieth century Newark was a prosperous working-class city of approximately 420,000, the majority of its citizens of German, Italian, Slavic, and Irish extraction. Blacks and Jews composed two of the smallest groups in the city. From the 1930s to the 1950s, the Jews lived mainly in the predominantly Jewish Weequahic section.

1938   Philip enters kindergarten at Chancellor Avenue School in January.

1942   Roth family moves to second-floor flat of two-and-a-half-family house at 359 Leslie Street, three blocks west of Summit Avenue, still within the Weequahic neighborhood but nearer to semi-industrial boundary with Irvington.

1946   Philip graduates from elementary school in January, having skipped a year. Brother graduates from high school and chooses to enter U.S. Navy for two years rather than be drafted into the peacetime army.

1947   Family moves to first-floor flat of two-and-a-half-family house at 385 Leslie Street, just a few doors from commercial Chancellor Avenue, the neighborhood's main artery. Philip turns from reading sports fiction by John R. Tunis and adventure fiction by Howard Pease to reading the left-leaning historical novels of Howard Fast.

1948   Brother is discharged from navy and, with the aid of G.I. Bill, enrolls as commercial art student at Pratt Institute, Brooklyn. Philip takes strong interest in politics during the four-way U.S. presidential election in which the Republican Dewey loses to the Democrat Truman despite a segregationist Dixiecrat Party and a left-wing Progressive Party drawing away traditionally Democratic voters.

1950   Graduates from high school in January. Works as stock clerk at S. Klein department store in downtown Newark. Reads Thomas Wolfe; discovers Sherwood Anderson, Ring Lardner, Erskine Caldwell, and Theodore Dreiser. In September enters Newark College of Rutgers as pre-law student while continuing to live at home. (Newark Rutgers was at this time a newly formed college housed in two small converted downtown buildings, one formerly a bank, the other formerly a brewery.)

1951   Still a pre-law student, transfers in September to Bucknell University in Lewisburg, Pennsylvania. Brother graduates from Pratt Institute and moves to New York City to work for advertising agency. Parents move to Moorestown, New Jersey, approximately seventy miles southwest of Newark; father takes job as manager of Metropolitan Life's south Jersey district after having previously managed several north Jersey district offices.

1952   Roth decides to study English literature. With two friends, founds Bucknell literary magazine, *Et Cetera*, and becomes its first editor. Writes first short stories. Strongly influenced in his literary studies by English professor Mildred Martin, under whose tutelage he reads extensively, and with whom he will maintain lifelong friendship.

1954   Is elected to Phi Beta Kappa and graduates from Bucknell magna cum laude in English. Accepts scholarship to study English at the University of Chicago graduate school, beginning in September. Reads Saul Bellow's *The Adventures of Augie March*, and under its influence explores Chicago.

1955   In June receives M.A. with Honors in English. In September, rather than wait to be drafted, enlists in U.S. Army for two years. Suffers spinal injury during basic training at Fort Dix. In November, is assigned to Public Information Office at Walter Reed Army Hospital, Washington, D.C. Begins to write short stories "The Conversion of the Jews" and "Epstein." *Epoch*, a Cornell University literary quarterly, publishes "The Contest for Aaron Gold," which is reprinted in Martha Foley's *Best American Short Stories 1956*.

1956   Is hospitalized in June for complications from spinal injury. After two-month hospital stay receives honorable discharge for medical reasons and a disability pension. In September returns to University of Chicago as instructor in the liberal arts college, teaching freshman composition. Begins course work for Ph.D. but drops out after one term. Meets Ted Solotaroff, who is also a graduate student, and they become friends.

1957   Publishes in *Commentary* "You Can't Tell a Man by the Song He Sings." Writes novella "Goodbye, Columbus." Meets Saul Bellow at University of Chicago when Bellow is a classroom guest of Roth's friend and colleague, the writer Richard Stern. Begins to review movies and television for *The New Republic* after magazine publishes "Positive Thinking on Pennsylvania Avenue," a humor piece satirizing President Eisenhower's religious beliefs.

1958   Publishes "The Conversion of the Jews" and "Epstein" in *The Paris Review*; "Epstein" wins *Paris Review* Aga Khan Prize, presented to Roth in Paris in July. Spends first summer abroad, mainly in Paris. Houghton Mifflin awards Roth the Houghton Mifflin Literary Fellowship to publish the novella and five stories in one volume; George Starbuck, a poet and friend from Chicago, is his editor. Resigns from teaching position at University of Chicago. Moves to two-room basement apartment on Manhattan's Lower East Side. Becomes friendly with *Paris Review* editors George Plimpton and Robert Silvers and *Commentary* editor Martin Greenberg.

1959   Marries Margaret Martinson Williams. Publishes "Defender of the Faith" in *The New Yorker*, causing consternation among Jewish organizations and rabbis who attack magazine and condemn author as anti-Semitic; story collected in *Goodbye, Columbus* and included in *Best American Short Stories 1960* and *Prize Stories 1960: The O. Henry Awards*, where it wins second prize. *Goodbye, Columbus* is published in May. Roth receives Guggenheim fellowship and award from the American Academy of Arts and Letters. *Goodbye, Columbus* gains highly favorable reviews from Bellow, Alfred Kazin, Leslie Fiedler, and Irving Howe; influential rabbis denounce Roth in their sermons as "a self-hating Jew." Roth and wife leave U.S. to spend seven months in Italy, where he works on his first novel, *Letting Go*; he meets William Styron, who is living in Rome and who becomes a lifelong friend. Styron introduces Roth to his publisher, Donald Klopfer of Random House; when George Starbuck leaves Houghton Mifflin, Roth moves to Random House.

1960   *Goodbye, Columbus and Five Short Stories* wins National Book Award. The collection also wins Daroff Award of the Jewish Book Council of America. Roth returns to America to teach at the Writers' Workshop of the University of Iowa, Iowa City. Meets drama professor Howard Stein (later dean of the Columbia University Drama School), who becomes lifelong friend. Continues working on *Letting Go*. Travels in Midwest. Participates in *Esquire* magazine symposium at Stanford University; his speech "Writing American Fiction," published in *Commentary* in March 1961, is widely discussed. After a speaking engagement in Oregon, meets Bernard Malamud, whose fiction he admires.

1962   After two years at Iowa, accepts two-year position as writer-in-residence at Princeton. Separates from Margaret Roth. Moves to New York City and commutes to Princeton classes. (Lives at various Manhattan locations until 1970.) Meets Princeton sociologist Melvin Tumin, a Newark native who becomes a friend. Random House publishes *Letting Go*.

1963   Receives Ford Foundation grant to write plays in affiliation with American Place Theater in New York. Is legally separated from Margaret Roth. Becomes close friend of Aaron Asher, a University of Chicago graduate and editor at Meridian Books, original paperback publisher of *Goodbye, Columbus*. In June takes part in American Jewish Congress symposium in Tel Aviv, Israel, along with American writers Leslie Fiedler, Max Lerner, and literary critic David Boroff. Travels in Israel for a month.

1964   Teaches at State University of New York at Stony Brook, Long Island. Reviews plays by James Baldwin, LeRoi Jones, and Edward Albee for newly founded *New York Review of Books*. Spends a month at Yaddo, writers' retreat in Saratoga Springs, New York, that provides free room and board. (Will work at Yaddo for several months at a time throughout the 1960s.) Meets and establishes friendships there with novelist Alison Lurie and painter Julius Goldstein.

1965   Begins to teach comparative literature at University of Pennsylvania one semester each year more or less annually until the mid-1970s. Meets professor Joel Conarroe, who becomes a close friend. Begins work on *When She Was Good* after abandoning another novel, begun in 1962.

1966   Publishes section of *When She Was Good* in *Harper's*. Is increasingly troubled by Vietnam War and in ensuing years takes part in marches and demonstrations against it.

1967   Publishes *When She Was Good*. Begins work on *Portnoy's Complaint*, of which he publishes excerpts in *Esquire*, *Partisan Review*, and *New American Review*, where Ted Solotaroff is editor.

1968   Margaret Roth dies in an automobile accident. Roth spends two months at Yaddo completing *Portnoy's Complaint*.

1969   *Portnoy's Complaint* published in February. Within weeks becomes number-one fiction best seller and a widely discussed cultural phenomenon. Roth makes no public appearances and retreats for several months to Yaddo. Rents house in Woodstock, New York, and meets the painter Philip Guston, who lives nearby. They remain close friends and see each other regularly until Guston's death in 1980. Renews friendship with Bernard Malamud, who like Roth is serving as a member of The Corporation of Yaddo.

1970   Spends March traveling in Thailand, Burma, Cambodia, and Hong Kong. Begins work on *My Life as a Man* and publishes excerpt in *Modern Occasions*. Is elected to National Institute of Arts and Letters and is its youngest member. Commutes to his classes at University of Pennsylvania and lives mainly in Woodstock until 1972.

1971   Excerpts of *Our Gang*, satire of the Nixon administration, appear in *New York Review of Books* and *Modern Occasions*; the book is published by Random House in the fall. Continues work on *My Life as a Man*; writes *The Breast* and *The Great American Novel*. Begins teaching a Kafka course at University of Pennsylvania.

1972   *The Breast*, first book of three featuring protagonist David Kepesh, published by Holt, Rinehart, Winston, where Aaron Asher is his editor. Roth buys old farmhouse and forty acres in northwest Connecticut, one hundred miles from New York City, and moves there from Woodstock. In May travels to Venice, Vienna, and, for the first time, Prague. Meets his translators there, Luba and Rudolph Pilar, and they describe to him the impact of the political situation on Czech writers. In U.S., arranges to meet exiled Czech editor Antonin Liehm in New York; attends Liehm's weekly classes in Czech history, literature, and film at College of Staten Island, City University of New York. Through friendship with Liehm meets numerous Czech exiles, including film directors Ivan Passer and Jiří Weiss, who become friends. Is elected to the American Academy of Arts and Sciences.

1973   Publishes *The Great American Novel* and the essay "Looking at Kafka" in *New American Review*. Returns to Prague and meets novelists Milan Kundera, Ivan Klíma, Ludvík Vaculík, the poet Miroslav Holub, and other writers blacklisted and persecuted by the Soviet-backed

Communist regime; becomes friendly with Rita Klímová, a blacklisted translator and academic, who will serve as Czechoslovakia's first ambassador to U.S. following the 1989 "Velvet Revolution." (Will make annual spring trips to Prague to visit his writer friends until he is denied an entry visa in 1977.) Writes "Country Report" on Czechoslovakia for American PEN. Proposes paperback series, "Writers from the Other Europe," to Penguin Books USA; becomes general editor of the series, selecting titles, commissioning introductions, and overseeing publication of Eastern European writers relatively unknown to American readers. Beginning in 1974, series publishes fiction by Polish writers Jerzy Andrzejewski, Tadeusz Borowski, Tadeusz Konwicki, Witold Gombrowicz, and Bruno Schulz; Hungarian writers György Konrád and Géza Csáth; Yugoslav writer Danilo Kiš; and Czech writers Bohumil Hrabal, Milan Kundera, and Ludvík Vaculík; series ends in 1989. "Watergate Edition" of *Our Gang* published, which includes a new preface by Roth.

1974 Roth publishes *My Life as a Man*. Visits Budapest as well as Prague and meets Budapest writers through Hungarian PEN and the *Hungarian Quarterly*. In Prague meets Václav Havel. Through friend Professor Zdenek Strybyrny, visits and becomes friend of the niece of Franz Kafka, Vera Saudkova, who shows him Kafka family photographs and family belongings; subsequently becomes friendly in London with Marianne Steiner, daughter of Kafka's sister Valli. Also through Strybyrny meets the widow of Jiří Weil; upon his return to America arranges for translation and publication of Weil's novel *Life with a Star* as well as publication of several Weil short stories in *American Poetry Review*, for which he provides an introduction. In Princeton meets Joanna Rostropowicz Clark, wife of friend Blair Clark; she becomes close friend and introduces Roth to contemporary Polish writing and to Polish writers visiting America, including Konwicki and Kazimierz Brandys. Publishes "Imagining Jews" in *New York Review of Books*; essay prompts letter from university professor, editor, writer, and former Jesuit Jack Miles. Correspondence ensues and the two establish a lasting intellectual friendship. In New York, meets teacher, editor, author, and journalist Bernard Avishai; they quickly establish a strong intellectual bond and become lifelong friends.

1975   Aaron Asher leaves Holt and becomes editor in chief at
          Farrar, Straus and Giroux; Roth moves to FSG with Asher
          for publication of *Reading Myself and Others*, a collection
          of interviews and critical essays. Meets British actress Claire
          Bloom.

1976   Interviews Isaac Bashevis Singer about Bruno Schulz for
          New York Times Book Review article to coincide with pub-
          lication of Schulz's *Street of Crocodiles* in "Writers from
          the Other Europe" series. Moves with Claire Bloom to
          London, where they live six to seven months a year for
          the next twelve years. Spends the remaining months in
          Connecticut, where Bloom joins him when she is not act-
          ing in films, television, or stage productions. In London
          resumes an old friendship with British critic A. Alvarez
          and, a few years later, begins a friendship with American
          writer Michael Herr (author of *Dispatches*, which Roth
          admires) and with the American painter R. B. Kitaj. Also
          meets critic and biographer Hermione Lee, who becomes
          a friend, as does novelist Edna O'Brien. Begins regular
          visits to France to see Milan Kundera and another new
          friend, French writer-critic Alain Finkielkraut. Visits Israel
          for the first time since 1963 and returns there regularly,
          keeping a journal that eventually provides ideas and ma-
          terial for novels *The Counterlife* and *Operation Shylock*.
          Meets the writer Aharon Appelfeld in Jerusalem and they
          become close friends.

1977   Publishes *The Professor of Desire*, second book of Kepesh
          trilogy. Beginning in 1977 and continuing over the next
          few years, writes series of TV dramas for Claire Bloom:
          adaptations of *The Name-Day Party*, a short story by
          Chekhov; *Journey into the Whirlwind*, the gulag autobi-
          ography of Eugenia Ginzburg; and, with David Plante,
          It Isn't Fair, Plante's memoir of Jean Rhys. At request
          of Chichester Festival director, modernizes the David
          Magarshack translation of Chekhov's *The Cherry Orchard*
          for Claire Bloom's 1981 performance at the festival as
          Madame Ranyevskaya.

1979   *The Ghost Writer*, first novel featuring novelist Nathan
          Zuckerman as protagonist, is published in its entirety in
          The New Yorker, then published by Farrar, Straus and Gi-
          roux. Bucknell awards Roth his first honorary degree;
          eventually receives honorary degrees from Amherst,

Brown, Columbia, Dartmouth, Harvard, Pennsylvania, and Rutgers, among others.

1980   *A Philip Roth Reader* published, edited by Martin Green. Milan and Vera Kundera visit Connecticut on first trip to U.S.; Roth introduces Kundera to friend and *New Yorker* editor Veronica Geng, who also becomes Kundera's editor at the magazine. Conversation with Milan Kundera, in London and Connecticut, published in *New York Times Book Review*.

1981   Mother dies of a sudden heart attack in Elizabeth, New Jersey. *Zuckerman Unbound* published.

1982   Corresponds with Judith Thurman after reading her biography of Isak Dinesen, and they begin a friendship.

1983   Roth's physician and Litchfield County neighbor, Dr. C. H. Huvelle, retires from his Connecticut practice and the two become close friends.

1984   *The Anatomy Lesson* published. Aaron Asher leaves FSG and David Rieff becomes Roth's editor; the two soon become close friends. Conversation with Edna O'Brien in London published in *New York Times Book Review*. With BBC director Tristram Powell, adapts *The Ghost Writer* for television drama, featuring Claire Bloom; program is aired in U.S. and U.K. Meets University of Connecticut professor Ross Miller and the two forge strong literary friendship.

1985   *Zuckerman Bound*, a compilation of *The Ghost Writer*, *Zuckerman Unbound*, *The Anatomy Lesson*, with epilogue *The Prague Orgy*, published. Adapts *The Prague Orgy* for a British television production that is never realized.

1986   Spends several days in Turin with Primo Levi. Conversation with Levi published in *New York Times Book Review*, which also asks that Roth write a memoir about Bernard Malamud upon Malamud's death at age seventy-two. *The Counterlife* published; wins National Book Critics Circle Award for fiction that year.

1987   Corresponds with exiled Romanian writer Norman Manea, who is living in Berlin, and encourages him to come to live in U.S.; Manea arrives the next year, and the two become close friends.

1988   *The Facts* published. Travels to Jerusalem for Aharon Ap-
        pelfeld interview, which is published in *New York Times
        Book Review*. In Jerusalem, attends daily the trial of Ivan
        Demjanjuk, the alleged Treblinka guard "Ivan the Terri-
        ble." Returns to America to live year-round. Becomes
        Distinguished Professor of Literature at Hunter College
        of the City University of New York, where he will teach
        one semester each year until 1991.

1989   Father dies of brain tumor after yearlong illness. David
        Rieff leaves Farrar, Straus. For the first time since 1970,
        acquires a literary agent, Andrew Wylie of Wylie, Aitken,
        and Stone. Leaves FSG for Simon and Schuster. Writes a
        memoir of Philip Guston, which is published in *Vanity
        Fair* and subsequently reprinted in Guston catalogs.

1990   Travels to post-Communist Prague for conversation with
        Ivan Klíma, published in *New York Review of Books*. *De-
        ception* published by Simon and Schuster. Roth marries
        Claire Bloom in New York.

1991   *Patrimony* published; wins National Book Critics Circle
        Award for biography. Renews strong friendship with Saul
        Bellow.

1992   Reads from *Patrimony* for nationwide reading tour, ex-
        tending into 1993. Publishes brief profile of Norman
        Manea in *New York Times Book Review*.

1993   *Operation Shylock* published; wins PEN/Faulkner Award
        for fiction. Separates from Claire Bloom. Writes *Dr. Hu-
        velle: A Biographical Sketch*, which he publishes privately
        as a thirty-four-page booklet for local distribution.

1994   Divorces Claire Bloom.

1995   Returns to Houghton Mifflin, where John Sterling is his
        editor. *Sabbath's Theater* is published and wins National
        Book Award for fiction.

1997   John Sterling leaves Houghton Mifflin and Wendy Stroth-
        man becomes Roth's editor. *American Pastoral*, first book
        of the "American Trilogy," is published and wins Pulitzer
        Prize for fiction.

1998   *I Married a Communist*, the second book of the trilogy,
        is published and wins Ambassador Book Award of the
        English-Speaking Union. In October Roth attends three-

day international literary program honoring his work in Aix-en-Provence. In November receives National Medal of Arts at the White House.

2000   Publishes *The Human Stain*, final book of American trilogy, which wins PEN/Faulkner Award in U.S., the W. H. Smith Award in the U.K., and the Prix Medicis for the best foreign book of the year in France. Publishes "Rereading Saul Bellow" in *The New Yorker*.

2001   Publishes *The Dying Animal*, final book of the Kepesh trilogy, and *Shop Talk*, a collection of interviews with and essays on Primo Levi, Aharon Appelfeld, I. B. Singer, Edna O'Brien, Milan Kundera, Ivan Klíma, Philip Guston, Bernard Malamud, and Saul Bellow, and an exchange with Mary McCarthy. Receives highest award of the American Academy of Arts and Letters, the Gold Medal in fiction, given every six years "for the entire work of the recipient," previously awarded to Willa Cather, Edith Wharton, John Dos Passos, William Faulkner, Saul Bellow, and Isaac Bashevis Singer, among others. Is awarded the Edward McDowell Medal; William Styron, chair of the selection committee, remarks at the presentation ceremony that Roth "has caused to be lodged in our collective consciousness a small, select company of human beings who are as arrestingly alive and as fully realized as any in modern fiction."

2002   Wins the National Book Foundation's Medal for Distinguished Contribution to American Letters.

2003   Receives honorary degrees at Harvard University and University of Pennsylvania. Roth's work now appears in thirty-one languages.

2004   Publishes novel *The Plot Against America*, which becomes a best seller and wins the W. H. Smith Award for best book of the year in the U.K.; Roth is the first writer in the forty-six-year history of the prize to win it twice.

2005   *The Plot Against America* wins the Society of American Historians' James Fenimore Cooper Prize as the outstanding historical novel on an American theme for 2003–04. On October 23, Roth's childhood home at 81 Summit Avenue in Newark is marked with a plaque as a historic landmark and the nearby intersection is named Philip Roth Plaza.

2006   Publishes *Everyman* in May. Becomes fourth recipient of PEN's highest writing honor, the PEN/Nabokov Award. Receives Power of the Press Award from the New Jersey Library Association for Newark *Star-Ledger* eulogy to his close friend, Newark librarian and city historian Charles Cummings.

2007   Receives PEN/Faulkner Award for *Everyman*, the first author to be given the award three times. Wins the inaugural PEN/Saul Bellow Award for Achievement in American Fiction and Italy's first Grinzane-Masters Award, an award dedicated to the grand masters of literature. *Exit Ghost* is published.

2008   Roth's seventy-fifth birthday is marked by a celebration of his life and work at Columbia University. *Indignation* is published.

2009   Honored in program at Queens College, "A 50th Anniversary Celebration of the Work of Philip Roth." Receives the Charles Cummings Award from the Newark Preservation and Landmarks Committee, the sponsor of semi-annual tours of "Philip Roth's Newark." Publishes *The Humbling*. Wins the annual literary prize of the German newspaper *Die Welt*.

2010   Receives *Paris Review*'s Hadada Award in April. Publishes *Nemesis* in September. Retires from writing fiction.

2011   In March receives the National Humanities Medal at the White House. Wins the Man Booker International Prize.

2012   Receives Library of Congress Creative Achievement Award. In October, wins Spain's Prince of Asturias Award for Literature.

2013   Named *Commandeur de la Légion d'Honneur* of France. Awarded the Emerson-Thoreau Medal of the American Academy of Arts and Sciences. Receives PEN/Allen Foundation Literary Service Award for "his personal involvement in promoting freedom of expression in Eastern Europe." Eightieth birthday celebration, organized by the Philip Roth Society in conjunction with the Newark Preservation and Landmarks Committee, is held at the Newark Museum.

2014   Receives honorary degree from Jewish Theological Seminary in New York. Awarded Yaddo Art Medal.

Note on the Texts

This volume contains thirty-seven essays, interviews, and speeches by Philip Roth. For this book, Roth has selected the contents from among his nonfiction writings, including texts, some of them nominally revised, from *Reading Myself and Others* (New York: Farrar, Straus and Giroux, 1975; exp. ed., New York: Penguin, 1985). The conversations in *Shop Talk: A Writer and His Colleagues and Their Work* (2001), appear here in the original text, whereas *Rereading Saul Bellow* and previously published pieces in *Explanations* appear in slightly different form. The following list provides information about the first publication for each of the selections in this volume.

FROM READING MYSELF AND OTHERS

"I Always Wanted You to Admire My Fasting"; or, Looking at Kafka. *American Review*, May 1973.

Writing American Fiction. *Commentary*, March 1961.

New Jewish Stereotypes. *American Judaism*, Winter 1961, as "The New Jewish Stereotypes."

Writing About Jews. *Commentary*, December 1963.

On *Portnoy's Complaint. New York Times Book Review*, February 23, 1969.

In Response to Those Who Have Asked Me: How Did You Come to Write That Book, Anyway? *American Poetry Review*, July–August 1974.

Imagining Jews. *New York Review of Books*, September 29, 1974.

Writing and the Powers That Be. *American Poetry Review*, July–August 1974.

After Eight Books. *Ontario Review*, Fall 1974.

Interview with *Le Nouvel Observateur*. *Le Nouvel Observateur*, May 1981.

Interview with *The London Sunday Times*. *London Sunday Times*, February 19, 1985.

Interview with *The Paris Review. Paris Review*, Fall 1985.

Interview on *Zuckerman*. Asher Z. Milbauer and Donald G. Watson, eds., *Reading Philip Roth* (New York: St. Martin's, 1988), as "An Interview with Philip Roth."

SHOP TALK

Conversation in Turin with Primo Levi. *New York Times Book Review*, October 12, 1986, as "A Man Saved by His Skills: An Interview with Primo Levi."

Conversation in Jerusalem with Aharon Appelfeld. *New York Times Book Review*, February 28, 1988, as "Walking the Way of the Survivor: A Talk with Aharon Appelfeld."

Conversation in Prague with Ivan Klíma. *New York Review of Books*, April 12, 1990, as "A Conversation in Prague."

Conversation in New York with Isaac Bashevis Singer about Bruno Schulz. *New York Times Book Review*, February 13, 1977, as "Roth and Singer on Bruno Schulz."

Conversation in London and Connecticut with Milan Kundera. *New York Times Book Review*, November 30, 1980, as "The Most Original Book of the Season."

Conversation in London with Edna O'Brien. *New York Times Book Review*, November 18, 1984, as "A Conversation with Edna O'Brien: The Body Contains the Life Story."

An Exchange with Mary McCarthy. *New Yorker*, December 28, 1998–January 4, 1999.

Pictures of Malamud. *New York Times Book Review*, April 20, 1986.

Pictures by Guston. *Vanity Fair*, October 1989, as "Breast Baring."

Rereading Saul Bellow. *New Yorker*, October 9, 2000.

EXPLANATIONS

Juice or Gravy? Talk at Lotos Club, New York, 1994, published as afterword to twenty-fifth anniversary edition of *Portnoy's Complaint* (New York: Vintage, 1994) and in *The New York Times Book Review*, September 18, 1994.

Patrimony. Acceptance speech, New Jersey Historical Society annual award, October 5, 1992. Previously unpublished.

Yiddish/English. Lifetime Achievement Award acceptance speech, YIVO Institute for Jewish Research, December 4, 1997. Previously unpublished.

"I Have Fallen in Love with American Names." Acceptance speech, National Book Foundation Medal for Distinguished Contribution to American Letters, November 20, 2002. Previously unpublished.

My Uchronia. *New York Times Book Review*, September 19, 2004, as "The Story Behind 'The Plot Against America.'"

Eric Duncan. Remarks at Roth's seventy-fifth birthday celebration at Columbia University, April 11, 2008. Previously unpublished.

Errata. The first section was first published as "An Open Letter to Wikipedia" on the "Page-Turner" blog of *The New Yorker*, September 6, 2012, http://www.newyorker.com/books/page-turner/an-open-letter-to-wikipedia. The rest of the essay is published here for the first time.

"Tyranny Is Better Organized than Freedom." *New York Times*, April 20, 2013, as "In Memory of a Friend, Teacher and Mentor."

A Czech Education. Acceptance speech, PEN Literary Service Award, 2013 PEN Literary Gala, April 30, 2013. Previously unpublished.

The Primacy of *Ludus*. Acceptance speech, Emerson–Thoreau Medal, read by Stephen Greenblatt at ceremony of the American Academy of Arts and Sciences, October 11, 2013. Previously unpublished.

Interview on *The Ghost Writer*. *The Book Haven* blog, February 3, 2014, as "An Interview with Philip Roth: The Novelist's Obsession Is with Language," https://bookhaven.stanford.edu/2014/02/an-interview -with-philip-roth-the-novelists-obsession-is-with-language/.

Interview with *Svenska Dagbladet*. *Svenska Dagbladet* (Stockholm; in Swedish), March 2, 2014, with publication the same day in English in the *New York Times Book Review*.

Forty-Five Years On. *T: The New York Times Style Magazine*, November 6, 2014, as part of "Old Books, New Thoughts," which featured Roth and six other writers reflecting on their earlier works.

The Ruthless Intimacy of Fiction. Speech given at Roth's eightieth birthday celebration at the Newark Museum, March 19, 2013, first published in *Philip Roth at 80* (New York: Library of America, 2013).

Notes

In the notes below, the reference numbers denote page and line of this volume (the line count includes chapter headings). Quotations from Shakespeare are keyed to *The Riverside Shakespeare*, ed. G. Blakemore Evans (Boston: Houghton Mifflin, 1974).

READING MYSELF AND OTHERS

6.6　Karl Rossmann, his American greenhorn.] Immigrant protagonist of Kafka's unfinished novel *The Man Who Disappeared*, which was given the title *Amerika* when it was first published posthumously in 1927 by his close friend, literary executor, and biographer Max Brod (1884–1968).

6.8–10　escape . . . Great Nature Theatre of Oklahoma?] In a chapter of *Amerika* that Max Brod titled "The Nature Theatre of Oklahoma," Rossmann leaves New York after being hired by the Theatre of Oklahoma, where according to its recruitment advertisement "Everyone is welcome! [. . .] If you want to be an artist join our company!"

6.11–12　Mann . . . Princeton] The German novelist Thomas Mann (1875–1955) was a lecturer at Princeton University, 1938–40.

6.16　once bid Max Brod to dispose of] In two separate documents, Kafka instructed Brod to burn his unpublished manuscripts after his death, a request that Brod did not carry out.

6.19　Mann's unmatched "religious humorist"] From "Homage," Mann's preface to the 1940 English translation of Kafka's novel *The Castle*.

6.25　K.] The protagonist of Kafka's novel *The Castle* (1926) is known only as "K." Joseph K., protagonist of *The Trial* (1925), is also sometimes referred to simply as "K."

11.38–40　*As Franz Kafka awoke one morning . . . Jew.*] Cf. the opening line of Kafka's novella *The Metamorphosis* (1915): "As Gregor Samsa awoke one morning from uneasy dreams he found himself transformed in his bed into a gigantic insect" (translation by Edwin and Willa Muir, 1933).

15.22　"aces up"] A street game played with a rubber ball.

17.17　V-mail] Printed forms for correspondence with military personnel that were microfilmed and sent overseas, then enlarged and delivered.

18.5　*gelt*] Yiddish: money.

19.39　W.P.A.] Works Progress Administration, a federal agency founded during the New Deal that provided work for, among others, artists and performers.

20.5 *Waiting for Lefty*] Play (1935) by left-wing American playwright and screenwriter Clifford Odets (1906–1963).

23.8 *The Way of All Flesh*] Semi-autobiographical novel (1903) by the English writer Samuel Butler (1835–1902).

25.3–4 death of two teenage girls.] Barbara Grimes, fifteen, and her sister, Patricia, thirteen, disappeared in the Brighton Park neighborhood of Chicago on the night of December 28, 1956. Their bodies were found in Willow Springs, Illinois, on January 22, 1957. No one was ever charged in their murders, and the case remains open. Their mother, Loretta Grimes, died in 1989.

25.20–21 Dixie Dugan] Long-running newspaper comic strip by the writer J. P. McEvoy (1897–1958) and the illustrator John H. Striebel (1891–1962), derived from McEvoy's popular novel *Show Girl* (1928).

27.24 Charles Van Doren] The son of a prominent literary family, Van Doren (b. 1926), an instructor of English at Columbia University, achieved national stardom for his performance on the television quiz show *Twenty-One* in 1956–57. Because of suspicions about the fairness and honesty of *Twenty-One* and other TV quiz shows, the program was investigated by a Manhattan grand jury and later the U.S. House Committee on Interstate Commerce. In a November 1959 congressional hearing Van Doren testified that the outcomes on *Twenty-One* had been rigged.

27.24 Roy Cohn and David Schine?] New York attorney Roy Cohn (1927–1986) was the chief counsel for the Senate Subcommittee on Investigations when it was chaired by Senator Joseph McCarthy, 1953–54. McCarthy announced an investigation into alleged Communist infiltration of the army in 1954 after the army refused Cohn's request to grant special privileges to his friend David Schine (1927–1996), a recently drafted private; the subsequent Army-McCarthy hearings addressed Cohn's and McCarthy's conduct in their dealings with the army and caused McCarthy's national influence to wane after his erratic performance during the televised proceedings. Cohn resigned as committee counsel in August 1954 and went into private law practice.

27.24–25 Sherman Adams and Bernard Goldfine?] Sherman Adams (1899–1986) resigned his position as White House chief of staff in 1958 when it was learned that he had accepted expensive gifts from the textiles manufacturer Bernard Goldfine (1890–1967), then under investigation for violations of Federal Trade Commission regulations.

28.24–26 When Edmund Wilson says . . . this country] In the essay "The Author at Sixty" (1956) by the American literary critic Edmund Wilson (1895–1972).

28.39–29.1 *Cash McCall . . . Advise and Consent*] The novels *Cash McCall* (1955) by Cameron Hawley (1905–1969); *The Man in the Gray Flannel Suit* (1955) by Sloan Wilson (1920–2003); *Marjorie Morningstar* (1955) by Herman Wouk (b. 1915); *The Enemy Camp* (1958) by Jerome Weidman (1913–1998); and *Advise and Consent* (1959) by Allen Drury (1918–1998).

29.21 "Dover Beach"] Poem (1851) by the English poet and critic Matthew Arnold (1822–1888).

29.26 *amor-vincit-omnia*] Latin: love conquers all.

31.14 Gregory Corso] American Beat poet (1930–2001).

34.6–7 Herbert Gold . . . Grace Paley] The American fiction writers Herbert Gold (b. 1924), author of *The Optimist* (1959) and *Therefore Be Bold* (1960); Arthur Granit (b. 1917), author of *The Time of the Peaches* (1959); Thomas Berger (1924–2014), author of *Crazy in Berlin* (1958) and *Little Big Man* (1964); and Grace Paley (1922–2007), author of the story collections *The Little Disturbances of Man* (1959) and *Enormous Changes at the Last Minute* (1974).

36.18 Lord Chesterfield] British statesman and man of letters (1694–1773).

44.28–29 Moishe Oysher or Eddie Fisher?] Moishe Oysher (1906–1958), Russian-born cantor and actor in the Yiddish theater; popular Jewish-American singer Eddie Fisher (1928–2010).

46.10 "melon-breasted." (See Thomas Wolfe.)] See, for example, chapter 53 of Wolfe's *Of Time and the River* (1935), which describes the "melon-heavy breasts" of "potent young Jewesses, thick, hot, and heavy with a female odour."

47.18–19 phrases are Lionel Trilling's] From the essay "On the Teaching of Modern Literature" by American literary critic Lionel Trilling (1905–1975), collected in *Beyond Culture* (1965); it was first published in *Partisan Review* (Jan.–Feb. 1961) under the title "On the Modern Element in Modern Literature."

48.22 Adolf Eichmann] SS officer (1906–1962) who headed the Jewish Department of the Reich Main Security Office in Nazi Germany, 1939–45, and played a major role in organizing the deportation of European Jews to extermination camps. He was captured in Argentina by Israeli operatives on May 11, 1960, and taken to Israel, where he was tried for crimes against humanity in 1961 and hanged on May 31, 1962.

48.22–23 Sal Mineo as a Jewish freedom fighter.] The American actor Sal Mineo (1939–1976) played the role of Dov Landau, a member of the Irgun, in the movie adaptation (1960) of Leon Uris's *Exodus*.

54.27 *Sayings of the Fathers*] A tractate of the Talmud.

63.10 Governor Wallace] Segregationist politician George Wallace (1919–1998), governor of Alabama, 1963–67, 1971–79, and 1983–87, independent candidate for president in 1968, and a candidate for the Democratic presidential nomination in 1964, 1972, and 1976.

67.27 Chekhov distinguishes] In a letter to A. S. Suvorin, December 23, 1888.

69.17 *The Second City comics*] Chicago-based comedy troupe founded in 1959.

69.21–26 Lenny Bruce . . . "case."] Comedian Lenny Bruce (1925–1966) was arrested numerous times on obscenity charges.

69.23 Joseph K.] See note 6.25.

72.6 *Abie's Irish Rose*] Long-running Broadway comedy (1922) by playwright Ann Nichols (1891–1966).

79.25 Leonard Lyons] A columnist for the *New York Post,* Leonard Lyons (1906–1976) wrote "The Lyons Den" from 1934 to 1974.

82.20–22 first book . . . Ali McGraw movie] A movie adaptation of *Goodbye, Columbus,* directed by Larry Peerce (b. 1930) and starring Ali McGraw (b. 1939), was released in 1969.

84.30–32 Arnold Rothstein's fixing . . . World Series.] The gangster Arnold Rothstein (1882–1928) was alleged to have been involved in the fixing of the 1919 World Series, when eight players for the Chicago White Sox, including star outfielder "Shoeless Joe" Jackson (1889–1951), deliberately lost games against the Cincinnati Reds. Rothstein won about $350,000 by betting on the Reds in the series.

84.35 *sechel*] Yiddish: sense, smarts, wits.

89.33–34 Philip Rahv's categories . . . paleface] See the essay "Paleface and Redskin" (1939) by editor and critic Philip Rahv (1908–1973).

97.35 *pittrice*] Italian: woman painter.

102.2 Goebbels-Streicher script] Joseph Goebbels (1897–1945) was the Nazi minister of propaganda, 1933–45. Goebbels committed suicide in Berlin on May 1, 1945. Julius Streicher (1885–1946), an early member of the Nazi party, was publisher of the virulently anti-Semitic newspaper *Der Stürmer,* 1923–45. Streicher was convicted of crimes against humanity at Nuremberg and hanged on October 16, 1946.

102.24 Weizmann] Chaim Weizmann (1874–1952), chemist and statesman who was the first president of Israel, 1949–52.

102.24 Jabotinsky] Zionist leader Vladimir Jabotinsky (1880–1940).

102.25 Moshe Dayan] Israeli military commander and political leader (1915–1981) who served as chief of staff of the Israel Defense Forces, 1953–58, defense minister, 1967–74, and foreign minister, 1977–79; he was regarded as a hero of the Sinai and Six Day wars.

102.26 Meir Kahane] American-born rabbi (1932–1990) who founded the militant Jewish Defense League in 1968 and immigrated in 1971 to Israel, where he founded the extreme right-wing Kach political party. Kahane was assassinated in New York City in 1990 by an Egyptian-American terrorist.

107.8 *Deep Throat*] Pornographic movie (1972) starring Linda Lovelace, stage name of Linda Susan Boreman (1949–2002).

109.23–24 Gabriel Heatter] Radio host (1890–1972) of a program based at WOR in New York City; optimistic in tone, the show began with the catch-phrase "There is good news tonight" during World War II.

110.18 *New York Post*] Under the ownership of Dorothy Schiff (1903–1989), 1939–76, the *Post* was an editorially liberal newspaper.

113.24 Leslie Fiedler] Literary critic (1917–2003), author of *Love and Death in the American Novel* (1960).

113.24–25 Mark Schorer] Literary critic (1908–1977), biographer and professor of English at the University of California, Berkeley, author of *Sinclair Lewis: An American Life* (1961).

113.26–27 Alan Lelchuk] American novelist (b. 1938), whose books include *American Mischief* (1973) and *Miriam at Thirty-Four* (1974).

114.6 "lice of literature," Dickens called them] In a letter to the English actor William Charles Macready, April 1, 1842.

114.27–28 "Reviewing," Virginia Woolf] The essay was first published in 1939 and later collected in *The Captain's Death Bed* (1950).

115.33–35 "collection of opinions . . . book."] From "The Literary Worker's Polonius: A Brief Guide for Authors and Editors" (1935), collected in Wilson's *The Shores of Light* (1952).

118.4 *Urn-Burial*] Treatise (1658) by the English writer Sir Thomas Browne (1605–1682).

119.4 *Orlando*] Novel (1928) by Virginia Woolf.

125.19 "L'art . . . *Gide.*] Cf. an 1896 journal entry by the French writer André Gide (1869–1951): "L'oeuvre d'art est une idée qu'on exagère" ("The work of art is the exaggeration of an idea").

125.28 woman activist] Vivian Gornick (b. 1935); her essay was published in the *Village Voice*, December 6, 1976.

136.5 Sonny Liston] American boxer (1932–1971) who was world heavy-weight champion, 1962–64.

146.36 Jack Benny] American entertainer (1894–1974), star of vaudeville and movies and the host of the weekly *Jack Benny Program* on radio, 1932–58, and television, 1950–65.

146.40 U.J.A.] United Jewish Appeal.

147.1 Céline] Louis-Ferdinand Céline (pseud. Louis Ferdinand Destouches, 1894–1961), French novelist and physician, author of *Journey to the End of the Night* (1932).

147.24–25   the Genet that Genet presents himself as] The French poet, essayist, and novelist Jean Genet (1910–1986), an illegitimate son of a prostitute, was a petty criminal before becoming a writer. He wrote candidly of his homosexuality and life as a hustler in autobiographical novels such as *The Miracle of the Rose* (1946) and *The Thief's Journal* (1949).

147.25–26   unsavory Molloy impersonated by Beckett.] In Beckett's novel *Molloy* (1951).

147.27–28   Rebecca West was writing about Augustine] In the monographic study *St. Augustine* (1933) by the British writer Rebecca West (1892–1983).

147.31   Colette] French novelist (1873–1954), author of *The Vagabond* (1910), *The Shackle* (1913), and *Chéri* (1920).

147.32–35   Gombrowicz . . . Konwicki] The Polish novelists Witold Gombrowicz (1904–1969), author of *Ferdydurke* (1937), *Trans-Atlantyk* (1953), and *Pornografia* (1960), and Tadeusz Konwicki (1926–2015), author of *A Dreambook for Our Time* (1963), *The Polish Complex* (1977), and *A Minor Apocalypse* (1979).

149.17–18   Olivia . . . c'est moi.] Cf. the quote attributed to the French writer Gustave Flaubert (1821–1880) about his novel *Madame Bovary* (1857): "Madame Bovary, c'est moi!"

150.17   Life is long and art is shorter.] A reversal of the dictum from antiquity *Ars longa, vita brevis* (art is long, life is short).

150.24–25   the author of *The Naked and the Dead*] Norman Mailer.

151.34   John Berryman said] In an interview in the *Paris Review*'s winter 1972 issue.

153.21   *Oblomov*] Novel (1859) by Russian writer Ivan Goncharov (1812–1891).

155.25   Abbie Hoffman] American political activist and prankster (1936–1989).

157.28   Camus's plague] As depicted in *The Plague* (1947), novel by the French philosopher and novelist Albert Camus (1913–1960).

158.7   June Allyson] American actor (1917–2006) cast in wholesome roles in musicals such as *Two Girls and a Sailor* (1944) and *Good News* (1947).

159.31   Falklands crisis] Argentine forces seized the Falkland Islands, a British overseas territory in the South Atlantic, on April 2, 1982, beginning an armed conflict that ended when the British recaptured the islands on June 14, 1982.

164.16   "The March of Time."] Series of short films (1935–51) that combined documentary footage with dramatic reenactments of current events.

165.7–8   Louis L'Amour] American writer (1908–1988), a prolific and popular writer of Western novels.

169.29–30   witness Lawrence on American literature] Chiefly in D. H. Lawrence's book *Studies in Classic American Literature* (1923).

171.37–38   an attack on *Portnoy's Complaint*] In two essays published in the Israeli newspaper *Haaretz* shortly after the novel was published.

175.8   Josef Škvorecký] Czech writer (1924–2012) who fled Czechoslovakia in the late 1960s and settled in Canada; his novels include *The Cowards* (1958) and *The Engineer of Human Souls* (1977).

SHOP TALK

190.38–39   catastrophe of the Italian armistice of September 8, 1943] The surrender of Italy to the Allies was publicly announced on September 8, 1943, which was followed by the German occupation of most of the country.

191.4   Mussolini's racial laws] Anti-Semitic laws enacted in Italy in 1938–39 that were modeled on the Nazi Nuremberg Laws of 1935.

196.14–16   Momigliano wrote . . . thought they were."] In "The Jews of Italy," essay first published in English in the *New York Review of Books*, October 24, 1985, by the Italian historian Arnaldo Momigliano (1908–1987).

197.4   *emarginato*] Italian: an outcast.

198.13   Joseph Roth] Jewish novelist and journalist (1894–1939) born in the Austro-Hungarian Empire, author of the novels *Job* (1930) and *The Radetzky March* (1932).

198.13   Potok] Chaim Potok, American novelist (1929–2002), whose books include *The Chosen* (1967) and *My Name Is Asher Lev* (1972).

199.14   *The Confessions of Zeno*] Novel (*La coscienza di Zeno*, 1923) by the Italian writer Italo Svevo, pseudonym of Ettore Schmitz (1861–1928), under the title with which it was first published in English translation.

199.26–27   Moravia . . . nom de plume] Alberto Pincherle (1907–1990) wrote under the pseudonym Alberto Moravia.

202.25   according to Max Brod, "spellbound in the family circle"] From *Franz Kafka: A Life* (1937) by Max Brod (see note 6.6).

204.27   Martin Buber] Jewish philosopher and theologian (1878–1965), author of *I and Thou* (1923).

204.28   Stefan Zweig's] Stefan Zweig (1881–1942), Vienna-born Jewish writer whose many books include the novel *Beware of Pity* (1939) and the memoir *The World of Yesterday* (1942).

206.26   Kosinski's *Painted Bird*] Novel (1965) by the Polish-born Jewish writer Jerzy Kosinski (1933–1991) recounting a boy's horrific journey through Eastern Europe during World War II.

206.29–30   landscape as uncongenial . . . Beckett's *Molloy.*] In *Molloy* (1951), the title character and the detective Moran wander through desolate landscapes that offer little comfort; both commit murders.

210.2   Agnon] S. Y. Agnon (1888–1970), Israeli writer born in Galicia who was awarded the Nobel Prize in Literature in 1966; his novels include *The Bridal Canopy* (1931) and *To This Day* (1952).

212.40–213.1   Sergius O'Shaughnessy . . . Stephen Rojack] Sergius O'Shaughnessy, protagonist of Norman Mailer's novel *The Deer Park* (1955) and short story "The Time of Her Time" (1959); Stephen Rojack, narrator and hero of his novel *An American Dream* (1965).

213.2   Lepke Buchalter or Gurrah Shapiro, he's Gary Gilmore.] Louis "Lepke" Buchalter (1897–1944) and Jacob "Gurrah" Shapiro (1899–1947) founded the gang of hired killers known as "Murder Incorporated"; Gary Gilmore (1940–1977), the subject of Mailer's *The Executioner's Song* (1979), was executed in Utah for two murders committed during armed robberies.

216.13   the "black milk" of the poet Paul Celan, morning, noon, and night] Recurring phrase in poem "Todesfuge" ("Death-fugue"), published in 1948, by Romanian-born Jewish poet Paul Celan (pseud. Paul Antschel, 1920–1970).

217.4   Jan Kott called a "European education"] In reference to the Polish writer Tadeusz Borowski (1922–1951), who was imprisoned at Auschwitz and later committed suicide; see Kott's afterword to a story by Borowski in *American Poetry Review*, November–December 1975. Kott (1914–2001) was a Polish theater critic best known for *Shakespeare Our Contemporary*, essays first published in book form in French translation in 1962, then in English in 1964.

219.13   "Gooseberries"] Story (1898) by the Russian writer Anton Chekhov (1860–1904).

219.25   Milan Kundera's] See the interview with Kundera in this volume, pp. 255–63.

226.29–30   "the muse of censorship"] The title of a 1984 lecture by George Steiner (b. 1929), Paris-born American literary critic and fiction writer.

228.31   Škvorecký] See note 175.8.

230.17   the occupation in 1968.] On August 21, 1968, under orders from Moscow, Warsaw Pact troops invaded Czechoslovakia to quash the "Prague Spring" movement championed by Alexander Dubček (1921–1992), who upon his appointment as the first secretary of the Czechoslovak Communist Party in January 1968 had begun instituting reforms in accord with a vision of "socialism with a human face."

230.20–22   the memory of Munich and the Western powers' desertion of Czechoslovakia] According to an agreement signed in Munich on September 30, 1938, by the leaders of Nazi Germany, Italy, France, and Great Britain, the largely German-speaking "Sudetenland" region of Czechoslovakia was ceded to Germany; British prime minister Neville Chamberlain (1869–1940) declared upon his return to England that the agreement would ensure "peace in our time." Germany occupied the remainder of Czechoslovakia on March 15, 1939.

231.18   signed Charter 77.] In December 1976 a group of Czechoslovak dissidents drafted Charter 77, a declaration calling on the Czechoslovak government to uphold the basic human rights it had agreed to respect in the 1975 Helsinki Accords and in other international conventions. When Vaclav Havel (1936–2011), Pavel Landovský (1936–2014), and Ludvík Vaculík (1926–2015) attempted to deliver the declaration, which had been signed by more than two hundred individuals, to the Federal Assembly building in Prague on January 6, 1977, they were arrested and interrogated by the state security police. The text of Charter 77 was banned in Czechoslovakia but circulated in samizdat versions and was published in the West. Members of the Charter 77 movement were continually harassed and sometimes imprisoned by the authorities until the overthrow of the Communist regime in the "Velvet Revolution" of 1989.

232.29   Capek . . . Hasek] Journalist, playwright, and novelist Karel Čapek (1890–1938), author of the play *R.U.R.* (1920); Jaroslav Hašek (1883–1923), author of the unfinished comic novel *The Good Soldier Švejk* (1920–23).

233.30   Tadeusz Borowski] See note 217.4.

234.1   Konwicki, Danilo Kis] Konwicki, see note 147.32–35; Serbian fiction writer Danilo Kiš (1935–1989), author of *A Tomb for Boris Davidovich* (1976).

236.9–10   an extensive essay . . . a play about his love affair with Felice Bauer.] The essay "The Swords Are Approaching: Franz Kafka's Sources of Inspiration" (1985) and the play *Kafka and Felice* (1983).

237.9   Milena Jesenska] Czech writer Milena Jesenská (1896–1944), who began corresponding with Kafka after asking if she could translate his story "The Stoker" from German to Czech. Their relationship ended when she refused to leave her husband for him. See pp. 7–8 in this volume.

238.30   Werfel] Prague-born novelist, poet, and playwright Franz Werfel (1890–1945) who wrote in German, best known for his novel *The Song of Bernadette* (1941).

238.30   Einstein] Albert Einstein lived in Prague from 1911 to 1912.

240.13   President Husak] Gustav Husák (1913–1991), general secretary of the Czechoslovak Communist Party, 1969–87, and president of Czechoslovakia, 1975–89.

241.9   Tomáš Masaryk] Czech statesman, military leader, and writer (1850–1937), the first president of the Republic of Czechoslovakia, 1918–35.

241.35   Charter 77] See note 231.18.

242.3   Civic Forum] Czech political movement and party cofounded by Václav Havel in 1989, which grew out of the Charter 77 movement.

242.8–17   Alexander Dubček . . . second-highest function in the state.] Alexander Dubček (see note 230.17) served as chairman of the Federal Assembly in Czechoslovakia, 1989–92.

244.12   Cortázar] The Argentine writer Julio Cortázar (1914–1984), author of the novel *Hopscotch* (1963), the story collection *Blow-Up and Other Stories* (1968), and many other books.

246.31   Agnon] See note 210.2.

247.27–28   if Kafka was ever translated into Yiddish.] Very few of Kafka's works were translated into Yiddish; *Der Prozes*, a translation of Kafka's *The Trial* by the Yiddish poet Melech Ravitch (pseud. Zekharye Khone Bergner, 1893–1976), was published in New York in 1966.

249.5   Litvaks] Lithuanian Jews.

249.33–34   Gombrowicz] See note 147.32–35.

251.35–36   Kafka's remark] From an entry in his diary, January 8, 1914.

253.38–39   Isaac Babel in Russia] Babel (1894–1940) became famous in the Soviet Union during the 1920s for the stories collected in *Konarmia* (1926, translated as *Red Cavalry*, 1929) and *Odessa rasskazy* (1931). He was arrested by the NKVD on May 15, 1939, and falsely accused of belonging to a secret Trotskyite organization and of spying for Austria and France. Babel confessed to the charges after seventy-two hours of interrogation, but later recanted his confession. Sentenced to death at a secret trial on January 26, 1940, he was shot the following day.

253.39   in Czechoslovakia, Jirí Weil] Czech Jewish writer (1900–1959), author of the novel *Life with a Star* (1949), who spent much of World War II in hiding in German-occupied Prague.

254.20   Hadassah] Zionist women's organization.

255.31–32   Russian invasion of 1968] See note 230.17.

256.23   Musil's] Robert Musil (1880–1942), Austrian writer best known for his unfinished multivolume novel *The Man Without Qualities*, the first three books of which were published in 1930, 1933, and 1943, respectively.

259.15–17   André Breton . . . talked about the glass house in which he wished to live.] See *Nadja* (1927): "I myself shall continue living in my glass house where you can always see who comes to call; where everything hanging from the ceiling and on the walls stays where it is as if by magic, where I sleep nights in a glass bed, under glass sheets, where *who I am* will sooner or later appear etched by a diamond."

261.39   Georges Bataille] French writer and philosopher (1897–1962), author of *Story of the Eye* (1928), *Blue of Noon* (1935, pub. 1957), and *L'Erotisme* (1957).

264.20–22   famous lyrical photograph . . . Virginia Woolf] A portrait of

Woolf (then Virginia Stephen) at the age of twenty taken in 1902 by the British photographer George Charles Beresford (1864–1938).

268.31–32   Joyce said that Ireland is the sow that eats its farrow.] Cf. *A Portrait of the Artist as a Young Man* (1916), ch. 5.

269.12   Yeats's line—"Romantic Ireland's dead and gone"] Repeated line in Yeats's "September 1913" (1913).

269.15   Frank Tuohy] Irish novelist (1925–1999) and biographer of Yeats.

269.33   a little book edited by T. S. Eliot] *Introducing James Joyce: A Selection of Joyce's Prose* (1942).

270.39   "the second sex"] Title of foundational feminist study by the French philosopher and intellectual Simone de Beauvoir (1908–1986).

271.39–272.1   Heathcliff/Mr. Rochester syndrome . . . pain and separation.] Men whom the protagonists of Emily Brontë's *Wuthering Heights* (1847) and Charlotte Brontë's *Jane Eyre* (1847), respectively, fall in love with and are separated from.

272.17   Marina Tsvetayeva] Russian poet, playwright, and essayist (1892–1941) who lived in exile, 1922–39, mostly in Paris; after her return to the Soviet Union her husband was executed and her daughter Alya imprisoned. Evacuated to a small town outside Moscow during the Nazi invasion, she was suspected of being a spy. Unable to support herself or her teenage son, she hanged herself on August 31, 1941.

272.21   Leonard Woolf] English colonial administrator, writer, and publisher (1880–1969), the husband of Virginia Woolf.

272.28–29   Flaubert's description of his room echoing with curses and cries of distress] In Flaubert's letter to Alfred LePoittevin, May 13, 1845: "I myself suffered a long period of suffocation: the walls of my room in the rue de l'Est still echo with the frightful curses, the foot-stampings, the cries of distress I gave vent to when I was alone there."

273.27   Philip Rahv] Critic and editor (see note 89.33–34), cofounder of *Partisan Review*; his essays are collected in *Image and Idea* (1949), *The Myth and the Powerhouse* (1965), and *Literature and the Sixth Sense* (1969).

274.28   Leon [Botstein]] American conductor and writer (b. 1946), since 1975 the president of Bard College.

278.29   "who never stopped hurting"] From Malamud's story "Angel Levine" (1955).

279.15–17   "He tried to say . . . black-painted window."] The penultimate paragraph of Malamud's story "The Bill" (1951).

280.31–32   "A child throwing a ball straight up saw a bit of pale sky"] From the opening paragraph of "The Bill."

281.12–13   an essay about American Jewish writers] "Imagining Jews"; see pp. 78–103 in this volume.

281.33–34   Blake says, "Opposition is true friendship,"] In the long poem *The Marriage of Heaven and Hell* (1790–93).

289.14–15   Uriah Heepisms] Insincere phases; in Charles Dickens's *David Copperfield* (1850), Uriah Heep is an obsequious clerk who secretly connives against his employer Mr. Wickfield.

289.39   Mutt and Jeff] Protagonists of a long-running comic strip, 1907–83.

290.6   John Mitchell] Lawyer and government official (1913–1988), attorney general in the Nixon administration, 1969–72, and head of the Nixon reelection campaign in 1972. He was convicted of perjury, conspiracy, and obstruction of justice for his role in the Watergate affair.

302.16   Teilhard de Chardin] French Jesuit theologian Pierre Teilhard de Chardin (1881–1955), author of *The Divine Milieu* and *The Phenomenon of Man*, published posthumously in 1957 and 1959, respectively.

304.37   Rudolf Steiner's anthroposophy] Spiritual belief system founded by the Austrian philosopher and religious thinker Rudolf Steiner (1861–1925).

306.38   Verga] Sicilian fiction writer and playwright Giovanni Verga (1840–1922).

EXPLANATIONS

313.22–23   Faisal . . . Wilson.] Faisal II (1935–1958), king of Iraq, 1939–58; Władysław Gomułka (1905–1982), general secretary of the Polish Communist Party, 1943–48, and a political prisoner, 1951–54, was readmitted to the party in July 1956 during a period of unrest in Poland and was reinstated as party leader in October; Swedish statesman Dag Hammerskjöld (1905–1961), secretary-general of the United Nations, 1953–61; Makarios III (1913–1977), Greek Cypriot religious and political leader; Dmitri Shepilov (1908–1995), Soviet minister of foreign affairs, 1956–57; Jawaharlal Nehru (1889–1964), prime minister of India, 1947–64; Charles E. Wilson (1890–1961), U.S. secretary of defense, 1953–57.

333.35–36   1927 poem . . . Stephen Vincent Benét] "American Names."

336.3   Arthur Schlesinger's autobiography] *A Life in the Twentieth Century: Innocent Beginnings, 1917–1950* (2000) by the historian Arthur Schlesinger Jr. (1917–2007).

339.29   Harry Guggenheim] American financier, publisher, and philanthropist (1890–1971).

355.18–19   what Henry James called "the germ"] See the opening of James's preface (1908) to *The Spoils of Poynton* and two other works collected in the New York Edition of his novels and tales.

358.14   Here Comes Everybody Jewish.] A nickname of the character Humphrey Chimpden Earwicker in James Joyce's *Finnegans Wake* (1939) is "Here Comes Everybody."

358.14   Leon Klinghoffer.] On October 7, 1985, four members of the Palestine Liberation Front (PLF) hijacked the Italian cruise liner *Achille Lauro* in the eastern Mediterranean and threatened to kill the ship's passengers if their demand for the release of fifty Palestinian prisoners was not met. The next day the hijackers murdered Leon Klinghoffer (1916–1985), a disabled Jewish American passenger, and threw his body overboard.

358.14–15   Jonathan Pollard.] Pollard (b. 1954), a civilian analyst working at a U.S. naval intelligence center in Suitland, Maryland, met in the late spring of 1984 with an Israeli air force officer studying in the United States and offered to supply Israel with highly classified information. Pollard became an agent of Lakam (Bureau of Scientific Liaison), an intelligence unit within the Israeli ministry of defense, and eventually gave his handlers more than one million pages of documents, including detailed information about Soviet weapons, Arab military capabilities, and U.S. intelligence collection methods. Despite assurances that he would be "taken care of" if discovered, Pollard's Israeli contacts quickly left the country after he fell under suspicion; when Pollard and his wife sought asylum in the Israeli embassy in Washington, D.C., on November 21, 1985, they were refused entry, and he was arrested by the FBI. After pleading guilty to espionage charges, Pollard said that he was motivated by concern for the security of Israel, while admitting that he had accepted cash payments of $1,500 a month (later increased to $2,500), as well as thousands of dollars in travel expenses and jewelry. Sentenced to life imprisonment in 1987, Pollard was released on parole on November 20, 2015.

358.15   Meir Kahane.] See note 102.26.

358.15   Eliot's Bleistein.] Jewish character in T. S. Eliot's poem "Burbank with a Baedeker: Bleistein with a Cigar" (1920), which contains anti-Semitic lines such as "On the Rialto once. / The rats are underneath the piles. / The Jew is underneath the lot. / Money in furs."

358.18–20   Elias Canetti . . . different from each other."] From Canetti's *Crowds and Power* (1960), a study of crowd psychology by the Bulgarian novelist Elias Canetti (1905–1994).

358.32   Joseph O'Neill] Irish novelist (b. 1964), author of *Neverland* (2008) and *The Dog* (2014).

361.35   Newark riots of 1967] Riots beginning on the evening of July 12, 1967, which spread from Newark's Central Ward to other sections of the city. After six days 23 people were killed, with 725 injured and 1,500 arrested.

362.24–25   Boudin . . . young daughter's career as a notorious antiwar terrorist] Katherine Boudin (b. 1943) was a member of Weatherman (later called the Weather Underground), a violent splinter faction of the leftist Students for a Democratic Society (SDS). She was involved in the "Days of Rage," a series of violent demonstrations staged by Weatherman in Chicago in October 1969, and survived a botched bomb-making operation that caused an explosion at a Greenwich Village townhouse on March 6, 1970, which killed three other members of Weatherman; the bombs were reportedly intended for an attack on a military dance at Fort Dix, New Jersey, and possibly on the main administration building at Columbia University. Boudin remained underground until October 20, 1981, when she and nine other revolutionaries staged a robbery in Nyack, New York, in which a security guard and two police officers were killed. Arrested at the scene, Boudin pled guilty to felony murder and was sentenced to twenty years to life. She was paroled in 2003.

364.1 "*Tyranny Is Better Organized than Freedom*"] From *Un nouveau théologien, M. Fernand Laudet* (1911) by the French writer Charles Péguy (1873–1914).

366.25 Norman Corwin] American writer, producer, director, and narrator of poetic, topical nonfiction radio programs (1910–2011); his hourlong special "On a Note of Triumph," broadcast on May 8, 1945, the day World War II ended in Europe, was heard by some sixty million Americans.

366.25–26 Howard Fast] American writer (1914–2003), author of popular historical novels such as *Citizen Tom Paine* (1943) and *Spartacus* (1951). A member of the Communist Party from 1943 to 1956, he served three months in prison for refusing to cooperate with the House Un-American Activities Committee in 1950 and ran for Congress as a candidate of the American Labor Party in 1952.

371.2–3 Emerson . . . none to beauty,"] From "Compensation" in *Essays: First Series* (1841).

372.24 "an original relation to the universe."] From Emerson, *Nature* (1836), as is the quote that follows.

376.37–377.1 Tina Brown] English magazine editor (b. 1953), editor of *Vanity Fair*, *The New Yorker*, and *The Daily Beast*.

378.11 Bleeding Kansas] Fighting in Kansas between pro-slavery and anti-slavery factions in the years following the Kansas-Nebraska Act (1854), which repealed the prohibition against slavery in federal territory north of 36°30'. Kansas was eventually admitted to the Union as a free state in January 1861.

378.11 Judge Taney and Dred Scott] In *Dred Scott v. Sandford* (1857), the U.S. Supreme Court ruled that Congress could not prohibit slavery in federal territories, and that free Negroes were not citizens of the United States. In the opinion of the Court in the case, Chief Justice Roger B. Taney (1777–1864) wrote that blacks "had no rights which the white man was bound to respect."

378.19 Armour and Swift] Founders of large rival meatpacking firms established in the Midwest in the middle of the nineteenth century: Philip Danforth Armour (1832–1901) and Gustavus Swift (1839–1903).

378.19   the Haymarket riot] On May 4, 1886, a crowd assembled in Chicago's Haymarket Square to protest the police shooting of several striking laborers the previous day. A bomb was thrown, shooting ensued, and seven policemen and at least four workers were killed. Although the actual bomb-thrower was not identified, eight anarchists were convicted of conspiracy to commit murder. Four of the defendants were hanged, one committed suicide in prison, and the remaining three were pardoned in 1893 by the newly elected governor, John P. Altgeld, who called their trial unjust.

378.23   Tilden-Hayes election and the Compromise of 1877] The contested 1876 presidential election between Democrat Samuel Tilden (1814–1886) and Republican Rutherford B. Hayes (1822–1893) was resolved via a compromise that awarded twenty disputed electoral votes to Hayes in exchange for the withdrawal of federal support for Republican state governments in the South, effectively ending Reconstruction.

381.29   Kafka's famous conundrum] "A cage went in search of a bird": from the collection of aphorisms (1917–18) that Max Brod posthumously titled *Reflections on Sin, Suffering, Hope, and the True Way*, now known as *The Zürau Aphorisms*.

385.37–38   "In the struggle . . . bet on the world."] From *The Zürau Aphorisms* ("Im Kampf zwischen Dir und der Welt, sekundiere der Welt").

394.18   what Shakespeare called the "fangs of malice."] *Twelfth Night*, I.v.184.

394.37–38   what I once described elsewhere as "that lubricious sensation that is fluency."] In *Operation Shylock*.

396.6   Finkielkraut] Alain Finkielkraut (b. 1949), French philosopher and intellectual whose interview with Roth is included in this volume, pp. 123–34, was one of the speakers at Roth's birthday celebration.

396.28–29   "The meaning of life is that it stops."] Not by Kafka himself but from the essay "Legible Death" (1980) by the American writer Leonard Michaels (1933–2003), discussing Kafka's aphorism "A cage went in search of a bird."

Index

*This book is set in 10 point ITC Galliard, a face
designed for digital composition by Matthew Carter and based
on the sixteenth-century face Granjon. The paper is acid-free
lightweight opaque that will not turn yellow or brittle with age.
The binding is sewn, which allows the book to open easily and lie flat.
The binding board is covered in Brillianta, a woven rayon cloth
made by Van Heek–Scholco Textielfabrieken, Holland.
Composition by Dedicated Book Services.
Printing and binding by Edwards Brothers Malloy, Ann Arbor.
Designed by Bruce Campbell.*

THE LIBRARY OF AMERICA SERIES

The Library of America fosters appreciation of America's literary heritage by publishing, and keeping permanently in print, authoritative editions of America's best and most significant writing. An independent nonprofit organization, it was founded in 1979 with seed funding from the National Endowment for the Humanities and the Ford Foundation.